P9-DVY-166

THE BEST
AMERICAN
MAGAZINE
WRITING
2007

THE BEST AMERICAN MAGAZINE WRITING

2007

Compiled by the American Society of Magazine Editors

Columbia University Press   New York

Columbia University Press
Publishers Since 1893
New York   Chichester, West Sussex
Copyright © 2007 American Society of Magazine Editors
All rights reserved

Library of Congress Cataloging-in-Publication Data
ISSN 1541-0978
ISBN 978-0-231-14391-2 (pbk. : alk. paper)

∞

Columbia University Press books are printed on permanent and durable
acid-free paper.
This book is printed on paper with recycled content.
Printed in the United States of America
p 10 9 8 7 6 5 4 3 2 1

References to Internet Web sites (URLs) were accurate at the time of writing.
Neither the author nor Columbia University Press is responsible for URLs
that may have expired or changed since the manuscript was prepared.

Contents

Cynthia Leive

Acknowledgments

very year the country's top magazine editors and writers put on their best black-tie finery and gather in New York City for the National Magazine Awards—and every year press coverage of the event invariably describes it as "the Oscars of the magazine industry."

For my money, we have the Oscars beat, and the book you are holding in your hands is the reason why. Magazines produce some of the most lovely and lasting writing of our time; though it's true that there's nothing better than a quick dip into a magazine when you're stuck on the cross-town bus in rush-hour traffic, the best magazine pieces also stand the test of time, working their particular brand of magic years after their time on the newsstand is gone. The stories collected in this volume—all finalists or winners of the 2007 National Magazine Awards—do what magazines do best, chronicling and influencing our culture, and they're just as rich and rewarding on the second or third reading as they were on that bus, on the first.

This anthology—the eighth annual collection produced by the American Society of Magazine Editors—would not have been possible without the energy and enthusiasm of the 270 magazine editors who spent three long days this spring judging the awards for ASME. Credit also goes to Nicholas Lemann, dean of the Columbia University Graduate School of Journalism,

x
Cynthia Leive

which cosponsors the awards, and NMA administrator Robin Blackburn, who organized the 1,774 entries before judging. We are deeply grateful to our book agent, David McCormick of Mc-Cormick & Williams, and our publisher, Columbia University Press, for their support of magazine journalism. And above all, this volume is the work of Marlene Kahan, the "magazine queen" and executive director of ASME, who selected these stories and who champions the work of editors everywhere.

Happy reading. If you're lucky, it'll be a long commute.

Cynthia Leive
President, American Society of Magazine Editors
Editor-in-Chief, *Glamour*

Marlene Kahan

Introduction

Ever since the days of Ben Franklin, the American magazine has been a major force in shaping society— and has proven to be a most resilient medium. Today, with the dramatic explosion of digital technology, consumers can read anything, anytime. But there is something unique about magazines—they create a relationship with the reader, one he or she looks forward to renewing with each new issue.

Magazines have the power to deepen our understanding of the world around us and touch our most personal interests and passions. In fact, a magazine can be a reflection not only of current times but of times to come. They can do this because writers have the luxury of space to explore the crucial nuances that shed light on the meaning and importance of a subject.

Which brings us to this collection of the best magazine articles of 2006. The pieces included in this anthology represent outstanding work by some of the most eminent writers in America as well as rising literary and journalistic talents. Wide-ranging in their style and subjects, these pieces inform, surprise, entertain, and provide new perspectives on what is happening in our world. They also reflect elements that distinguish the best in magazine writing: moral passion, vivid characters and settings, zealous reporting, and artful narrative that transforms information into a compelling story.

In addition, they show on many levels the power of journalists who will go to almost any lengths to find their story. The beneficiary of this dedication and determination is you, the reader. And the reward to those who will read what follows is having in one place articles that resonate as much today as when they originally appeared.

Many of these pieces were published in a year when man's inhumanity toward man preoccupied the world and, accordingly, was reported on in magazines. Readers will not soon forget C. J. Chivers's astonishing and chilling account in *Esquire* of the three-day siege by Chechen terrorists at School No. 1 in the Russian town of Beslan; William Langewiesche's reconstruction in *Vanity Fair* of the events leading up to the massacre at Haditha; and Andrew Corsello's harrowing portrait in *GQ* of Robert Mugabe's mad rule in Zimbabwe and two men—a white farmer and a fiery black priest—who strive for forgiveness instead of hate. Several other pieces reported on different tragedies: Tom Junod's take on the ripple effects of the Katrina disaster in *Esquire*; Eric Konigsberg's sensitive look in the *New Yorker* at why a gifted child committed suicide; Christopher Hitchens's profile in *Vanity Fair* of survivors of Agent Orange; and Caroline Alexander's heart-wrenching profile in *National Geographic* of Reinhold Messner, the man who epitomized modern mountaineering.

On the lighter side, you will be treated to Vanessa Grigoriadis's hilarious portrait of fashion icon Karl Lagerfeld in *New York Magazine*; Sandra Tsing Loh's incisive look at the affluent modern woman in her book review in the *Atlantic Monthly*; and Paul Theroux's wry essay in *Smithsonian* on the delights and challenges of living with geese.

The anthology also includes Janet Reitman's investigation for *Rolling Stone* that yielded a rare, uncensored view of the usually secretive Church of Scientology; and Susan Casey's revelation in *Best Life* of a virtually unknown, Texas-sized garbage dump resting at the bottom of the Pacific ocean.

What these stories share is an amazing ability to make the words on paper come alive ... from the very beginning the reader is transported into the lives and places described in this collection. We hope you enjoy the journey.

Marlene Kahan
Executive Director
American Society of Magazine Editors

THE BEST
AMERICAN
MAGAZINE
WRITING

2007

New York Magazine

WINNER—PROFILE WRITING

With sparkling, elegant prose, Vanessa Grigoriadis creates a revealing portrait of fashion icon Karl Lagerfeld and the rarified world he inhabits, that is, by turns, comic and surprisingly poignant. This profile stands out for its innovative structure and impressively economical use of detail. As Lagerfeld himself might say, "It's dee-vvvine."

Vanessa Grigoriadis

Karl Lagerfeld, Boy Prince of Fashion

Down Fifth Avenue they come, the fragrant and bejeweled hordes, having said their bons mots at Derek Lam's cocktail party at Barneys and a Tom Ford perfume launch at Saks, and now clippity-clopping their way ever closer to the opening of the exquisite new Fendi boutique on Fifty-third Street. It is eight P.M., still early enough for tourists to stroll about and city buses to zoom by, and also too early for the arrival of Karl Lagerfeld, designer of Chanel, Fendi, Lagerfeld Collection, a new Karl Lagerfeld line, and "the reason we are all here!" Half an hour before the event is supposed to end, Lagerfeld remains at his suite at the Mercer, and it's whispered that he will not leave because he cannot find a thing to wear. Soon, Silvia Fendi, the handsome blonde daughter of the LVMH-owned house, is packed in a Town Car and sent downtown to work some magic, or at least appeal to Lagerfeld's nobler side, because Lagerfeld is nothing if not noble.

What can one talk about while waiting for Lagerfeld? Lagerfeld, of course. "Karl has the energy of . . . what? Twenty-five thousand Turkish elephants!" says socialite Anne Slater, wearing her big blue glasses and grinning up a storm. "He's magnetic and powerful. I think he's absolutely, devastatingly attractive."

"At our dinner for Karl at Schiller's, firemen had to stand at the door to stop people from coming in because everyone

4
Vanessa Grigoriadis

wanted to see him," says Robert Burke, the recently departed
Bergdorf Goodman head of fashion. "Karl said the firemen
were the best-dressed people from the whole evening!"

"Karl is a genius!" exclaims Lindsay Lohan, whose name has
been lobbed recently as the new face of Chanel ("I prefer Nicole
Kidman and that generation at the moment," Lagerfeld later
tells me dryly). "I want to have everything that he makes. Everything! I go into stores and grab all his things."

"Karl is the one person that makes me shy," says throaty Bun-
galow 8 owner Amy Sacco. "I think I've conquered—I've run the
gamut on people that I speak to, and very few times have I been
shy. But Karl is beyond, and I'm afraid I'd bore him to tears."

Giorgio Armani, André Leon Talley, Anna Wintour with her
pretty daughter, Bee. "A conversation with Karl is not a fashion
conversation—it's a conversation, a conversation that embraces
the culture of life," says Talley. Amanda Cutter Brooks, Celerie
Kemble, Anh Duong. "Karl defended me once. He said, 'Do not
forget that Anh is not only a beautiful woman but also an artist!'" exclaims Duong. Sophie Dahl, Cecilia Dean, Liv Tyler.
"I'm starting to feel a little tired and overwhelmed, and I wonder
if I slip out if anyone would notice," lisps Tyler, with one of her
coy half-smiles. An emissary from Planet Not Obsessed With
Karl: Chuck Close plants his wheelchair two inches from the
exit door. "I'm not very interested in fashion," says Close, sur-
veying the crowd. He sighs. "This event is making me want to
start smoking again."

But then there he is—Karl! His stiff silver tie glitters like a
saber. His black leather gloves are good for murder. He poses for
the cameras wearing a ghastly grimace, an entourage of twenty
Frenchmen and foxes waiting behind. Guests with fingers curled
around champagne glasses jostle to catch a glimpse, not quite
crying the way they did in Tokyo last year at the opening of the
biggest Chanel store in the world, but certainly eager to be en-
tertained. "I think his hair is powdered, like from the 1800s,"

says one socialite. "In fact, it is from the 1800s," titters her friend. Paparazzi are yelling "Karl!" and bystanders are yelling "Karl!" and PETA is yelling "Karl!" the loudest. A dreadlocked white guy with Rollerblades slung over his shoulder streaks down the sidewalk and snarls, "Blood for money, that's what Karl Lagerfeld wants. Karl is greedy! Karl is evil! Karl is wicked! Karl is . . . the devil!"

Lagerfeld stops in the doorway, puckering his bulbous German lips, which is what he does when he is mad—well, not mad, exactly, but frustrated with other people, who, he has found, are frequently idiots. "You eat meat and wear leather, so shut up," he says to a German reporter. "I have no time for zis foolishness."

. . .

Lagerfeld is too busy, too smart, and too old to be brought into any foolishness, at least not that which is not of his own making. At sixty-seven—or seventy-two, if the 1933 birth date on a baptismal record unearthed by German tabloids is to be believed—he is one of the most professionally self-realized people alive, keeping busy with an incredible twelve or so collections each year, an extensive photography career, a Paris-based bookshop, personal museum-quality furniture collections, the management of six homes, and staying skinny. Lagerfeld lost ninety pounds four years ago on a low-calorie diet—his book on the subject was a best seller in Europe—and has put on ten or so since. The new, skinny Karl is an improved Karl. The creepy fat guy hiding behind a fan has been replaced by a boogying hipster who hangs out with Stephen Gan and Hedi Slimane. "My people are zee cool ones, the rockers," says Lagerfeld. "I get along with everyone except for men my age, who are bourgeois or retired or boring, and cannot follow the evolution of time and mood."

As much as Lagerfeld would like to ignore his association with such men—and aging and death in general—his role as a vital elder statesman has much to do with his importance in the world of fashion. He is the King of Fashion, if you will, though he would prefer to be called its eternal Prince. Lagerfeld is the last of the old-world couturiers, with Valentino his only remaining contemporary, and the last of the big high-fashion names, with Yves Saint Laurent in retirement, Tom Ford in transition, and Helmut Lang disappeared. He is also a terrific pop cartoon— a scolding great-uncle, Dave Navarro the elder, the S&M George Washington. His look is an extremely conscious metaphor for his philosophy of fashion and life: Here, watch as I bring together the old, in my tall eighteenth-century collar and bizarre powdered hair, with the new, as seen in my ponytail and $2,500 Agatha leather pants, "the most expensive leather pants in the world," he declares, with a laugh exactly like Count Chocula's in its length and ridiculousness. Without the indecipherable French-German accent, he would be made for reality TV, although one would think he'd resist on grounds that philistines should not even be aware that he exists. His iconography grows and grows: first, menacing larger-than-life portraits at H&M; then, Los Angeles's Museum of Contemporary Art gift shop, where one could buy a pin with his face on it.

"In the whole world, there is nowhere I can go," says Lagerfeld, in a tone that should have him fluttering that old fan. "Everybody has a camera, and it is flash-flash-flash, and I am a puppet, a marionette, Mickey at Disneyland for children to play with. In Japan, they touch me. I have Japanese women pinch my ass, so now I must say, 'You can have the photo, but please don't touch me.' You cannot pinch the ass of a man my age! And I cannot go out without something for my eyes, because someone might throw chemicals in my face, and I would be like my childhood French teacher whose wife burnt him with acid, Mr. Pommes-Frites, can you believe the name. I can cross the street nowhere in the world, I can never go into a shop. Oh, it's horrible, horrible." Lagerfeld, the master of the contrapuntal, grins a bit and then whispers, "In fact, I do like it. It's very flattering, and very fun."

·　　·　　·

The place where Lagerfeld will likely be fending off excitable fans next is New York, though he will not say so directly. "I can tell you all sort of bullshit, but I work only from feelings and motivations and creations and needs and opportunities," he declares. Nevertheless, last year, while working on the show of Chanel couture at the Met, he bought one of the John Pawson–designed apartments in Ian Schrager's updated Gramercy Park Hotel, which he will decorate only with German design from 1905 to 1915 and move into in April. "I must have a key to the park, because you know I cannot walk in the street," he says. (Of the Met show, Lagerfeld says, "I do not care if they say I was a fascist and all this—if you did not like it, you could have walked out.") Lagerfeld has been spending a lot of time here these days, making a trip about every six weeks, to stay at the Mercer, dine at diet-friendly restaurants like Omen, and occasionally go to nightclubs where young people ask him to sign their clothes with Sharpies. "I like New York these days," he says. "At least the way I see it, it is perfect, though I am not down in the streets, so don't ask me about that. I like how the people don't call me by Monsieur here. It's always just the first name—Karl!"

Lagerfeld also now has offices in New York, since he sold Lagerfeld Gallery—recently renamed Lagerfeld Collection—to Tommy Hilfiger for $30 million (Hilfiger has no creative say). It was all very sudden, says Hilfiger: "I was at Karl's home in Paris, and we were telling each other our dreams. I said, 'You know, I would like to buy another brand.' He said, 'Buy mine.'" And why not? It may have beefed up Hilfiger's December sale to Apax Partners, and who owns what and what they plan to do is of little interest to Lagerfeld, who intends to do exactly what he wants regardless. "Groups are groups," he says, with a wave of his hand.

One very good thing Lagerfeld got out of the Hilfiger deal was some of the most stunning office space in New York, on the seventeenth floor of the Starrett-Lehigh Building. Lagerfeld's true nature is revealed in his walk, a curious, energetic bourrée performed on the balls of his feet, and on a recent afternoon he dashes to and fro in the offices, drinking in the stunning Hudson River–to–Empire State Building views. "Dee-vvvine," he pronounces, to the tiny claps of assistants (divine is one of Lagerfeld's favorite words, never used ironically). "I must be in Milan, Paris, and New York. To show in one city is a problem, because you cannot go to every party the same night. You cannot dance on every bar. But you can dance in different cities on different bars. I think that is the modern way, and I am organized for it."

The organization of which he speaks is a support system of a half-dozen image-makers, casting directors, public-relations officers, and graphic designers who travel the world with him, hooking up with creative satellites to consult on projects. Today in the studio, there's Stephen Gan and *Harper's Bazaar* senior fashion editor Melanie Ward, consultants on Lagerfeld Collection and the Karl Lagerfeld line, which includes denim and T-shirts and is overseen by Ward and will be sold in top-tier department stores beginning in March. As with Chanel and Fendi, Lagerfeld controls every aspect of the image-making, from photography to the concept of the ad campaign. The team follows him from city to city like a rap star's posse. Their look is sleek Euro professional, all with close shaves, slim-cut sport jackets, and starched collars. Most wear some sort of chunky silver Chrome Hearts jewelry, a Lagerfeld obsession since he met codesigner Laurie Stark at a fashion show and she bent over in her leather pants to show him the tartan letters spelling KARL across her butt. Today Lagerfeld wears a sterling-silver belt of the American flag with the Pledge of Allegiance engraved on the back—"Dee-vine!"—and a pendant around his neck. He unscrews it to reveal a stack of seaweed pills and pops one in his mouth.

"Our job is to be the team of Karl," declares Lagerfeld Collection publicist Caroline LeBar, an imposing Frenchwoman in Libertine suits and one of Lagerfeld's long-term protectors ("I do not like strangers," he explains). Over a catered sushi lunch—Lagerfeld sits apart from the group, waving a silver fork over pineapple and asparagus in Chinese-takeout boxes that are, oddly, colored black—a member of his team talks about Lagerfeld's recent photo shoot with Christina Aguilera. "She is horrible!" she exclaims. "She did not even kiss Karl good-bye. She just sticks out her head from the door, 'Bye!' "

"Oh, well," I say. "She is a pop star."

"*Karl* is a pop star," she declares.

On the roof for the photo shoot, it is perfectly mild, and the city seems at peace, with helicopters floating overhead and boats moving slowly down the river. An androgynous model climbs onto a fire escape in a Lagerfeld Collection floor-length black dress cut down the center, fluttering in the wind. It's inspired by the clothes that Lagerfeld began to wear when he got skinny: skintight pants and long vampiric frock-coats, all Berlin all the time. "A little young Bonaparte!" says Lagerfeld of the model, whispering with Gan. "She is beautiful, but as a model she has a flaw. Her legs are too short. But nobody notices. How perfect she is for this! How divine!"

The model turns her angular body into the sun, and you can see the outline of a tattoo down her belly through the gauzy fabric. "I want to see it—it looks like lacing," Lagerfeld tells Ward. "Now, I have nothing against tattoo, as long as I don't have to put it on my body. And her nose-pierce, well, we can move with a computer, though I don't know if you have a cold if it is very pleasant. Some of them have pierces in the nipples also—and uh-oh—in other areas too!" He laughs his Count Chocula laugh and shakes his head. "That's modern."

.   .   .

For all his interest in being modern, Lagerfeld can be quite old-fashioned. He does not drive or use a cell phone, nor does he smoke, drink, or take drugs. He takes great solace in the proprieties of social life and is always telling everyone what can and cannot be done. For example, there were plans for a dinner at LVMH head Bernard Arnault's new Manhattan apartment after the Fendi store opening, but Lagerfeld squashed them upon hearing that Arnault's mother had died. "They say it is an apartment Arnault has not yet lived in so it is okay, but I say you cannot go to somebody's private house without him, knowing that his mother is dead, sitting there eating his food—no, no, one cannot do this," declares Lagerfeld. With those who are refined, he is refined—"Karl is a great storyteller, a gentleman, and a true wit," says Nicole Kidman. "Working with him and dining with him are equal pleasures"—and with those who are not, he is delighted to be naughty. Says Helena Christensen, "At a shoot with all these important clients around, he will whisper some really perverted joke in my ear, or say, 'Did you see her breasts, her on the left? Or him, look at him, isn't it perverted how he is pushing his torso towards us?'" Lagerfeld socializes with royalty, like Prince Charles and Camilla Parker Bowles, and fits right in. "The public does not know who Camilla is," he declares. "She is the life of the party! She's sparkling, she's witty, she's ready for everything, and not pretentious, not one bit. If you had to make a choice to live with somebody, this is the one." Of Princess Diana, he says, "She was pretty and she was sweet, but she was stupid."

Before he ruled the world of fashion, Lagerfeld was a pampered little prince. The heir to a German condensed-milk fortune, he was raised on a 12,000-acre estate near the Danish border. At four, he insisted on having his own valet because he liked to change clothes several times a day. The family remained on the estate during World War II, suffering no casualties or hardships; Lagerfeld insists that he barely even knew there was a war. But all was not sunshine and rainbows. His mother was a villain and her crimes many: He was not allowed to chatter on when talking to her, because "you may be six years old, but I am not"; she refused to let him wear glasses although he was shortsighted, saying, "Children with glasses are the ugliest thing in the world"; she scolded him for smoking as a teenager, because "if you smoke, you show the hands, and as yours are not beautiful . . . you should not." Among Mater's few judicious comments was that homosexuality was "nothing, just like hair color, some are black and some are blonde, who cares," and this Lagerfeld repeats with some pride. He doesn't talk about his sexual orientation and maintains that he never had sexual congress with the man he calls the love of his life, the Parisian "It" dandy Jacques de Bascher, who called Lagerfeld "Mein Kaiser" and died of AIDS in 1989. When Lagerfeld says he "hated the nineties, for some reasons," it is code for many miserable years suffering with a broken heart, partially expressed by naming his Hellenic-inspired villa in Hamburg "Jako," an amalgam of their names, and briefly selling a perfume of the same appellation. In fact, De Bascher was the reason Lagerfeld gained weight to begin with. He writes in *The Karl Lagerfeld Diet* that directly before De Bascher's death, "I started to lose interest in my appearance, because I knew what was going to happen. I lost interest in myself and trivial matters. I felt old-fashioned in my proper made-to-measure Italian clothes. I started to buy my clothes from Matsuda, Comme des Garçons, and Yohji Yamamoto. I went from small to medium, medium to large, then to extra-large."

When Gan and Slimane met Lagerfeld, six or seven years ago, he was extra-large, and in fashion circles there is no question that the new friendships—and what is whispered to be an ob-session with Slimane—sparked Lagerfeld's desire to lose weight. About six months after Gan introduced Slimane to Lagerfeld, Lagerfeld greeted Gan at his Paris studio in a Dior Homme tie. "The tie was unusually narrow for his width at the time," says Gan. "He said, 'Look! I'm wearing your friend's tie!'" Six months later in Paris, Lagerfeld was wearing a Dior Homme jacket, and six months later it was the pants. "I have never felt an age dif-ferentiation with Karl—hanging out with him is like hanging out with a buddy," says Gan, who is about thirty years his junior. "Now he shops for clothes the way some people shop for choco-lates."

Says Lagerfeld, "My only ambition in life is to wear size twenty-eight jeans."

. . .

At fourteen—or, you know, nineteen—Lagerfeld moved in with a family friend in Paris, a woman who had been his mother's vendeuse at Molyneux. Two years later, in 1954, he entered a contest sponsored by the International Wool Secretariat and won the prize for a coat (Yves Saint Laurent won in the dress category). He began his career in the couture studios of Pierre Balmain, where he learned dress-making methods of the twen-ties and thirties before becoming the head designer of Patou. Fashion was a good job for him, his mother said—"It shows you have no pretension or ambition." While Kenzo and Saint Lau-rent built empires, Lagerfeld remained under the radar, design-ing for Krizia and Charles Jourdan in the early sixties and Chloé and Fendi in the seventies. "Lagerfeld is not a designer, he's a mercenary" is the famous kiss-off by Pierre Bergé, Saint Lau-rent's former business partner–majordomo–lover. In 1983, La-gerfeld was hired by Chanel's corporate head, Alain Wertheimer, to reinvent the Chanel brand, moribund since Coco's death in

1971. He promised to be modern. "Respect is not creative," he told Wertheimer, according to Jane Kramer in *Vogue*. "Chanel is an institution, and you have to treat an institution like a whore—and then you get something out of her."

In the same way that Lagerfeld's collection for H&M made it safe for Stella McCartney and other high-fashion designers to go downmarket, his vast accomplishments at Chanel have set the standard for all the old European houses frantically trying to reinvigorate aging brands with a hot young designer—Alber Elbaz at Lanvin, Olivier Theyskens at Rochas. No other designer has been able to exploit a house's legacy in quite the same way as Lagerfeld, and it has been said that Chanel, owned by the press-averse Wertheimer family, is the largest luxury company in the world, with annual revenues of more than $4 billion.

Fashion people will tell you about Lagerfeld's "weird psychic connection" with Coco Chanel and how he "channeled Coco" to reinvent the brand, but Lagerfeld does not wear Chanel himself. "In Chanel, I look like my mother," he says, grimacing. Like his mother, Coco Chanel was master of the grand pronouncement—"Luxury is not the opposite of poverty, but the opposite of vulgarity" was perhaps her most famous aphorism. Chanel, the fabled orphan-grisette-demimondaine-superstar, is credited with inventing modern style in the 1910s with simple, uncorseted dressing, giving rise to the little black dress, bouclé jacket, and later accoutrements like red lipstick, a perpetual tan, and Chanel No. 5. After surviving the scandal that she spent World War II at Paris's Ritz with a Nazi boyfriend—"Really, a woman my age cannot be expected to look at his passport if she has a chance of a lover," she explained—she staged a slow but solid comeback in the fifties, but her selfish nature and disappointment in love eventually got the better of her, and she died a bitter spinster.

Lagerfeld is determined to end his life differently. He says he will not participate in retrospectives of his work, create any foundations, write an autobiography, or keep archives. "I do not like funerals, and I do not want anyone to come to mine," he says. "Do what you want with the ashes. Send them down the garbage chute." Nevertheless, he seems to like talking about death an awful lot. The top book on his nightstand is Joan Didion's *The Year of Magical Thinking*, which he declares, of course, divine. "I have finished it three times in less than a month!" he says. He bangs the table repeatedly as he begins to count off the age of death of his ancestors—two grandparents at ninety-eight and one hundred; his father at almost ninety; and his mother at eighty-two, killed by her own fidelity to propriety. "The doctor told her she must stay in bed, but instead she got her hair done and when he arrived, crossed the room to greet him at the door, dying there," he says. "Also I had a godfather who lived to 104, and his brother to 102, and their mother to 108. When my godfather died, he was totally normal, chic and everything. He got up early and dressed every day. After lunch he slept one hour and walked one hour afterwards." He stops banging on the table, and leans back in his chair. "That is a long time they lived," he says softly. "They saw a lot. I would like to see as much."

·　　·　　·

Paris in the wintertime, raw and windy. Lagerfeld is no longer leasing his eighteenth-century hotel particulier, site of countless galas and unforgettable private dinners. Now he lives in a long, narrow, glassed-in apartment on Quai Voltaire—"like a space in the hospital for early-born babies," he says—that he has furnished with postmillennial furniture by Ronan and Erwan Bouroullec and Marc Newson. He does not want to be owned by things, he says. In the past decade and a half, he has sold off his eighteenth-century-furniture collection ($21.7 million), his collection of the Italian postmodern design group Memphis ($280,000) and Art Deco pieces ($4 million), as well as the château in Brittany where his mother and De Bascher are buried. "In the future, I want only apartments like hotel suites," he says. "I want to be light. I want nothing." The riots are going on, and Lagerfeld doesn't want to talk about them. Paris is dreary, mired in the past. "Now they make the ugliest sixties building landmarked," he says. "The Chanel building on Avenue Montaigne is the ugliest building in the world, all I want is to see it go, but they do nothing. You never hide against progress, because then you will be lost."

The Chanel-headquarters building on Rue Cambon is a bit mired in the past as well, although Lagerfeld had the salon renovated in 2002. The modernist beauty of the ground-floor boutique, filled with happy Asian and American customers, disappears in the offices, where thin girls in pedal pushers sit at cramped desks, pounding on keyboards. "They do not wear these pants in America yet?" asks an assistant, laughing. "In a few months, they will." Another sign of olden times: a butler, whose entire job seems to be carrying a platter that holds a crystal goblet filled with Pepsi Max expressly for Karl.

Lagerfeld is fitting his Paris–New York collection, a new line that he has added to Chanel's five collections a year because he knows the Chanel customer can bear it, that they will buy almost anything he sells (in the boutique, a cloth coat was priced at 36,814 euros, and there was only one left). The mannequins cabines, young girls with bodies more terrifying than Nicole Richie's, put on dresses behind filmy curtains as Lagerfeld makes tiny adjustments. Devendra Banhart, an American neo-folk singer Lagerfeld has taken under his wing, hangs around waiting to be fitted in a suit he will wear to perform in the show. "How about if I wear just my underwear?" he asks.

"Oh-ho!" says Lagerfeld.

Chanel's high-energy Belgian accessories designer dashes about wearing multiple scarves and belts and fake earrings from the collection, trying to get Lagerfeld's attention. "Look at these!" she says, shaking to make things jingle. "How beautiful!"

"*J'adore!*" exclaims Lagerfeld. "If you go out to a nightclub like this, the ladies will go crazy for it. *Très jolie, très New York.*"

Throwing on three rhinestone bracelets and sticking her hands into a white fur muff, she vamps across the room. "I look great," she says. "I resemble—"

"You resemble an American!" he says.

She puffs out her cheeks. "When do we eat?" she asks.

"Oh, la!" laughs Lagerfeld.

Lagerfeld rarely shows up at Chanel before late afternoon, and it is eight when he begins taking the photos for the collection's press packet in Mademoiselle's old flat, preserved as she left it on the office's top floor—the Coromandel screens, Oriental tables, the quilted suede sofa, a silver box lined in gold (a gift from one of her lovers, the Duke of Westminster). The models in their forties-era New York looks parade through Coco's suites, and the shoot extends for hours, far past midnight, and afterward Lagerfeld insists on writing captions for each shot with Chanel's Parisian publicist. "Please tell him that captions are not modern," she begs me.

Lagerfeld summons the butler for his Pepsi Max and waits for his camera to be reloaded. "Marc Jacobs and all, they will have to wait," he declares from the couch, sitting down for the first time all night. "This is not an easy job, because I have the understanding about Chanel and couture design that nobody has anymore. I have the training that nobody else has. This job is not free." He takes a sip from his goblet. "I am not going anywhere."

Vanity Fair

WINNER—PUBLIC INTEREST

With brutal precision, moral clarity and tremendous literary force, William Langeswiesche reconstructs the events leading up to a massacre of Iraqi civilians at the hands of battle-scarred U.S. Marines. By creating a microcosm of the American occupation, he helps us understand not just what happened at Haditha, but what it tells us about the war and why the occupation has gone so disastrously wrong.

William Langewiesche

Rules of Engagement

I. One Morning in November

The Euphrates is a peaceful river. It meanders silently through
the desert province of Anbar like a ribbon of life, flanked by the
greenery that grows along its banks, sustaining palm groves and
farms, and a string of well-watered cities and towns. Fallujah,
Ramadi, Hit, Haditha. These are among the places made famous
by battle—conservative, once quiet communities where American power has been checked, and where despite all the narrow
measures of military success the Sunni insurgency continues to
grow. On that short list, Haditha is the smallest and farthest
upstream. It extends along the Euphrates' western bank with a
population of about 50,000, in a disarray of dusty streets and
individual houses, many with walled gardens in which private
jungles grow. It has a market, mosques, schools, and a hospital
with a morgue. Snipers permitting, you can walk it top to bottom in less than an hour, allowing time enough to stone the
dogs. Before the American invasion, it was known as an idyllic
spot, where families came from as far away as Baghdad to while
away their summers splashing in the river and sipping tea in the
shade of trees. No longer, of course. Now, all through Anbar,
and indeed the Middle East, Haditha is known as a city of death,
or more simply as a name, a war cry against the United States.

November 19, 2005, is the date people remember. Near the center of Haditha the U.S. Marines had established a forward operating base they called Sparta. It was manned by the roughly 200 Marines of Kilo Company of the Third Battalion, First Marine Division, out of Camp Pendleton, California. This was Kilo Company's third tour in Iraq. It had participated in the invasion, in the spring of 2003, and again in the hard-fought battle for Fallujah in the fall of 2004. Because of normal rotations, however, only about two-thirds of its current members had been to Iraq before. The average age was twenty-one. The company commander was a captain, an Annapolis graduate named Lucas McConnell, who was thirty-two and, like all but one of his lieutenants, was on his first tour at war. McConnell was a can-do guy, more of a believer than a thinker, disciplined, moderately religious, somewhat moralistic, and deeply invested in his beloved Marine Corps.

Winter was coming. At dawn Haditha was cool and clear. McConnell dispatched a convoy of four armored Humvees on a routine mission to deliver hot breakfasts and a radio-coding card to an observation post, a fortified checkpoint about three miles away, on River Road south of town. Some of the Humvees were equipped with top-mounted machine guns; two were "high-back" vehicles with open rear beds like those of pickup trucks, designed to carry troops and supplies, and wrapped in high protective siding. Between them the four Humvees held a squad of twelve heavily armed Marines, which was considered to be the minimum desirable force even for such a milk run as this. The men carried grenades, nine-mm pistols, and variations of the basic assault rifle, the M16. They were led by a sergeant named Frank Wuterich, aged twenty-five, who of all the sergeants of Kilo Company was known to be the most unassuming and considerate, the slowest to anger. He was another first-timer at war.

They rolled south toward the outpost, rattling through sleeping neighborhoods in single file, spaced well apart. Any insurgents watching them from the houses—and there likely were some—would have perceived the men behind the top-mounted guns as robotic figures swaddled in protective armor and cloth, and would barely have glimpsed the others through the small panes of thick, dusty, bulletproof glass, or above the armored high-back sides. Over the years on the streets of Iraq, living outside the American protective bubbles, I have often imagined that killing Americans is easier for their anonymity, because it allows insurgents to take on the machines or the uniforms without dwelling on the individuals inside. This was the experience of Resistance fighters when slaughtering hapless German conscripts during World War II in France, and presumably also of the mujahideen when killing Russians in Afghanistan. But the men on the receiving end of an attack have a different view of the effects. They know one another as individuals and friends. Even the newcomers to Kilo Company, for instance, had spent at least six months together already, and had grown so close that they could identify one another on sight, from behind, when all geared up and walking on patrols at night.

·   ·   ·

It was a fifteen-minute drive from Sparta Base to the outpost south of town. Sergeant Wuterich's squad unloaded the hot breakfasts and other supplies, and picked up several Iraqi soldiers from the apprentice Iraqi Army—trainees attached to the company, who lived in their own compound adjoining that of the Marines. The Iraqis were armed with the ubiquitous Iraqi weapon, the banana-clip, Russian-designed AK-47. After a brief delay the squad headed up River Road for Sparta Base. It is possible to judge the mood. Because the conflict in Iraq is a guerrilla war without progressive front lines, and American combat troops operate from immobile forts with fixed zones of responsibility, most patrols consist of predictable out-and-returns.

The pattern is well known to the insurgents. Routes can be varied, but the choices typically are limited, especially if the patrols
must stick to the roads and the distances are short. As a result,
one of the basic facts of life for those troops who are actually in
the fight is that the return to base is the most dangerous trip in
Iraq: if the mujahideen are going to hit you at all, the chances
are they'll hit you then. Nonetheless, for individual soldiers even
in places as threatening as Haditha, most days are quiet, and
weeks can go by with little sign of the enemy. There is no reason
to believe that Wuterich's men were pumped up for the drive
home. Were they alert? Sure, why not, but another fact of life is
that you cannot see much out of an armored Humvee, and even
if you could, you have no chance of identifying the enemy until
first you come under attack. You've got all these weapons, and
you've been told that you're a mighty warrior, a Spartan, but
what are you going to shoot—the dogs? You're a Marine without
a beach. So you sit zipped into a filthy Humvee, trusting the
guys up on the guns to watch the rooftops and the traffic on the
road, trusting your driver to keep his eyes on the ground ahead,
holding your M16 muzzle-up between your knees, calmly enduring the ride. The radio crackles. Your head bobs with the
bumps. You don't talk much. There's not much to say. If you're
dumb you trust your luck. If you're smart you're fatalistic. Either
way it usually works out fine.

They turned west off River Road, onto a street known to
them as Route Chestnut—a wide thoroughfare running through
a district of clustered houses. It was 7:15 in the morning. Up
ahead and unbeknownst to them, insurgents had planted a land
mine, probably weeks before. In the bureaucratized language of
this war, such mines are known as improvised explosive devices,
or I.E.D.'s. The ordinary ones are made from small artillery
rounds, and rigged to detonate upon reception of an electronic
signal from a short-range line-of-sight transmitter—a cordless
telephone, a garage-door opener, a toy-car remote control. The

insurgents of Haditha produced plenty of them; Kilo Company had discovered dozens in the previous weeks, and in the following weeks would discover many more. Most had been laid hastily and were poorly tucked into soft dirt or trash beside the roads, sometimes with wires showing. But the land mine this morning was different. It was a sizable propane tank stuffed with high explosives. More important, it had been buried directly in the road, and so lovingly paved over that apparently no surface disturbance was visible. The first Humvee rolled across it without incident. On board were three Marines, named Salinas, Rodriguez, and Sharratt. The second Humvee crossed, carrying Mendoza, De La Cruz, and Tatum. The third Humvee was the command vehicle. It crossed, with Wuterich, Graviss, and a medic named Whitt. Somewhere in these vehicles sat the Iraqi soldiers as well.

The fourth Humvee carried the final three Marines. It was a high-back model. At the steering wheel was a veteran of the Fallujah fight, a plump twenty-year-old named Miguel Terrazas, from El Paso, Texas, who was one of the most popular soldiers in Kilo Company, known for certain kills he had made, and yet also for his irrepressible good humor. Sitting to his right was another Fallujah veteran, James Crossan, aged twenty, from North Bend, Washington. Crossan was frustrated with the mission in Haditha, which he saw as an attempt to play policeman in the midst of an active war. In the open back was Salvador Guzman, aged nineteen, a first-timer to Iraq, who was known as a typically easygoing Marine. Guzman was from Crystal Lake, Illinois. He faced rearward in the Humvee pointing his weapon over the protective siding, watching the street behind.

As this trio passed unsuspectingly over the buried land mine, a spotter watching from nearby, probably in one of the houses, pushed a button. With a boom that shook the surrounding neighborhood, the device detonated directly under Terrazas in a fireball of violently expanding gases. The blast simultaneously lifted the Humvee and split it in two, separating the top half from the bottom. Guzman was blown clear and landed in the dirt behind the wreckage. He lay there bruised and stunned, with a broken foot but no serious injury. Crossan, in the right front seat, was not so fortunate. He was blown through the right door and then had part of the Humvee fall on him. He lay pinned under the heavy steel, suffering from multiple bone fractures and internal injuries. Others from the squad came running up. He heard someone shouting, "Get some morphine!" and he passed out.

The morphine can only have been meant for Crossan, because Guzman was not so badly hurt, and Terrazas was already beyond such needs. It is a requirement of understanding the events in Haditha—and the circumstances of this war—not to shy away from the physical realities here, or to soften the scene in the interest of politics or taste. Terrazas was torn in half. His bottom half remained under the steering wheel. His top half was blown into the road, where he landed spilling his entrails and organs. He probably did not suffer, at least. He must have lost consciousness instantly and have died soon after hitting the ground. He had a hole in his chin. His eyes were rolled back. He did not look peaceful at all. He looked bloody and grotesque.

Get morphine? No, not for Terrazas. For Wuterich and the nine intact members of the squad, Terrazas's fate was extremely disturbing. They were all of them professional soldiers who had willingly assumed the risk. But just a minute ago Terrazas had been driving home, relaxed and good-humored as usual, and now in a flash he was irretrievably gone. Such is the nature of death in Iraq: you are alive, and the streets seem calm and normal, until suddenly, inevitably, with no warning, you are dead or maimed for the rest of time. With no distant thunder to approach, the loss seems worse for the lack of any ability to prepare.

.   .   .

The wreckage smoked black. The air smelled of cordite, dust, and burned rubber. Wuterich called for backup, and for medical helicopters to evacuate the casualties. He did what a squad leader is supposed to do. A few Marines struggled to free Crossan. After a period of confusion the others crouched with weapons to their shoulders, scanning the nearby rooftops, walls, and windows in the hope of spotting the spotter, and alert to the possibility of further attack. They ordered the Iraqi soldiers to do the same. The Iraqis complied, but somewhat reluctantly, as if perhaps they thought this was not really their fight. In any case, though much remains confused about the immediate aftermath of the attack, and indeed about the hours that followed, what is nearly certain is that at first the squad took no fire. When reinforcements arrived from Sparta Base, after about ten minutes, one of them was able to kneel gently over Terrazas's remains. He said, "You are my brother by another mother. I love you, man." He covered Terrazas with a poncho, closing him off from sight.

By that time the killing of Iraqis had already begun, though here again uncertainty reigns. From transcripts, conversations, documents, press reports, and above all a sense for the plausible in Iraq, it is possible to reconstruct a lot. Nonetheless, given the complexities of guerrilla war, and the confusion that exists in the minds of those closest to battle, only the barest facts are indisputable. After the land-mine explosion, Wuterich's Marines remained in the immediate vicinity throughout the morning and beyond. Over the next few hours, until maybe around lunchtime, they killed twenty-four Iraqis. To accomplish the job, they used a few grenades, and maybe a pistol, but primarily their assault rifles. They suffered not a single casualty during this time. Five of the dead were young men who had approached in a car. The remaining nineteen were people from the neighborhood, found and killed in the rooms or yards of four family houses, two on the south side of the road, and two on the north. They included nine men, four women, and six children. Many had been sleeping, and were woken by the land-mine blast. Some were shot down in their pajamas. The oldest man was seventy-six. He was blind and decrepit, and sat in a wheelchair. His elderly wife was killed, too. The dead children ranged in age from fifteen to three. They included boys and girls. The Marines later delivered the corpses to the morgue, where they were catalogued by the local coroner. Photographs and videos were taken independently by Americans and Iraqis in the neighborhood and at the morgue. The images showed blood-splattered rooms, as well as victims. The dead did not look peaceful. They looked bloody and grotesque. You are my brother by another mother, you are my daughter by my wife. The dead were buried by angry, grieving crowds.

.   .   .

On the second day, a Marine Corps press officer at the big base downriver in Ramadi issued a wildly misleading statement attributing the civilian deaths to the enemy's I.E.D., as if the families had crowded around the device before it exploded. That statement was later held out to be a deliberate lie, a cover-up, but in fairness it resulted from the isolation of the base, and was more self-delusional than underhanded. The press statement was not seen by Captain McConnell or his men, who had no chance therefore to correct it. Once it was issued, it became an official truth that the Marine Corps, even today, has rigidly refused to retract, despite the fact that within the Corps a more plausible official truth existed almost from the start: the day after the press statement was issued, McConnell visited the battalion headquarters at a dam five miles north of Haditha, where he gave his commander, Lieutenant Colonel Jeffrey Chessani, a PowerPoint briefing on the action, explaining that some number of civilians had been killed by Wuterich's squad while they suppressed a "complex ambush" that had started with the explosion of the land mine and had continued with an attack by hidden gunmen. Most of the briefing concerned other small firefights that had erupted in Haditha the same day. Chessani authorized the maximum compensation payments of $2,500 to the families for each of the dead who could be certified not to have been insurgents. A Marine major was assigned to do at least that much of an investigation. McConnell's version was passed up the chain of command. McConnell returned to his fight for Haditha.

But one month later a reporter at *Time* magazine's Baghdad bureau, Tim McGirk, viewed a gruesome video of the aftermath, which suggested that people had been shot and killed inside the houses. Such is the nature of this war, with its routine collateral horrors, that had McGirk been privy to McConnell's report the video might not have surprised him. But with only the press statement about a land mine to go by, it was obvious that something about the official description was very wrong. McGirk's initial queries to the Marine Corps were rebuffed with an e-mail accusing him of buying into insurgent propaganda, and, implicitly, of aiding and abetting the enemy in a time of war. Whoever wrote the e-mail was out of his league. Negative publicity does indeed help the insurgency, but it's the killing of bystanders that really does the trick. Iraq is a small country with large family ties. After three years of war, the locals hardly needed *Time* to tell them the score. Rather, it was the Americans back home who needed help—any little insight into why the war kept getting worse. McGirk and others in the Baghdad bureau continued with their inquiry, focusing increasingly on the possibility that a massacre and cover-up had occurred. They did not draw conclusions, but laid out what was known and, in mid-March 2006, published the first of several carefully considered accounts.

Knowing that the articles were coming, the Marine Corps had been forced to accept two independent military investigations, one led by an Army general, concentrating on the responsibilities of command, and the other by the criminal investigative branch of the Navy, which focused on reconstructing events on the ground. News from the investigations occasionally emerged, and did not look good for the Marines. Pennsylvania congressman John Murtha, a former Marine and a powerful friend of the Pentagon, stated bluntly that his sources were telling him that a massacre had indeed occurred; he said that there had been no firefight, and that Wuterich's squad had simply gone berserk. Murtha's larger point was that impossible pressure was being placed on U.S. troops, and that they should be withdrawn from a self-destructive war. Following his statements, Haditha became yet another test in a polarized nation, and never mind the details: if you liked President George W. Bush, you believed that no massacre had taken place; if you disliked him, you believed the opposite. As part of the package, *Time* came in for Internet attacks, hate-filled attempts to find any small discrepancies in its reporting, and, again, never mind the underlying truth.

Amid the vitriol came allegations of other U.S. atrocities in Iraq, some of which turned out to be real. The Iraqi prime minister, Nuri Kamal al-Maliki, who had enjoyed the strong support of the U.S. government, stated publicly what has long been obvious on the streets—that the abuse of Iraqi civilians by American soldiers is routine. He did not say what is equally obvious—that abuse of Iraqis by Iraqis is even more routine, and that, along with horrors inflicted by Sunni groups, much of the worst is done by Shiite militias, who constitute a significant portion of the government's own forces as Iraq slips into civil war.

Al-Maliki vowed to launch his own independent investigation of the Haditha killings—wishful thinking for a government leader forced to hunker down in Baghdad's fortified Green Zone. But tempers were fraying in both Iraq and the United States.

Meanwhile, Kilo Company and the rest of the Third Battalion had returned to California on schedule in the early spring of 2006, and had been greeted with the usual fanfare. But one week later the division's top general relieved Captain McConnell and Lieutenant Colonel Chessani of their commands, stating that he had lost confidence in their abilities to lead. The two officers remained on duty in other roles, though straining against bitterness, and anxious about the future. McConnell hoped that by remaining silent he might prevail, standing against the assault as a Spartan would. Semper fi. Nonetheless, it seems eventually to have dawned on him that his own beloved Corps might not be at his side. Reluctantly, McConnell hired a private defense lawyer, as did Wuterich and others. The naval investigation dragged on, and in midsummer produced a 3,500-page report. The report has not been made public, but apparently suggests that some members of the squad had engaged in murder, and that afterward they and perhaps others had agreed on a narrative to hide the crime. The Marine Corps began to ready charges, and to prepare for military trials and lesser career-ending disciplinary actions. The trials will take place at Pendleton, probably sometime before spring. The penalties may include capital punishment and prison for life. In the most general terms the outcome is already known. A former officer close to McConnell said to me, "The Corps has this reflex when it feels threatened at home. It has a history of eating its young."

II. The Fallujah Legacy

Who among these young should be eaten, and how, are questions that Marine Corps justice will decide. But the story of

Haditha is about more than the fate of just a few men, the loss of their friend, or the casualties they inflicted along the Euphrates River one cool November morning. More fully explored, it is about the observable realities of an expanding guerrilla war—about mistakes that have been made and, regrettably, about the inability to fix what is wrong. Those limitations appear to be inherent in the military, and though they certainly have much to do with the reactions and resentments of the least competent soldiers, they also, in a different way, apply to the very best. No matter how sophisticated or subtle our military thinkers may be, ultimately they have use of only this very blunt device—a heavy American force that is simply not up to suppressing a popular rebellion in a foreign land. Despite all the fine words and intentions, the U.S. military turns out to be a tool that is too large and too powerful to be sharpened. Our soldiers collectively did not want this war, and many have come to believe that it cannot be won, but they are not in positions to act on those thoughts, and have no choice but to perform their assignments as their capacities allow.

The starting point of the Haditha killings is early 2004, when the occupation was nearly a year old, and the Marines were brought back to Iraq to take over from the U.S. Army west of Baghdad, in the Sunni strongholds of Anbar Province. Anbar was said to be restive, but it was already dangerous as hell. The Army had blundered there. Soon after the invasion, in April 2003, soldiers from the Eighty-second Airborne Division had gone into the center of Fallujah, where they set up an observation post in a schoolhouse. The best account yet of the consequences, and indeed of the entire war, is contained in the recent book *Fiasco*, written by Thomas E. Ricks of *The Washington Post*. Ricks quotes the Army colonel in command, who said, "We came in to show presence just so the average citizen would feel safe." But it didn't work out that way, as it has not worked out for all the iterations of "presence" ever since.

This is an aspect of the war still poorly accepted by the military, and by critics who believe that by sending more troops the U.S. might have done a better job, or could do so today. The view from the street has always been different. Iraq steps aside to let soldiers pass by, and then immediately fills in the void behind them. The soldiers are targets as hapless as any German conscript ever was. Reduced to giving candy to children, and cut off by language and ignorance from the culture around them, they work in such isolation that the potentially positive effects of their presence usually amount to nil. The potentially negative effects, however, are significant. Back in April 2003, the U.S. colonel's average Iraqi citizen might have told him, "You don't know what you don't know, and, sir, you don't know a lot."

The colonel's soldiers had set up the observation post high in the schoolhouse, from which they could see over the tops of garden walls and into family compounds where unveiled women did housework and hung laundry to dry. The soldiers did not understand that this amounted to a violation of the local women, and a serious insult to their men. An angry crowd gathered in front of the school to demand the soldiers' withdrawal. From their positions in the building, the soldiers eyed the demonstrators warily for a while, but then rifle rounds began to hit the walls, fired perhaps from both a rooftop and the street, and the soldiers responded by firing directly into the crowd. Massive response had been the norm during the recent invasion, when the opponents were enemy troops, but times had changed and these were mostly noncombatants on the street. As many as seventy-one people were wounded, and between five and seventeen died, depending on the truth of the American or Iraqi versions. The commander of the Eighty-second Airborne, General Charles Swannack Jr., later claimed that his men's marksmanship had been precise—and indeed so accurate that every one of the casualties (he counted five or six) was an identifiable instigator who deserved what he got. In other words, within the Army there was no question of disciplinary action. But the school-house shootings had given the insurgency a cause, and the guerrilla war had begun.

•   •   •

By the time the Marines arrived in early 2004, nearly two years before the killings in Haditha, the war was out of hand. This was true not just in Anbar but all through central Iraq, where it was obvious that the crude tactics of the Army were failing, and playing into the insurgents' plans. Individual soldiers were brave, but the Army as an institution was averse to risk, and it was making a show of its fear by living on overprotected bases, running patrols only in armored vehicles, and overdoing its responses to the pinprick attacks by the insurgents—arresting far too many men, and answering rifle fire with tanks, rockets, artillery, and air strikes. It became so common to call down precision bombs against even individual suspected insurgents (for instance, someone spotted by drone, walking with a shovel along a road at night) that a new term was coined, based on the physical effects that could sometimes be observed on video. "Pink misting," some soldiers called it, and in their growing frustration they said it with glee.

Excessive force was employed not merely because the weapons were available but also because high technology had led Americans to expect low-casualty wars. Especially in the context of a conflict that had never been adequately explained, the U.S. military for political reasons could not afford any implication that it was squandering its soldiers' lives in Iraq. It is difficult to argue publicly that the military's caution was not a good thing. Strictly in gaming terms, however, there was a problem: by squandering innocent Iraqi lives instead, in order to save American soldiers, the Army in particular was spawning untold numbers of new enemies who would mount more frequent attacks against those same soldiers in the future. This was happening, and fast. The Army was locked into a self-defeating cycle by the very need to keep its casualties down. Meanwhile, the insurgent campaign was expanding in proportion to the number of noncombatants dishonored, brutalized, or killed. It was expanding in proportion to outrage.

Perhaps because of their history in irregular wars, the Marines seem to have a special sense for such cycles of violence. Despite their public image as leathernecks and fighters, they possess a contemplative strain, and their organization, because it is relatively small, is also relatively amenable to change. When they returned to Iraq in 2004, they knew that the fight had grown much trickier than before, and they announced that in Anbar they would demonstrate a new approach to winning the war. They would shed the excess of armor, use military precision rather than power, get out of their vehicles and walk through the towns, knock on doors rather than break them down, and go out of their way to accommodate the Iraqi culture. They would base their tactics on good intelligence. They would not overreact when provoked. They would shoot insurgents, and even enjoy the kills, but they would be careful not to hurt innocent bystanders. They would provide the necessary stability to allow a civil Iraqi society to grow. They would be understood, and they would make friends.

It was to be a textbook counterinsurgency campaign. In abstraction the strategy made sense, and it was the obvious choice—indeed, the only potentially productive one remaining. In practice, however, it quickly encountered an uncooperative Iraq. With its population of 250,000, Fallujah was particularly tough. In addition to all the native insurgents there, it contained foreign fighters from elsewhere in the Middle East, who had arrived to do battle under the banners of God. Within a couple of weeks the Marines were being forced by hostile fire back into their armored vehicles, and were encountering the same frustrations that the Army had, of not speaking Arabic, not having reliable translators, not knowing whose advice to trust, and not being able to distinguish between the enemy and ordinary people on the streets. As for the Iraqis in Anbar, the distinction so dear to the American forces, between the Army and the Marines, meant little to them. The view from the rooftops was that all these guys wore the same stars and stripes, and were crusaders for Zionists and oilmen, if not necessarily for Christ. Recently on Capitol Hill, John Murtha, the congressman and former Marine who has been so vocal about the killings in Haditha, mentioned those early encounters with reality to me. He said, "The Marines came over here to my office and said, 'Jesus, they're shooting at us!' And I said, 'Well, where did you *think* you were going?'"

The Marines did not formally abandon their strategy, but they saw it torn from their grasp. On March 31, 2004, precisely two years before Captain McConnell and his Kilo Company came home from their momentous tour in Haditha, four American employees of a security firm called Blackwater were ambushed and killed in Fallujah. Their corpses were hacked apart and burned, and two of them were hung from a bridge amid celebrations on the street. Images were beamed around the world. Judging correctly that it could not leave the insult unanswered, the Bush administration, after brief consideration of the options, decided on an all-out assault against the city. That decision continues to stand as one of the worst of the war, ranking only below the decision to disband the Iraqi Army and the initial decision to invade. At the time, for those of us living independently in Iraq outside of the American security zones, and with some sense therefore of the mood on the streets, it demonstrated once again the inability of officials to imagine the trouble that the United States was in, and the astonishing insularity of Washington, D.C.

.　　　.　　　.

The Marines knew better. They wanted to respond to the Blackwater ambush by going after the individual killers, and then following through with a well-crafted counterinsurgency campaign to stabilize and mollify the city. But when they were overruled and ordered to do the opposite—to mount an immediate full-frontal offensive—they set aside their theories, and as professional soldiers they dutifully complied. It was a disaster. Backed up by tanks and combat aircraft, the Marines went into Fallujah dealing destruction, and quickly bogged down in house-to-house fighting against a competent and determined foe. To make matters worse, the showcase battalion of the new Iraqi Army mutinied and refused to join the fight. The battle cost several dozen American dead and many more wounded, and did immeasurable damage to the prospects for American success. It turned into a humiliation for the United States when, after four days of struggle, the Marines were ordered by a nervous Washington to withdraw. Again they dutifully complied. Afterward, the jubilant insurgents took full public control of the city, and with the help of the foreign fighters turned it into a fortified haven which U.S. forces did not dare to enter.

To get a feeling for Kilo Company and the killings in Haditha, it is necessary to remember this. After the spring battle was lost, Fallujah became an open challenge to the American presence in Iraq. There were plenty of other challenges, and to speak only of Fallujah is grossly to simplify the war. Still, Fallujah was the most obvious one, and the United States, unless it was to quit and go home, had no choice but to take the city back. Everyone knew it, on all sides, and for months the antagonists prepared. Because of the fortifications and the expectation of active resistance, there was no question this time of a patient counterinsurgency campaign: the Marines were going to have to go in and simply smash the city down. In November of 2004, they did just that, with a force about 10,000 strong. Before attacking they gave the city warning, and allowed an exodus to occur. Nearly the entire population fled, including most of the insurgents, who spread into Baghdad or up the Euphrates to carry on the rebellion, leaving behind, however, a rear guard of perhaps 1,000 gunmen who, exceptionally, wanted to make a stand. This was their mistake. The Marines attacked with high explosives and heavy weapons. Over the ten days it took to move through Fallujah, and the following weeks of methodical house-to-house clearing, they wrecked the city's infrastructure, damaged or destroyed 20,000 houses or more, and did the same to dozens of schools and mosques. They were not crusaders. They did not Christianize the place. They turned Fallujah into Stalingrad.

Many insurgents survived the initial assaults and emerged to contest the Marines at close quarters, room to room and in the rubble. It is said to have been the most intense battle by American forces since Vietnam. The insurgents were trapped inside cordon upon cordon of American troops, and they fought until death. For the Marines the rules of engagement were necessarily loose. Rules of engagement are standing orders that limit the targets of soldiers, defining the difference between appropriate and inappropriate killing according to strategic and tactical goals, and between legal and illegal killing according to interpretations of international law. In Fallujah the rules allowed Marines to kill anyone they believed to be dangerous, and others who got in the way. In addition to those seen carrying weapons, in practice this meant everyone in every structure from which hostile fire came, and any military-age male seen moving toward the Marines or running away. Obviously, the Marines were not allowed to kill wounded prisoners, but in a televised case one of them did, and Marine Corps justice averted its gaze.

The men of Kilo Company fought through the thick of Fallujah. Lance Corporals Terrazas and Crossan, and most of the other men of future Haditha note, ran the course from start to finish. Kilo Company lost four Marines killed and at least twenty seriously wounded, and was involved in the best-known close-quarters combat of the battle—a desperate attempt to clear insurgents from the rooms of a house, which came to be known as the Hell House fight. Toward the end of it, a New York–based photographer named Lucian Read snapped an iconic picture of a blood-drenched sergeant who had been shot seven times and blasted with an enemy grenade, but who nonetheless was emerging on foot from the house, holding a pistol in one hand, supported by a Marine on each side. The photograph showed the Marines as they like to be seen, and as some like to see themselves. There's a lot to be said for going to war with a photographer in tow, until something happens that you would rather forget.

·　　　·　　　·

Fallujah was a victory for the Marine Corps, but a victory narrowly defined. The reality is that a quarter-million people were forced from their homes and, when they returned, were faced with a city in ruins, surrounded by concertina wire and watched over by armed men in towers. Marine general John Sattler, who had led the assault, claimed that the insurgency had been broken. But as the seasons slid by in 2005, guerrillas slipped back into Fallujah, or sprang up from its ruins, and they surged forward through all the other towns of Anbar, including Haditha. Sattler was wrong, and embarrassingly so. Within more contemplative circles of Marines, the battle of Fallujah became less of a triumph than a warning. The consequences were not difficult to discern.

A hard-pressed combat officer once put it this way to me: "Yeah, we won Fallujah. But before that we *made* Fallujah. And we definitely can't afford to make another."

The hell of it was that the reasonable alternative—a nuanced counterinsurgency campaign—was not showing much promise either. At its core, the counterinsurgency campaign asked a lot. On the Iraqi side, it required the people of Anbar to place their faith in a United States government that had repeatedly blundered over the previous few years, and that was unable to protect collaborators from the insurgents' knives. On the American side, it required young Marines with little worldly experience to show trust in a foreign population on alien streets where they were being shot at and blown up. Indeed, the formula asked so much from everyone involved that it was becoming difficult to know when it was realistic anymore. Specialists in Washington advocated patience and wisdom, and said the standard thing about our instant-gratification society. Officials in the Green Zone highlighted the slightest positive signs. But on the ground in Anbar the trends were all wrong.

III. First, Do No Harm

After Fallujah and the Hell House fight, Kilo Company flew home to California, spent a half-year retraining under its new captain, Lucas McConnell, and then returned to Iraq in September 2005, with Haditha in its sights. Haditha at that point had been largely ignored by the Marines for nearly a year. It was being ruled by an uncompromising group of insurgents who had instituted Islamic law and done some good deeds, but had also carried out public floggings and beheadings, and were using Haditha as a base from which to launch attacks in the region. In April of 2005 they had taken nineteen Shia fishermen to a soccer field and slaughtered them all. The few policemen in town had resigned or fled to avoid similar fates. Then, on

August 1, roughly two months before Kilo Company returned to Iraq, six Marine snipers from an Ohio-based company of reservists had been ambushed and killed on the outskirts of the city, in a scene that was videotaped by the insurgents and made available on DVDs in the market. Two days later another fourteen Marines from the same reserve company were killed when their armored personnel carrier was destroyed by an improvised mine. By the end of its tour, primarily around Haditha, that company had suffered twenty-three dead and thirty-six wounded, earning it the unfortunate distinction of having been the most badly mauled of any company in the war thus far. Upon returning to Ohio, one of the sergeants described his rage after the destruction of the personnel carrier. He had busted into a nearby house and had barely restrained himself from shooting two women and a teenage boy whom he found inside. He said he realized then that he had been too long in Iraq. He had been there seven months. He left in September 2005, when Kilo Company arrived.

.   .   .

The Marines decided to clean out Haditha once and for all. At the start of October they positioned about 3,000 troops in an arc to the south, west, and north, around the town. Roughly 700 of the troops were from Pendleton's Third Battalion under its new commander, Lieutenant Colonel Chessani. The men of Kilo Company were assigned the lead. They waited in the desert west of the city center. Before the offensive began, they knelt with their helmets off and prayed. They expected intense resistance in the form of rifle fire and rocket-propelled grenades. The plan called for them to advance on foot on a broad front, and to push the insurgents through the city until they were backed against the Euphrates, where they would surrender or die. The strategy was odd—as if the Marines had forgotten exactly which war they were in. Before dawn three bridges that crossed the river were bombed to cut off the enemy's escape. Later, at a Baghdad press briefing, Major General Rick Lynch said, "We took out a portion of each of those bridges to deny the terrorists and foreign fighters—the insurgency—the ability to come from north to south, or south to north, across the Euphrates River. It was a precision strike so that when we indeed defeat the insurgency in these areas—and we're on a glide path to do that—we can go back and replace those segments of the bridges so that the people in that area can regain their own freedom of movement." It was a tidy plan for an orderly war, everything in its place. Lynch continued, "Put that original chart up, please, the one that I just took down."

When the Marines advanced into Haditha, on the first day of Ramadan, October 4, 2005, they encountered a town so peaceful that at first it seemed deserted. They knew that it was not—that they were being watched from behind the compound walls, and that the residents were playing it safe by staying off the streets. The frustration was that the insurgents were lying equally low, and not standing to fight or run away, as conventional combatants would. They could do this because of a reality soon evident to ordinary grunts but stubbornly denied by the U.S. command, which was that in Haditha the insurgency enjoyed widespread public support, and all the more so now with American soldiers suddenly walking around. The insurgents did not need to consult with experts to understand guerrilla war. Why bother to confront these Americans immediately, when you could let them pass by and later hunt them down? Why bother to go north to south or south to north when you could simply stay at home?

Within hours the Marines had walked all the way through Haditha and had reached the Euphrates with little to show. Over the next two weeks Chessani's battalion remained in town, searching house to house and encountering hardly any opposition.

Evidence of the insurgency was all around. By the time the offensive was formally called off, the Marines had netted 119 improvised mines, several facilities for making them, two car bombs, fourteen weapons caches, and a propaganda shop equipped with computers, copiers, and several thousand blank CDs and audiotapes. They had found a note pinned to the door of a mosque, on which a former policeman renounced his collaboration with the invaders and begged the insurgents for their forgiveness. Finally, they had detained about 130 suspects, of whom they released about half and shipped off the others for interrogation. Against the scale of the rebellion, these were illusory accomplishments.

·   ·   ·

When Chessani's battalion withdrew in mid-October, it shifted a few miles to the north and settled into its comfortable quarters at the dam above Haditha. McConnell and his Kilo Company were left behind to maintain a full-time presence in the center of town. They set up Sparta Base in a former school administration building, in a walled compound that could accommodate their generators and Humvees. The perimeter was reinforced with coils of concertina wire, sandbagged machine-gun emplacements, and blast walls made of HESCO barriers—large dirt-filled cubes heavy enough to limit the effects of mortars and rockets. The administration building was H-shaped and low-slung. It contained about fifteen rooms of various sizes, all with linoleum floors and painted concrete walls. One of the rooms was made into the company's office and called the Combat Operations Center. Two others were made into a chow hall and a kitchen. The kitchen once burned because the cooks were not paying attention, but the food that was served was surprisingly good, and later sometimes included crab. Most of the building was made into general living quarters, where the men slept on cots and kept their personal gear, including an abundance of iPods, video games, and DVD players. As a final special touch there was even a makeshift photography studio where Lucian Read, who had rejoined the company, shot individual portraits of the men. Despite all that is said about difficulties endured by American forces in Iraq, as time passed the Marines at Sparta Base tended to feel that, if anything, they were not roughing it enough.

A sign on the wall read:

Habits of Thought

1. Sturdy Professionalism
2. Make yourself hard to kill.
3. No Better Friend, No Worse Enemy
4. First, Do No Harm
5. The Iraqi People are not our enemy, but our enemy hides amongst them.

Corollary 1: You have to look at these people as if they are trying to kill you, but you can't treat them that way.

Corollary 2: Be polite, be professional, have a plan to kill everyone you meet.

This was standard Marine Corps stuff, passed down from above. It was meant as a guide to the war in Iraq, but it was unclear and overwrought. The men of Kilo Company had a culture of being assertive and tough, partly because of the Hell House fight and the publicity that had followed. But now that this latest offensive had fizzled, they were being asked to do exactly what? They were wandering around Haditha just waiting to get hit. Lieutenant Colonel Chessani, up at the dam, was a strange guy to them. He had a reputation of being standoffish, intensely religious, and uncommunicative; he seemed to know the enlisted men only by the nametags on their chests, and they felt he offered them little guidance at best. Captain McConnell was a different story. He was seen as an accessible and straightforward guy, but also as a military lifer, whose talks to his men, though intended to be inspirational, were dulled by Marine Corps clichés and prefabricated thoughts. He was always talking about responsibility and honor. He seemed sincerely to believe that in Haditha they were fighting the global war on terror—oh yes, and winning it, too. He insisted that the insurgents were cowards who lacked values, when the opposite was evidently true. He made Wagnerian vows like "We will not falter in the clashing of spears." At Sparta Base sometimes it got a little thick, especially for a place with no enemy in sight. In fairness, however, officers who can inspire enlisted Marines are rare, and McConnell, because he was new, was perhaps just trying too hard.

．　　　　　．　　　　　．

Meanwhile, the Marines mounted patrols every day, often for no better reason than to spot something unusual on streets that to them remained strange. This was said to be an intelligence-based war, but the intelligence was poor. Sometimes the Marines detained men whose names appeared on their lists; more often they went into houses, asked a few questions, and walked away empty-handed. Officially their rules of engagement were only slightly more restrictive than those that had applied to the free hunting in Fallujah, with their tolerance for the killing of people who got in the way. In Haditha, however, there were civilians all around. Reflexively the city was known as a battle space, and perhaps it was one, but if so it was barely recognizable. Simply put, though Haditha was still largely controlled by the insurgents, during all the weeks prior to the killings of November 19, the Marines of Kilo Company saw very little action there. Battle space? They killed one man—a town idiot who insisted on crossing their perimeter wire. They found some munitions caches in sandy soil along the riverbanks. They talked to some tribal leaders. But the largest measure of their success was a circular one—the continuing discovery of improvised land mines, which were laid each night, but which would not have been planted in the first place were it not for the presence of American troops in town. Indeed, the whole war had become a chicken-or-egg question, around and around with no answer possible.

The enlisted men of Kilo Company rarely philosophized. Many had joined the Corps in response to the September 11 attacks, now four years past, but the emotions that once had motivated them had been reduced by their participation in an enormously bureaucratic enterprise, and by the tedium of war. Fine—they were probably better soldiers for it. These were not the taut warriors portrayed in action movies. As they shed their helmets and body armor, they emerged as ordinary five-foot-nine-inch, 150-pound middle-class Americans, sometimes pimple-faced, and often sort of scrawny. Some of them were mentally agile, and some quite obviously were not. By the stringent standards of the U.S. military, they were not always well behaved. At Sparta Base there was a bit of illicit drinking, a touch of pornography. There are rumors about the use of narcotics as well. But the unit's morale was good enough, largely because the men had become close friends. They liked motorcycles, they liked cars, they liked guns. They especially liked girls a lot. Some could not speak without fuck. For instance, they fucking did not want to be in Iraq. Not anymore, if they ever did. Those who were returning felt they had come back way too fucking soon. And no, they did not respect the Iraqi culture—who the fuck would? Iraqi men wear man-dresses. Iraqi men think everyone wants to eye-fuck their precious wives. Iraqi men kill their own people, then turn around and kill Marines. It's fucking bullshit. God should paintball the genuine bastards so the Marines could then blow them away. Sometimes on the streets of Haditha it seemed like every man would get splattered.

But the Marines did not sit around Sparta Base and worry this to death. They talked about other things, their exploits, their party binges, the really dumb moves of their friends. They laughed and gave each other hard times. They gave each other names. When they mounted their patrols, they went up and down the designated streets and did their jobs as they were told. Be polite and have a plan to kill everyone you meet? Yes, sir, roger that, and on streets like these that would mean shooting the guy from up close, sir, at any false move on his part—is that what you mean by a plan? If the counterinsurgency mission in Haditha seemed half-cocked, so did any real chance for success in Iraq, but that was for others to decide—not for the soldiers who had to carry out the fights. The Marines of Kilo Company were well-intentioned guys who took pride in their conventional battlefield skills and, partly as a result, now just wanted to go home. As a group they were not like people who join the police for the satisfaction of hurting others. They were more like people who join Outward Bound. Until the killings of November 19, there is no evidence that in Haditha they abused the fucking Iraqis even once.

Then suddenly on Route Chestnut Guzman and Crossan were wounded, Terrazas was torn in two, and Sergeant Wuterich was calling for backup. The events that followed will never be reconstructed completely, no matter what the courts may find. Through the dust and noise on that Haditha street, they played out in a jumble of semi-autonomous actions, complicated by perceptions that had been narrowed by the attack and further confused by the ambiguities associated with fighting a guerrilla war on foreign ground. Some of the Marines may have suspected that a line had been crossed, and that crimes might have been committed, but in the urgency of the moment it would have seemed less likely then than it seems now, and even today the principal view of those involved is anger that the accusations are cheap, and that Kilo Company has been unfairly singled out.

There is probably a feeling of remorse as well, but, to generalize, it is regret that the killing of noncombatants had so little to do with the intentions of the men, and that the story cannot somehow be taken back and run all over again.

IV. From House to House

The boom of the land mine exploding was heard throughout Haditha. Immediately afterward the city went quiet, except near the convoy, from which the Marines piled out shouting. Some ran back to the shattered Humvee to render aid as they could; the others quickly settled down, and indeed milled around uncertainly until Wuterich ordered them to spread out into defensive positions. It was still barely 7:15 in the morning, the Humvee boiled with black smoke, and the possibility existed that its destruction marked the start of an ambush that would now expand into overlapping attacks with automatic fire and rocket-propelled grenades. All through Iraq the insurgents were laying such lethal traps. For the moment, the houses on both sides of the street showed no sign of activity, though certainly they contained people lying low, if only out of fear.

Again it is important to face the realities here. According to counterinsurgency doctrine, these people were not necessarily the enemy, but Terrazas was nonetheless spilling his guts into their street. Among these very houses was one where the Marines had discovered a bomb factory just a few days before. Moreover, even if the neighbors were not directly involved, they must have known the location of this land mine, which could not have been planted without the locals taking notice. Surely some residents could have found a way to warn the patrol; if they were not the enemy, surely some could have acknowledged that Kilo Company during its stay in Haditha had been showing goodwill and restraint. But no, it was apparent that to these people Terrazas was just another dead American, like roadkill, and good riddance to him. For Wuterich's squad the silence of the neighborhood was therefore less reassuring than ominous. It was the quiet before the storm, the prelude to an attack. The Marines were angry and tense. They sighted their rifles at the walls and rooftops, thinking every variation of fuck and waiting for the incoming rounds.

Instead, a white Opel sedan came driving up the street. It was an unmarked taxi carrying five young men, four of them college students bound for school in Baghdad, the fifth their driver. They were only about a hundred yards away from the blast site when they happened upon the scene. Through their windshield—dirty, bug-splattered, against the sun—they would have seen one of the most dangerous sights in Iraq: smoke rising from a shattered Humvee, a stopped convoy, and American soldiers in full fighting mettle coming at them down the street. The Marines halted the car from a distance. When soldiers do this in Iraq, they are supposed to follow a progressive escalation of force, with hand signals first, followed by raised weapons, then warning shots with tracers visible, then shots to the engine block, and finally, if the car keeps coming, shots directly into the driver. Because of the risk of car bombs, however, the procedure is typically shortened: weapons go up, and if the car doesn't stop, the driver and other occupants are liberally sprayed with fire. Those are the rules of the road, and so be it; given the circumstances, they are well enough understood to seem fair.

This time the driver stopped, as most drivers do. Some witnesses in the nearby houses later said that he tried to back away but then desisted. The Marines came running up, shouting and cursing. Presumably they told the occupants to get out of the car and to kneel on the street with their hands on their heads. What the Marines thought of them is not clear. Later they said they believed the men were associated with the land-mine explosion, and were perhaps the spotters who had pushed the button, or were following up now with a car-bomb attack.

This strains credulity for several reasons, not the least of which is that five people in a car are about four too many for either purpose. Equally unlikely was another explanation sometimes mentioned, that these were insurgents driving up to do battle. But the truth is that the Marines neither knew nor needed to know why they stopped the car. The stop was legitimate. It was a necessary act to limit the risks to the squad, and to keep the confusion from growing.

The problem is what happened next, after a quick search revealed that the car contained no weapons or explosives, or any other evidence that linked the men to the insurgency. The Iraqis perhaps should have been held for a while or, better yet, allowed to take their car and leave. Instead, all five of them were shot dead by the Marines. Later, the Marines reported that they killed them because they had started to run away. Even if true, by normal standards this raises the question of what threat these men could have posed when they were fleeing unarmed—or at least what threat could have justified shooting them down. But in Iraq the question was moot, and for reasons that give significance to the Haditha story beyond mere crime and punishment. The first and simplest reason is that, because of reluctance to second-guess soldiers in a fight, the rules of engagement allow for such liberal interpretations of threat that in practice they authorize the killing of even unarmed military-age males who are running away. The second reason derives from the first. It is that the killing of civilians has become so commonplace that the report of these particular ones barely aroused notice as it moved up the chain of command in Iraq. War is fog, civilians die, and these fools should not have tried to escape.

.   .   .

The incident reemerged only because of the insistent inquiries of *Time* magazine. During the subsequent military investigations that were forced onto the Marine Corps in the spring and summer of 2006, grainy images from an aerial drone were found that appeared to show the five bodies lying clustered together beside the sedan, with one sprawled partly atop another. Perhaps they had been dragged back and placed there, but this was not part of the original story. Certainly the pattern as seen from overhead was not one of men killed while trying to scatter. Equally troubling were the statements of one of the Iraqi soldiers who was with the convoy, and who four months later was questioned by a naval investigator. The questioning was incomplete, full of opportunities never pursued, and further weakened by an incompetent interpreter. A lawyer in court could tear such testimony apart. Nonetheless, what emerged was a picture of murder. The Iraqi soldier said he had been only about twenty-five yards away from the Opel sedan, and had watched the entire scene. It was obvious to him that the Iraqis were noncombatants—otherwise, why would they have driven up like this? He said the Marines had yanked open the Opel's doors, taken the men out, forced them to kneel with their hands on their heads, and, without bothering to search them, had quickly gunned them down. The investigator said, "Bang, bang, bang, bang, bang." Well yeah, well no, well actually the Iraqis were sprayed with rifle rounds. The M16 is a light, clip-fed weapon with a plastic stock and a metal barrel. It fires a three-round burst when it is switched to automatic. It does not bang then, but ripples sharply. The Iraqi soldier said he saw a head come apart and a face split in two. He also said that one of the Marines used a pistol, and he called that man a captain, but he did not appear to know any of the squad members' names, and this element he seems to have gotten wrong. By my calculation, there were no officers yet on the scene.

Errors are too easy to make when assigning individual blame. Sergeant Wuterich, for instance, has been repeatedly singled out. If the five Iraqi civilians from the car were summarily slain, Wuterich was probably elsewhere, closer to the center of concern, placing his men into defensive positions and watching the houses for hostile fire. Indeed, it is wrong to brand any of the Marines of his squad without knowing what each was doing, and where each one was. I do not know those details, though by now the military prosecutors must. It appears that only a few of the Marines handled the people from the car, and that, while all of them were angry, only two let loose with their guns. The killing was not agreed upon or planned. It started without warning and finished too fast to stop. Claims have been made of an extensive conspiracy to cover up murders and protect the Marine Corps from embarrassment—but no such conspiracy was necessary, and it is unlikely that any occurred. As for the killings of the car's occupants, all that would have been required was a shift at the outset contained in two simple words. They ran. It would not matter who first uttered the words, or if these were the ones actually spoken. Among the men of Wuterich's squad the elegance would immediately have been understood. We are brothers by other mothers. The dead do not return to life, but some mistakes can be undone. Killing is not wrong in Iraq, if you can say the rules allowed it.

.   .   .

Within minutes the force from Sparta Base arrived. It was a squad of about the same size as Wuterich's, led by the only officer present on Route Chestnut the entire morning, a young lieutenant named William Kallop. Like other lieutenants in Kilo Company, Kallop was junior in all but rank to the senior enlisted men, to whom he naturally deferred. He had a reputation of being a little soft, a little lost. He was the pleasant son of a wealthy New York family, who had joined the Marine Corps, it was believed in Kilo Company, to prove something to himself before returning to a life of comfort. As a soldier he was said to be average. When the allegations against Kilo Company surfaced in the spring of 2006, his parents vigorously reacted. They hired a New York public-relations firm that specializes in legal cases, and then engaged a defense attorney who is a former Marine general and was once one of the top lawyers in the Corps. The implicit warning may have had some effect. While McConnell and Chessani were humiliated and relieved of their commands, and Wuterich was fingered in public, Kallop was left untouched, though technically upon his arrival at Route Chestnut on November 19 he had become the commander on the scene.

Apparently his command didn't amount to much. For the most part he remained on the street by the Humvees with the rest of his squad and allowed Wuterich and his men to work their way through the four houses where, to repeat the number, they killed the additional nineteen Iraqis—children, women, and men. It is virtually certain that none of the dead were combatants, but little else about the case is so straightforward. Strange though it seems at first glance, the military courts will probably have a very difficult time deciding if war crimes were committed inside the houses. The difficulty will not be due to a Marine Corps agenda. Indeed, the expedient solution for the entire U.S. military would be to treat Wuterich and his men as criminals, and to destroy McConnell and Chessani as well, thereby avoiding the alternative conclusion, that the debacle in Haditha is related to normal operations in the war. But it just does not seem plausible, as John Murtha and others have claimed, that these particular Marines, who had enjoyed a relatively low-key tour, went so berserk after Terrazas's death that, having already slaughtered the five Iraqis by the car, they proceeded without specific reason or provocation to enter people's houses and execute even the children at point-blank range in a feverish rampage sustained for several hours, even while Lieutenant Kallop and the other recent arrivals listened to the rippling of gunfire and the screams of the soon dead. The killings in the houses on November 19 were probably nothing so simple as that.

Wuterich may have explained it best, because he has insisted that his Marines came under AK-47 attack, and defended themselves as they had been trained to do, by returning fire and surging forward to suppress the aggressors. Critics have expressed skepticism, pointing out that there was little evidence of exterior damage to the houses, and that certain neighborhood witnesses heard no firefight before the first house was stormed. Other witnesses, however, did hear firing, and the same Iraqi soldier who gave the damning description of executions by the car, and who was certainly no friend of the Marines, repeatedly described coming under attack from the south side of the street.

When the naval investigator asked for details, the interpreter summarized the soldier's answers. He said, "Fire open at them. Shots were shooting at them. Fighting between them and forces are fighting at us, shooting at us. The Americans spread through the houses, and they stayed. They were going to take care of this. So they went where the fire was coming, receiving fire, in that direction. . . . Somebody's shooting at us, we're shooting at them, but they are just shooting at us and we're shooting back."

The investigator said, "Okay. And how many Marines did that?"

Translating directly now, the interpreter said, "It was all mixed up. Even I was a little shake. . . . I didn't see who's shooting at us."

"Did you shoot your weapon at all?"

"I shot in the air. Yeah, we shot, but we shot in the air."

"Why did you shoot in the air?"

"He says, Who am I going to shoot? I got to see somebody I'm shooting."

"Okay. So why shoot at all?"

"When they start firing, the Marines were like, 'Oh come on, you shoot too.' Everybody shot five, six rounds."

Maybe this investigator had not been around the Iraqi Army before. He said, "In the air?"

"In the air, yes, sir I mean, we have no effect when we go out there. We have no effect on anything because they take orders from whatever they tell us." The Iraqi soldier obviously wanted to make it clear that he had not killed any of the dead.

"So you shot in the air?"

"Yes, I did."

"Who told you to shoot in the air?"

"They told."

"But who told you?"

"Not all, not everybody, sir."

Evidently the investigator tried to recover his balance. He said, "Did you ever see anybody—you said that you were taking shots from the neighborhood. Did you ever see anybody shooting at you or the Marines?"

"No, I haven't seen. I know the fires were coming at us, but from where, I don't know."

"But you're sure that you were being shot at?"

"Yes, yes. They want to kill us."

"Was it a lot of shots or just here and there?"

"Spray. It was spray continuous."

"Spray continuous. For about how long?"

"When we first received spray, and then after that, hell break loose. All Americans were firing and everything. I couldn't tell which one's which."

"Okay. And you shot in the air?"

"Yes, sir."

The testimony rings all too true, with compensation for some light twisting of facts. It is very likely that the Marines did indeed begin taking fire on Route Chestnut, a short while after the occupants of the car were killed, and possibly in angry response. Someone is bomb me, I am shoot him, but he is just shoot at me, and I am just shoot him back. This is the kind of fight that Donald Rumsfeld could not imagine.

.   .   .

It was now perhaps 7:30 in the morning. Kallop had arrived with his reinforcements. The fire seemed to come from a house on the south side of the street. In hindsight we know that no insurgents were discovered there, but chances are they were present nonetheless, if not in that house, then in others nearby. The evidence remains uncertain, but Wuterich, for one, insists that his men believed the house contained aggressors, and that they proceeded with a by-the-book operation to clear them out, exactly as the rules of engagement allowed. This may very well be. If you assume it is true, you can watch Haditha play out from there, largely within the legal definition of justified killing—a baseline narrative that becomes the happiest possible version of the morning's events.

With Kallop in place among the Humvees, Wuterich led his men from the front. They got to the house, kicked through the door, and in the entranceway came upon the owner, a middle-aged man, whom one of them shot at close range, probably with a three-round burst to the chest. The Marine's M16 would barely have kicked in his hands. Beyond the sound of the shots, he might have heard the double pops of the rounds entering and exiting the man, the heavier snap of bullets against bone, perhaps the metallic clatter of spent cartridges hitting the ground. The Iraqi was not thrown by the rounds as people are thrown in the movies. If no bones were broken, he may not have felt much pain, except for some stinging where his skin was torn. Unless he was struck in the heart, he did not die immediately, but soon succumbed to massive hemorrhaging. Chances are his blood first splattered against the wall, then flowed into a dark-scarlet puddle beneath him until his heart stopped pumping.

The power was out in the house, and the light inside was dim, all the more so for the Marines, who were piling in from the sunshine of the street. Inside a hostile house, survival requires fast reactions. The Marines fired on a figure down the hall, who turned out too late to be an old woman. There could have been a message there, but guerrilla wars are tricky, and the Marines were not about to slow down. She screamed when she was hit, apparently in the back, and then she died. The Marines were shouting excitedly to one another. They worked down the hall-way until, busting open a door, they came upon a room full of people. Later some of the squad said they had heard AK-47s be-ing racked, though whatever they heard turned out not to be that. The room was dim, and the people were glimpsed rather than clearly seen. The Marines rolled in a grenade, hugged the hallway for the blast, and then charged into the dust and smoke to mop up with their rifles as they had been trained to do. This is my weapon, this is my gun. It was the Hell House fight all over again, though, as it happened, without the opposition. Nine people had sheltered in that room, three generations of the same family, from an ancient man paralyzed by a stroke to an infant girl just three months old. When the grenade exploded, it blew some of them apart, wounded others with penetrating shrapnel, and littered the room with evil-smelling body parts. In the ur-gency of the moment the old man forgot that he was paralyzed and tried to stand up. He took rounds to the chest, vomited blood as he fell, and then lay on the floor twitching as he died. In that room four residents survived. A young woman left her husband behind, grabbed the infant girl, and managed to run away; a ten-year-old girl and her younger brother lay wounded beside their dead mother and remained conscious enough to be terrified.

The Marines went on to the neighboring house, still seeking insurgents, as they believed. What happened there was a repeat of what had just happened next door, only this time the Americans knocked before they shot the man at the gate, and a grenade tossed into an empty bathroom ignited a washing machine, and a grenade tossed into the room where the family was sheltering failed to go off, and perhaps only one American came in and sprayed the room with automatic fire. This time there was just a single survivor, a girl of about thirteen, who later was able to provide some details of her family's death. There was a lot of smoke, but:

Daddy was shot through the heart. He was forty-three.

Mommy was shot in the head and chest. She was forty-one.

Aunt Huda was shot in the chest. She was twenty-seven.

My sister Nour was shot in the right side of her head. She was fifteen.

My sister Saba was shot through the ear. She was eleven.

My brother Muhammad was shot in the hand and I don't know where else. He was ten.

My sister Zainab was shot in the hand and the head. She was five.

My sister Aysha was shot in the leg and I don't know where else. She was three.

The brains of at least one of the little girls were shoved through fractures in her skull by the impact of a bullet. This is a standard effect of high-velocity rounds fired into the closed cavity of a head. Later that day, when a replacement Marine came in to carry out the bodies, the girl's brains would fall onto his boot.

Wuterich's men pursued the search to the north side of Route Chestnut, where they put the women and children under guard and killed four men of another family. There on the north side they found the only AK-47 that was discovered that day— apparently a household defensive weapon, of the type that is legal and common in Iraq. No one has claimed that the rifle had been fired.

On Route Chestnut the killing was over, and the cleanup began. Nearly a year later, the Marines who were involved unanimously insist that it was just another shitty Anbar morning. By narrow application of military law, the upcoming trials may indeed leave it as such. If so, however, those trials will have to justify the shootings around the car and, furthermore, will have to account for certain statements by witnesses that call into question the scenes inside houses as I have described them in the happiest possible version of the events. Those statements, which again are full of contradictions and uncertainties, raise the possibility that, behind the privacy of the walls, Wuterich's men were carrying out deliberate executions and laughing about it, that one aimed and said "You! You!" before he shot the old man down, that they made return trips to the killing rooms to finish people off, and that on the north side of the road they herded their victims into a wardrobe before shooting them through the door. Unless the Marines of Wuterich's squad suddenly start confessing to war crimes, these are questions only the courts will be able to decide.

V. A Thanksgiving Prayer

On the afternoon of November 19, when the reports of civilian casualties reached Captain Lucas McConnell, it did not cross his mind that anything unusual had occurred: the killing by American forces of noncombatants in Iraq is simply so commonplace. Sergeant Wuterich reported on the fight as he defined it. Lieutenant Kallop acquiesced. An intelligence sergeant who surveyed the carnage said much the same thing. Captain McConnell scarcely reacted, because this slaughter seemed to lie within the rules of engagement, and in that sense was little different from any other. McConnell inhabited a military world, full of acronyms and equipment, and peopled by identifiable combatants— a place where spears clashed and civilians unfortunately sometimes came to harm. For him it had been a very active day. Soon after the land-mine explosion that had killed Terrazas, ambushes and firefights erupted elsewhere in Haditha, and all four of his platoons were engaged.

The main thread started at 8:35 in the morning, when an explosives-and-ordnance squad heading to Route Chestnut for a post-blast analysis came under fire from a palm grove. The squad returned fire and drove on. Twenty-five minutes later, and slightly to the south, an aerial drone observed ten men meeting on a palm-grove trail between River Road and the Euphrates. The men appeared to be MAMS, or military-age males, and clearly were not just farmers. Two came on foot, one by motorcycle, and seven by car. They loaded gear into the car and, leaving three men behind, drove slowly south along the trail. McConnell called this "egressing." The drone circled lazily overhead, performing well in the global war on terror. The time was approximately 9:12. At 9:48, about a kilometer away, a Kilo Company patrol was attacked by small-arms fire, and the Marines shot back, resulting, they believed, in three enemy wounded in action, or E.W.I.A., though all of them got away.

The men in the car on the palm-grove trail were in no particular hurry. They stopped beside other cars on the trail, presumably to coordinate future attacks. Eventually they came to River Road, not far south of Route Chestnut, where they parked the car and entered two houses. McConnell called the houses "safe houses," perhaps because the men calmly entered them. There was little doubt that all seven men were insurgents, but it was impossible to tell who else was in the houses, and specifically whether families were sheltering inside. Force-protection standards precluded the possibility of checking, and since the rules of engagement sanctioned collateral casualties with the enemy so near, a flight of Cobra helicopters arrived and fired two AGM-114 Hellfire missiles, one into each house, to soften things up. Kilo Company Marines then rushed forward to clear the rooms as required. The first house was empty, but as they approached the second one they were greeted by small-arms fire and grenades.

The Marines pulled back—way back—and called in an AV-8B Harrier jet to drop a guided 500-pound GBU-12 Paveway bomb. The bomb crashed into the house with impressive precision, but did not explode.

At this point the drone saw two MAMs leave through the back door and run into a little palm-grove patch to hide. The Marines brought the Harrier around to pink-mist these guys with a second 500-pound bomb—this one guided into the patch—but it, too, turned out to be a dud. Undaunted, the troops switched weapons and hit the patch with a $180,000 air-launched AGM-65 Maverick missile. The strike resulted in one E.K.I.A. The surviving MAM egressed the patch and ingressed the house again. It was ridiculous. The Harrier came back around and dropped a third 500-pound bomb directly through the roof, blowing the whole house and everyone in it to bloody shreds.

This was McConnell's reality as Haditha settled down for the night. He gave a talk at Sparta Base, in which for once he did not overstretch. He said: Men, we've had a tough day, it's sad about Terrazas, but everyone functioned pretty well, so good job and keep at it. He did not mention—and apparently did not much think about—all the noncombatants who had died. Look, this was Iraq. The clearing operations on Route Chestnut did not stand out as being significantly different from the other main act of the day, the use of missiles and bombs against a house that may well have contained a family. God knows there were enough body parts now scattered through the ruins. Killing face-to-face with an M16 allows you at least some chance to desist from slaughtering women and children, which is not true once a bomb is called down on a house. But there is no evidence that McConnell was even thinking about these matters. The photographer Lucian Read, who had been traveling elsewhere in Anbar, returned the day after the killings and later snapped digital pictures of shrouded corpses in the houses by Route Chestnut. Read believes McConnell was aware of the pictures; if so, he did not try to suppress them or to limit their distribution. McConnell was such a company man, such a by-the-book Marine, that, like the entire chain of command above him, he was numb to the killings of noncombatants so long as the rules of engagement made the killings legal. If there was a failure here, it was not that of McConnell but of the most basic conduct of this war.

Five days after the killings, Kilo Company celebrated Thanksgiving with a turkey dinner, including stuffing and potatoes. The occasion was recorded on video. Before the meal McConnell led the men in prayer. He said, "Father, we thank you for this food which you have prepared for us. Please bless this food with your great grace, and please let us take the sustenance that you provide for us, and go forth and do great things in your name. We are very grateful here in Kilo Company for many things. We thank you for the mission that you have provided for us, to leave America and go into foreign lands and try to do good things for the world and for our country. It's our greatest honor, and we thank you for that. We thank you for our families, who support us back in the States, and the brotherhood that we have here. It is our greatest strength, and we thank you for that as well. We also want to thank you for the veterans and those who have gone before us, because without them there would be no Marine Corps legacy, and there wouldn't be that great standard to uphold. So we thank you for that because it guides us, it keeps us on the right track, and it's that steering factor that helps us go forth and do great things. We thank you for the memory and the life of Lance Corporal Miguel Terrazas, who did great things in his life, did great things for all of us, was a great friend and a great Marine. We just ask that you help us take this food that you've provided us here today, help it maintain, sustain our bodies so we can uphold that legacy that our fallen comrades have provided for us. We say all these things in your great name. Amen."

The men answered with Marine Corps *Hoo*-rahs and Amens.

McConnell said, "Hey, please enjoy the meal. Make sure you pat the cooks on the back. They work hard. And if you see someone from the Four shop here in the near future that you know, pat them on the back, because they get all that stuff out here, and it's not the most safest place to be pushing food around. But I appreciate you all being here, and first and foremost Happy Thanksgiving. Go forth and do great things. *Hoo*-rah!"

· · ·

Hoo-rah. Iraqis live in an honor-bound society, built of tight family ties. When noncombatants are killed, it matters little to the survivors whether the American rules allowed it, or what the U.S. military courts decide. The survivors go to war in return, which provokes more of the same in a circular dive that spirals beyond recovery. Haditha is just a small example. By now, nearly one year later, hatred of the American forces in the city has turned so fierce that military investigators for the trials at Pendleton have given up on going there. That hatred is blood hatred. It is the kind of hatred people are willing to die for, with no expectation but revenge. This was immediately apparent on a video that was taken the day after the killings by an Iraqi from the neighborhood—the same video that was later passed along to *Time*. The Marine Corps was wrong to dismiss the video as propaganda and fiction. It is an authentic Iraqi artifact. It should be shown to the grunts in training. It should be shown to the generals in command. The scenes it depicts are raw. People move among the hideous corpses, wailing their grief and vowing vengeance before God. "This is my brother! My brother! My brother!" In one of the killing rooms, a hard-looking boy insists that the camera show the body of his father. Sobbing angrily, he shouts, "I want to say this is my father! God will punish you Americans! Show me on the camera! This is my father! He just bought a car showroom! He did not pay all the money to the owner yet, and he got killed!"

A man cries, "This is an act denied by God. What did he do? To be executed in the closet? Those bastards! Even the Jews would not do such an act! Why? Why did they kill him this way? Look, this is his brain on the ground!"

The boy continues to sob over the corpse on the floor. He shouts, "Father! I want my father!"

Another man cries, "This is democracy?"

Well yeah, well no, well actually this is Haditha. For the United States, it is what defeat looks like in this war.

Best Life

FINALIST—PUBLIC INTEREST

Zeroing in on a virtually unknown Texas-sized garbage dump lying becalmed in the Pacific and the man who discovered it, author Susan Casey ensnares even the most jaded reader. "Our Oceans Are Turning Into Plastic . . . Are We?" takes an environmental problem whose very familiarity has bred inaction and turns it into an issue that's far too alarming to ignore.

Susan Casey

Our Oceans Are Turning Into Plastic . . . Are We?

Fate can take strange forms, and so perhaps it does not seem unusual that Captain Charles Moore found his life's purpose in a nightmare. Unfortunately, he was awake at the time, and 800 miles north of Hawaii in the Pacific Ocean.

It happened on August 3, 1997, a lovely day, at least in the beginning: Sunny. Little wind. Water the color of sapphires. Moore and the crew of *Alguita*, his fifty-foot aluminum-hulled catamaran, sliced through the sea.

Returning to Southern California from Hawaii after a sailing race, Moore had altered *Alguita*'s course, veering slightly north. He had the time and the curiosity to try a new route, one that would lead the vessel through the eastern corner of a 10-million-square-mile oval known as the North Pacific subtropical gyre. This was an odd stretch of ocean, a place most boats purposely avoided. For one thing, it was becalmed. "The doldrums," sailors called it, and they steered clear. So did the ocean's top predators: the tuna, sharks, and other large fish that required livelier waters, flush with prey. The gyre was more like a desert—a slow, deep, clockwise-swirling vortex of air and water caused by a mountain of high-pressure air that lingered above it.

The area's reputation didn't deter Moore. He had grown up in Long Beach, forty miles south of L.A., with the Pacific literally in his front yard, and he possessed an impressive aquatic résumé: deckhand, able seaman, sailor, scuba diver, surfer, and finally captain. Moore had spent countless hours in the ocean, fascinated by its vast trove of secrets and terrors. He'd seen a lot of things out there, things that were glorious and grand; things that were ferocious and humbling. But he had never seen anything nearly as chilling as what lay ahead of him in the gyre.

It began with a line of plastic bags ghosting the surface, followed by an ugly tangle of junk: nets and ropes and bottles, motor-oil jugs and cracked bath toys, a mangled tarp. Tires. A traffic cone. Moore could not believe his eyes. Out here in this desolate place, the water was a stew of plastic crap. It was as though someone had taken the pristine seascape of his youth and swapped it for a landfill.

How did all the plastic end up here? How did this trash tsunami begin? What did it mean? If the questions seemed overwhelming, Moore would soon learn that the answers were even more so, and that his discovery had dire implications for human—and planetary—health. As *Alguita* glided through the area that scientists now refer to as the "Eastern Garbage Patch," Moore realized that the trail of plastic went on for hundreds of miles. Depressed and stunned, he sailed for a week through bobbing, toxic debris trapped in a purgatory of circling currents. To his horror, he had stumbled across the twenty-first-century Leviathan. It had no head, no tail. Just an endless body.

•   •   •

"Everybody's plastic, but I love plastic. I want to be plastic." This Andy Warhol quote is emblazoned on a six-foot-long magenta and yellow banner that hangs—with extreme irony—in the solar-powered workshop in Moore's Long Beach home. The workshop is surrounded by a crazy Eden of trees, bushes, flowers, fruits, and vegetables, ranging from the prosaic (tomatoes) to the exotic (cherimoyas, guavas, chocolate persimmons, white figs the size of baseballs). This is the house in which Moore, fifty-nine, was raised, and it has a kind of open-air earthiness that reflects his sixties-activist roots, which included a stint in a Berkeley commune. Composting and organic gardening are serious business here—you can practically smell the humus—but there is also a kidney-shaped hot tub surrounded by palm trees. Two wet suits hang drying on a clothesline above it.

This afternoon, Moore strides the grounds. "How about a nice, fresh boysenberry?" he asks, and plucks one off a bush. He's a striking man wearing no-nonsense black trousers and a shirt with official-looking epaulettes. A thick brush of salt-and-pepper hair frames his intense blue eyes and serious face. But the first thing you notice about Moore is his voice, a deep, bemused drawl that becomes animated and sardonic when the subject turns to plastic pollution. This problem is Moore's calling, a passion he inherited from his father, an industrial chemist who studied waste management as a hobby. On family vacations, Moore recalls, part of the agenda would be to see what the locals threw out. "We could be in paradise, but we would go to the dump," he says with a shrug. "That's what we wanted to see."

Since his first encounter with the Garbage Patch nine years ago, Moore has been on a mission to learn exactly what's going on out there. Leaving behind a twenty-five-year career running a furniture-restoration business, he has created the Algalita Marine Research Foundation to spread the word of his findings. He has resumed his science studies, which he'd set aside when his attention swerved from pursuing a university degree to protesting the Vietnam War. His tireless effort has placed him on the front lines of this new, more abstract battle. After enlisting scientists such as Steven B. Weisberg, Ph.D. (executive director of the Southern California Coastal Water Research Project and an expert in marine environmental monitoring), to develop methods for analyzing the gyre's contents, Moore has sailed *Alguita* back to the Garbage Patch several times. On each trip, the volume of plastic has grown alarmingly. The area in which it accumulates is now twice the size of Texas.

At the same time, all over the globe, there are signs that plastic pollution is doing more than blighting the scenery; it is also making its way into the food chain. Some of the most obvious victims are the dead seabirds that have been washing ashore in startling numbers, their bodies packed with plastic: things like bottle caps, cigarette lighters, tampon applicators, and colored scraps that, to a foraging bird, resemble baitfish. (One animal dissected by Dutch researchers contained 1,603 pieces of plastic.) And the birds aren't alone. All sea creatures are threatened by floating plastic, from whales down to zooplankton. There's a basic moral horror in seeing the pictures: a sea turtle with a plastic band strangling its shell into an hourglass shape; a humpback towing plastic nets that cut into its flesh and make it impossible for the animal to hunt. More than a million seabirds, 100,000 marine mammals, and countless fish die in the North Pacific each year, either from mistakenly eating this junk or from being ensnared in it and drowning.

Bad enough. But Moore soon learned that the big, tentacled balls of trash were only the most visible signs of the problem; others were far less obvious, and far more evil. Dragging a fine-meshed net known as a manta trawl, he discovered minuscule pieces of plastic, some barely visible to the eye, swirling like fish food throughout the water. He and his researchers parsed, measured, and sorted their samples and arrived at the following conclusion: By weight, this swath of sea contains six times as much plastic as it does plankton.

This statistic is grim—for marine animals, of course, but even more so for humans. The more invisible and ubiquitous the pollution, the more likely it will end up inside us. And there's growing—and disturbing—proof that we're ingesting plastic toxins constantly, and that even slight doses of these substances can severely disrupt gene activity. "Every one of us has this huge body burden," Moore says. "You could take your serum to a lab now, and they'd find at least 100 industrial chemicals that weren't around in 1950." The fact that these toxins don't cause violent and immediate reactions does not mean they're benign: Scientists are just beginning to research the long-term ways in which the chemicals used to make plastic interact with our own biochemistry.

·　　·　　·

In simple terms, plastic is a mix of monomers linked together to become polymers, to which additional chemicals can be added for suppleness, inflammability, and other qualities. When it comes to these substances, even the syllables are scary. For instance, if you're thinking that perfluorooctanoic acid (PFOA) isn't something you want to sprinkle on your microwave popcorn, you're right. Recently, the Science Advisory Board of the Environmental Protection Agency (EPA) upped its classification of PFOA to a likely carcinogen. Yet it's a common ingredient in packaging that needs to be oil- and heat-resistant. So while there may be no PFOA in the popcorn itself, if PFOA is used to treat the bag, enough of it can leach into the popcorn oil when your butter deluxe meets your superheated microwave oven that a single serving spikes the amount of the chemical in your blood.

Other nasty chemical additives are the flame retardants known as poly-brominated diphenyl ethers (PBDEs). These chemicals have been shown to cause liver and thyroid toxicity, reproductive problems, and memory loss in preliminary animal studies. In vehicle interiors, PBDEs—used in moldings and floor coverings, among other things—combine with another group called phthalates to create that much-vaunted "new-car smell." Leave your new wheels in the hot sun for a few hours, and these substances can "off-gas" at an accelerated rate, releasing noxious by-products.

It's not fair, however, to single out fast food and new cars. PBDEs, to take just one example, are used in many products, incuding computers, carpeting, and paint. As for phthalates, we deploy about a billion pounds of them a year worldwide despite the fact that California recently listed them as a chemical known to be toxic to our reproductive systems. Used to make plastic soft and pliable, phthalates leach easily from millions of products—packaged food, cosmetics, varnishes, the coatings of timed-release pharmaceuticals—into our blood, urine, saliva, seminal fluid, breast milk, and amniotic fluid. In food containers and some plastic bottles, phthalates are now found with another compound called bisphenol A (BPA), which scientists are discovering can wreak stunning havoc in the body. We produce 6 billion pounds of that each year, and it shows: BPA has been found in nearly every human who has been tested in the United States. We're eating these plasticizing additives, drinking them, breathing them, and absorbing them through our skin every single day.

Most alarming, these chemicals may disrupt the endocrine system—the delicately balanced set of hormones and glands that affect virtually every organ and cell—by mimicking the female hormone estrogen. In marine environments, excess estrogen has led to *Twilight Zone*-esque discoveries of male fish and seagulls that have sprouted female sex organs.

On land, things are equally gruesome. "Fertility rates have been declining for quite some time now, and exposure to synthetic estrogen—especially from the chemicals found in plastic products—can have an adverse effect," says Marc Goldstein, M.D., director of the Cornell Institute for Reproductive Medicine. Dr. Goldstein also notes that pregnant women are particularly vulnerable: "Prenatal exposure, even in very low doses, can cause irreversible damage in an unborn baby's reproductive organs." And after the baby is born, he or she is hardly out of the woods. Frederick vom Saal, Ph.D., a professor at the University of Missouri at Columbia who specifically studies estrogenic chemicals in plastics, warns parents to "steer clear of polycarbonate baby bottles. They're particularly dangerous for newborns, whose brains, immune systems, and gonads are still developing." Dr. vom Saal's research spurred him to throw out every polycarbonate plastic item in his house, and to stop buying plastic-wrapped food and canned goods (cans are plastic-lined) at the grocery store. "We now know that BPA causes prostate cancer in mice and rats, and abnormalities in the prostate's stem cell, which is the cell implicated in human prostate cancer," he says. "That's enough to scare the hell out of me." At Tufts University, Ana M. Soto, M.D., a professor of anatomy and cellular biology, has also found connections between these chemicals and breast cancer.

As if the potential for cancer and mutation weren't enough, Dr. vom Saal states in one of his studies that "prenatal exposure to very low doses of BPA increases the rate of postnatal growth in mice and rats." In other words, BPA made rodents fat. Their insulin output surged wildly and then crashed into a state of resistance—the virtual definition of diabetes. They produced bigger fat cells, and more of them. A recent scientific paper Dr. vom Saal coauthored contains this chilling sentence: "These findings suggest that developmental exposure to BPA is contributing to the obesity epidemic that has occurred during the last two decades in the developed world, associated with the dramatic increase in the amount of plastic being produced each year." Given this, it is perhaps not entirely coincidental that America's staggering rise in diabetes—a 735 percent increase since 1935—follows the same arc.

•   •   •

This news is depressing enough to make a person reach for the bottle. Glass, at least, is easily recyclable. You can take one tequila bottle, melt it down, and make another tequila bottle. With plastic, recycling is more complicated. Unfortunately, that promising-looking triangle of arrows that appears on products doesn't always signify endless reuse; it merely identifies which type of plastic the item is made from. And of the seven different plastics in common use, only two of them—PET (labeled with #1 inside the triangle and used in soda bottles) and HDPE (labeled with #2 inside the triangle and used in milk jugs)—have much of an aftermarket. So no matter how virtuously you toss your chip bags and shampoo bottles into your blue bin, few of them will escape the landfill—only 3 to 5 percent of plastics are recycled in any way.

"There's no legal way to recycle a milk container into another milk container without adding a new virgin layer of plastic," Moore says, pointing out that, because plastic melts at low temperatures, it retains pollutants and the tainted residue of its former contents. Turn up the heat to sear these off, and some plastics release deadly vapors. So the reclaimed stuff is mostly used to make entirely different products, things that don't go anywhere near our mouths, such as fleece jackets and carpeting. Therefore, unlike recycling glass, metal, or paper, recycling plastic doesn't always result in less use of virgin material. It also doesn't help that fresh-made plastic is far cheaper.

Moore routinely finds half-melted blobs of plastic in the ocean, as though the person doing the burning realized partway through the process that this was a bad idea, and stopped (or passed out from the fumes). "That's a concern as plastic proliferates worldwide, and people run out of room for trash and start burning plastic—you're producing some of the most toxic gases known," he says. The color-coded bin system may work in Marin County, but it is somewhat less effective in subequatorial Africa or rural Peru.

"Except for the small amount that's been incinerated—and it's a very small amount—every bit of plastic ever made still exists," Moore says, describing how the material's molecular structure resists biodegradation. Instead, plastic crumbles into ever-tinier fragments as it's exposed to sunlight and the elements. And none of these untold gazillions of fragments is disappearing anytime soon: Even when plastic is broken down to a single molecule, it remains too tough for biodegradation.

Truth is, no one knows how long it will take for plastic to biodegrade, or return to its carbon and hydrogen elements. We only invented the stuff 144 years ago, and science's best guess is that its natural disappearance will take several more centuries. Meanwhile, every year, we churn out about 60 billion tons of it, much of which becomes disposable products meant only for a single use. Set aside the question of why we're creating ketchup bottles and six-pack rings that last for half a millennium, and consider the implications of it: *Plastic never really goes away.*

·   ·   ·

Ask a group of people to name an overwhelming global problem, and you'll hear about climate change, the Middle East, or AIDS. No one, it is guaranteed, will cite the sloppy transport of nurdles as a concern. And yet nurdles, lentil-size pellets of plastic in its rawest form, are especially effective couriers of waste chemicals called persistent organic pollutants, or POPs, which include known carcinogens such as DDT and PCBs. The United States banned these poisons in the 1970s, but they remain stubbornly at large in the environment, where they latch on to plastic because of its molecular tendency to attract oils.

The word itself—*nurdles*—sounds cuddly and harmless, like a cartoon character or a pasta for kids, but what it refers to is most certainly not. Absorbing up to a million times the level of POP pollution in their surrounding waters, nurdles become supersaturated poison pills. They're light enough to blow around like dust, to spill out of shipping containers, and to wash into harbors, storm drains, and creeks. In the ocean, nurdles are easily mistaken for fish eggs by creatures that would very much like to have such a snack. And once inside the body of a bigeye tuna or a king salmon, these tenacious chemicals are headed directly to your dinner table.

One study estimated that nurdles now account for 10 percent of plastic ocean debris. And once they're scattered in the environment, they're diabolically hard to clean up (think wayward confetti). At places as remote as Rarotonga, in the Cook Islands, 2,100 miles northeast of New Zealand and a twelve-hour flight from L.A., they're commonly found mixed with beach sand. In 2004, Moore received a $500,000 grant from the state of California to investigate the myriad ways in which nurdles go astray during the plastic manufacturing process. On a visit to a polyvinyl chloride (PVC) pipe factory, as he walked through an area where railcars unloaded ground-up nurdles, he noticed that his pant cuffs were filled with a fine plastic dust. Turning a corner, he saw windblown drifts of nurdles piled against a fence. Talking about the experience, Moore's voice becomes strained and his words pour out in an urgent tumble: "It's not the big trash on the beach. It's the fact that the whole biosphere is becoming mixed with these plastic particles. What are they doing to us? We're breathing them, the fish are eating them, they're in our hair, they're in our skin."

Though marine dumping is part of the problem, escaped nurdles and other plastic litter migrate to the gyre largely from land. That polystyrene cup you saw floating in the creek, if it doesn't get picked up and specifically taken to a landfill, will eventually be washed out to sea. Once there, it will have plenty of places to go: The North Pacific gyre is only one of five such high-pressure zones in the oceans. There are similar areas in the South Pacific, the North and South Atlantic, and the Indian Ocean. Each of these gyres has its own version of the Garbage Patch, as plastic gathers in the currents. Together, these areas cover 40 percent of the sea. "That corresponds to a quarter of the earth's surface," Moore says. "So 25 percent of our planet is a toilet that never flushes."

·   ·   ·

It wasn't supposed to be this way. In 1865, a few years after Alexander Parkes unveiled a precursor to man-made plastic called Parkesine, a scientist named John W. Hyatt set out to make a synthetic replacement for ivory billiard balls. He had the best of intentions: Save the elephants! After some tinkering, he created celluloid. From then on, each year brought a miraculous recipe: rayon in 1891, Teflon in 1938, polypropylene in 1954. Durable, cheap, versatile—plastic seemed like a revelation. And in many ways, it was. Plastic has given us bulletproof vests, credit cards, slinky spandex pants. It has led to breakthroughs in medicine, aerospace engineering, and computer science. And who among us doesn't own a Frisbee?

Plastic has its benefits; no one would deny that. Few of us, however, are as enthusiastic as the American Plastics Council. One of its recent press releases, titled "Plastic Bags—A Family's Trusted Companion," reads: "Very few people remember what life was like before plastic bags became an icon of convenience and practicality—and now art. Remember the 'beautiful' [*sic*] swirling, floating bag in *American Beauty*?"

Alas, the same ethereal quality that allows bags to dance gracefully across the big screen also lands them in many less desirable places. Twenty-three countries, including Germany, South Africa, and Australia, have banned, taxed, or restricted the use of plastic bags because they clog sewers and lodge in the throats of livestock. Like pernicious Kleenex, these flimsy sacks end up snagged in trees and snarled in fences, becoming eyesores and worse: They also trap rainwater, creating perfect little breeding grounds for disease-carrying mosquitoes.

In the face of public outrage over pictures of dolphins choking on "a family's trusted companion," the American Plastics Council takes a defensive stance, sounding not unlike the NRA: Plastics don't pollute, people do.

It has a point. Each of us tosses about 185 pounds of plastic per year. We could certainly reduce that. And yet—do our products have to be quite so lethal? Must a discarded flip-flop remain with us until the end of time? Aren't disposable razors and foam packing peanuts a poor consolation prize for the destruction of the world's oceans, not to mention our own bodies and the health of future generations? "If 'more is better' and that's the only mantra we have, we're doomed," Moore says, summing it up.

Oceanographer Curtis Ebbesmeyer, Ph.D., an expert on marine debris, agrees. "If you could fast-forward 10,000 years and do an archaeological dig . . . you'd find a little line of plastic," he told *The Seattle Times* last April. "What happened to those people? Well, they ate their own plastic and disrupted their genetic structure and weren't able to reproduce. They didn't last very long because they killed themselves."

Wrist-slittingly depressing, yes, but there are glimmers of hope on the horizon. Green architect and designer William McDonough has become an influential voice, not only in environmental circles but among Fortune 500 CEOs. McDonough proposes a standard known as "cradle to cradle" in which all manufactured things must be reusable, poison-free, and beneficial over the long haul. His outrage is obvious when he holds up a rubber ducky, a common child's bath toy. The duck is made of phthalate-laden PVC, which has been linked to cancer and reproductive harm. "What kind of people are we that we would design like this?" McDonough asks. In the United States, it's commonly accepted that children's teething rings, cosmetics, food wrappers, cars, and textiles will be made from toxic materials. Other countries—and many individual companies—seem to be reconsidering. Currently, McDonough is working with the Chinese government to build seven cities using "the building materials of the future," including a fabric that is safe enough to eat and a new, nontoxic polystyrene.

Thanks to people like Moore and McDonough, and media hits such as Al Gore's *An Inconvenient Truth*, awareness of just how hard we've bitch-slapped the planet is skyrocketing. After all, unless we're planning to colonize Mars soon, this is where we live, and none of us would choose to live in a toxic wasteland or to spend our days getting pumped full of drugs to deal with our haywire endocrine systems and runaway cancer.

None of plastic's problems can be fixed overnight, but the more we learn, the more likely that, eventually, wisdom will trump convenience and cheap disposability. In the meantime, let the cleanup begin: The National Oceanographic and Atmospheric Administration (NOAA) is aggressively using satellites to identify and remove "ghost nets," abandoned plastic fishing gear that never stops killing. (A single net recently hauled up off the Florida coast contained more than 1,000 dead fish, sharks, and one loggerhead turtle.) New biodegradable starch- and corn-based plastics have arrived, and Wal-Mart has signed on as a customer. A consumer rebellion against dumb and excessive packaging is afoot. And in August 2006, Moore was invited to speak about "marine debris and hormone disruption" at a meeting in Sicily convened by the science advisor to the Vatican. This annual gathering, called the International Seminars on Planetary Emergencies, brings scientists together to discuss mankind's worst threats. Past topics have included nuclear holocaust and terrorism.

. . .

The gray plastic kayak floats next to Moore's catamaran, *Alguita*, which lives in a slip across from his house. It is not a lovely kayak; in fact, it looks pretty rough. But it's floating, a sturdy, eight-foot-long two-seater. Moore stands on *Alguita*'s deck, hands on hips, staring down at it. On the sailboat next to him, his neighbor, Cass Bastain, does the same. He has just informed Moore that he came across the abandoned craft yesterday, floating just offshore. The two men shake their heads in bewilderment.

"That's probably a $600 kayak," Moore says, adding, "I don't even shop anymore. Anything I need will just float by." (In his opinion, the movie *Cast Away* was a joke—Tom Hanks could've built a village with the crap that would've washed ashore during a storm.)

Watching the kayak bobbing disconsolately, it is hard not to wonder what will become of it. The world is full of cooler, sexier kayaks. It is also full of cheap plastic kayaks that come in more attractive colors than battleship gray. The ownerless kayak is a lummox of a boat, fifty pounds of nurdles extruded into an object that nobody wants, but that'll be around for centuries longer than we will.

And as Moore stands on deck looking into the water, it is easy to imagine him doing the same thing 800 miles west, in the gyre. You can see his silhouette in the silvering light, caught between ocean and sky. You can see the mercurial surface of the most majestic body of water on earth. And then below, you can see the half-submerged madhouse of forgotten and discarded things. As Moore looks over the side of the boat, you can see the seabirds sweeping overhead, dipping and skimming the water. One of the journeying birds, sleek as a fighter plane, carries a scrap of something yellow in its beak. The bird dives low and then boomerangs over the horizon. Gone.

Esquire

WINNER—REPORTING

In "The School," C. J. Chivers recounts, in astonishing and chilling detail, the progress of the three-day siege by Chechen terrorists at School No. 1 in the Russian town of Beslan. Told with economy yet packed with detail, "The School" presents scenes and images that compel the reader's attention, and may haunt them for decades to come.

C. J. Chivers

The School

September 1. Afternoon. The Gym.

Kazbek Misikov stared at the bomb hanging above his family. It was a simple device, a plastic bucket packed with explosive paste, nails, and small metal balls. It weighed perhaps eight pounds. The existence of this bomb had become a central focus of his life. If it exploded, Kazbek knew, it would blast shrapnel into the heads of his wife and two sons, and into him as well, killing them all.

Throughout the day he had memorized the bomb, down to the blue electrical wire linking it to the network of explosives the terrorists had strung around them hours before. Now his eyes wandered, panning the crowd of more than eleven hundred hostages who had been seized in the morning outside the school. The majority were children, crouched with their parents and teachers on the basketball court. The temperature had risen with the passing hours, and their impromptu jail had become fetid and stinking with urine and fear. Many children had undressed. Sweat ran down their bare backs.

His eyes settled on his captors. Most of the terrorists had left the gym for defensive positions in the main school building, leaving behind a handful of men in athletic suits or camouflage pants. These were their guards. They wore ammunition vests and slung Kalashnikov rifles. A few were hidden behind ski masks, but as the temperature had risen, most had removed them, revealing faces. They were young. Some had the bearing of experienced fighters. Others seemed like semiliterate thugs, the sort of criminal that had radiated from Chechnya and Russia's North Caucasus during a decade of war. Two were women wearing explosive belts.

Kazbek studied the group, committing to memory their weapons, their behavior, their relations to one another, and the configuration of their bombs. A diagram of their handiwork had formed in his head, an intricate map that existed nowhere else. With it was a mental blueprint of the school, in which he had studied as a boy. This was useful information, if he could share it, and Kazbek thought of fleeing, hoping he might give the Special Forces gathering outside a description of the bombs and defenses. Already Kazbek assumed this siege would end in a fight, and he knew that when Russia's soldiers rushed these rooms, their attack would be overpowering and imprecise. He knew this because he once was a Russian soldier himself.

He evaluated the options. *How does my family get out?* Escape? Passivity? Resistance? His wife, Irina Dzutseva, and their sons, Batraz, fifteen, and Atsamaz, seven, were beside him. Kazbek was a tall man with neat dark hair and a mustache, and Batraz, who was growing tall as well, had the hint of a beard. Kazbek had made him remove his shirt, exposing a boyish frame. He hoped this would convince the terrorists that, unlike his father, Batraz was not a threat, and he would not be rounded up with the men. Kazbek's mind was engaged in this sort of agonizing calculus, trying to determine the best way to save his children from a horror with too many variables and too many unknowns. How best to act? Yes, he had information to share. But even if he escaped, he thought, the terrorists might identify his wife and sons. And then kill them. They had already shot several people, including Ruslan Betrozov, who had done nothing more than speak. No, Kazbek thought, he could not run. He also knew that any uprising by the hostages would have to be swift and complete. There were few terrorists in the gym, but by

Kazbek's count at least thirty more roamed the school. How could all of these terrorists be overcome by an unarmed crowd, especially when even before rigging the bombs the terrorists had created an immeasurable psychological advantage? "If any of you resists us," one had warned, "we will kill children and leave the one who resists alive." There would be no resistance. Who, after all, would lead it? Already the adult male captives were dying. Many had been executed. Most of the others were in the main hall, kneeling, hands clasped behind their heads.

Kazbek was lucky. The terrorists had overlooked him during the last roundup. He had been spared execution.

Now his mind worked methodically. He wanted no one to see what he planned to do. Slowly, almost imperceptibly, his hand moved over the floor to the blue wire. Kazbek was forty-three. He had been a Soviet sapper as a younger man. He knew how bombs worked. He also knew how to disable them. The bomb overhead was part of a simple system, an open electric circuit rigged to a motor-vehicle battery. If the terrorists closed the circuit, current would flow from the battery through the wires and detonate the bombs. But if Kazbek pulled apart the wire inside its insulation, no current could flow. Then, he knew, if the circuit snapped closed, the bomb above his family would not explode. Kazbek had spent much of the day folding the wire back and forth, making a crimp. It was only a matter of time.

He lifted the wire. Back and forth he folded the notch, working it, looking directly at the men who would kill him if they knew what he was doing. He would disconnect this bomb. It was a step. Every step counted. His mind kept working. *How does my family get out?*

9:10 A.M. The Schoolyard

Morning marked a new school year at School No. 1 in Beslan, beginning with rituals of years past. Returning students, second through twelfth graders, had lined up in a horseshoe formation beside the red brick building. They wore uniforms: girls in dark dresses, boys in dark pants and white shirts. The forecast had predicted hot weather; only the day before, the administration had pushed the schedule an hour earlier, to the relative cool of 9:00 A.M. Students fidgeted with flowers, chocolates, and balloons, waiting for the annual presentation, when first graders would march before their schoolmates for the opening of their academic lives.

Zalina Levina took a seat behind the rostrum and greeted the milling parents. Beslan is an industrial and agricultural town of about thirty-five thousand people on the plain beneath the Caucasus ridge, part of the Russian republic of North Ossetia and one of the few places in the region with a modicum of jobs. For the moment, work seemed forgotten. Parents had come to celebrate. Irina Naldikoyeva sat with her daughter, Alana, four, and glimpsed her son, Kazbek, seven, in the formation with his second-grade class. Aida Archegova had two sons in the assembly. Zalina was baby-sitting her two-and-a-half-year-old granddaughter, Amina. They had not planned on attending, but the child had heard music and seen children streaming toward the school. "Grandma," she had said, "let's go dance." Zalina put on a denim dress and joined the flow. Already it was warm. The first graders were about to step forward. The school year had begun.

The terrorists appeared as if from nowhere. A military truck stopped near the school and men leapt from the cargo bed, firing rifles and shouting, "*Allahu akhbar!*" They moved with speed and certitude, as if every step had been rehearsed. The first few sprinted between the formation and the schoolyard gate, blocking escape. There was almost no resistance. Ruslan Frayev, a local man who had come with several members of his family, drew a pistol and began to fire. He was killed.

The terrorists seemed to be everywhere. Zalina saw a man in a mask sprinting with a rifle. Then another. And a third. Many students in the formation had their backs to the advancing gunmen, but one side did not, and as Zalina sat confused, those students broke and ran. The formation disintegrated. Scores of balloons floated skyward as children released them. A cultivated sense of order became bedlam.

Dzera Kudzayeva, seven, had been selected for a role in which she would be carried on the shoulders of a senior and strike a bell to start the new school year. Her father, Aslan Kudzayev, had hired Karen Mdinaradze, a video cameraman for a nearby soccer team, to record the big day. Dzera wore a blue dress with a white apron and had two white bows in her hair, and was on the senior's shoulders when the terrorists arrived. They were quickly caught.

For many other hostages, recognition came slowly. Aida Archegova thought she was in a counterterrorism drill. Beslan is roughly 950 miles south of Moscow, in a zone destabilized by the Chechen wars. Police actions were part of life. "Is it exercises?" she asked a terrorist as he bounded past.

He stopped. "What are you, a fool?" he said.

The terrorists herded the panicked crowd into a rear courtyard, a place with no outlet. An attached building housed the boiler room, and Zalina ran there with others to hide. The room had no rear exit. They were trapped. The door opened. A man in a tracksuit stood at the entrance. "Get out or I will start shooting," he said.

Zalina did not move. She thought she would beg for mercy. Her granddaughter was with her, and a baby must mean a pass. She froze until only she and Amina remained. The terrorist glared. "You need a special invitation?" he said. "I will shoot you right here."

Speechless with fear, she stepped out, joining a mass of people as obedient as if they had been tamed. The terrorists had forced the crowd against the school's brick wall and were driving it through a door. The people could not file in quickly enough, and the men broke windows and handed children in. Already there seemed to be dozens of the terrorists. They lined the hall, redirecting the people into the gym. "We are from Chechnya," one said. "This is a seizure. We are here to start the withdrawal of troops and the liberation of Chechnya."

As the hostages filed onto the basketball court, more terrorists came in. One fired into the ceiling. "Everybody be silent!" he said. "You have been taken hostage. Calm down. Stop the panic and nobody will be hurt. We are going to issue our demands, and if the demands are implemented, we will let the children out."

Rules were laid down. There would be no talking without permission. All speech would be in Russian, not Ossetian, so the terrorists could understand it, too. The hostages would turn in their cell phones, cameras, and video cameras. Any effort to resist would be met with mass executions, including of women and children.

When the terrorist had finished, Ruslan Betrozov, a father who had brought his two sons to class, stood and translated the instructions into Ossetian. He was a serious man, forty-four years old and with a controlled demeanor. The terrorists let him speak. When he stopped, one approached.

"Are you finished?" he asked. "Have you said everything you want to say?"

Betrozov nodded. The terrorist shot him in the head.

9:20 A.M. The Administrator's Office.

Irina Dzutseva, Kazbek Misikov's wife, huddled near the desk, embracing Atsamaz, her first-grade son. Atsamaz was quiet and waiflike but dressed like a gentleman in black suit and white shirt. Irina could feel his fear. They hid amid papers and textbooks, listening to the long corridor. Doors were being opened, then slammed. They heard gunshots. Atsamaz clung to a balloon. "Where are Papa and Batik?" he asked. "Were they killed?"

The first graders and their parents had been standing at the main entrance and were among the first to see the attack. Irina had turned back into the school and bolted down the corridor as the shooting began, charging down the hall in high heels, pulling her son by his hand. She heard screams and a window shatter. Glass tinkled on the floor. The corridor was long and still; their footfalls echoed as they passed each door, the entrance to the gym, the cafeteria, and the restrooms. At the end of the hall they rushed upstairs to the auditorium and crouched behind the maroon curtain on the stage with other mothers and students. Balloons were taped to the ceiling. Posters decorated the wall. Behind the curtain was a door, and they pushed in and settled into an office packed with books. *Short Stories by Russian Writers. Methods of Teaching. Literature 5.* Irina looked at the others: four adults and six children. They were cut off and could only guess at what was happening outside. They sat in the stillness, waiting to be saved.

After about half an hour, someone pushed against the door. A child called out hopefully: "Are you ours?"

The door swung open. Three terrorists stood before them, beards hanging beneath masks. "God forbid that we are yours," one said, and the group was marched down to the gym with terrorists firing rifles into the ceiling.

In the gym they encountered a scene beyond their imagination. Almost the entire student body had been taken captive, a mass of distraught human life trapped as if it were under a box. Children's cries filled the air. The gym was roughly twenty-eight yards long by fifteen yards wide, and its longer sides each had a bank of four windows, ten feet by ten feet, with panes made from opaque plastic. Light came in as a glow. A wide streak of blood marked the area where Betrozov's corpse had been dragged. Irina hurried with Atsamaz to the far corner and found

Batraz, her older son. She understood that their lives would be leveraged in a test of wills against the Kremlin. Hope rested with negotiations, or with Russia's security forces, not known for tactical precision or regard for civilian life. The last time a Chechen group had seized hundreds of hostages, at a theater in Moscow in 2002, Russian commandos attacked with poisonous gas. At least 129 hostages died.

Two young women wearing explosive belts roamed the wooden floor, wraithlike figures dressed in black, their faces hidden by veils. Irina shuddered. Russia has an enduring capacity to produce ghastly social phenomena; these were the latest occurrence of the *shahidka*, female Islamic martyrs who had sown fear during the second Chechen war. The Russian news called them black widows, women driven to militant Islam and vengeance by the loss of Chechnya's young men. The hostages noticed an incongruity: The black veil worn by one *shahidka* framed the neatly sculpted eyebrows of what seemed a teenager who had recently visited a beauty salon.

Two terrorists entered the room with backpacks and began unloading equipment: wire and cable on wooden spools, bombs of different sizes, including several made from plastic soda bottles and two rectangular charges, each the size of a briefcase. With pliers and wire cutters, they set to work, assembling the components into a system. Their plans became clear. Many of the small bombs would be daisy-chained together and hoisted above the crowd, and a line of larger explosives would be set on the floor. The hanging bombs served two purposes: They were a source of mass fear, forcing obedience from the hostages underneath. And elevation ensured that if the bombs were to explode, they would blast shrapnel down from above, allowing for no cover. Virtually everyone would be struck by the nuts, bolts, ball bearings, and nails packed inside. The terrorists assigned the tallest hostages, including Kazbek, who is six foot three, to lift the bombs. The choice of suspension showed malign ingenuity:

They strung cables from one basketball hoop to the other, dangling the bombs on hooks. Kazbek realized the terrorists had inside information. Not only had they planned the basketball hoops into their design, but the cables and wires were precut to size, as if they knew the dimensions before they arrived. The bombs were a custom fit.

The weight of the rig at first caused bombs to sag near the children's heads. "Do not touch them," a terrorist warned, and then instructed Kazbek and others to pull the slack out of the system. The network was raised higher, higher, and then nearly taut, until the deadly web was up and out of reach. Kazbek assessed the trap: It was like a string of Christmas lights, except where each bulb would go was a suspended bomb. A terrorist stood on the trigger, and the system was connected to a battery. If the triggerman were to release his foot, Kazbek knew, the circuit would close. Electricity would flow. The bombs would explode.

Afternoon. The Main Hall.

Aslan Kudzayev carried a chair through the long blue hall under the watch of his guards. He was hurrying through his tasks. He had been put in a work gang the terrorists formed from adult male hostages and ordered to barricade the classroom windows. The terrorists worried that Russian Special Forces would attack. The hostages proved to be a useful labor pool. Aslan wore white pants, a white shirt, and white shoes. He was thirty-three and lanky, with short brown hair. As he lugged the chair, a terrorist with a bandaged arm pointed a Makarov nine-mm pistol in his face. Aslan stopped. "You have short hair," the terrorist said. "You are a cop."

Aslan shook his head. "No," he said. "No."

The terrorist told him to empty his pockets, and Aslan showed him a wallet, money, and keys. He owned a building-supply store. Nothing about him said cop. The terrorist signaled him to return to work.

Once the windows were blocked, the men were ordered to sit in the hall, hands behind their heads. By now the terrorists were emerging as individuals; the hostages were forming a sense of their captors. There were the leaders and the led, and the led were organized into teams. Some specialized in explosives. Others were jailers, controlling the hostages in the gym. The largest group was in the main building: a platoon preparing to fight off a Russian assault. They had come with packs of food, coffee, and candy, as well as sleeping bags, gas masks, and first-aid kits. Each had a rifle and wore a vest bulging with ammunition. Some had hand grenades. A few had forty-mm grenade launchers mounted under their rifle barrels.

Aslan began to understand their command structure. All of them deferred to a light-footed and muscular man with a bushy reddish beard whom they called the Colonel. He paced the corridor with a cocky strut, his shaved head topped with a black skullcap, exuding the dark charisma of the captain of a pirate sloop. He was charged with energy and power and seemed fired with glee. Beneath him were midlevel commanders, including a Slav who used the name Abdullah and had pointed the pistol at Aslan's face. Aslan grudgingly marveled at their discipline and skill. They had taken the school, laced it with bombs, and made it a bunker in half a day. *Say what you want about these bastards, but they are not stupid*, he thought. *They know what to do.*

He and two other hostages were ordered to their feet and taken down the hall to the library, where they were given axes and picks and told to tear up the floorboards. Aslan wondered whether the terrorists had a cache of weapons under the planks, but he could see nothing in the hole he made and was led back to sit. Captive in the corridor, growing tired and cramped, Aslan realized he had come to the end of his life. He fell to reverie. Slowly he reviewed the things that made him what he had been:

his marriage, the birth of his two daughters, the success of his business. He felt regret that he had not yet had a son. An Ossetian was supposed to have a son. Now and then he was startled by nearby rifle fire, but he could not tell where it came from. He returned to daydreaming. He thought: *What will they say at my funeral?*

Early Afternoon. The Gym.

The terrorist was sick of Larisa Kudziyeva. She had been shouting, even after they had ordered everyone to be quiet. She was lean and beautiful in a quintessentially Caucasus way, with fine skin and dark hair and brown eyes, a look intensified by her black blouse and skirt. She did not look her thirty-eight years. The terrorist was one of the young men guarding the hostages. He wore his mask. He walked toward her to quiet her, for good.

Larisa had spent the first hours of captivity tending to Vadim Bolloyev, a father who had been shot near the right shoulder. He lay on the basketball court silently, holding in his pain. His white shirt was soaked red. He was growing weak. "Why did they shoot you?" she had asked him.

"I refused to kneel," he said.

Larisa urged him to lie back and placed her purse under his head. She inspected his wound. The bone had been shattered. Blood flowed freely. She tried using a belt as a tourniquet but could not position it. Sweat beaded his forehead. His son, Sarmat, six, sat beside him in a white shirt and black vest, watching his father slip away.

Larisa had not wanted to come to school that day. Her six-year-old son, Zaurbek, was starting first grade, but she had asked Madina, her nineteen-year-old daughter, to bring him. Her husband had died of stomach cancer in April. She was in mourning and felt no urge to celebrate. But after they left, Larisa looked outside at the crowds moving to the school. Go with them, a voice told her, and she rushed to her balcony. "Wait for me!" she called down.

Now she leaned over a bleeding man, struggling to save him. Her daughter was enrolled at a medical academy. "You are a future doctor," Larisa whispered. "What do I do?"

"There is no way to save him," Madina said. "His artery is damaged. He needs an operation."

Larisa felt fury. She would not let him die. She shouted at a terrorist across the room. "We need water and bandages!" she said. No one answered. She shouted again. She was breaking rules. The terrorist approached. "Why are you yelling?" he said.

"I need bandages," she said.

"Are you the bravest person here, or the smartest?" he said. "We will check." His voice turned sharp: "Stand up!"

Bolloyev grabbed her shirt. "Do not go," he said. Larisa slipped free and stood, and the terrorist shoved her with his rifle toward a corner where confiscated cameras and phones had been piled and smashed.

"What are you doing?" she demanded.

He ordered her to kneel. "No," she said.

For this Bolloyev had been shot. "I told you," he said. "Get on your knees."

"No," she said.

For a moment they faced each other, the terrorist and the mother, locked in mental battle. She looked into his mask; freckles were visible near his eyes. A hush fell over the gym. The hostages had seen Betrozov's murder. Now came Larisa's turn. The terrorist raised his Kalashnikov, past her chest, past her face, stopping at her forehead. He pressed the muzzle against her brow. Larisa felt the circle of steel on her skin.

Bolloyev propped himself on an elbow. Larisa's children looked on. She reached up, grasped the barrel, and moved it away. "What kind of spectacle are you playing here, and in front of whom?" she snapped. "There are women and children here who are already scared."

The terrorist paused. Thinking quickly, she tried to convince him that Ossetians were not enemies of Chechens, a difficult task, given that enmity between Ossetians, a Christian people with a history of fidelity to Moscow, and the Islamic Chechens and Ingush, who have long been persecuted, is deep. "Your children rest in our sanatoriums," she said. "Your women give birth here."

"Not our wives and children," the terrorist said. "They are the spawn of Kadyrov."

The word stung. *Kadyrov*—the surname of former rebels who aligned with Russia and became the Kremlin's proxies. The separatists despised them with a loathing reserved for traitors. Larisa was stumped. Abdullah had been rushing across the gym; he stepped beside them. "What is happening here?" he said.

"This guy wants to execute me because I asked for water and bandages for the wounded," she said. Abdullah studied the two: his young gunman, the woman who stared him down.

"There is nothing for you here," he said. "Go back and sit down and shut up."

She pointed to his bloodied arm. "Your arm is bandaged," she said. "Give me some of those bandages."

"You did not understand me?" he said. "There is nothing for you here. Go back and sit down and shut up."

Larisa returned to her place. Her children stared at her. Bolloyev lay back down. His lips were violet, his forehead coated in sweat. His death could not be far away. She was enraged.

Afternoon. The Gym.

Zalina Levina could not console her granddaughter, Amina, and did not know what to do. She had stripped the pink skirt and red shirt from the toddler's sweaty skin. It was not enough. Amina cried on, filling Zalina with dread. The terrorists had grown more irritable, and their threats were multiplying. "Shut your bastards up or I will calm them down fast," one had said. Zalina worried the child would be shot.

Zalina knew Chechnya firsthand, having lived in Grozny, its capital, before the Soviet Union collapsed. She remembered its mountain vistas and orderly atmosphere. The city had industry, a university, an oil institute, a circus, a soccer stadium, and rows of apartment buildings on tree-lined streets. She also remembered its brutality. Nationalism had sprouted anew as Moscow's grip weakened. Old animosities reemerged. In the early 1990s, before the first Chechen war, a group of Chechen men had stolen her brother-in-law's car. "We give you a month to leave," one had said, "or we will return and burn down your house." The family fled to Beslan, sixty-five miles away, across what would become a military front. Zalina thought she had escaped the war.

Now Amina kept crying and Zalina's anxiety grew. There seemed no reason for hope. The terrorists were demanding a withdrawal of federal troops from Chechnya, and if the hostages knew anything about Vladimir Putin, Russia's president, they knew he was unlikely to do this. Putin's success rested in part on his reputation for toughness. He was not one to grant concessions, certainly not to separatists, for whom his disdain was well known.

As they waited, the hostages were miserable in the heat. The gym was too crowded to allow for much movement, which forced them to take turns extending their legs. Others leaned back-to-back. The terrorists gave little relief. Sometimes they made everyone display their hands on their heads, fingers upright, like rabbit ears. Other times, when the gym became noisy with crying children, they selected a hostage to stand, then warned everyone: Shut up or he will be shot. But silence, like a federal withdrawal, was an almost impossible demand. Children can stay quiet for only so long.

Amina cried and cried. *I have to save this child,* Zalina thought. She opened her dress and placed a nipple under Amina's nose. Zalina was forty-one years old and not the toddler's mother. But she thought that maybe Amina was young enough, and a warm nipple familiar enough, that any nipple, even her dry nipple, would provide comfort. Naked and sweaty, Amina took the breast. She began to suck. Her breathing slowed. Her body relaxed. She fell asleep. *Be still*, Zalina thought. *Be still*.

Afternoon. The Gym.

Larisa Kudziyeva's defiance made her known to her captors, and in the hours after she was nearly shot, she noticed a terrorist staring at her. He was not wearing a mask and often turned his eyes toward her. He was just less than six feet tall, thick-armed and meticulous, possessing a seriousness the other terrorists seemed to respect. His camouflage pants were pressed. His black boots were laced tight. He had a freshly trimmed beard and eyes that lacked some of the bloodlust evident in the others. Larisa thought he must be in his early thirties, old enough to have waged guerrilla war for ten years. He was a negotiator and spent much of the time talking on a mobile phone with Russians outside. Between calls his eyes settled on Larisa.

Her anger had not subsided. She had kept working on Bolloyev, pressing rags to his wound. Each came away soaked. The blood grew sticky and spoiled in the heat; Larisa never knew a man's blood could smell so bad, like a butcher's drain. She shouted for aid again, for water, for bandages, but no one listened. As he was dying, Bolloyev asked for his daughters, who were also in the gym, and Larisa called to them. The terrorists punished her by posting a *shahidka* beside her with a pistol and instructions to shoot if she made another noise. Bolloyev weakened further and asked his son, Sarmat, to recite his address and names of relatives, as if he knew he would die and wanted the boy to rehearse his lines to rescuers, should they find him alone.

As Bolloyev faded, pallid and shivering, Abdullah ordered him dragged away. "Where are you taking him?" Larisa demanded.

"To the hospital," he said.

She knew it was not true, and fumed. Later, as the temperature soared, she took a group of children to the bathroom. Returning, she sat beside the one who stared. There was a connection here. She intended to use it.

"You are probably the only person who can tell us something about our fate," she said.

He looked at her, up close for the first time. She had washed away Bolloyev's blood. "You will stay here until the last federal troops leave Chechnya," he said.

"That is not a one-day matter," she said.

"Once negotiations start, you will have everything," he said. "Food. Water. Everything."

He sat with his rifle and phone, an underground fighter who had stepped into view. Men like this lived in Russia's shadows, biding time, praying, emerging on occasion to kill. Once a constant presence on television, they had disappeared into their insurgency. Now the hostages' lives were under his control. "What is your name?" she asked.

"Ali," he said. It was not a name common to the mountains.

"Is that a name or a nickname?"

"I see you are a wise woman," he said.

"Answer the question," she said. "A man should have a name. This is what differentiates him from an animal."

"It is a nickname," he said. "Now I am Ali. In the previous time, I was Baisangur."

"And your real name?" she said.

"I no longer need it," he said. "There is not a person left alive who can call me by my name."

Baisangur—a legendary Chechen warrior who had fought Russia in the nineteenth century, part of a generation revered in separatist lore. The most famous of these fighters had been Imam Shamil, whose name passed through generations to Shamil Basayev, the one-footed separatist commander whose wisecracking practice of terrorism made him Russia's most wanted man.

Basayev planned hostage seizures and recruited *shahidkas*; the terrorists in this gym prepared under his command. Baisangur's martial pedigree was more pure. The original Shamil had been captured and accepted a pardon from the czar. Baisangur fought to his death.

Yes, once he had been Baisangur, and before that he used his real name. But years ago, Ali said, as Russia was trying to quell their rebellion, a warplane took off from this area and dropped bombs on a Chechen village. There were no men where the bombs landed. But the village was not empty. It was crowded with families. Those bombs, he said, exploded among his wife and five children. Everyone who loved him was dead. He looked at Larisa, the incandescent one. "My wife looked just like you," he said. "Even twins do not look so alike."

Larisa needed information; she pushed. "What is the name of your village?" she asked.

"You do not need to know it," he said. "You do not know what is happening in Chechnya."

August 30. Shortly After Dawn. Chechnya.

The road to Grozny runs southward across a plain toward the sparkling and snowcapped Caucasus ridge, a setting so empyreal that had history been different it might be a land of fable. As the road continues on, crossing the swirling Terek River, bunkers and checkpoints appear, first occasionally and then frequently, from which sunburned Slavic soldiers look wearily out. Chechnya is a dot on Russia's vastness, an internal republic the size of Connecticut. But the Kremlin covets and fears it, and has flowed soldiers and police over its borders, ringing it with layers of security and denying most access to outsiders. It is a war zone and a region whose recent inner workings are largely unknown.

Short of the capital, the terrain becomes steep and scarred with artillery trenches, from which Russian batteries long ago fired their barrages. The city beyond these hills is a ruin, a warren of rubble and shattered buildings in which many of the remaining inhabitants camp in the wreckage of their homes. In the annals of recent conflict, few places have seen such a multiplicity of horrors and then fallen so swiftly from the public discourse. After Chechnya declared independence in 1991, prompting Russia to invade three years later, the Chechens became a source of fascination in the West. They were tribesmen who merged mountain traditions with modern life, an Islamic people speaking their own language, bound by ancient codes of honor and hospitality, and seeking independence as they fought armored columns in front of their homes. Their symbol was the wolf, but they were underdogs, local people who seemed to win skirmishes against a world power with little more than rifles and the force of will.

No matter those moments of military success, the Chechens' separatist urges have led nearly to their destruction. Russia and the rebels signed a cease-fire in 1996, and the Russian military withdrew, leaving behind a rebel-led government. Chechen independence and self-governance had been born. The result was disastrous. The young government, which inherited formidable problems and had little aid or revenue, was largely abandoned by the Kremlin, which seemed eager for it to fail. Inexperienced and prone to internal quarrels, it proved barely capable of governing and flashed an affinity for ancient notions of Islamic law, going so far as to show public executions on TV. Crime soared, corruption was unchecked, and ransom kidnappings became common enough to have the feel of an approved line of work.

Whatever the merits of the conventional portrait of the Chechen rebel, war and rackets warped many of them out of popular form, leading them to lives of thuggery and organized crime. Chechnya's people waited for autonomy to improve their lot. But nationalism led to warlordism, and warlordism to more sinister associations. Some prominent commanders, including Shamil

Basayev, allied themselves with international Islamic movements that had taken root in Pakistan and Afghanistan, steering the republic deeper into isolation and attracting foreign jihadis to the slopes of the Caucasus. With Basayev's blessing, a dark-maned Arab field commander who used the name Ibn al-Khattab and had fought in Afghanistan and Tajikistan opened training camps in the mountains. Recruits arrived from Chechnya and elsewhere in the Caucasus, especially from nearby Ingushetia, and from Turkey, Central Asia, and Arabia. They studied weapons, tactics, and the manufacture of bombs. Under the sway of fighters, autonomous Chechnya was recognized by only one foreign government: Afghanistan's Taliban.

Spurred by Prime Minister Putin, who was soon to become president, Russia sent its armor back to Chechnya in 1999. This time Russia fought unsparingly. With little regard for life or property, its military surrounded Grozny and pounded the capital with rockets, artillery, and aircraft, collapsing the city around the rebels. Sweeps and barrages destroyed villages and towns. The destruction was of an order not seen since World War II; Grozny's sagging hulks invited comparisons to Warsaw, 1944. The city fell early in 2000, and Putin, by then president, declared the battle ended. A new policy took shape. Russia would garrison troops and equipment and provide money, instructions, and political support. But local administration was to be handed over to Chechens deemed sufficiently loyal, a formula flowing from the institutional memory of a weakened empire. The appointment of proxies was accompanied by a message that became more hollow the more it was repeated on state TV: *There is no war. We have won.*

No verified casualty counts exist for the wars, but all agree the human toll has been vast, ranging from tens of thousands of Chechens killed to more than two hundred thousand. Setting aside the numbers, the years of violence and atrocities made clear that as public policy, little could be less wise than extensive killing in Chechnya, where tradition asks blood to be washed in blood. Chechens are bound by *adat*, an oral code that compels families to avenge the killing of their relatives. By the time President Putin claimed victory, enough blood had been spilled for a fury lasting generations. It mixed not just tribal urges for revenge and independence but racism and militant Islam.

The war that did not exist continued. Unable to defend Grozny conventionally, the rebels formed guerrilla bands, hiding amid the local populace and in nearby Russian republics and traveling between Azerbaijan, Georgia, and Turkey, where the Chechen diaspora is large. Islamic unrest expanded through Russia's territory in the Caucasus, and underground *jamaats* with connections to the Chechens formed in at least six of the region's internal republics. A rhythm emerged. Almost daily the separatists or their allies would stage small attacks or plant mines, and occasionally they would mass for large raids. In response to a spreading insurgency, the Russians set out to annihilate it, raiding homes in search of young men and generating complaints of rape, torture, robbery, and abduction. Macabre profiteering took hold, including sales of corpses back to families for burial.

Terrorism had been part of the separatists' struggle since before the first war. Basayev's debut was as an airplane hijacker in 1991; mass hostage taking began in 1995. But as death tolls rose and separatists were driven further underground, more turned to terrorism, then suicide terrorism. The rebels destroyed Chechnya's seat of government with a truck bomb in 2002 and assassinated the Kremlin-backed president in 2004. At the center was Basayev, sardonic and lame. His terrorist group, the Riyadus-Salakhin Reconnaissance and Sabotage Battalion of Chechen Martyrs, included ethnic fighters from the Caucasus and foreigners, including Arabs and a few Europeans.

A nationalist turned nihilist, Basayev made clear he thought Russian civilians were fair targets. After scores of hostages died at the theater in Moscow, he suggested Russia suffered what it deserved. "It turned out that these were innocent civilians who had gone to the theater for recreation," he wrote. "In this regard, you have to ask yourself: Who are the more than three thousand children aged under ten who died during the three years of the brutal and bloody war in Chechnya? Who are the more than four thousand children who lost their legs, arms, eyes, who ended up paralyzed? Who are the thirty-five hundred missing people who have been abducted from their homes or detained in the streets by the Russian occupiers and whose fate remains a mystery? Who are the two hundred thousand slain women, elderly, ill, children, and men? Who are they?"

Blood meets blood. Such were the rules in Basayev's war. And this time he was not sending terrorists to a theater. He had ordered them to a school.

Evening. The Execution Room.

Sometime after 5:00 P.M., while sitting in the hall with other male hostages, Aslan Kudzayev overheard the terrorists listening to the news on a radio. The announcer was discussing the siege, and Aslan understood that the world knew the students of Beslan were hostages. It was his first taste of the outside world since the siege had enveloped them, and it gave him a vague sense that they would be helped.

A few minutes later the Colonel appeared and ordered him and Albert Sidakov, another hostage, down the hall. Their walk ended in a literature classroom on the second floor, where eight dead men, broken by bullets, lay in a pool of blood. A portrait of Vladimir Mayakovsky, the revolutionary poet, hung on the far wall, which had been chipped by bullet impacts. Aslan understood. Throughout the day, men had been led off in small groups. Those who had not returned had been taken here and shot. As he and the others had sat downstairs, fingers interlocked behind their necks, the terrorists had realized the job of fortifying the school was done. Male hostages had become expendable. They were being culled.

"Open the window and throw these corpses out," the Colonel said.

Aslan and Albert lifted the first body to the sill and shoved it out. They moved to the next. So this is how Aslan would spend the last minutes of his life: When the eighth body was pushed onto the grass, he knew, he and Albert would be shot. Time was short. He glanced around the room. The Colonel was gone. A lone terrorist guarded them. Aslan assumed the terrorists would not throw out the bodies themselves, for fear of snipers. He and Albert were valuable for a few minutes more. They pushed out two more of the bullet-riddled men, including one who seemed to still be alive. Aslan leaned and pretended to retch.

The terrorist had removed the magazine from his Kalashnikov and was reloading it, round by round. "Let's jump out the window," Aslan whispered to Albert.

Albert was silent. "Let's jump," he whispered again.

"How?" Albert said, looking overwhelmed.

Aslan realized that if he was going to leap, he was going to leap alone. Their guard's rifle was unloaded. This was it. He bent to another corpse, then rushed toward the bloody sill. He hit in a push-up position and propelled himself out. The drop was eighteen feet, and he descended and slammed onto the bodies in a crouch. A bone in his foot popped. He rolled toward the school wall, reducing the angle the terrorist would have to fire at him, and began crawling away from the window. He worried the terrorist would drop a grenade. Gunfire sounded.

The terrorist's mask appeared in the window. The wall was nearly two feet thick, making it difficult for him to fire near the foundation without leaning far. He opted to try. His barrel blasted. Bullets thudded near Aslan. Bits of soil and grass jumped beside him. He scurried to the building's corner. Before him was a parking lot. He crawled on, putting cars between him and the window. The terrorist did not know where he was and fired into several cars, searching.

Aslan heard shouts. At the edge of nearby buildings, local men with the police and soldiers waved him to safety. He was so close, but an instant from death. The police had been told that if they harmed a terrorist, hostages would be executed in return. They held their fire. More bullets struck cars. A soldier threw a smoke grenade, hoping to obscure the terrorist's line of sight. It sent up a plume, which drifted the wrong way. Someone threw another, and a third, and a cloud rose between Aslan and his tormentor. He crawled with all of his speed and reached a railroad ditch in front of the school. He rolled in and lay still on the dirt. His white outfit was covered with grass stains and blood. Aslan was out. His wife, two daughters, and mother-in-law were still inside.

Evening. The Main Hall and Execution Room.

Karen Mdinaradze was not supposed to be here. He kneeled in the hall, his nose near the plaster, hands behind his head. Male hostages were lined up the same way to his right. To his left was a thin older man. Beyond him stood a *shahidka*, keeping watch.

Karen's luck was worse than bad. He was not a resident of Beslan. He was a videographer, hired to videotape Aslan's daughter Dzera during her role as bell ringer. He had not wanted the job, but Aslan persisted, and finally Karen gave in. He had been framing the girl in his viewfinder when the terrorists arrived. So far he was untouched, but he suffered a banal affliction. Karen was highly allergic to pollen, and many children had come to school with flowers and had carried them to the gym when they were captured, surrounding him with irritants. His eyes had reddened. His breathing was short. He felt luck running down. At about 3:00 P.M. a terrorist ordered him to the hall. Although he looked strong—he was built like a wrestler—his allergies drained him. Fatigue settled over him with the arrival of dusk.

The woman near him exploded.

There had been no warning. One second she was standing there, a veiled woman in black. The next she was not, having been torn apart in a roaring flash. The explosives cut her to pieces, throwing her head and legs into the geography classroom. Much of her flesh splashed along the walls. Shrapnel and heat shot out from the belt, striking the men in the corridor as well as another terrorist who guarded them, who was knocked to the floor. The other *shahidka* was also pierced with shrapnel. She fell, blood running from her nose. Karen felt heat and debris smack his left side. His left eye went dim. But the older man between him and the *shahidka* had absorbed much of the shrapnel, creating a shadow in which Karen was spared the worst. He was briefly unconscious, but came to, slumped forward against the wall. He thought he was dying and traced his palms along his face and head. His eyelid was torn, and he had shrapnel in his face and left calf. Heat had seared his salt-and-pepper hair, making it feel like brittle wire. Someone handed him a handkerchief and he wiped his face, pulling out plaster. "If I die, tell my mother and wife I love them very much," he told the man.

He surveyed the gruesome space. The thin man beside him, who had shielded him, breathed fitfully. His hips and legs faced the wrong direction, as if his lower spine had spun around. Karen knew he was in the last minutes of life. The injured terrorist had been set on a door removed from its hinges, and Abdullah knelt beside him, reading in Arabic in the lilting rhythm of prayer. Someone produced a syringe. The terrorist was given an injection, became still, and was carried away. After a few minutes a terrorist addressed the wounded. "Go to the second floor and we will provide you medical assistance," he said.

Karen stood with those who were able and limped upstairs to the Russian-literature classroom, and saw dead hostages piled on the floor. The injured men were given an order: "Lie down."

Their lives ended in an instant. A masked terrorist stepped forward, shouted, *"Allahu akhbar!"* and fired bursts from fifteen feet away, sweeping his barrel back and forth. The air filled with their cries and the thwacks of bullets hitting heavy flesh. The men rolled and thrashed. Errant bullets pounded the wall. At last the hostages were motionless, and the terrorist released the trigger. He pulled a chair to the door and straddled it with the hot barrel resting in front of him. He was listening. A moan rose from the pile. He fired again.

He remained for a few minutes, watching, listening. The room fell still. The night was warm. He rose and walked away.

Night. The Palace of Culture.

Outside the school, Russia's local and federal authorities struggled to react to the hostage crisis, whose scale and ferocity had overwhelmed them.

Although the main Beslan police station was practically next to the school, its officers had not mustered a coordinated effort to aid the women and children. Federal soldiers from the Fifty-eighth Army in Vladikavkaz, North Ossetia's capital, had flowed into Beslan during the day, joined by commandos from the former KGB, members of the famed units known as Alpha and Vympel. But so far the most anyone had done was form a disorganized perimeter, a cordon with uncertain orders and under uncertain command. The tactical leaders on the ground, in fact, seemed so unschooled in tactics that their cordon's outer limit was within range of the terrorists' small-arms fire, and families of the missing, who roamed the edges, were occasionally exposed to the forty-mm grenades the terrorists fired out. A sense of logistics escaped these officials as well. No fire-fighting equipment was staged. There were few ambulances. Many of the soldiers were lightly equipped, without the helmets or body armor they would need in a close-quarters fight.

Just beyond the window from which Aslan Kudzayev had leapt, within earshot of the executions, a vigil had formed. Relatives massed at the Palace of Culture, a grandly named Soviet movie house, consoling one another and worrying over the possibility of a Russian assault. They were a living picture of fear. Some were numb. Some were despondent. Hundreds paced. Many displayed the deflated calm of the helpless, people whose families were at stake but who had no influence over what came next. Now and then gunfire would sound. There would be a collective flinch. A few women would wail. Every few hours, Russian and local officials would leave the administration building, walk past the statue of Lenin, and brief the families in the palace. Each time they assured them they were doing all they could. And each time they said the terrorists had seized roughly 300 hostages, which was a lie.

Night. The Execution Room.

Karen Mdinaradze lay in the spreading pool of blood. It was dark. The room was quiet. The terrorist had fired without taking precise aim, relying on the automatic rifle to cut through the pile of men, and had missed one man. As bullets killed everyone around Karen, he fell behind a man who must have weighed 285 pounds. This man had been struck. Karen was not. He survived his own execution. After his executioner walked away, he lost sense of time. He saw the chair in the doorway and the open window and wanted to leap out. But he heard footsteps and was afraid.

In time the terrorist returned with two more hostages and ordered them to dump the bodies. Corpse by corpse they lifted the dead to the sill and shoved them out. The pile grew on the grass below. Three corpses remained when they came to Karen. He did not know what to do. He assumed the two men would be shot when their task was done and assumed he would be shot if he was discovered alive. But he knew he could not be thrown out the window; the drop was eighteen feet. The men bent to lift him. He felt a pair of hands clasp behind his neck and hands tighten on his ankles. He rolled forward and stood.

The men gasped. Karen rocked on his feet.

The terrorist told Karen to come near and stared at him, eyes moving under his mask as he surveyed his intact frame. "You walk under Allah," he said.

"Now throw out the rest of the corpses and I will tell you what to do next."

Two bodies remained, including that of the heavy man behind whom Karen had fallen. He lifted him by the belt as the other two took the legs and head and pushed him out. Another terrorist appeared, and the two captors pointed excitedly; Karen realized they had decided not to kill him. The three hostages were ordered downstairs to wash, then led to the gym.

Karen sat. His head was cut and bruised, his left eye blinded, his clothes drenched in blood. A woman near him whispered— "Did they hit you with a rifle butt?"—and he passed out.

September 2. Before Dawn. The Bathroom.

Zalina Levina rose at midnight. Rain was falling. Many of the children slept. The terrorists had not granted bathroom privileges for hours, but now the gym was quieter, and she wanted to try again. The bathroom was not lined with bombs; she thought she might hide with her granddaughter there. None of the terrorists stopped her, and she carried Amina into the room and sat. Her neighbor Fatima Tskayeva was already there, cradling her baby, Alyona, as rain pattered outside.

Whispering in the darkness, Fatima told of signs of dissent in the terrorists' ranks. The *shahidkas*, she said, seemed to have been deceived, as if they had not known they would be targeting children. One of them had used the bathroom in the evening, and was menstruating and upset. Now, Fatima said, the *shahidkas* were dead, killed in an explosion hours before. Fatima also said that some of their captors were capable of compassion. Her other daughter, Kristina, ten, whose heart was weak, had fainted earlier. Abdullah had picked up the girl and given her a tablet of validol, an herbal medicine for tension and heart pain. None of this made sense to Zalina, and she wondered about her own daughter. What would she think of Zalina bringing Amina to the school? Amina was not a student. There was no reason for her to be here. *I have to save this child*, she thought.

Under a desk stacked in the barricade she saw a lump of dried chewing gum. Zalina peeled it free, rolled it into a ball, and put it in her mouth. Slowly she worked it between her teeth, softening it with saliva. A faint taste of sugar spread on her tongue. It was food. She kept pressing and rolling it between her teeth, restoring it to something like what it had been. The gum absorbed more saliva and softened. It was ready. She plucked it from her lips and fed it to the toddler in her arms.

Morning. The Gym.

The Colonel stormed onto the court. Negotiations, he said, were failing. Russia was not responding, and was lying, saying only 354 hostages were in this room. "Your president is a coward," he snarled. "He does not answer the phone."

For these reasons, he said, he had announced a strike. There would be no more water and no food for the hostages. Bathroom privileges had ceased. The terrorists had told Russia's negotiators, he said, that in solidarity with their cause the hostages had agreed to these terms.

Late Morning. The Gym.

Abdullah pulled aside Larisa Kudziyeva, the commanding presence in a gym full of fear. He wanted to know who she was. A Chechen, or perhaps a member of another of the Islamic mountain people in the Caucasus?

"Do you have your passport with you?" he asked.

"Why should I bring my passport to a school?" she said.

"Are you Ingush?" he asked.

"No," she said.

"What is your last name?"

"Kudziyeva."

He studied her black clothes. "Why are you dressed like that?" he asked.

"It is how I choose," she said. Her defiance was almost reflexive.

Abdullah proceeded with his offer. The *shahidkas* were dead, but an explosive belt remained. This hostage, who could look into her executioner's barrel without flinching, was a candidate to wear it.

"We will release your children, and if you have relatives, we will release them, too," he said. "But for this you will have to put on a suicide belt and a veil and become one of our suicide bombers."

Larisa wondered about the *shahidkas*. "Where are yours?" she asked.

"Yesterday your soldiers tried to storm the building and they died," he said. It was a lie.

"I am afraid I may spoil everything—I am not a Muslim," she said. "How much time do I have to decide?"

"You have time," he said. "Sit down and think."

She returned to her children. The women nearby were curious. The temperature had risen again. The crowd was weak. "What did he want?" a woman asked. Larisa told them. "Do it," the woman said. "Maybe they will let us go."

Afternoon. The Gym.

Kazbek Misikov felt the wire separate between his fingers. His task was done: Inside its insulation, the wire had broken. But chance contact, he knew, might still allow a spark to jump across, and he needed to be sure the two ends could not meet incidentally. This required a finishing touch, and Kazbek grasped the blue plastic on either side of the crimp and stretched it like licorice, putting distance between the severed ends inside.

Now a new problem presented itself. Stretching the plastic had turned it a whitish blue. The defect was obvious. The terrorists had inspected the wires and bombs several times, and if they checked again, they would discover his subterfuge.

He felt a surge of worry. He and his wife had made it this far and had agreed on a plan: If the Russians attacked, Irina would help Batraz, their older son, and Kazbek would help Atsamaz, their first grader. Atsamaz was exhausted and dehydrated. Kazbek often looked into his eyes, and at times they seemed switched off. But he had found a way to keep him going. Other adults had whispered that it was possible to drink small amounts of urine. Kazbek had collected their pee. "I want a Coke," Atsamaz had said when told to drink it.

"After we leave, I will buy you a case of Coke," Kazbek said. The boy drank.

Now Kazbek had put them in fresh danger and would have to take another risk. When a terrorist strolled past him, he addressed him politely. "This wire lies across the passage," he said. "They are tripping on it. Neither you nor we need these to explode."

"What can be done?" the terrorist said.

"If we had a nail, the wire could be hung," Kazbek said.

The terrorist returned with a hammer and spike. Kazbek stood and drove the spike into the wall. He lifted the wire from the floor and laid a few turns around the shank, taking care to wrap with the whitish-blue section. He put a wooden spool on the spike and pressed it tight. The severed portion of wire was hidden. Kazbek had succeeded. He sat back with his family beneath the disconnected bomb.

Afternoon. The Bathroom.

Zalina Levina and Fatima Tskayeva hid in the bathroom with their small children. Hours passed; more breast-feeding mothers with babies pushed in, seeking relief from the heat. The place became a nursery.

Abdullah passed by and taunted them. "Maybe we have something to tell you," he said. Fatima begged for information. He laughed. Two hours later he offered a hint. "If they let him come in, maybe we will let the breast-fed children out," he said.

Zalina's mind whirled. *Who was coming?*

At about 3:00 P.M., a new man passed the door. He was tall and well built, with a thick mustache and graying hair. He wore a clean gray sport coat. They recognized him at once: Ruslan Aushev, the former president of Ingushetia, a republic bordering Chechnya, and a decorated Soviet veteran from Afghanistan. Aushev commanded respect among both his people and Chechnya's separatists. But he had been ousted by Putin, replaced by a loyalist from the KGB. Aushev's career stalled. In the nursery, he was the most important man in the world.

Zalina felt hope. *Aushev!* she thought. *We will be let go!* Applause sounded in the gym. Aushev stopped before them. A terrorist pointed in. "Here are the women with breast-fed children," he said.

"Do you know who I am?" Aushev asked.

"Of course," a mother said. He turned and left. The women rose, holding their babies, shaking with anticipation. They had been captives for more than thirty hours, without food, with little water, and with no sleep. There had been shooting and explosions. Their babies could take no more. Soon they might start to die. Abdullah stood at the door. "We will release you," he said. "But if you point out our photographs to the police, we will know immediately, and we will kill fifty hostages. It will be on your conscience."

"Now," he said, "one breast-fed child with one woman." He motioned for them to go.

Fatima was near the door. She did not move. "Let me take all of my children," she pleaded, reminding Abdullah of her two others, including Kristina, with the weak heart. "You helped her yourself," she said. "Let us all go."

"No," he said.

"Let my children out. I will stay."

"No."

Fatima sobbed now. "Then let Kristina leave with my baby," she begged.

Abdullah's anger flashed. "I told you, bitch, no," he said. "Now I am not releasing anyone because of you."

He looked at the other women. "Everyone back to the gym," he said. Panic flowed through Zalina. Sweeping up her granddaughter, she stepped past Abdullah. Rather than turning left for the gym, she turned right, toward the main school. She had decided. *I am leaving*, she thought. *Let them shoot me in the back.*

Another terrorist blocked her. "Where are you going?" he said.

She tilted her head at Abdullah. "He allowed me," she said, and brushed past. The main hall was a few yards away. The walk seemed a kilometer. Zalina passed through the door and saw

Aushev by the exit at the end of the hall. She moved toward him. He waved her on.

Zalina walked barefoot in quick strides, Amina's cheek tight to her own. Her heart pounded. Would she be shot? She did not look back. The corridor was littered with bits of glass. She did not feel it nicking her feet. Behind her the other women followed. A chain of mothers and babies was making its way out, twenty-six people in all.

Zalina focused on the door. She passed Aushev, who stood with the Colonel. "Thank you very much," she said. The exit was barricaded with tables, and a terrorist slid them aside and opened the door. Air tumbled in, and light. She stepped out.

Behind her in the corridor, Fatima Tskayeva wailed as she carried Alyona, her infant. She could not go any more. Sobbing, she handed the baby to a terrorist in a black T-shirt and mask. She had two more children here. She had decided to stay. The terrorist carried Alyona down the hall to Aushev and handed him the child. Fatima's cries pierced the corridor.

Outside, Zalina rushed Amina past the place where the assembly had been the day before. Discarded flowers were on the ground. A man shouted from a roof. "There are snipers," he said. "Run!"

The line of women followed, and together they approached the perimeter. An aid station was waiting with medicine, food, and water. Zalina knew nothing of it. She trotted for her apartment, which was inside the perimeter, reached the entrance, climbed the stairs, and stood at her door. She had no key. She banged. It had been a mistake to bring Amina to school. It had been a mistake to have been taken hostage. But the terrorists had mistaken her for a breast-feeding mother. It was their mistake that she was out. They were free. Amina was alive. Who had a key? She descended the stairs to the entrance. Four Russian troops approached.

"Give me the child," one said, extending his arms. Amina saw their camouflage and began to howl. "Do not touch her," Zalina snapped. "No one will touch her."

Evening. The Gym.

Karen Mdinaradze slipped in and out of consciousness. Once he awoke to see a woman over him, fanning him, another time to find children cleaning his wound with a cloth soaked in urine. He awoke again. A teenaged girl thrust an empty plastic bottle to him and asked him to urinate in it.

"Turn your eyes away," he said, and he pressed the bottle against himself and slowly peed. He finished and handed the bottle back. The girl and her friends thanked him and quickly poured drops to wash their faces. Then each sipped from the bottle, passing it among themselves, and returned it to him. Karen's dehydration was advanced; his throat burned. He poured a gulp of the warm liquid into his mouth and across his tongue, letting it pool around his epiglottis. The moisture alleviated some of the pain. He swallowed.

He looked at the bottle. A bit remained. A very old woman in a scarf was gesturing to him, asking for her turn. He passed the bottle on.

September 3. Past Midnight. The Weight Room.

Irina Naldikoyeva picked her way by the hostages dozing on the floor. Her daughter, Alana, was feverish. The gym was connected to a small weight-lifting room, which had become an informal infirmary. Irina asked permission from a terrorist to move Alana there. He nodded, and she carried the drowsy child and laid her on the room's cool floor. Perhaps fifty people rested in the space, mostly children and elderly hostages.

A water pipe was leaking, and, unsolicited, a small boy came to them and gave Alana a cup of water. She drank thirstily and lay down. Gradually her breathing slowed and deepened. She drifted to sleep. Irina returned to the gym, retrieved her son, and placed him beside his sister.

After several hours caressing the children, Irina dozed off, the first time since they were taken hostage that she had slept. Her father appeared. He had died several months earlier, but his face hovered before her, an apparition with gray hair. He did not speak. Nor did she. They looked into each other's eyes.

After perhaps twenty minutes, she woke. Her father, Timofey Naldikoyev, had been a gentle man, quiet and kind. She had never dreamed of him before. She wondered: *What does it mean?*

Morning. The Gym.

Forty-eight hours after the hostages had been taken captive, the survivors were sliding to despair. They were beginning their third day without food, and their second without water. Almost all had slept only in snatches through two nights. They were dehydrated, filthy, weak, and drained by fear. They slumped against one another and the walls. The terrorists seemed tired, too, frayed and aware that their demands were being ignored. They had become nastier and drove the hostages out of the weight room to the gym, shoving some with rifles.

As the sun climbed and the temperature again began to rise, the two terrorists who specialized in explosives roamed the court. Their explosives were arranged in at least two circuits— the more visible one connecting the hanging bombs. A second circuit wired together a string of bombs on the floor, including two large bombs. The terrorists moved this second chain near one of the walls. Irina Naldikoyeva watched, struggling to stay alert. She was massaging her son, waiting for a sign.

Minutes After 1:00 P.M. The Gym.

The explosion was a thunderclap, a flash of energy and heat, shaking the gym. Twenty-two seconds later a second blast rocked the gym again. Their combined force was ferocious. Together they blew open the structure, throwing out the plastic windows, splattering the walls with shrapnel, and heaving people and human remains through the room. One of the blasts punched a seventy-eight-inch-wide hole through a brick wall twenty-five inches thick, cascading bricks and mortar onto the lawn. It also lifted the roof and rafters above the hole, snapping open a corner of the building like a clam before gravity slammed the roof back down. Much of the ceiling fell onto the hostages below.

Scores of hostages were killed outright. Their remains were heaped near the fresh hole and scattered across the basketball court. But most survived, hundreds of people in various states of injury. At first they hardly moved. Many were knocked senseless. Some were paralyzed by fright. Others, worried about another blast, pressed to the floor. At last they began to stir, and escape.

Dzera Kudzayeva, the first-grade girl who was to have been the bell ringer, had been near the blast that knocked out the wall. She had been asleep under her grandmother, Tina Dudiyeva, whose body had seemed to rise above her with the shock wave. The child stood now, and seeing sunlight through the hole, she scampered out, over the shattered bricks and onto the lawn. She began to run. She had arrived on Wednesday in a dress with a white apron and ribbons; she left now in only panties, filthy, streaked in blood, sprinting. She crossed the open courtyard and lot and came to the soldiers who ringed the school. She was free. The sound of automatic weapons began to rise.

The hole was only one route. The pressure of the explosions had thrown the windowpanes clear of their frames, exposing the room to light and air. The hostages reacted instinctually. A desperate scramble began. The sills were a little more than four feet above the floor, and throughout the room many of those who were not badly injured rushed to the sills, pulled themselves up, and dropped out to the ground.

Karen Mdinaradze had been unconscious on the floor and had not been struck by shrapnel. He woke, heard moaning, and found himself surrounded by gore. Human remains had rained down; two girls near him were covered by a rope of intestine. He saw people hurdling the windows, mustered his energy, stumbled to the sill, and followed them out.

He landed in the courtyard and ran in a panicked human herd. A mother weaved in front, pulling her small boy. Bullets snapped overhead. They dashed across the courtyard toward the far corner, following those in front toward a gap in the fence. The mother went down. Her son stopped. "Mama!" he screamed. Karen bent and scooped the boy with his right hand as he ran past, pulling him tight like a loose ball. He charged for the fence opening and passed through it and out of the line of fire. Beside him was a small metal garage. He placed the boy inside. The mother ran around the corner. She had not been shot. She had stumbled. She fell atop her boy, sobbing. Soldiers, police officers, and local men were hunched and running toward them; Karen stumbled on, one-eyed and bloody, until a man hooked an arm under him and steered him down the street to an ambulance, which drove him away.

The first rush of escapes was over. Back in the gym, Aida Archegova had been leaning against the wall opposite a large bomb and had been stunned by the explosions. A piece of ceiling had fallen on her. She woke to glimpse her older son, Arsen, eleven, scrambling out. She recognized him by his blue briefs, which she had folded dozens of times. She did not see her younger boy. She pushed aside the ceiling and scanned the room. Where is Soslan? Gunfire boomed. A terrorist stood at the door, shouting. "Those who are alive and want to live, move to the center of the gym," he said.

Aida picked her way through the corpses and mortally injured, looking for Soslan. He was not among them. A boy about four years old told her he was looking for his brother. She took his hand and led him to the door and told him to wait. Another boy approached her, and a girl about twelve. "I am scared," the boy said. The girl said her sister was dying. Bullets zipped through the gym, the tracers glowing red, smacking walls. "Lie down here and wait," she said. "You may be killed."

Terrorists clustered in the hall, and Abdullah approached and ordered the hostages to follow. They formed a line, and he led them down the long hall to the cafeteria, a light-blue room where perhaps forty hostages were sitting or lying on the floor. Terrorists ducked behind barricades at the windows, firing out. Buckets of water rested on the table, with cookies and salted cabbage. The children took bowls and dipped them. Some drank six or seven bowls, unable to slake their thirst, and then began to eat with their hands.

Abdullah ordered the women to the windows. "Put the children there as well," he said. Aida froze. Bullets buzzed and popped through the air, pecking the brick facade, pocking the plaster walls. "If children are there, then they will not shoot and you will be safe," Abdullah said.

Six large windows faced the front of the school, each with steel bars, which prevented escape. Aida stepped to a middle window, lifted a boy who appeared to be about seven, and laid him on the sill. She took her place beside him. She made a highly visible target, her black hair falling on a red blouse. Her feet were on broken glass. The Russians were advancing. Abdullah ordered her to shout to them. She found a piece of curtain and held it through the bars, waving it. Other mothers were being used the same way. Beside her, Lora Karkuzashvili, a waitress at a local restaurant, frantically waved a strip of cloth. They were human shields. "Do not shoot!" the women screamed. "Do not shoot!"

1:10 P.M. The Gym and the Weight Room.

Atsamaz stood over his unconscious father. "Papa!" he shouted. "Papa!"

His father, Kazbek, was stunned. Inside his haze he heard the boy and remembered his agreement with his wife. He was to get Atsamaz out. He opened his eyes. The bomb overhead had not exploded. It still hung there. He saw Atsamaz and looked for his wife, Irina, crawling to Batraz, their older son, who was curled lifelessly on the floor. She rolled him over. "Batik!" she screamed.

Both of her eardrums had been ruptured, making even her own voice seem muffled. "Batik!" she shouted. He did not move. He was wearing only black pants. Blood ran from his left knee. "Batik!"

Batraz stirred. Irina cradled him, urging him toward alertness.

The survivors were in motion. At the opposite wall, children were going out the window, using the body of a fat old woman as a step. One by one they scrambled over the corpse, becoming silhouettes in the window frame, and then were gone. Tracers zipped in; Kazbek worried his family would be shot.

He wrapped Atsamaz with his arms and lurched to the weight room. Putting Atsamaz down, he saw that the boy was covered in someone else's blood. Kazbek inspected himself. A chunk of his left forearm was gone, as if it had been cut away with a sharp scoop. Blood pulsed from the wound. His right arm was injured, too; a bullet, he thought, must have passed through it.

He felt weak. If he were to keep bleeding like this, he knew, he did not have much time. He pulled a bright orange curtain toward him, made bandages, and tried to stop his bleeding. His head was injured, too, with cuts and burns. After dressing his arms, he tied a piece across his scalp, making a garish turban, and sat down. There were three windows, each covered with bars. They were trapped.

About a dozen hostages were in the room, including Larisa Kudziyeva and her family, and Sarmat, Vadim Bolloyev's small son. Larisa had been at the entrance to the weight room at the instant of the first explosion, standing beside Ibragim, one of the terrorists. The blast had knocked them to the floor together and entangled their legs. Ibragim had seemed surprised. After the second blast, he rolled free of Larisa and stood. "Are you blowing us up?" she asked him.

"No, it is yours," he said.

Ibragim disconnected a bomb at the doorway and rested it on the floor. "Make sure the children do not touch it," he said to her, and left.

The terrorists had staged equipment in the weight room, and Larisa rummaged through their backpacks, finding candy, raisins, dried apricots, and cookies. She handed food to the hostages. The battle flowed around them; they devoured the terrorists' supplies. A boy came to Larisa. "Where is my mother?" he said.

"At this moment I am as good as your mother," she said. "Sit. Eat."

Kazbek was slumped on a wrestling mat, fighting for consciousness. His bandages were soaked. Shooting roared at the windows. He knew Russian soldiers were closing in. *Soon they will be tossing grenades through windows,* he thought, *and then asking who is inside.* His wife was nearby. Blood ran from her ears. A bone in her neck had been cracked. The building shook from explosions, and he was falling asleep. He saw Irina's face, her soft cheeks and warm brown eyes. It was beautiful.

"Do not die!" she said.

1:25 P.M. The Gym.

Irina Naldikoyeva had been lying among corpses for at least twenty minutes, covering her son, Kazbek. Her niece, Vika Dzutseva, fifteen, was beside her, in a sleeveless blue dress, with Alana. Flames were spreading in the ceiling. The children wore only soiled briefs.

The children had been asleep on the floor at the moment of the first explosion, and were protected. But the first blast sent shrapnel into Irina's leg; the second sent more metal into her neck and jaw. She was light-headed and unsure what to do. Helicopters thumped overhead. She worried one would be disabled and slam into the gym. She had watched other hostages being led away and was wary of following the terrorists, but was running out of choices. The gym was afire.

Abdullah entered, looking for survivors. "Those who are alive, stand and go to the cafeteria," he shouted. His eyes met Irina's. *This means you.*

She took Kazbek by his hand and told Vika to take Alana, and they made their way to him. Broken bodies were packed in a wide arc around the hole in the wall, so many that Irina and Vika had trouble finding places to put down their feet. Several times they had to lift the children over the tangle.

In the main hall Vika collapsed with Alana, but a terrorist drove Irina on to the cafeteria, where she looked in and saw bloodied hostages and terrorists firing through the windows. Her instinct was to hide. She kept moving, heading upstairs to the auditorium and slipping behind the maroon curtain on the stage. Perhaps twenty hostages were there. A girl came to Irina, tore off a piece of her black skirt, and bandaged her leg. Irina held Kazbek and waited. Bullets pecked against the school's outer walls.

Before 2:00 P.M. The Coach's Office.

With so many armed terrorists inside, School No. 1 was difficult for rescuers and the Special Forces to approach, especially because they had been caught unprepared. At the moment of the first explosion, two T-72 tanks had been parked with engines off on Kominterna Street, one block east of the school. Their crews had reacted with as much astonishment as the civilians clustered nearby, and argued over what to do. Inside a five-story apartment building overlooking the gym from the northeast, a Russian sniper team had also been taken unaware, and rushed to a balcony to see what had happened. They began to provide covering fire to hostages climbing out. A group of Special Forces soldiers, who had been rotated from the perimeter to a training range at a nearby army base, began speeding back, scrambling to a fight that had started while they were out of position.

Along the uneven perimeter, held by a disorganized mix of Ossetian police officers, traffic cops, conscript soldiers, local men with rifles, and Special Forces teams, disorder and confusion reigned. Some men were ordered to advance, while men beside them were ordered to hold their fire. Gradually, however, a sense that the final battle had begun took hold, and the men moved forward. Volleys of bullets smacked into the school, kicking up red dust. Litter bearers followed.

After an hour the Russians were pressing near the gym, and the volume of their fire, coming from so many directions, had begun to reduce the terrorists' numbers and push them out from many rooms. Several terrorists were injured, and others were dead. The gym, with flames crackling on its ceiling, had become untenable to defend. The terrorists were making a stand in the cafeteria, where the windows had iron bars.

For this they wanted hostages as shields, and Ibragim returned to the weight room to retrieve the group hiding there. He was a dark-haired young man, appearing younger than twenty-five, wearing a T-shirt and an ammunition vest. He entered the room and shouted at the hostages on the floor. Kazbek was there, wrapped in orange bandages, looking near death. Others looked capable of walking out. "Those who want to live, come," he shouted. No one complied.

"Get the people out!" he shouted. "The ceiling is on fire."

"You leave," Larisa said. "We will stay."

"The roof will collapse," he said.

Larisa worried that if they did not follow his orders, Ibragim would begin to kill. She led a group to the door and was joined by Ivan Kanidi, the school's physical-education instructor. Ibragim signaled for them to move low along the wall, ducking at windows so no one would be shot. Heat radiated from above. Flaming pieces of ceiling fell. Larisa's daughter, Madina, held three children by the hand, but a boy shook free to hide among the dead.

Ibragim forced them on, mustering more hostages he found alive on the floor. At the far end of the gym, he directed them to the coach's office, where he looked out the window to see what he could of the Russian advance. When he turned, Ivan Kanidi lunged.

Ivan was seventy-four years old, but he retained the muscularity of a lifelong athlete. He seized Ibragim's rifle with two thick hands, trying to rip it from his grasp. The rifle barrel swung wildly as they struggled and spun. "Get the children out!" Ivan shouted.

"Let go, old man, or I will kill you!" Ibragim snarled.

Back and forth they fought, pushing and pulling each other around the room by the rifle. Basketballs and other sports equipment littered the floor. After what seemed a minute, Ivan fell backward with the rifle in his hands. He was a nimble man, big-chested but lean, with a finely trimmed gray mustache. Before he could turn the rifle, Ibragim drew a pistol and shot him in the chest. He was motionless. Ibragim leaned down, retrieved his rifle from the dead man's hands, and looked at the group. "Everybody out," he said.

They began the walk to the cafeteria. Kira Guldayeva, a grandmother Ibragim had rousted from the gym, was suspicious, and when Ibragim looked away, she pulled her grandson, Georgy, six, into a classroom. Larisa and Madina remained under Ibragim's control, arriving at the cafeteria under his escort.

The place was a horror. Each element of the siege—from the capture of the children to the enforced conditions of their captivity among the bombs to the murders of their fathers and teachers in the literature classroom to the explosions that ripped apart people by the score—had been a descent deeper into cruelty, violence, and near-paralyzing fear. Now they had reached the worst. Women stood at windows, screaming and waving white cloths. Bullets struck the walls. Dust and smoke hung in the air. Glass covered the floor, much of it splattered with blood. The room stunk of gunpowder, rotting food, and sweat. Terrorists raced through the haze, bearded, whooping, firing, and yelling instructions. Larisa had her son, Zaurbek, by the hand, and apprehended their new conditions; Madina had the two children she had brought from the weight room. She did not know their names. They rushed around a corner near the dish-washing room, where at least twenty other hostages were massed tight. Two girls were trying to squeeze themselves into a massive soup pot. Dead women and children were strewn on the kitchen tiles. The Kudziyeva family took a place on the floor.

Just After 2:00 P.M. The Weight Room.

Kazbek Misikov tried to focus. He had fainted from blood loss, but Atsamaz revived him by dumping water on his face. He knew he had to rally himself. Roughly a dozen hostages remained in the weight room, but only three were adults, and he was the only man. Heat and orange glow emanated from the gym. Sounds of battle boomed outside. They were in a seam, forgotten but alive.

The barred windows offered no escape. Irina found paper and made a sign with red lipstick. *DETI*, it read, Russian for "children." She held it up at a window so they would not be shot. Kazbek staggered beside her, put his head at the window, where it was exposed. "There are children here!" he shouted. "Do not shoot!"

He was wearing a bloody turban and wondered if he would be mistaken for an Arab. Peering into the narrow alley, he saw the district prosecutor looking back. They both were startled. "Alan!" Kazbek said.

The prosecutor rushed to the window. "What can we do?" he said.

He was accompanied by a man with a rifle, and Kazbek asked him to aim at the door, in case a terrorist returned. He was weak but managed to lift a barbell and pass it between the bars. The men outside used it as a lever and popped the frame free. An escape route was open. Irina started handing out children: First the little ones, and then the adults helped her with a badly burned teenage girl. When the last child was out, the adults followed.

The Misikovs emerged behind the school. Soldiers passed them going the other way, rushing to penetrate the building through the hole they had made. The fire in the gym roof, which had spread slowly, was now a conflagration. Smoke rose over the neighborhood. Kazbek moved woozily to a stretcher, lay down, and slipped out of consciousness.

The children were handed from rescuer to rescuer in a chain. Atsamaz was passed along with the others until he ended up in the arms of Slavik, his uncle, a face he knew in the chaos. Slavik embraced him. Atsamaz realized he had been saved. He clung to the man. "Papa promised me I could have a Coke," he said.

After 2:00 P.M. The Cafeteria.

Less than fifteen minutes after Irina Naldikoyeva and her son found refuge in the auditorium, the terrorists forced them downstairs to the cafeteria and its tableau of misery. Hostages crowded the room, partially dressed, soiled, riddled with shrapnel, shot, burned, dehydrated, and stunned. Irina saw her niece, Vika, slumped beneath a window, her long black hair matted with sweat. "Where is Alana?" she asked.

"Here," Vika said, pointing to a child, naked except for dirty panties, curled under a table.

Bullets were coming in from the Russians firing outside. Irina grabbed her children and scrambled with them along the floor, stopping against a large freezer, panting. A terrorist handed her a bucket of water, and she tilted it and gave each child a drink. They gulped voraciously. At last it was her turn, and she put the bucket to her lips, poured the cool water onto her tongue, eager for it to hit her parched throat. But instead the water splashed onto her floral blouse. Irina did not understand and reached under her chin and felt the place where shrapnel had passed through. The bottom of her mouth was an open hole. Blood and water soaked her torso. She put the bucket aside.

Around her were at least six dead children, and she knew this place was not safe. She crawled to the dish-washing room, pushed the children under the sinks, and lay her body across them. Bullets kept coming. Some skipped off window frames or iron bars and whirred by, ricochets. One plunked the sink above her son.

A terrorist was on his back on the floor, motionless with his mouth open, showing gold teeth. His head had been bandaged. In the cupboards along the floor were more small children, hiding with pots and pans. The terrorist stood and lurched back to fight. On the other side of the door, Lora Karkuzashvili stood at a window. Aida Archegova was to her right. Abdullah was ducking and shooting, moving between them. Ibragim was in the corner, firing through the bars, his arms streaked in blood. Volleys of bullets came back in. Lora was struck in the chest, dropped, and did not move. Aida was standing, shouting and waving a cloth. A boy sat beside her, exposed. "Do not shoot!" Aida screamed.

Aida had been at the window for at least twenty minutes; somehow the bullets missed her and the child. She did not know his name; only once had he spoken. "I do not want to die," he said. Every chance she had, she put him on the floor. Always Abdullah told her to put him back. But Abdullah looked away again, and Aida swung the boy off the sill and placed him under a table. She stood upright and felt a tremendous slap on the left side of her face. The impact spun her head. Much of her jaw was gone. She had been hit. She looked at Abdullah, who was using her for cover. "May I sit now?" she tried to ask. "I am bad."

"I do not care if you are bad or good," he said. "Stand if you want to live."

She was dizzy. There was an explosion. Aida fell.

Everyone was wounded, cowering, or dead. A creaking and rumbling sounded outside, and the turret of a T-72 tank appeared near the fence bordering the school grounds. Its barrel flashed. There was a concussive boom. The entire facade shook. Dust fell from the ceiling. The shell had struck another room.

Midafternoon. The Gym.

Pushed away by flame, sniper fire, and charging infantry, the terrorists yielded the gym. The place in which they had confined more than eleven hundred people, the pen with its matrix of bombs, was no longer theirs. Flames rolled along its ceiling and roof. Beneath the fire, on the basketball court, corpses and gravely injured hostages were spread across the floorboards, partially dressed or nearly naked, twisted into unnatural shapes. Heat seared the room.

For a long time almost no one moved, but at last Marina Ka-nukova, a first-grade teacher who had been feigning death with a third-grade girl, stirred. The heat had become too much, and she had heard a soldier's voice telling those who were alive to crawl to safety. The bodies were too thick to crawl over, so she took the child by the hand, crouched, and with flames roaring overhead they stepped across the dead to the weight room, where they were met by soldiers and local men, who directed them out a window. Behind her, bit by bit, coals and the flaming roof were dropping onto the injured and the dead. The air filled with smells of burning plastic and roasting hair and flesh.

Flanked by the Special Forces, a BTR-80 had arrived on the gym's western side. An eight-wheeled armored vehicle with a 14.5-mm machine gun on a turret, it rolled toward the door where the hostages had first been forced into the school, its gun firing as it advanced, and rammed the wall and windows.

Soldiers and local men climbed into the bathroom and freed a group of screaming, terrified hostages, many slicked in blood and shit. Teams of soldiers pushed into the school. The Russians were inside at last, possessing opposite ends of the gym. Their storm had come late. On the basketball court, burning bodies were before them by the score.

Midafternoon. The Cafeteria.

The survivors slumped in the corner by the dish-washing room, perhaps twenty-five people crammed in a tiny space. Still the bullets kept coming. A crash sounded along the outside wall; they noticed that the iron bars on the window in the left corner were gone. Three Russian commandos climbed in.

They were a fit and nimble trio, carrying rifles and wearing body armor and helmets. They stood among the dead and the injured, weapons ready, blood, broken glass, and spent shells around their feet. One of them bled from his hand. "Where are the bastards?" one whispered.

A door to the storerooms swung open. Ibragim was there. Simultaneously, the commandos and the terrorist opened fire over the hostages. Ibragim stepped aside, then reappeared, holding two hand grenades. Bullets hit him as he let them go.

Time seemed to slow.

Larisa Kudziyeva watched one of the grenades, a smooth metal oval about the size of a lime, as it passed over her, fell to the floor, and bounced off the kitchen tile toward the soldiers. Her son was beneath her and her daughter beside her. She squeezed the boy, threw her leg and arm over him, and swung her other hand over her daughter's face.

A hand grenade is a small explosive charge surrounded by a metal shell, whose detonation is controlled by a fuse with a few-second delay. When the charge explodes, it shatters the metal exterior, turning it into bits of shrapnel that rush away at thousands of feet per second, accompanied by a shock wave and heat. It can kill a man fifteen yards away. The nook was less than six yards across.

The grenade exploded.

After the wave of metal hit her, Larisa was encased in something like silence, a state in which the absence of sound was overlaid by the ringing in her ears, leaving her to feel an effect like a struck crystal glass. How easy it is to die, she thought. But she did not die, not immediately, and as if in a dream she ran an arm over her son, who was beneath her. He was alive. "Mama," he said. "Mamochka."

The shrapnel had blasted the right side of her face, tearing part of it off, and ruined her right arm. Larisa did not want the boy to see what had become of her and turned away and raised her left hand to her face. Her fingertips felt wet flesh and exposed bone. The bone fragments were sharp enough to prick. She passed out.

Her daughter crawled to her. A teacher beside Larisa was missing a leg. One of the commandos was dead. The children Madina had escorted in were dead. One of Larisa's neighbors was dead. Another teacher was dead. The grisly mess extended through the room.

Larisa looked dead, but Madina checked her pulse, finding life. More commandos climbed in. They told the survivors to follow them out. "My mother is still alive," Madina said.

"We will take care of her," a soldier said.

Madina picked up her little brother, handed him out the window to a man outside. The man helped her down, too, and the brother and sister ran out into the neighborhood. They were saved.

Inside the dish-washing room, Irina Naldikoyeva had felt the wall shake, but she remained on top of her children, holding them down, unsure what had happened. There were two doors into the tiny room, and after a few minutes a man's head appeared along the floor at one of them. It was a commando, crawling. He wore a helmet. His face was sweaty. Irina understood: Russians were inside. The children hiding with the pots understood, too. The cupboard doors flew open and they scuttled out and bounded past him, looking for a way out.

Irina followed with Kazbek and Alana, out the door, past the mangled corpses, to the window. She handed out the children and then shinnied down. She was out, in autumnal air, standing on grass. She walked unsteadily and turned the corner at the first house on Kominterna Street. She did not know where her children had gone. She sat on the ground. Someone came and led her away.

Late Afternoon. A Classroom.

Kira Guldayeva hid with Georgy in the classroom as the sound of gunfire rose and fell. Six Kalashnikovs were stacked against the wall. Camouflage clothing was strewn on the floor. The walls were streaked with blood, as if during the battle injured terrorists had congregated here. Kira pulled Georgy close. He was a small boy, wearing only underpants. She checked him for injuries and found tiny holes where shrapnel had entered his back, buttocks, and one of his feet. Blood beaded from each wound. Her injuries were worse, a catalog of the afternoon's hazards: She had been shot twice, and one bullet had passed through her arm. Shrapnel had struck her shoulder. She had been burned.

She sat for a long time, afraid the terrorists might return and wondering when the rescuers might reach them. "Stay here," she told the boy, and crept to the door.

A Russian soldier stood across the hall. They appraised each other, two faces in the chaos. He dashed toward her.

As he crossed the open, gunfire boomed. A bullet slammed into his head. He staggered into the room, dropped his rifle, grasped for his helmet, and collapsed. He did not move. His dropped rifle pointed at Kira and Georgy; she pushed it away with a board.

Another soldier followed him in and leaned against the wall. He was injured, too. "Lie down," he said to them, and began applying a bandage to his leg. A microphone hung at his throat, into which he spoke in clipped tones. More soldiers entered. The school was falling under Russian control.

They put Kira and Georgy on stretchers, and she was handed through a window. Litter bearers ran with her, tripped, and dropped her to the ground. "Where is the boy?" she screamed. "Where is the boy?"

Late Afternoon. The Cafeteria.

Larisa Kudziyeva awoke, unsure how much time she had spent on the floor. The hostages near her were all dead. She tried to move, but her right arm felt as if someone were atop it.

Much of her face was gone; soldiers stepped past her as if she were a corpse. They seemed calmer, having for the moment taken control of the room. One stood above her, a blurry form. She raised her left hand to wipe blood from her eyes. He glanced down, surprised. "Girl, be patient," he said. "They will bring stretchers."

His voice sounded kind. *If he can call me girl when I look like this*, she thought, *then I can wait.* She drifted to sleep.

Late Night. A Hospital Room in Vladikavkaz.

Nikolai Albegov arrived at the door and surveyed his son's wife. He was sixty-six, a retired truck driver, fidgeting where he stood. The thin frame of Irina Naldikoyeva, his daughter-in-law, was extended on the bed. Her head and her neck were wrapped in gauze. She was foggy from painkillers. An IV snaked into her arm.

Throughout Beslan and Vladikavkaz a fresh horror was descending. The morgue in Beslan was overflowing, and bodies were laid on the grass. Vladikavkaz's morgue also had a growing display of corpses waiting to be claimed. The dashes out of the school, and the rescues, had been so spontaneous and disorganized that many families were not sure whether their spouses and children had survived. The families also heard of blackened remains encased on the basketball court under the collapsed roof. The living roamed among the dead, peering at the unclaimed, looking for their own.

Nikolai's family had been spared this. For nine years Irina had lived in his home. She had borne the family a son and a daughter and performed much of the daily labor. Nikolai kept one of the most traditional households in Beslan, and under the mountain customs he observed, he was the *khozyain*, the elder of his domain. Irina was not allowed to address him. She had never spoken to him unless he had asked her a question. They had never embraced.

He stood at the door in a suit, a leathery, strong-handed old man in his very best clothes, assessing the woman who had come into his home. He did not yet know what had happened in the school. But she had brought his family out. Tears ran down his dark face. He walked to her bed, found a spot on her face where there was no bandage, and gave her a kiss.

September 4. Evening. A Hospital Room in Vladikavkaz.

The doctor assessed Larisa Kudziyeva. Twice they had operated on her, but she had remained in a coma. Shrapnel had cut too many holes through her; blood transfusions leaked out. Her blood pressure had sunk. She was near death. The hospital was overwhelmed with patients, and at last Larisa was triaged. Nurses washed her and put a tag on her toe.

But Larisa Kudziyeva would not die, and hours later another doctor found her alive where she had been left for dead. Early on September 4 she was put back on an operating table. Much of her eye socket was gone. The right side of her face was mashed. Her right arm was shredded and broken in three places. Her middle finger was snapped. Her side had absorbed a shock wave and shrapnel blast. But the metal had missed her main arteries and her right lung. She stabilized before sunrise.

Now she was awake, barely. The surgeon questioned her, running through a simple neurological exam.

"What is your birthday?" he asked.

"The fourteenth," she said.

"What month?"

"May," she said. It was true. But it was not.

"No, forget that day," the doctor said. "Your birthday is September fourth."

Epilogue

The Beslan siege claimed a greater toll of human life than all but one act of modern terrorism, the destruction of the World Trade Center. The terrorists' actions and the bungled rescue efforts ended with the deaths of 331 people, not counting the 31 terrorists the Russian government says were killed. Among the dead were 186 children and 10 members of Russia's Special Forces, whose individual acts of courage were undermined by the incompetence of their government's counterterrorism response. More than seven hundred other people were injured, most of them children.

The siege ended with no victor. Faith in Russia's government, and the ability of its security agencies to protect its citizens, has been shaken. Sympathy for Chechen independence has shrunk. Even some of Chechnya's separatist fighters, men claiming loyalty to Shamil Basayev, have questioned the utility and rationale of such tactics, although the underground rebel government, unwisely, has not distanced itself from Basayev, who was appointed its first deputy prime minister in 2005. His retention of such a post, no matter his earlier guerrilla prowess, discredits the separatists and is grounds for shame.

The Russian and North Ossetian parliaments have opened investigations into the terrorist act, which thus far have led to inconclusive findings and drawn accusations of cover-ups from survivors and the bereaved. Official lies have eroded public confidence, including the insistence during the siege that only 354 hostages were seized, and an enduring insistence that the T-72 tanks did not fire until all the survivors were out, which is false. It remains unclear, and a source of acrimonious debate, what caused the first two explosions and the fire in the gym, although the available evidence, on balance, suggests that the blast damage and the majority of the human injury were caused by the terrorists' bombs. There is similar uncertainty about the reason behind the explosion of the *shahidka*. Other points of contention include what help, if any, the terrorists received from inside Beslan, whether the terrorists hid weapons in the school before the attack, how many terrorists were present, and whether several of them escaped. A third of the dead terrorists have not been publicly identified, and their names are officially unknown. Ibragim was killed; this is clear. But many hostages, including Larisa Kudziyeva and Kazbek Misikov, have studied the known pictures of the dead terrorists and insist that Ali, previously known as Baisangur, and others were not among the dead and were not seen on the last day of the siege.

Almost all of the surviving hostages remain in North Ossetia, and many continue to receive treatment, including Larisa, who had endured fourteen surgeries through early April 2006 and is expecting two more. Aida Archegova, who became a human shield after searching for her son Soslan, was rescued and later learned that Soslan escaped. Her face has been rebuilt, with bone from her hip grafted to fashion a replacement jaw. She has never again seen the boy who was a human shield with her and does not know whether he is alive. Sarmat Bolloyev survived. Lora Karkuzashvili, the human shield shot in the chest by rescuers, did not. Alina Kudzayeva, the wife of Aslan Kudzayev, who jumped from the window of the literature classroom, was freed with their nineteen-month-old daughter and other breast-feeding mothers; the remains of her mother, Tina Dudiyeva, who shielded Dzera, the bell ringer, were found in the gym. Albert Sidakov, who opted not to jump with Aslan, was killed, as were both sons of Ruslan Betrozov, the man who stood to translate the terrorists' instructions. Fatima Tskayeva, who sent out her infant but stayed behind with her two other children, died with her daughter Kristina. Makhar, Fatima's three-year-old son, was saved. Karen Mdinaradze, who survived execution, was questioned by a detective at the hospital, who thought that he might be a terrorist masquerading as a fleeing hostage; he was eventually treated properly. His ruined left eye has been replaced with an artificial one. Even up close it looks real. Kazbek Misikov and his family recovered from most of their injuries, although Kazbek's arms remain damaged and he is classified an invalid. On January 22, 2006, his wife, Irina Dzutseva, gave birth to a third son, Elbrus, who is named, like his father, for a mountain that soars above the others on the Caucasus ridge.

The New Yorker

FINALIST—PROFILE
WRITING

In a masterful marriage of writer's voice and lively subject, Ian Parker's wonderful romp captures the idiosyncratic appeal of the irascible Christopher Hitchens, one of the nation's most controversial political analysts. As he emerges in the hands of Parker, Hitchens is a man who walks (and stumbles) along the thin line separating brilliant from just plain nuts.

Ian Parker

He Knew
He Was Right

Until not long ago, Christopher Hitchens, the British-born journalist, was a valued asset of the American left: an intellectual willing to show his teeth in the cause of righteousness. Today, Hitchens supports the Iraq war and is contemptuous of those who do not—a turn that has confused and dismayed former comrades, and brought him into odd new alliances. But his life looks much the same. He still writes a great deal, at a speed at which most people read. And, at fifty-seven, he still has an arrest-photograph air about him—looking like someone who, with as much dignity as possible, has smoothed his hair and straightened his collar after knocking the helmet off a policeman.

At a dinner a few months ago in San Francisco with his wife, Carol Blue, and some others, Hitchens wore a pale jacket and a shirt unbuttoned far enough to hint at what one ex-girlfriend has called "the pelt of the Hitch." Hitchens, who only recently gave up the habit of smoking in the shower, was working through a pack of cigarettes while talking to two women at his end of the table: a Stanford doctor in her early thirties whom he'd met once before, and a friend of hers, a librarian. He spoke with wit and eloquence about Iranian politics and what he saw as the unnecessary handsomeness of Gavin Newsom, the mayor of San Francisco.

Hitchens writes on politics and literature; and in both lines of work he tends to start from textual readings of a subtle and suspicious-minded kind. When he is not writing, he talks in the same measured, ironic voice as his prose, with the same fluency and intellectual momentum, as if he were troubled by the thought that he might never find another audience. Hitchens likes to have his say: he takes his arguments to the cable-news channels, to West Point cadets, to panel discussions in window-less hotel conference rooms. He stays at public meetings until the crowd—dehydrated and faint—has no more questions to ask, and then he gives out his e-mail address. He is a fine, funny orator, with the mock-heroic manner of an English barrister sure of his ground ("by all means," "if you will"), using deri-sion, a grand diction, and looping subclauses that always carry him back to the main path. He also has the politician's trick of eliding the last word of one sentence to the first of the next, while stressing both words, in order to close a gate against inter-ruption. In more private settings, the rhetoric is the same—except that there are filthy jokes drawn out to twenty minutes, and longer quotations from his vast stock of remembered English poetry. He seems to be perpetually auditioning for the role of best man. Ian McEwan, the novelist, recently said of Hitchens, "It all seems instantly, neurologically available: everything he's ever read, everyone he's ever met, every story he's ever heard."

In the noisy front room of the North Beach restaurant where the friends had met, Hitchens made a toast: "To the Constitu-tion of the United States, and confusion to its enemies!" The conversation was amiable and boozy; Hitchens might be said to care more for history than for individual humans, but he was in an easy mood, after a drive, in beautiful early-evening light, from Menlo Park. (He and Blue, a writer working on a novel, live with their thirteen-year-old daughter in Washington, D.C., but spend the summer in California, where her parents live.) During the ride, he had discussed with the Pakistani-born taxi driver the virtues and vices of Benazir Bhutto, while surreptitiously using a bottle of Evian to put out a small but smoky fire that he had set in the ashtray.

And then the young doctor to his left made a passing but sympathetic remark about Howard Dean, the 2004 presidential candidate; she said that he had been unfairly treated in the American media. Hitchens, in the clear, helpful voice one might use to give street directions, replied that Dean was "a raving nut bag," and then corrected himself: "A raving, sinister, demagogic nut bag." He said, "I and a few other people saw he should be destroyed." He noted that, in 2003, Dean had given a speech at an abortion-rights gathering in which he recalled being visited, as a doctor, by a twelve-year-old who was pregnant by her father. ("You explain that to the American people who think that parental notification is a good idea," Dean said, to applause.) Dean appeared not to have referred the alleged rape to the police; he also, when pressed, admitted that the story was not, in all details, true. For Hitchens, this established that Dean was a "pathological liar."

"All politicians lie!" the women said.

"He's a *doctor*," Hitchens said.

"But he's a politician."

"No, excuse me," Hitchens said. His tone tightened, and his mouth shrunk like a sea anemone poked with a stick; the Hitchens face can, at moments of dialectical urgency, or when seen in an unkindly lit Fox News studio, transform from roguish to sour. (Hitchens's friend Martin Amis, the novelist, has chided Hitchens for "doing that horrible thing with your lips.") "Fine," Hitchens said. "Now that I know that, to you, medical ethics are nothing, you've told me all I need to know. I'm not trying to persuade you. Do you think I care whether you agree with me? No. I'm telling you why I disagree with you. That I do care about. I have no further interest in any of your opinions. There's nothing you wouldn't make an excuse for."

"That's wrong!" they said.

"You know what? I wouldn't want you on my side." His tone was businesslike; the laughing protests died away. "I was telling you why I knew that Howard Dean was a psycho and a fraud, and you say, 'That's O.K.' Fuck off. No, I mean it: fuck off. I'm telling you what I think are standards, and you say, 'What standards? It's fine, he's against the Iraq war.' Fuck. Off. You're MoveOn.org. 'Any liar will do. He's anti-Bush, he can say what he likes.' Fuck off. You think a doctor can lie in front of an audience of women on a major question, and claim to have suppressed evidence on rape and incest and then to have said he made it up?"

"But Christopher . . ."

"Save it, sweetie, for someone who cares. It will not be me. You love it, you suck on it. I now know what your standards are, and now you know what mine are, and that's all the difference—I hope—in the world."

•   •   •

What happened to Christopher Hitchens? How did a longtime columnist at *The Nation* become a contributor to the *Weekly Standard*, a supporter of President Bush in the 2004 election, and an invited speaker at the conservative activist David Horowitz's forthcoming Restoration Weekend, along with Ann Coulter and Rush Limbaugh? Or, to put it another way, how did Hitchens come to be a "Lying, Self-Serving, Fat-Assed, Chain-Smoking, Drunken, Opportunistic, Cynical Contrarian"? (This is from the title of an essay posted on CounterPunch, a Web site coedited by Hitchens's former friend and *Nation* colleague Alexander Cockburn.) The question, in polite and impolite forms, goes around and around at Washington dinner parties: did Hitchens maintain high principles while the left drifted from him, or did he lose himself in vanity and ambition? The matter has even inspired a forthcoming anthology of attack and coun-terattack, *Terror, Iraq, and the Left: Christopher Hitchens and His Critics.*

On the time line of the Hitchens apostasy, which runs from revolutionary socialism to a kind of neoconservatism, many dates are marked in boldface—his reassessment cannot be fixed to any one of them—and those familiar with Hitchens's work know that he has always thrived on sectarian battles, and always looked for "encouraging signs of polarization," a phrase he has borrowed from his late friend Israel Shahak, the Israeli activist. But, when I talked with Hitchens, our conversation began with events in 2001. By that year, Hitchens said, he had begun to doubt if his future lay in political journalism. He had, by then, published fifteen books, including one on the Elgin Mar-bles dispute, and slim, scornful volumes—modern versions of eighteenth-century pamphleteering—making the case against Henry Kissinger (mass murderer), Bill Clinton (sex criminal), and Mother Teresa (friend of despots). He had written, but not yet published, an admiring book about George Orwell's political clear-sightedness. He had a column for *Vanity Fair*, in addition to his "Minority Report" for *The Nation*, which he had started in 1982, a year after moving to America. But, he said, political commentary had become "increasingly boring. There were times when I was due to write a *Nation* column and I hadn't got a hugely strong motive to write." He no longer described himself as a socialist, an identity he had formed as a teenager, in the late sixties. He had taken to describing capitalism as the world's only true revolutionary force.

"I was becoming post-ideological," Hitchens recalled. "And I thought, Well, what I want is to write more about literature— not to dump politics, because one can never do that, but I re-member thinking that I would make a real effort to understand Proust." Wherever possible, Hitchens writes as an oppositionist, which means that his panegyrics are delivered in the form of a bodyguard's shove against intruders; and in this case he had decided on a book-length riposte to Alain de Botton's *How Proust Can Change Your Life*. Hitchens finished writing his notes on September 9, then flew to Walla Walla, Washington, to give a lecture on Henry Kissinger that coincided with the filing of a federal lawsuit against Kissinger and other Nixon Administration officials by the family of René Schneider, the Chilean military commander murdered in 1970. "I made a speech to an excited audience, and I ended, 'I like to think that tomorrow, 11th September 2001, will be remembered for a long time as a landmark day in the struggle for human rights'—a prescient remark, I hope you'll agree. I got a standing ovation, signed a few books, kissed a few people, went to bed reasonably contented. You know the rest."

He went on, "The advice I've been giving to people all my life—that you may not be interested in the dialectic but the dialectic is interested in you; you can't give up politics, it won't give you up—was the advice I should have been taking myself. Because I did know that something like 9/11 would happen." So "it was goodbye to Marcel for a bit." (He has not written his Proust book, but, in 2004, he published a limpid essay on a new translation of *Swann's Way*: "Through his eyes we see what actuates the dandy and the lover and the grandee and the hypocrite and the poseur, with a transparency unexampled except in Shakespeare or George Eliot," he wrote in *The Atlantic*. "And this ability, so piercing and at times even alarming, is not mere knowingness. It is not, in other words, the product of cynicism. To be so perceptive and yet so innocent—that, in a phrase, is the achievement of Proust.")

In a 2003 interview, Hitchens said that the events of September 11 filled him with "exhilaration." His friend Ian Buruma, the writer, told me, "I don't quite see Christopher as a 'man of action,' but he's always looking for the defining moment—as it were, our Spanish Civil War, where you put yourself on the right side, and stand up to the enemy." Hitchens foresaw "a war to the finish between everything I love and everything I hate." Here was a question on which history would judge him; and just as Orwell had (in his view) got it right on the greatest questions of the twentieth century—communism, fascism, and imperialism—so Hitchens wanted a future student to see that he had been similarly scrupulous and clear-eyed. (He once wrote, "I have tried for much of my life to write as if I was composing my sentences to be read posthumously.") His enemies stood in two groups: first, the forces of jihad, and, second, those in "the Chomsky-Zinn-Finkelstein quarter," as he has put it— the cohort of American leftists who seemed too ready to see the attacks as a rebuke to American imperialism. In his first *Nation* column after September 11, Hitchens wrote that "the bombers of Manhattan represent fascism with an Islamic face. . . . What they abominate about 'the West,' to put it in a phrase, is not what Western liberals don't like and can't defend about their own system, but what they do like about it and must defend: its emancipated women, its scientific inquiry, its separation of religion from the state. Loose talk about chickens coming home to roost is the moral equivalent of the hateful garbage emitted by Falwell and Robertson."

Many American liberals would have had no argument with that; nor, indeed, with the way Hitchens jabbed at the filmmaker Oliver Stone at a public meeting in Manhattan a few weeks later, when Stone referred to the "revolt of September 11." ("Excuse me. Revolt? It was state-supported mass murder, using civilians as missiles.") Nevertheless, Hitchens felt compelled formally to remove himself from the American left. In a clarifying sign-off a few months later, he dropped his *Nation* column. This may have been largely a change of address rather than a change of mind—moving out of the house long after the divorce—but he detected some inner shift in 2001. "For the first time in my life, I felt myself in the position of the policeman," he told me. In part, this was a response to America's panic. "Nobody knew what was going on. This giant government, and huge empire. Bush was missing. Panic, impotence, shame. I've never known any feeling like it. What does one do when the forces of law and order have let you down, and the whole of society is stunned and terrified? Simply, I must find out what it's like to think like a cop. It shifts the angle, in a way that can't really be wrenched back again." During the I.R.A. bombing campaigns on the British mainland, which began in the 1970s, this had not happened. Then he had "kept two sets of books: I didn't like bombs, I didn't like the partition of Ireland." Now he felt as if he had "taken an oath to uphold and defend the Constitution against all enemies, foreign and domestic."

We were in Hitchens's home in Washington. His top-floor apartment, with a wide view that includes No. 1 Observatory Circle, the vice-presidential residence, is large and handsome: sparely furnished, with a grand piano, books piled on the floor, a few embassy invitations on the mantelpiece, and prints and paintings propped against the walls rather than hung from them; these include an oil painting of Hitchens and Blue (a dark-haired, darkly dressed woman—a young Susan Sontag) with coffee, whiskey, and cigarettes on a table in front of them.

Hitchens has the life that a spirited thirteen-year-old boy might hope adulthood to be: he wakes up when he likes, works from home, is married to someone who wears leopard-skin high heels, and conducts heady, serious discussions late into the night. I arrived just after midday, and Hitchens said that it was "time for a cocktail"; he poured a large drink. His hair flopped over his forehead, and he pushed it back using just the tips of his fingers, his hand as unbending as a mannequin's.

He noted that he never likes going to bed. "I'm not that keen on the idea of being unconscious," he said. "There's plenty of time to be unconscious coming up." In Washington, his socializing usually takes place at home. "I can have some sort of control over who comes, what gets talked about, what gets eaten, what gets drunk, and the ashtrays," he said. "Call me set in my ways." (Hitchens's predominant tone is quietly self-parodying. Even his farewells are ironic: "It's been real," "Stay cool.") Guests at the Hitchens salon include people he first knew in London, who call him "Hitch," including Salman Rushdie, Ian McEwan, and his great friend Martin Amis ("The only blond I have ever really loved," Hitchens once said); long-standing American friends like Christopher Buckley and Graydon Carter; an international network of dissidents and intellectuals; and, these days, such figures as David Frum, the former Bush-administration speechwriter, and Grover Norquist, the conservative activist. In September, he hosted Barham Salih, a Kurd who is a deputy prime minister of the new Iraqi government. Many guests can report seeing Hitchens step out of the room after dinner, write a column, then step back almost before the topic of conversation has changed.

Rushdie recalled an evening last year. "I met Paul Wolfowitz," he said, laughing. "And I discovered, to my immense surprise, that he's a very nice man." Wolfowitz, the neoconservative who served as the deputy secretary of defense between 2001 and 2005, and who now runs the World Bank, was a primary architect of the invasion of Iraq; he has become the emblem of Hitchens's new political alignments. Wolfowitz respected Hitchens's record as a writer on human rights. He called Hitchens in the fall of 2002, at the prompting of Kevin Kellems, then his special adviser, and now an adviser at the World Bank. "It felt like Cold War espionage," Kellems recalled. "Contacting someone on the other side you think might want to defect." Hitchens accepted an invitation to lunch at the Pentagon. "I snuck him in," Kellems said. "We didn't put his name on the schedule."

As Wolfowitz knew, Hitchens was a longtime observer of the cruelty of Saddam Hussein, and had spoken publicly for his removal since 1998. He supported the cause of Kurdish independence, and had been to Halabja and seen the injuries caused there by Iraqi chemical weapons; and he was friendly with dissident Iraqis in exile, including Ahmed Chalabi, of the Iraqi National Congress, which aggressively promoted the notion, now widely discounted, that Saddam was poised to become a nuclear power. After September 11, and the subsequent defeat of the Taliban in Afghanistan (upon which Hitchens addressed the British antiwar left in the pages of the *Guardian*, "Ha ha ha, and yah, boo"), he had thrown himself into the debate over Iraq, making speeches and writing for *Slate*. Brandishing the 1930s slogan "Fascism Means War," he argued that Saddam was something more than another tyrant; though he did not have nuclear weapons, he aspired to have them; his regime was on the verge of implosion, and better that it should implode under supervision, with the West providing "armed assistance to the imminent Iraqi and Kurdish revolutions." Hitchens told me, "The number of us who would have criticized Bush if he hadn't removed Saddam—that's certainly the smallest minority I've ever been a member of."

I mentioned the Pentagon meeting. "Wolfowitz was not asking my advice about Iraq—don't run away with that idea," Hitchens said. "He just felt that those who worked for the ousting of Saddam should get on closer terms with each other." According to Kellems, who attended the meeting, "Hitchens said, 'I was trying to signal you'"—through his writing—"and Wolfowitz said, 'I wondered.'" Hitchens disputes that memory; he does remember asking Wolfowitz for reassurances that, in the event of an invasion, the United States would protect the Kurds from the Turks. They talked about Rwanda and Bosnia, about the history of genocide and the cost of inaction. Kellems, who has since become a friend of Hitchens, described "two giant minds unleashed in the room. They were finishing each other's sentences." According to Hitchens, Wolfowitz is a "bleeding heart," and he went on, "There are not many Republicans, or

Democrats, who lie awake at night worrying about what's happening to the Palestinians, but he does." (Hitchens has been a decades-long agitator for the Palestinian cause; he coedited a book on the subject with Edward Said, the late Palestinian American scholar.) "And Wolfowitz wants America's human-rights ethic to be straight and consistent as far as possible. And if there's an anomaly he's aware of it."

On April 9, 2003, the day the statue of Saddam was pulled down in central Baghdad, Hitchens wrote, "So it turns out that all the slogans of the anti-war movement were right after all. And their demands were just. 'No War on Iraq,' they said—and there wasn't a war on Iraq. Indeed, there was barely a 'war' at all. 'No Blood for Oil,' they cried, and the oil wealth of Iraq has been duly rescued from attempted sabotage with scarcely a drop spilled." That July, Hitchens and a few other reporters flew to Baghdad with Wolfowitz. "It's quite extraordinary to see the way that American soldiers are welcomed," Hitchens told Fox News upon his return. "To see the work that they're doing and not just rolling up these filthy networks of Baathists and jihadists, but building schools, opening soccer stadiums, helping people connect to the Internet, there is a really intelligent political program as well as a very tough military one."

·   ·   ·

Three years later, Hitchens is still on Fox News talking about the Iraq war. He has not flinched from his position that the invasion was necessary, nor declined any serious invitation to defend that position publicly, even as the violence in Iraq has increased, and American opinion has turned against the intervention and the president who launched it. In this role, he has presented himself with an immense test of his rhetorical mettle—one can say that without doubting his sincerity. He often seems to have had more at stake, and certainly more oratorical energy, than anyone in the government. (In recent months, the trope of "Islamic fascism," which Hitchens has used frequently since his 2001 *Nation* column, has reached the top layers of government—in August, Bush said that the country was "at war with Islamic fascists"—and he has had to deny the charge that he is writing administration speeches.) Today, he always carries with him—like the Kurdistan flag in his lapel—debating points, worn smooth with use: Abdul Rahman Yasin, who was involved in the 1993 World Trade Center attack, took refuge in Iraq; Dr. Mahdi Obeidi, Saddam's senior physicist, had centrifuge parts buried in his garden; as late as 2003, Iraqi agents were trying to buy missiles from North Korea; Tariq Aziz, Iraq's deputy prime minister, offered Hitchens's friend Rolf Ekéus, the weapons inspector, a two-and-a-half-million-dollar bribe. "I feel like Bellow's Herzog, writing crazed letters," Hitchens said, smiling. "The occupation has not turned out as one would have liked, but the main problem is to have underestimated the utter evil of the other side. I wouldn't have believed they could keep up a campaign of murdering people at random."

Hitchens asks his opponents this: "We should have left Iraq the way it was? However I replay the tape, however much I wish things had been done differently, I can't get to that position." He acknowledged that his support of the war had caused him some intellectual discomfort. "The most difficult thing is having to defend an administration that isn't defensible," he said. On television and radio, he explained, "you're invited on to defend the administration's view on something and then someone's invited on to attack it. You don't want to begin by putting distance, because then it looks like you're covering your ass. You take the confrontation as it actually is. I'm not going to spend a few silky minutes saying, 'You know, I don't really like Bush and his attitude toward stem cells.' No. Wait. The motion before the house is this: Is this a just and necessary war or is it not?"

He went on, "I'm open to the prosecution of the administration, even the impeachment of some members, for the way they've fucked up the war, and also the way they exploit it domestically. But do not run away with the idea that my telling you this would satisfy any of my critics. They want me to immolate myself, and I sincerely believe that for some of them, when they see bad news from Iraq, the reaction is simply 'This will make Hitchens look bad!' I've been trying to avoid solipsism, but I've come to believe there are such people."

Hitchens finds support on the right, of course. Peter Wehner, a deputy assistant to the president and the director of the office of strategic initiatives in the White House, invited Hitchens to give a lecture to White House staff a few years ago, and now jokingly addresses him as "Comrade" in e-mails. Wehner admired Hitchens as a "fantastic political pugilist" even when they were on opposing camps in the eighties. Now, he said, "On the issues of greatest gravity and historical importance—the war against global jihadism and the liberation of Iraq—I am thrilled to be on the same side of the divide as Christopher."

To Hitchens's left, there is enmity and derision. This summer, a mock-obituary, published online, described him dying in the manner of Major Kong: riding a warhead out of a B-52 in a future American war in Iran. Another Internet tribute posted a photograph of him with the caption "Hitchens: 'I'll Kick Saddam's Fucking Teeth In.'" A parodic MySpace page introduces Hitchens this way: "I am a man of the Enlightenment. Words fall from my tongue and you eat them up like a starving kitten on the street." Last year, Hitchens was jeered when he debated the British M.P. George Galloway in New York. When he appeared on *Real Time with Bill Maher*, this summer, Hitchens said "Fuck you" to a hostile crowd and, to Maher, "Your audience, which will clap at apparently anything, is frivolous."

Many friends and former friends have been watching Hitchens's progress with disappointment, or something sharper. Colin Robinson, his former publisher at Verso Books, said, "I hope it might be possible to save some bits of Christopher. It's a terrible loss to the left—it's so rare to have someone in the mainstream media who could go out and give the other side a dusting." Using a similar tone of regret, Eric Alterman, a *Nation* columnist and an estranged friend, called him a "performance artist." Alexander Cockburn told me, "Between the two of them, my sympathies were with Mother Teresa. If you were sitting in rags in a gutter in Calcutta, who would be more likely to give you a bowl of soup?"

Hitchens claims to be unperturbed by his critics. "You'd think I'd driven over their pets and abducted their daughters," Hitchens said. "I'd like to know what brings that on." A pause. "So I could do it more." He added, "People say, 'What's it like to be a minority of one, or a kick-bag for the Internet?' It washes off me like jizz off a porn star's face." (Thomas Cushman, one of the editors of *Terror, Iraq, and the Left*, said of Hitchens, "What's great about him is that being despised is actually the source of his creativity.")

I asked Rushdie if recent events had taken their toll on his friend. "Christopher is well equipped to take care of himself," Rushdie said, "but I do think that some of the people that he is now aligned with are not really people that he's like. That must be very strange for him, and I worry about that."

When I told Hitchens that some friends were worried, he smiled through his annoyance. "I suppose it's nice to be worried about," he said. "It's almost like being cared about."

•　　　•　　　•

In 1982, Hitchens wrote an essay for *The Nation* about Evelyn Waugh's *Brideshead Revisited*, and the point he was most keen to make was that although the First World War predates the action of the novel, it remains at the center of the story. Hitchens quoted at length from Waugh's honeyed description of the excursion made by Charles Ryder and Sebastian Flyte to the

Venice of the early twenties, a passage of champagne cocktails and gondolas that ends with Sebastian saying, "It's rather sad to think that whatever happens you and I can never possibly get involved in a war."

I asked Carol Blue about this passage. She said that her husband, who was brought up in an English military family in the years following the Second World War, had an aspect of "those men who were never really in battle and wished they had been. There's a whole tough-guy, 'I am violent, I will use violence, I will take some of these people out before I die' talk, which is really key to his psychology—I don't care what he says. I think it is partly to do with his upbringing."

The Second World War was "the entire subject of conversation" when Hitchens was growing up, he told me: "I didn't know films were made out of anything else." Every Boxing Day, the family would toast the sinking of the German battleship *Scharnhorst*. Portsmouth, where he first lived, was still scarred by Nazi air raids. Hitchens's father was a career Navy man from a working-class family who reached the rank of commander and, with that, a foothold in the middle classes. He met Hitchens's mother, who was from a lower-middle-class Liverpudlian family, during the war. Commander Hitchens was not a garrulous man, but some observations of his have stuck with his son. "They are all kind of solid," Christopher said. "He said, 'Beware of girls with thin lips'; 'Don't let them see you with just your socks on'; and 'Socialism is founded on sand.'" His father also said that "the war was the only time when he knew what he was doing."

His parents, Hitchens said, were of a class that "resent but sort of envy the rich, but they're terrified of organized labor, and feel themselves to be the neglected, solid citizens." Commander Hitchens was a conservative of the peeved, country-going-to-the-dogs sort—a Thatcherite in waiting. Christopher abandoned that conservatism as a boy but perhaps absorbed the lesson that politics is a form of anger. "My father was not a misanthrope, exactly, but he thought that the whole thing"—that is, life—"was a bit overrated."

Commander Hitchens had a Baptist-Calvinist background. His wife was Jewish, but she never told her husband or her children. Hitchens learned this about her—and himself—only long after her death. ("On hearing the tidings, I was pleased to find that I was pleased," he has written.) She was more social than Hitchens's father, and more alert to signs of class slippage: it was vital to decant milk into a jug before taking it to the table, and to avoid saying "toilet." Hitchens once overheard an argument between his parents about the cost of boarding school, in which his mother said, "If there is going to be a ruling class in this country, then Christopher is going to be in it."

She succeeded: Christopher was privately and expensively educated (as was Peter, his younger brother, who is a prominent right-wing newspaper columnist in London) and now has the accent—and white suit—of the English upper-middle classes. Ian Buruma detects in Hitchens some mix of regard and disdain "for the 'real' officer class. Waugh had a bit of that, and Wodehouse—Christopher's favorite writers—which is one reason that Wodehouse ended up in America. America allows you to play the role of the fruity upper-class Englishman, whereas in England you'd feel vulnerable to exposure."

Hitchens went to boarding school, in Devon, at the age of eight. He was happy, but, he said, "a radicalizing thing for me was the realization that my parents had scrimped and saved to allow me to be the first member of my family to go to boarding school. I was surrounded by these sons of Lancastrian businessmen who thought it was their perfect right to be there. That had a huge effect: these fuckers don't even know when they're well off." He also saw through Mrs. Watts, his instructor on religious matters, "who told us how good it was of God to make all our vegetation green, because it was the color that was most restful for our eyes, and how horrible it would be if it was orange. I remember sitting there, in my shorts and sandals, and thinking, That *can't* be right." Hitchens has just finished a book informed by a lifetime of steely anticlerical thought, *God Is Not Great*, to be published next year, which begins with Mrs. Watts, and goes on to say of his religious friends, "I would be quite content to go to their children's bar-mitzvahs, to marvel at their Gothic cathedrals, to 'respect' their belief that the Koran was dictated, though exclusively in Arabic, to an illiterate prophet, or to interest myself in Wicca and Hindu and Jain consolations. And as it happens, I will continue to do this without insisting on the polite reciprocal condition—*which is that they in turn leave me alone. But this, religion is ultimately incapable of doing. As I write these words, and as you read them, people of faith are in their different ways planning your and my destruction. . . . Religion poisons everything.*"

Hitchens used to have, at times, a "pronounced" stutter. "One way of curing it was to force yourself to speak in public," he said. In his first school debate, Hitchens spoke against new immigration restrictions (nobody else would), and found that the techniques required—such as charm and the sudden, cutthroat withdrawal of charm—came naturally to him. His later success in America derived in part from his bruising rhetorical talents. In Britain, such qualities are on show every week at Prime Minister's Question Time, but in America Hitchens was a novel act. "It's extraordinary," he said. "I've been invited onto shows like *Crossfire* and told, 'Can't you hold it down a bit?'"

In 1964, he ran as the Labour Party candidate in his school's mock election (again, nobody else would). He lost, but the Labour Party won in the country. The new government quickly proved itself to be, in Hitchens's words, "completely corrupt and cynical"—backing President Johnson on Vietnam, for example.

His response was to join the party, thus starting a career of antagonistic idealism. "That's why you join a party, to take up the struggles within it," Hitchens explained. "And that's what pushed me to the left-the humiliation of the Labour Government." By the time he came to study politics, philosophy, and economics at Balliol College, Oxford—semi-official motto: "Effortless Superiority"—he had been invited to join a Trotskyist group, the International Socialists. (He was spotted while skillfully heckling a Maoist at a public meeting.)

As a student, Hitchens was good-looking and charismatic. He does not remember ever having met Bill Clinton, his Oxford contemporary, but he told me that there was a student who, at different times, was his girlfriend and Clinton's, before she began a lifetime of lesbianism. He met Martin Amis and, for a time, shared a house with James Fenton, the poet, whom Hitchens had brought into the International Socialists. "He wore a beret—I have to tell you that he did," Fenton said of Hitchens, remembering that his comrade "was not known as a stalwart of the 'getting up at six to go to the factory gates' brigade. I used to think that the revolution would break out and I'd be waking Christopher, trying to get him out of bed."

In fact, something a little like this happened. During the Paris uprisings of 1968, transport links with France were cut before many, including Hitchens, could cross the channel. "It's a big regret of my life," he said. Indeed, when he talks about the Cromwellian and American revolutions, his tone is almost nostalgic. (His personal identification with Thomas Paine is nearly as strong as it is with Orwell; his short study of Paine, published this year, was dedicated to Jalal Talabani—"first elected president of the Republic of Iraq; sworn foe of fascism and theocracy"—rather as "The Rights of Man" was dedicated to George Washington and the Marquis de Lafayette.) But wherever Hitchens might have been a witness to an explosion of popular feeling, either no explosion occurred or it was delayed until he left. He recalled flying out of Iraq the day before the deaths, in July 2003, of Saddam's sons, Uday and Qusay. When Hitchens described the celebrations that followed, you could hear a man struggling to transform a secondhand report into a firsthand one by force of will power alone: "I could have been there—it kills me! That night, the entire cityscape was a blaze of weapons being fired in celebration. It was like ten million Fourth of Julys . . ."

At times, Hitchens can look like a brain trying to pass as a muscle. He reads the world intellectually, but emphasizes his physical responses to it. Talking of jihadism, he said, "You know, recognizing an enemy—it's not just your mental cortex. Everything in you *physically* conditions you to realize that this means no good, like when you see a copperhead coming toward you. It's basic: it lives or I do." When Hitchens's prose hits an off note, it often includes the visceral or the pseudo-visceral, whether in a paean to oral sex for *Vanity Fair* ("I was at once bewitched and slain by the warm, moist cave of her mouth") or in commentaries on current affairs: "reeking fumes of the suicide-murderers," "the stench of common bribery, pungently reeking of crude oil." On these occasions, the bookish Hitchens is elbowed aside by an alternate self: a man as twitchingly alert as Trotsky at the head of the Red Army.

Such performances of masculinity don't appear exclusively on the page. Not long ago, in Baltimore, I saw Hitchens challenge a man—perhaps homeless and a little unglued mentally— who had started walking in step with his wife and a woman friend of hers while Hitchens walked some way ahead. Hitchens dropped back to form a flank between the women and the man, then said, "This is the polite version. Go away." The man ambled off. Hitchens pressed home the victory. "Go away *faster*," he said.

"Wouldn't it have been easier to cross the road?" Blue asked, innocently.

·   ·   ·

While still at Oxford, Hitchens wrote his first article for the *New Statesman*, a left-leaning weekly. Upon graduating and moving to London, he became an occasional contributor, while taking a number of jobs in mainstream journalism, and selling the *Socialist Worker* on street corners. The *New Statesman* was enjoying a golden moment: its staff and writers included Amis, Fenton, McEwan, and Julian Barnes, the novelist. The Friday-lunch gatherings of *Statesman* hot shots and other writers, in which they out-joked each other on matters of sex, literature, and nuclear disarmament, now have the status of literary legend. (The *Statesman* staff played a game in which the task was to think of the phrase least likely to be uttered by each member. For Hitchens: "I don't care how rich you are, I'm not coming to your party." For Amis: "You look a bit depressed, why don't you sit down and tell me all about it?")

Romantically, Hitchens described himself as playing second fiddle to an unstoppable Amis: "I'd basically be holding his coat and refilling his glass, and trying to learn from the Master." In fact, Hitchens's own appeal was considerable; among the girlfriends he had before his first marriage was Anna Wintour, who is now the editor of *Vogue*. Hitchens told me, "When I was younger—this will surprise you, seeing now the bloated carcass of the Hitch—I used to get quite a bit of attention from men. And, um. It was sometimes quite difficult, especially when you hadn't seen it coming. I was considered reasonably pretty, I suppose, between seventeen and twenty-five. I remember noticing when it stopped, and thinking, Oh dear. What? None of these guys want to sleep with me anymore?" Asked about his own activities, he said, "Nobody who's been to public school can pretend to know nothing of the subject. And even at university there was an epicene interlude. But it wasn't what I wanted at all." (In 1999, Alexander Cockburn wrote, "Many's the time male friends have had to push Hitchens's mouth, fragrant with martinis, away" during hellos and goodbyes; Hitchens said that he had no memory of "making a bid for the clean-limbed and cupid-lipped Alexander Cockburn.")

In December 1973, Hitchens, then twenty-four, published a lead article about Greek politics in the *New Statesman*. Datelined Athens, it was a serious, rather dry analysis of political developments following the ousting of the dictator George Papadopoulos. It avoided the kind of foreign-crisis writing he abhors. (His parody: "As I stand here pissed and weeping in this burning hell, the body of a child lies like a broken doll in the street.") Almost the only local color was a glimpse of civil and religious icons on the wall of an Athens police station.

Although the article does not hint at it, there was an awful reason for Hitchens seeing the police-station wall. He told me the story: Not long after Hitchens graduated from Oxford, his mother left his father, and moved in with another man. "He was a charmer, which my father was not. He was witty, burbling, could do music, poetry, but couldn't make a living. He was a flake, and not always so delicious. He had this dark, depressive side." In the fall of 1973, a friend called Hitchens one morning in his London apartment to say she'd just read a newspaper article about the death of a Mrs. Hitchens in Athens. Hitchens flew alone to Greece, to learn that, in a suicide pact, his mother had taken an overdose of sleeping pills in a bedroom of the Georges V Hotel, while, in the bathroom, her companion had done the same, and also cut himself severely. "It was a terrible Polanski scene," Hitchens said.

At the hotel, he said, "I went out of the bathroom to the window and had my first view of the Acropolis. It was a perfect view." He learned that his mother had tried his number in London many times in the previous days, but he had missed the calls. "Before the days of answering machines," he said. "If I'd picked up, it could have been enough to stop her, because I usually could make her laugh. That was a bitter reflection."

Athens was in political turmoil—"this mad, Costa-Gavras world." Hitchens, whose skills and taste in journalism draw him to penetrating quick studies, sized the city up. "You can learn a lot in a short time when there are tanks in the street," he said. He wrote the article when he got home. "Everyone said, 'Christopher, how could you?' I said, 'How could I not?' It was therapeutic to write. No—consoling. Useful." He added that, in the fifteen years before his father's death, Hitchens never again discussed with him the death of his mother.

When Turkey invaded Cyprus the following summer, Hitchens realized that he had neglected an important part of the story. Cyprus became a specialty, and, later, the subject of his first book, which described the island as having been betrayed by outside powers; an accusing finger was pointed at Henry Kissinger. Hitchens became a figure in radical Cypriot circles, where he met his first wife, Eleni Meleagrou, whom he used to introduce as "the terrorist." James Fenton sees Cyprus as decisive in Hitchens's political development, not only because he had the experience of becoming a "mini-celebrity" but because of his disappointment in the British failure to protect Cyprus during the invasion: in other words, the dishonorable failure of an imperial power to make a military intervention. Hitchens, unlike Fenton and most others on the British left, supported Margaret Thatcher's gunboat response to the Argentine occupation of the Falkland Islands, in 1982.

By then, Hitchens and Meleagrou had married and moved to America. Hitchens pounded away at Reagan and capital punishment as *The Nation*'s Washington columnist, and reported for other magazines from the Middle East, Central America, and Eastern Europe. The couple split up in 1989, not long after

Hitchens met Carol Blue in Los Angeles. (Meleagrou and their two children, now aged twenty-two and seventeen, live in London.) That winter, Hitchens and Blue flew to Eastern Europe, to be witness to the revolutionary events of the time. It may need to be said: These were events that Hitchens welcomed. In 2001, Peter Hitchens—who has Christopher's voice exactly, but is a churchgoer who is unpersuaded by Darwin—wrote an article in *The Spectator* ("O Brother, Where Art Thou?") that recalled "a Reagan-era discussion about the relative merits and faults of the Western and Soviet systems, during which Christopher said that he didn't care if the Red Army watered its horses in Hendon," a London suburb. On the occasion being described, as Christopher later tartly explained to readers of *Vanity Fair* (in an article entitled "O Brother, Why Art Thou?"), he had been telling a joke. The brothers did not speak for four years. Hitchens said to me, "I've spent far more time talking to *you* than to him in the last twenty-five years." Peter Hitchens said, "If we weren't related, I don't think we'd have much to do with each other," but he showed a kind of regard for what he sees as the consistency of his brother's position: "He's a Trotskyist, really, not in terms of being a Bolshevik revolutionary but in that he is an idealist and he is impressed by military command." (Peter, too, was once in the International Socialists.)

In a similar dispute, Martin Amis, in *Koba the Dread*, a nonfiction book on Stalin, cast Hitchens as, essentially, an apologist for Soviet communism. Hitchens was irritated. He had always been "solid" on the subject of the Soviet bloc, he said; he was as much a friend of the opposition there as he was of the opposition in South Africa or in El Salvador. "Everything I've *thought* is on the record," Hitchens went on. If he had been a Stalinist, "It would show, even if I was trying to conceal it." Hitchens wrote two barbed responses: one in *The Atlantic*, and the other in the *Guardian*, which was headlined "DON'T. BE. SILLY." He told me, "Martin does not know the fucking difference between

Bukharin and Bakunin." (His friendship with Amis survived this discord.)

In 1989, the Ayatollah Khomeini issued a fatwa against Salman Rushdie, on the ground that his novel *The Satanic Verses* defamed Islam. "There's a sense in which all this—Christopher's move—is partly my fault," Rushdie said. "The fatwa made Christopher feel that radical Islam was not only trying to kill his friend; it was a huge new threat to the kind of world he wanted to live in. And I have the sense he felt there was a liberal failure to get the point of what was happening." The fatwa split the left. As Ian Buruma put it, "The instinct was, whenever there was any conflict between Third World opinion and the Western metropole, you'd always favor the Third World. Yet here was a case where people were forced to take the opposite view." For Hitchens, that task was simplified by his contempt for religion.

Hitchens helped arrange a meeting between Rushdie and President Clinton, in 1993. But he had by then taken a position on the president, derived from policy difference and suspicion of Clinton's character (but also, possibly, from awareness of the gap in political potency between two Oxford contemporaries, one of them being the leader of the free world). Hitchens despised him, and charged him with drug running, rape, and other crimes. He also became one of the loudest critics of Clinton's bombing of the Al-Shifa pharmaceutical factory in Sudan at the time of the Monica Lewinsky scandal: Clinton had "killed wogs," he wrote, to save his skin. While Hitchens's literary and historical writing has allowed for nuanced appraisals, even forgiveness, of morally complex figures—in a 2005 book on Jefferson, for example, Hitchens finds his way past the fact of his slaveowning—the political present elicits prosecutorial zeal.

In 1992, Hitchens had begun a column for *Vanity Fair*; he was happy to discover that he could vastly increase his income and readership without having to watch his tongue—"a breakthrough for me," he said. The same year, he went to Bosnia at his own expense; as he called for armed intervention there, three years before the Clinton administration acted, he found himself endorsing the same petitions as many neoconservatives, including Wolfowitz. In 1999, in an incident that some see as the true start of Hitchens's political pilgrimage, he told House Judiciary Committee staff members who approached him that Sidney Blumenthal, a longtime friend who was then working in the Clinton White House, had gossiped to Hitchens about Monica Lewinsky being a "stalker." Blumenthal had testified that he had not made such remarks, so the claim put him at risk of a perjury charge and, potentially, strengthened the impeachment case against Clinton. It was possible to read Hitchens's action as a gesture of principle, but many who knew him saw it as a vicious act: he was "Snitchens." "He'd got to that moment in life when he was asking himself if he could Make A Difference," Alexander Cockburn told me, in an e-mail. "So he sloshed his way across his own personal Rubicon and tried to topple Clinton via a betrayal of his close friendship."

When I asked Hitchens about this period, he defended his actions but also said, "It seems to me to have happened to somebody else. That's true of a lot of the fights I took part in before 2001. Seemed like a good idea at the time, but it shrinks incredibly compared to Baghdad and Beirut and New York."

"That episode did hurt him," Buruma said. "He lost friends, he felt isolated in Washington, and I think there was a time when he really felt bruised."

Hitchens's splenetic Clinton book, *No One Left to Lie To*, was published months after the Blumenthal incident. Verso, his publishing house, threw a party at Pravda, a SoHo restaurant. Colin Robinson recalled, "It's the only launch party I've ever been to where people booed the author."

·   ·   ·

The Hitchens-Blue partnership has a grad-school air. It's hard to see who pays the bills or fills the fridge. Blue can get stuck at the post-shower, towel-wearing stage of the day. (Her husband, with affection: "Darling, you would be so much more convincing if you were dressed.") Hitchens is not hapless—he meets his many deadlines and catches his many planes—but it's unsettling to watch him rinse a single spoon for four minutes, or hear the pandemonium over the supply of cigarette lighters. (He has cut back from smoking three packs a day.) He is a late-learning and scary driver. He does not wear a watch, although he looks at his bare left wrist when trying to calculate the time.

One morning during the family's summer escape to Northern California—they stay in a guesthouse built next to the home of Blue's parents—Blue and I drove to a local supermarket. She walked the store's aisles with an air of rock-star puzzlement that may have been heightened for my benefit; she did not want to seem like a housewife. We left with sandwiches, a cherry pie, and two bottles of whiskey, and nothing that looked beyond the horizon of the next meal.

When we returned with our provisions, at about one o'clock, Hitchens, who had been working, was sitting at his desk with a drink. On the walls around him were some color printouts of kittens and puppies sitting in lines. He pointed to a manuscript of *God Is Not Great*, a book that he thinks may have more heft and permanence than anything he has written before, in a career of rapid responses and public lashings. "I have been, in my head, writing it for many years," he said. "Religion is going to be the big subject until the end of my life. And I wanted to make an intervention."

Hitchens had already finished the morning period of mail and e-mail he refers to as "telegrams and anger" (a quotation from *Howards End*). He had given his attention that day to the wiretap lawsuit brought by the American Civil Liberties Union against the National Security Agency; in January, he accepted the A.C.L.U.'s invitation to become a named plaintiff, denting his reputation as an administration cheerleader. He had also begun a review of Ann Coulter's *Godless: The Church of Liberalism*, for an obscure new British journal. He was not doing it for free, but the gesture was still generous; Hitchens, who is unusually lacking in professional competitiveness, makes himself available to younger writers and editors. He also teaches: he is presently a visiting professor at the New School, and he is supervising the Ph.D. thesis, on Orwell, of Thomas Veale, a U.S. Army major, who calls Hitchens the "only 1930s liberal in existence."

Hitchens had started writing an hour or so before, planning on leniency: "I was thinking of hammering her for the first half and being a bit gentle the second." (He shares Coulter's disregard for Joseph Wilson, the diplomat.) But he had written a thousand words, and he was not through hammering. "I thought I'd do a thousand words by lunchtime—my usual ambition if I'm doing a short piece," he said. But he now saw that he could get it all done before eating. "If I can't fuck up Ann Coulter before lunch then I shouldn't be in this business," he said. Not long afterward, he came into the kitchen and handed me the finished review.

We had lunch outside. Hitchens ignored the sandwiches and put his fork in the cherry pie, moving outward from the center. He had a postproduction glow. "Writing is mainly recreational," he said. "I'm not happy when I'm not doing it." He can entertain himself in other ways—he strained to remember them—such as "playing with the cats and the daughter. But if I take even a day away from it I'm very uneasy."

In the past few years, Hitchens has published, in addition to his books on Orwell, Jefferson, and Paine, a book of oppositionist advice entitled *Letters to a Young Contrarian*; a collection of his writings on the Iraq war; and a giant miscellany, *Love, Poverty, and War*. He wrote *God Is Not Great* in four months. He has contributed to dozens of publications (including *Golf*

Digest—he plays the game). He almost never uses the backspace, delete, or cut-and-paste keys. He writes a single draft, at a speed that caused his *New Statesman* colleagues to place bets on how long it would take him to finish an editorial. What emerges is ready for publication, except for one weakness: he's not an expert punctuator, which reinforces the notion that he is in the business of transcribing a lecture he can hear himself giving.

Earlier, in answer to a question I hadn't asked, Blue had said to me, "Once in a while, it seems like he might be drunk. Aside from that, even though he's obviously an alcoholic, he functions at a really high level and he doesn't act like a drunk, so the only reason it's a bad thing is it's taking out his liver, presumably. It would be a drag for Henry Kissinger to live to a hundred and Christopher to keel over next year."

Hitchens, too, brought up the subject of alcohol before I did. "You're going to want to talk about this," he said, not wrongly, pointing at his glass. (A writer likes a cooperative subject, but it can be dispiriting to make a portrait in the shadow of a gigantic self-portrait.) He was not a "piss artist," he explained, "someone who can't get going without a load of beer, who's a drunk—over-confident and flushed. I can't bear that." He went on, "I know what I'm doing with it. And I can time it. It's a self-medicating thing." I took his point. Hitchens does drink a very great deal (and said of Mel Gibson's blood-alcohol level at the time of his recent Malibu arrest—0.12 percent—"that's as sober as you'd ever want to be"). But he drinks like a Hemingway character: continually and to no apparent effect.

That evening at the guesthouse, Peter Berkowitz, the Straussian intellectual and Hoover Institution fellow, and Tod Lindberg, the editor of *Policy Review*, dropped by with family members. The back-yard pool was suddenly full of children. Someone had brought champagne, and Hitchens poured it with exaggerated disapproval. (A few years ago, he claimed that the four most overrated things in life were champagne, lobsters, anal sex, and picnics.) Hitchens went into the house and put on Bob Dylan's "Tryin' to Get to Heaven"; he stood in the doorway and sung quietly along. He quoted Philip Larkin on Dylan: a "cawing, derisive voice." He repeated Larkin's words a few times, approvingly. His daughter got out of the pool, and said, pleasantly, "Can we close the door, so nobody else has to hear this?"

She went back to her friends. "Look," Hitchens said happily. "They're waiting for us to die."

·　　·　　·

Hitchens and Blue flew back to Washington just after Labor Day. At the end of that week, in the Madison Hotel, Hitchens sat alongside William Kristol, the editor of the *Weekly Standard*, and others on a panel convened by the David Horowitz Freedom Center. Robert (Buzz) Patterson, the conservative author and former White House military aide, introduced the event, and was applauded for a passing dig at the A.C.L.U. Hitchens, whose remarks were delivered into a warm hum of approval—"too easy," he later said—described it as "a pleasure as well as a duty" to kill Islamic terrorists.

Horowitz has often spoken and written about his upbringing by communist parents. Hitchens's response, years ago, was to ask, "Who cares about his pathetic family?" But Horowitz holds no grudge, and the two men talked in the bar afterward, with the rapport that comes from being the only people in a ten-block radius who could say they had read all three volumes of Isaac Deutscher's biography of Leon Trotsky. Horowitz asked about Hitchens's commitment to his Restoration Weekend, in Palm Beach, later in the year. Hitchens would never apologize for sharing a platform with anyone, but he wanted to know what Horowitz saw in Ann Coulter: Hadn't he noticed the creationism in *Godless*?

"I didn't read the Darwin pages," Horowitz admitted. "It's nearly a third of the sodding book!" Hitchens said.

Hitchens had to be up early in the morning, and he began to make his way out. But a friend came up and asked him a favor, leading Hitchens to a group of young Horowitz fans. Hitchens sat down. "You really want to hear the most obscene joke in the world?" he asked them.

An hour later, Hitchens was at home, making a bacon sandwich. I asked him if he had felt a pang of envy when, in 2005, Michael Ignatieff, the author, public intellectual, and longtime U.K. resident, moved back to his native Canada to become a Liberal M.P.—and a likely future leader of his party. Hitchens replied, "Not a pang. A twinge." When he was a young man, Hitchens was once sounded out about standing for Parliament as a Labour candidate. He took another path, but in subsequent years has occasionally thought of the politician he did not become. And today in Britain the political furniture is arranged as he would like it to be; that is, with opposition to the Iraq intervention heard as loudly on the Conservative side as on the left, and—as he sees it—a Labour government acting in accordance with the radical, humanist, internationalist idealism of his youth. Earlier this year, Hitchens had a private meeting with Prime Minister Tony Blair.

I asked Hitchens if he would accept a life peerage and a seat in the House of Lords. "It would be fantastically tempting," he said, showing more eagerness than I'd expected. "I think I couldn't do it, even though it's no longer hereditary. I couldn't quite see the term 'Lord Hitchens.'" He added, with some feeling, "That I never had the right to walk into Parliament is something I'll always be sorry about."

This year is the twenty-fifth anniversary of Hitchens's move to America. Barring a last-minute complication, this will also be the year he becomes a citizen. He began the process not long after the attacks of 2001. The paperwork is done, he has passed the exam, and he was interviewed in June.

I asked if he'd vote in November. "I'll run in November," he said. "Don't rule it out." He added, "I can't be president. So we can relax about that."

National Geographic

Alexander's soaring profile of Reinhold Messner is both a nail-biting adventure yarn and the heart-wrenching story of a lion in winter. Full of fresh reporting and insight, Alexander guides Messner back to childhood conflicts with his Nazi father and to the tragic climb in which his brother died, to render a definitive portrait of the man who epitomized modern mountaineering.

Caroline Alexander

Murdering the Impossible

Beyond the walls of the sixteenth-century fortress, in northern Italy, the Dolomite range rose burnished and glowing in the late afternoon light. Within the walls, Reinhold Messner, the world's greatest mountaineer, was building a mountain. At his energetic direction, a backhoe lumbered back and forth in the dusty courtyard, heaving slabs of rock and depositing them in an artful pyramid that by the end of the exercise had formed a small mountain.

"This is Kailas, Holy Mountain," Reinhold said, while the backhoe filled the air with golden dust. He was relishing the scene—the whole scene; not just the satisfaction of seeing Tibet's most holy mountain assembled in miniature under his supervision but also, I suspected, the roar and rumble and chaos and dust and magnificent improbability of the undertaking. The Kailas installation is only one of the many features, fanciful and inspired, that will fill his latest Messner Mountain Museum, this one dedicated to the theme of "When Men Meet Mountains."

Reinhold Messner is well into what he has designated Stage Six of his already remarkable life, without, it would seem, a backward glance for Stage One, when he was one of the world's elite rock climbers, or Stage Two, when he was unquestionably the world's greatest high-altitude mountaineer. Today, at sixty-two, he is instantly recognizable from the multitude of publicity photographs taken over the past three decades—lean and fit and sporting an even longer mane of waving hair, now threaded with silver, than he did when younger. His features tend to alternate between two characteristic expressions: The first, a look of fierce intensity, which, combined with beetling eyebrows and flowing beard and hair, give him an air of Zeus-like authority. It was with this expression that he moved his mountain. The second is his trademark smile—a reflexive baring of his very white, even teeth behind his beard—which gleams on friend and foe without distinction, like the smile of a crocodile. It was the crocodile smile he was baring now, as he envisioned the climactic moment of opening night of the Messner museum: A violent explosion, simulating a volcanic eruption, was to rend the night from inside the castle walls. "There should be a lot of flames and smoke," he said, again with relish. "It should be at night so that the whole of Bolzano can see." He paused to savor the image of a fireworks blast that would appear to viewers as a catastrophic blowup. "Then my friends will say, 'It is a pity,' and my enemies will say, 'Good, finally, at last!'"

To non-climbers it may be difficult to convey the extent and grandeur of Reinhold Messner's accomplishments. Here's a start: His ascent, with longtime partner Peter Habeler, of Hidden Peak, the 26,470-foot (8,068-meter) summit of Gasherbrum I, one of the giants of the Himalaya, without any of the paraphernalia of traditional high-altitude climbing—porters, camps, fixed ropes, and oxygen—was hailed as forging a whole new standard of mountaineering. But that was back in 1975, before Messner and Habeler went on to climb Mount Everest without oxygen, a feat that took climbing to the absolute limit. That, in turn, was in May of 1978—three months before Messner climbed Nanga Parbat, the ninth-highest mountain on Earth, solo—a feat heralded as one of the most daring in mountaineering. That, however, was two years before he climbed Mount Everest without oxygen, equipped with a single small rucksack—and alone.

"It is very difficult to calibrate high-altitude climbing," said Hans Kammerlander, who has climbed seven of the world's fourteen 8,000-meter mountains with Messner. "There is no referee, there is no stopwatch. There were others—Buhl, Herzog, Forrer," he said, running through the names of climbing greats. "They did more solo climbs. But Reinhold had so many new ideas—he found new ways, new techniques. He imagined them, and then he put them into practice. So, all around, yes, he does deserve the title of being the greatest mountaineer in history."

Messner's contribution to his profession is not only a list of astonishing feats but also the unrelenting philosophy that lay behind them. "I'm only interested in our experiences and not in the mountains—I'm not a naturalist," he told me. "I'm interested in what's going on in the human beings. . . . William Blake wrote a line, when men and mountains are meeting, big things are happening," he said, paraphrasing a favorite quote from the eighteenth-century poet, and the philosophy behind his new museum. "If you have a highway on Everest, you don't meet the mountain. If everything is prepared, and you have a guide who is responsible for your security, you cannot meet the mountain. Meeting mountains is only possible if you . . . are out there in self-sufficiency."

In an essay he wrote when he was only twenty-seven, he decried the siege tactics that allowed even an unskilled climber to conquer a mountain bolt by bolt, issuing a plea for both the mountain that cannot "defend itself" and for the climber, who was being cheated of the opportunity to test the limits of his courage and skill. Titled "The Murder of the Impossible," the essay, now considered a minor classic, argued that the wielders of expansion bolts and pegs "thoughtlessly killed the ideal of the impossible." Messner's characteristic minimalism—he is adamant he has never put an expansion bolt in a face of rock, as he has never used bottled oxygen—was, therefore, a brash demonstration that the principles he preached could be put to spectacular practice. His landmark high-altitude alpine-style climbs liberated both the individual climber, by showing alternatives to the hugely encumbered and expensive classic expeditions, as well as the mountains themselves. The irony, of course, was that it was Messner who, by these very achievements, murdered and laid in the dust all traditional notions of what constituted "the impossible."

•   •   •

Thanks to the stream of books that followed his accomplishments, and aided by dark good looks that rendered him promotable, Messner achieved a celebrity status that extended far beyond subscribers to *Alpinist* and *Gripped*. In Europe, where frequent appearances on television have kept him in the public eye, as well as afforded him a platform for his often blunt outspokenness, he continues to evoke strong emotions, received by admirers with the adoration bestowed on rock stars and by his detractors with resentful charges of self-promotion. He receives both with equal enthusiasm. "Obstacles energize me," he told me. Tirelessly confrontational, he is famous for outbursts of towering rage. "I became so angry that I yelled in a way that the windows there, they were shivering," he told me with satisfaction of an encounter with a local foe. One could say fairly that Reinhold was conditioned from youth by the same phenomena that energize him now: obstacles, risk, and high-adrenaline rage.

Reinhold was born and raised in St. Peter's, a hamlet in the Villnöss Valley, in northern Italy's South Tirol, a place he still claims is the "most beautiful in the world." Wholly defining the valley, the ethereal Geislerspitzen range rises above the Alpine meadows in bare rock pinnacles and spires, as improbably strik-ing as the turrets of a distant fairy-tale kingdom. "The climbing had to do with two facts," Reinhold said. "My father was a climber—but not an extreme climber—so as children we heard about this. Secondly, we had no football place in the valley . . . we had no swimming pool—I'm still not able to swim. And the only possibility to do something to express ourselves was to go on the rocks. So we learned very early." Reinhold was five years old when, led by his father, he made his first summit, toiling some 3,000 feet up a peak in the Geislerspitzen; by thirteen he had overtaken his father and claimed the sport as his own.

South Tirol has a vexed political history, its identity split be-tween Italy and Austria. Even today its valleys and towns carry both Italian and German names, and most families grow up as the Messners did, Italian citizens but German speaking. Rein-hold's mother, Maria Troi, was better educated than was then traditional for girls. "My mother would give us the freedom to do what we had the feeling we had to do," said Reinhold, an at-titude unusual in the postwar valleys, where lives were directed by practical concerns of earning a living. Repeatedly, people described her as a calming, gentle force in a turbulent family.

Josef Messner, the family patriarch, was a complicated man, and his relationship with his sons was similarly complicated. As a boy, Josef had been a promising student, but family circum-stances prevented him from pursuing higher education. He be-came a schoolteacher and married Reinhold's mother, moving into an upper-story flat in a house her father owned. The grow-ing family lived here, with a new child born almost every other year. Their flat, where the only heat came from the kitchen's woodstove, was above a butcher's shop, and the animals were slaughtered in a shed beside the house. As did many in the val-ley, the Messners grew vegetables and kept chickens, which the young boys were taught to kill. While the single sister, Waltraud, helped the mother in the house, the boys were kept busy with outside chores, hauling wood and stones, each looking after his immediately younger brother. Reinhold's special charge was his brother Günther. In the Messner home, as in the rugged Tirol in general, self-sufficiency was a paramount virtue.

"The father was a devoted Catholic, but in a Calvinist manner," said Reinhold's former wife, Ursula Demeter, known as Uschi, who retains warm ties with Reinhold and his family. The mother was "quiet, peaceful, fatalistic—God had given her her station. But for the father, if you did not make money, if you did not succeed, God had turned from you."

Josef Messner's life was further complicated by his chosen politics. "In thirty-eight, Hitler and Mussolini came together, and they decided the South Tiroleans should take a chance to vote," Reinhold told me. "Who is voting for Italy stays in South Tirol; who is voting for Germany, for the Führer, he can leave, and he will get the same amount of land somewhere in Germany. And my father was one of the organizers of this option . . . in which 86 percent"—he leaned forward for emphasis—"of the South Tiroleans decided they would leave their homeland to go somewhere with the Nazis." He shook his head. "It is incredible." The war put an end to all such options. By voluntarily becoming a Nazi, Josef Messner had staked his hopes on a German future; ironically, his wartime duties had been to serve as an Italian translator. At war's end, he returned to his wife's house in the narrow valley and set about raising his family of nine children with their resolutely Teutonic names—Werner, Reinhold, Siegfried, Waltraud—on what was now a headmaster's salary.

"My father was an anxious man," said Hansjörg Messner, one of Reinhold's younger brothers and a psychotherapist in London. "His anxiety made him a strict man. He wasn't austere; he was a strict man in given moments, so his strictness, or even perhaps his violence at times, was, I think, a basic reaction to his anxiety." The flashes of violence took several forms—beatings, not uncommon in rural communities of that era, and verbal tirades. "My father had the ability not just to shout but to humiliate," Hansjörg said. When the young Reinhold failed his school exams because he had spent less time studying than climbing, the father had poured out the full violence of his scorn. "I remember Reinhold sitting at the wooden table in the kitchen, holding his head and just crying and crying," Hansjörg said. At that moment the father could triumph; he had been proven irrefutably right. Repeatedly, vehemently, over the years he had been telling his stubborn son that a life doing what he loved and did best—the life of a climber—was impossible.

"In the family, I told you, there was only one chance," Reinhold said. "To break, to be broken, or to be stronger than the father."

By the time Reinhold was thirteen and Günther eleven, they had formed an unassailable climbing partnership. Both precociously strong and talented, they differed sharply in personality. Reinhold was outspoken and confrontational—public—according to his brother Hubert Messner, head of neonatology at Bolzano Hospital, while Günther was closed. "Reinhold started to do everything he wanted to do. Günther was not this way," Hubert said. "Günther, because he was influenced more by our father— I think that was the big problem. He was not able to say, 'I don't like it, I don't do it.'"

From the rock towers of the Geislerspitzen, Reinhold and Günther moved to other Dolomite peaks, then farther afield onto classic ascents in the western Alps. In the Dolomites, they mastered freestyle rock climbing, but in the Alps they gained experience of mixed terrain and pure ice. When Reinhold was twenty and Günther eighteen, they were in a position to measure themselves against some of Europe's most experienced climbers. "When I had a chance to climb with them, or go on a similar route where a famous climber had been, I was only looking and learning," Reinhold said, and paused. "For a few years.

And I would say at twenty, twenty-three, we understood, there is nobody who can climb what we are climbing." Although the brothers continued as partners, Reinhold had taken to lightning-strike solo dashes to the summits, traveling as light and fast as possible. "Reinhold's solo climbs in the Dolomites from sixty-five to after seventy count as some of his best," said Hans Kammerlander, who is also from the South Tirol. "These experiences are often overlooked."

As the brothers racked up noteworthy ascents, what Hansjörg calls Reinhold's "triumphalism" became more pronounced. "There was a place in the village where we could go to watch a television," Hansjörg said. "And we used to watch the fights of Cassius Clay. You know how Clay used to call his fights: 'I'll take him in round six!' That's when Reinhold began to call his climbs. 'The Eiger face in ten hours!'"

Much of Reinhold's style—traveling light and quickly—depended on his uncanny speed. Just how fast he was capable of moving he would dramatically demonstrate many times over in the years ahead. One example: On an expedition in 1979 to Ama Dablam in Nepal, Reinhold and his friend Oswald Oelz conducted a spectacular rescue of Peter Hillary, son of the great explorer, and two companions. "Reinhold covered that ground that the New Zealand climbers had taken two and a half days to climb in six hours," recalled Nena Holguín, a witness of the rescue. "I mean he moved like lightning speed across the snow. You know how deer are light-footed—he would seem to spring; it seemed like he hardly touched the ground."

After Reinhold and Günther completed their schooling, they began to train, grudgingly, for professions, Reinhold as an architect at Padua University, Günther to work in a bank. But their real education continued on the rocks. "I trained also to stay days out—days and days without food," Reinhold said. "We went into the mountains without taking food with us; we had to carry it, so we learned to do without it." They also learned, as

Reinhold put it, "to handle situations," or retain emotional equilibrium.

"I think that courage is only the other half of fear," he said. "Only because I am afraid, I need courage. . . . If I am well-prepared, and if I'm living a long time in my visions, in my fantasy, with my challenge—before doing it, I'm living with it, I'm dreaming about it, planning, preparing, training. So when I start to climb—especially when I'm on a big wall, whatever difficulties—I am so concentrated that there is nothing else existing; there's only a few meters of wall where I am hanging and climbing; and in this concentration, everything seems quite logical. There is no danger anymore. The danger is gone. . . . But the concentration is absolute."

By 1969, Reinhold had obtained his diploma in architecture and was teaching mathematics in a local secondary school, an occupation he had chosen solely because it allowed him to climb. Then out of the blue came an invitation to join an expedition in the Himalaya. It was to be a turning point. "I see Reinhold in two phases, you see," Hansjörg said, carefully. "I see him before Nanga Parbat and after Nanga Parbat."

.   .   .

Climbers speak of a mountain's "line," the route up its face that unlocks the summit. The line of Reinhold Messner's life, that line that unlocks and defines him, is unquestionably the 1970 Austro-German Sigi Löw Memorial Expedition to Nanga Parbat. Rising in northern Pakistan, Nanga Parbat is one of the world's eight-thousanders, the fourteen mountains standing above 8,000 meters; at 8,126 meters (26,660 feet), it is the ninth highest in the world. Following numerous unsuccessful, sometimes fatal, expeditions, it was first summited in 1953, by the great Austrian climber Hermann Buhl. "In my time, the most technically demanding climb was not any one peak," Reinhold said. "It was surely, at least in the German-speaking world, the south face of Nanga Parbat, the Rupal Face." Even the victorious Buhl, who had climbed by way of the north side, had been intimidated by this massive wall, which he described with palpable amazement as "the highest mountain wall in the world, plunging 17,000 feet in one sheer sweep from the summit into the unplumbed depths."

The leader of the expedition, Karl Maria Herrligkoffer, was not himself a climber, but his half brother, Willie Merkl, had died on Nanga Parbat (his name is commemorated in several of the mountain's landmarks), and Herrligkoffer had come to cultivate the same attitude toward the mountain, vengeful and obsessive, as had Ahab to his whale. By June 26, 1970, the expedition's higher camps and ropes had been laboriously fixed, in very heavy weather, up to 7,350 meters, or as far as the Merkl Couloir, a long vertical gully that was to be the pathway to the summit. One summit attempt had been aborted, and the expedition was weeks behind schedule. Now, Reinhold, his brother Günther, and Gerhard Baur were huddled in the single three-man tent that constituted Camp Five, at the foot of the couloir, poised for a final attempt. At Reinhold's suggestion an elaborate plan of assault had been laid. On receiving the next day's weather report, Base Camp was to signal Camp Five, firing a red rocket for bad weather, a blue for good. If the rocket was red, Reinhold would make a solo strike for the summit, racing the weather. If the outlook was good, there would be a team ascent. At eight o'clock that night, a red rocket flared.

Reinhold set out in the darkness of the early morning with no equipment save crampons and an ice ax, while Günther and Baur began to prepare ropes in the first 200 meters of the couloir, to aid in the difficult descent. Until this moment, Günther had been with Reinhold every step of the way; now his elder brother—always the leader, always used to getting his way—was en route to the summit and glory, while he was left to handle a tangled mess of frozen rope. Something inside him snapped, and, dropping the ropes, he sprinted after his brother. In four hours, Günther covered the 600 vertical meters of the Merkl Icefield. "Surely," as Reinhold said, "he went at the limit of his possibilities to catch me."

The effects of Günther's extraordinary effort were soon apparent. It was five P.M., late in the day, when the brothers shook hands on the summit. An hour later—a long time—they began the descent. Sluggish and weakening, Günther balked at the difficult route they had ascended. Alarmed, Reinhold sought a quicker route to lower ground, leading them west of the summit ridge where, when darkness caught them, they huddled down for what would be the worst night of their lives. Under the hard, bright stars, the night temperature plunged to forty degrees below zero. Without a tent, their only protection was a single space blanket. They had no food or water and had been many hours in the "death zone." Günther began to hallucinate, pawing at an imaginary blanket on the ground.

"This is very hard," Reinhold said. "In high altitude, there's no oxygen going to the blood, so you cannot burn, you are not heated. Instinctively, you stay awake as long as possible. You force yourself that the blood is circulating, by thinking. We told also each other, 'Move the toes, don't sleep.' . . . If somebody would sleep, really sleep, it could easily be that he's passing by."

By daylight, Günther's condition was critical. Then suddenly, it seemed help was on the way. Below their bivouac site, the figures of Peter Scholtz and Felix Kuen appeared coming from Camp Four, laboring up the ascent route on the trail the brothers had broken. The ensuing miscommunication between the two parties, shouting back and forth across a divide roughly the length of a football field, remains one of the most unsatisfactorily explained incidents of the Nanga Parbat saga. Scholtz and Kuen are now dead, so their accounts cannot be subjected to inquiry. Somehow, the ascending climbers failed to comprehend the crisis. For their part, the Messners could not know that the red rocket for bad weather had been fired in error. The weather was in fact flawless, and Scholtz and Kuen had come for the summit, not for rescue.

Bypassed by his companions, Reinhold made a bold decision: He and Günther would descend by way of the Diamir Face, on the opposite side of the mountain. "When you are standing there up high, close to the summit, if you look to the Diamir side, it's a very gentle snow slope," said Steve House, an American who climbed the Rupal Face, alpine-style, with his partner, Vince Anderson, in 2005. "It's almost flat; it's easy walking," he said of the initial descent. "The Rupal Face is huge, dangerous, scary. It makes perfect sense to me why he followed that decision."

The Diamir Face had been climbed only twice before, and Reinhold was navigating by instinct. In the night, he and Günther made a second, brief bivouac at 6,500 meters. The next day, under a punishing sun, they continued downward. By 6,000 meters, Günther had partly recovered, and it seemed they were on the homestretch. "From the second bivouac, we could see more or less that there is a way down," Reinhold said. "You can overview a mountain from down, from a certain distance, but never from upwards, and this is very important to understand. . . . Coming from up, you see only abyss; you cannot know, 'I go right, or left'—and this was also the reason why I was forced on the way down to go ahead."

By his own assessment, Reinhold was at times over an hour ahead, out of sight and hearing. Although speed has always been his trademark, he may not yet have understood that his speed was preternatural. Stumbling down Nanga Parbat, moving with his instincts, he left Günther behind. Seeing a stream, he drank for the first time in four days. Relieved, he waited for Günther to catch up. But Günther was never to appear.

Hansjörg, using the clinical language of his profession, refers to Reinhold suffering a "breakdown" when he realized his brother had disappeared. Reinhold's own account is that he went insane. For a day and a night, he searched the place where Günther should have been, scrabbling with his hands in the debris of a recent avalanche. "I had always a strange feeling that he's around," Reinhold said. "I heard these steps behind me. When I looked back, he was not there. I heard sometimes his voice . . . and I went there, but he was not there. So my intelligence, my clear thinking, told me, 'Your brother's dead.' But my feelings told me, 'Your brother's here.'" At length, his most primitive survival instincts kicked in, and he staggered onward into the Diamir Valley, hallucinating. Two days later, villagers carried him out of the valley. Passed along into the hands of the police, he was on his way to the hospital when the police jeep caught up with the departing expedition, who had given the brothers up for dead. According to one member, Reinhold's first words were to sob: "Where is Günther?"

"I think Reinhold was terribly burdened by not being able to bring his brother home," Hansjörg said, "and I think my father out of his anxiety and a lack of reflection reinforced this guilt: 'Where did you leave Günther?'" He'd left his brother behind. The family's view was that Günther may have been stronger than Reinhold. "And it was, 'Why him, and why not Reinhold?'" Hubert said. Family members speculate that one cause of Günther's desperate summit run had been his unhappiness with his conventional job: "Günther wasn't able to break the rules," as Hubert said. "That was his dilemma. All these questions arise . . . and Reinhold—after this event, Reinhold closed himself up in the family."

·   ·   ·

For Reinhold, the Nanga Parbat expedition was life-changing. He had lost his brother and closest friend. He had seven frostbitten toes and three fingertips amputated. And he was yet more famous, for when the dust settled, it was Reinhold Messner who had successfully conquered the most challenging wall in the world and traversed an 8,000-meter mountain. The traversing of Everest by a large American expedition in 1963 was then the only comparable feat.

To complicate matters, Reinhold had fallen in love with Ursula Demeter, the wife of Max von Kienlin, who had accompanied the expedition as a paying guest. Shortly after the expedition's return, she left her husband and moved in with Reinhold. "I was a very simple mountain valley man, a young man," Reinhold said. "She knew the big world. And we built up very quickly a successful team. She was doing the correction of my books; she did the handling with my editors." In this era before corporate sponsorship, to earn a living by climbing required ingenuity and aggressiveness. Without her, he said, "my career, if I can call it a career, would be a different one."

In the fall of 1971, Reinhold took Uschi with him back to Nanga Parbat. "I was hoping that maybe after a dry summer, hopefully a dry summer, the body could come out of an avalanche," Reinhold said. After trekking into the Diamir Valley, they set up a tent, and Reinhold left early the following morning. "The sound of avalanches was thundering around us, night and day," Uschi recalled. Reinhold left the camp at dawn. When darkness descended, she built a bonfire from old lumber, made dinner, and waited. It was long after dark when Reinhold returned. "He was crying and shaking," Uschi said. "He wouldn't eat. He went inside and cried in the night; he cried in his sleep." This was repeated the next day. At week's end, having found no trace of Günther's body, they left.

"After Nanga Parbat the innocent enthusiasm for climbing was gone," Hansjörg said. "Reinhold became"—he paused a long time, searching for the right word—"he became more professional."

·   ·   ·

"I am sure that the real key for understanding climbing is the coming back," Reinhold told me. "It means if you are really in difficult places, in dangerous places, if you are in . . . thin air, and you come back, you feel that you got again a chance for life. You are reborn. And only in this moment, you understand deeply that life is the biggest gift we have." Reinhold was speaking from the perspective of a sage veteran of thirty-one 8,000-meter expeditions. There are few such veterans around. "In my generation, half of the leading climbers died in the mountains," he told me. For the twenty-five-year-old survivor of Nanga Parbat, however, there was no question he had returned to climb again.

"During the period when I was in the clinic," Reinhold told me, "I was still thinking, I will probably, after that time of recovery . . . be able to be self-sufficient—I can go to climb anything. And only during the year seventy-one, I understood this ability will never be like before . . . More than my feet, I lost a little bit of my finger, too, and they cut a little bit of bone, low down, and this bone is pressing on this point"—he held up the ring finger of his left hand. "So with this finger, I could not really work. If you have a little bit of pain on the fingertip, or somewhere, you're not anymore a good climber, because you're always out of concentration. I understood immediately I would never anymore be able to rock climb like in sixty-nine, my best year. And so I became a high-altitude climber." This had never been in the original plan: "High altitude was not interesting to me; it was not steep enough—it was hiking, and I would never want to hike a mountain."

•   •   •

Reinhold's own assessment of his most outstanding accomplishments in the high-altitude mountaineering that would define him include the double traverse with Hans Kammerlander of two 8,000-meter peaks, Gasherbrum II and Gasherbrum I, back to back, in 1984, and the solo climb of that mountain of his life, Nanga Parbat, in 1978. But the climb that captured popular imagination was the first ascent of Everest without oxygen, in the spring of 1978.

The very idea was revolutionary. In the 1970s, expeditions typically carried fifty kilos of oxygen per person, for use above 7,200 meters. According to physiologists, to attempt the biggest 8,000-meter peaks, such as Everest and K2, without oxygen was to risk permanent brain damage.

"It was based on nothing," Reinhold said of this view. He had his own experience to draw on. In 1977, while still acclimatized from an unsuccessful attempt on the formidable south face of Dhaulagiri, in Nepal, he had taken a flight over Everest in a small unpressurized plane. "I tried it, and I had a crisis at 7,800 meters," Reinhold said in his most matter-of-fact voice. The crisis was his feeling "a little bit insecure" and an inability to load new film in his Rolleiflex. "Afterwards, I felt quite well, and I was able to do photographs above the summit without a problem, without a blackout." The plane had eventually climbed to 9,000 meters.

The Austrian Alpine Club agreed to allow Reinhold and his partner, Peter Habeler, to accompany their 1978 Everest expedition as an independent two-man team. Habeler was from the North Tirol, the Austrian side of the Dolomites, and had known Reinhold for fifteen years and been his partner on hundreds of expeditions in Europe as well as several in the Himalaya. Along with Günther and Friedl Mutschlechner, Habeler was one of the few partners who could keep Reinhold's pace. In 1975, they had made history by climbing Gasherbrum I, the smallest team ever to summit an 8,000-meter peak. According to Habeler, the two had toasted each other at the end of the expedition with the words, "to Everest."

The expedition to Everest without oxygen electrified the public. Reinhold summed up: "It was like going to the moon without oxygen—how is it possible? . . . And in Germany, at least five doctors on television appeared before, going and telling

everyone they can prove it is not possible." He smiled his crocodile smile. "And so they prepared the field for a great success."

Physiological tests on Reinhold have revealed a strikingly ef-
ficient metabolism—possibly a result of having trained himself
to go without food—but nothing unusual regarding lung or
cardio capacity. On the other hand, as Reinhold noted with satisfaction, DNA markers from both the maternal and paternal
line were rare. ("Yes, the Messners are special," he said.) In his
prime, Reinhold trained by running hills—"a thousand meters
uphill in 30 minutes," as he told me—but no longer runs much
now. Apparently he does not need to. "He's experienced, his
body's experienced," Hubert said. Six years ago, they made an
8,000-meter expedition together, and after ten days in the
mountains, according to Hubert, Reinhold was "completely
fit—but he's only good in the mountains."

Climbing Everest without oxygen confirmed Reinhold's extraordinary adaptation to high-altitude mountains. For his part,
he was, as he said, "very, very happy. I was thinking—after Everest, I was feeling I could do anything."

.　　　•　　　•

One of the first things he did do was publicly alienate his entire
community. At a local festival held to honor the success of the
Everest expedition, Reinhold was asked why he had not carried
his country's flag. "In my answer, I said I didn't go up for Italy,
not for the South Tirol, not for Austria, not for Germany," Reinhold said, laughing hard enough to sputter. "I went up for myself. I took out my handkerchief: 'This is my flag.' Nobody's
going up for somebody on Everest. You go by yourself, and you
handle it yourself." His tone darkened. "All this nationalistic
chanting makes me angry. I cannot stand it." The necessity of
opposing "fascists" and "Nazis" is one of Reinhold's favorite
themes; he is fond of pointing out that the German Alpine Club

banned Jews from membership in 1921 and posted signs on remote mountain huts to this effect, and he credits acceptance of such actions to what he calls the German "sheeplike" reverence for authority. "My *übermensch* is a self-determined person who would never accept something, some rules from up high up," Reinhold said, paraphrasing Nietzsche. "He would say, This is my way, and I go this way. And this would be the great enemy of the fascist."

Extreme self-determinism, however, has drawbacks. Shortly after he and Peter Habeler made history, they fell out. They later reconciled, but the long estrangement was part of a professional pattern. "The expedition is one thing, but after the expedition is something else," Arved Fuchs said. In 1990, he and Reinhold had made the first crossing of the Antarctic continent on foot; Reinhold had moved on from mountaineering to Stage Three of his life, exploring the horizontal world. "This is something I just don't understand," Fuchs continued. "This man is known all over the world, he sets up new standards as far as mountaineering goes, he is very successful, probably very wealthy, but he has never made his peace with his success and with himself; and this I think is the tragedy of his life."

"Reinhold as an alpinist is the best, the finest in the world," Hans Kammerlander said. "But he has some weaknesses. I speak as a friend," he said in a tone of great gentleness. "He cannot take criticism, and he is quick to attack if he is criticized."

"I expose myself, I accept the natural powers as the rulers of my world," Reinhold said of being on the mountains. "There's no more human rulers if I'm out there. There's no religion which is controlling me and telling me how I have to behave. There's just pure nature, which I have to respect. The nature in myself, and the nature outside." The freedom of the mountains evidently means freedom from other people.

In 2003, Reinhold returned to Everest's Base Camp to celebrate the fiftieth anniversary of its conquest. "I needed more than two hours to go from one end of the base camp to the next," he said, his incredulity mixed with unconcealed contempt for what he calls the "city culture" that has infiltrated the mountains, destroying their solitude with its ubiquitous Internet connection to the world below.

For him, climbing Everest without oxygen opened the way for the ultimate feat of lonely self-determination: Climbing Everest solo, a dream inspired by heartfelt, lofty ideals—and also some down-to-earth competitiveness. What specifically galvanized Reinhold into action was an announcement by Japanese climber Naomi Uemura that he had obtained a permit for a solo attempt in 1980. In his book, Reinhold candidly records his own reaction: "How can it be true? It is my idea!"

The permit Reinhold obtained for a solo climb in 1980, by way of Everest's North Face, was one of the very first issued by the Chinese since their occupation of Tibet in 1950. He and his small party—a mandatory Chinese liaison officer, an interpreter, and one companion who also acted as a medical attendant—would be the only people on the north side of the mountain.

Reinhold's choice of companion was unconventional: Nena Holguín was a thirty-year-old American who had hiked across parts of South America and islands in the Pacific before working in the Himalaya, building schools for the Sir Edmund Hillary Foundation. Today the owner of a hiking-tour company in the Canadian Rockies, she and Reinhold had met in 1979, following his expedition to Ama Dablam. On Everest, their single-tent advanced base camp was set up at 6,500 meters; the two Chinese escorts remained at a lower camp. "It was only Reinhold and I and a wolf, who came to the camp when I was alone and was chewing on the bones outside of my tent," Holguín said. She had the full-time duties of expedition cook and all-purpose helper. They remained between the two camps for a month before Reinhold set out on the morning of August 18.

"Reinhold had already soloed about 2,000 mountains at that point," Holguín said. This included his remarkable solo ascent of Nanga Parbat. "People don't think of it as easier, but it's easier sometimes to do things alone because there is nobody you have to cooperate with, as long as you can get past the aloneness. He likes to do things exactly at his own pace and his own style. It's easy to do things alone if you already know you can do them. He trusted himself."

The historic climb got off to an almost fatally bad start when only 500 meters from camp, in the darkness, Reinhold slipped into a crevasse. Higher up, soft snow made the climbing arduous; being alone, there was no one to share the task of breaking trail. He would spend three nights on the mountain.

"In the Alps, it was easy," Reinhold said. "I started in the morning, and in the evening I was back. Being alone is becoming difficult in the nights. Climbing, there's no problem—you are climbing. Staying alone in dangerous places, icy, cold places for nights and nights and nights is much more difficult." Reaching the summit, Reinhold registered only dull emotions. Mist came in, and light snow blurred his footprints. He turned mechanically for the descent, conscious of deteriorating mental keenness, a dangerous indifference to his condition.

"I finally spotted him on the third day coming down," Holguín said. "I was watching him, and I was watching him, and I was watching him—and I blinked, and he was gone. And he had actually fallen down—he slipped almost the last 400 feet, but he self-arrested with his ice ax." Meeting her, he cried on her shoulder. "When I got him back to the tent, he said, 'Well, I'll never do that again; I'll never solo another mountain like that—I was at my limit.'"

In 1986, Reinhold climbed Lhotse, and in doing so became the first man to attain all fourteen of the 8,000-meter mountains. "When I finished the 8,000-meter peaks, I understood, now I could only repeat myself. What I did is boring now,"

Reinhold said. "But I like to go somewhere where everything is new, and to begin again an activity."

•   •   •

Reinhold's silver Mercedes SLK sped out of Bolzano, toward the mountains and Schloss Juval, his castle home. A striking key chain dangled from the car's ignition: an animal's talon attached to a lump of sand-colored fur. "It is a yeti claw," said Reinhold, and laughed. Stage Four of the Messner itinerary through life was devoted to holy mountains and myths, and included stalking the legendary yeti, the Himalayan equivalent of Bigfoot. This pursuit of what he eventually identified as the Himalayan brown bear earned Reinhold great ill will in German climbing circles. "The yeti story undermined him in elite alpine culture," Hans Kammerlander said. It seems that German climbers, stumbling back from their own mountain epics, had been greeted not with the acclaim, respect, and book offers of which they had dreamed but—thanks to Reinhold Messner—with the facetious question, "So, did you see a yeti?"

Like a brigand's retreat, Juval stands sternly on a 3,000-foot-high cliff, guarded by soaring, snow-streaked mountains and commanding a view over lesser mortals in the Senales Valley. Reinhold's acquisition of the thirteenth-century schloss in 1983 fulfilled several dreams. Here, with his impeccably managed organic fields, animals, and vineyards, he could be a farmer, something he claims he has always wanted to be: Mountain farming is Stage Five. More important, Juval offers "self-sufficiency," one of Reinhold's favorite terms, a place where he could, if necessary, hunker down and live well, keeping the rest of the world at bay.

Juval was also the site, in 1998, of a climbing tragedy. Locked out of his castle one rainy night, the world's greatest mountaineer scaled its walls and, dropping twenty feet into the darkness, landed badly and fractured his heel. The injury was severe enough to curtail him and still gives pain. The realization that he would not be in top form for many years partly prompted his decision to become a member of the European Parliament. The ability—as after Nanga Parbat—not merely to regroup but to turn his back on something he had long loved, seems the secret of his constant reinventions. Asked the issues on which he had made the most difference during this five-year tenure, Reinhold looked amused. "Nobody made any difference," he said. The political career, from 1999 to 2004, did not even warrant a life stage designation. In celebration of its conclusion he fulfilled an old dream, at the age of sixty, of crossing the Gobi desert.

Most of the year, Reinhold and his family live not in the mountains at Juval but in the attractive nearby town of Merano. On returning to his apartment there, Reinhold opened the door to a low, rumbling sound coming from the kitchen. "I don't know what is that noise," he said, perplexed. A baby dragon? Tibetan prayer flags whispering over a chorten? "I think it's a vacuum cleaner," I offered cautiously, and was reminded of an earlier statement he had made regarding his domesticity. "I would not know even where to go if the light is off or the heating does not function," he had said. "I'm really living like in my mother's house. That's very nice." The Messner household seemed well run and happy. "Our system is much stronger than a marriage," Reinhold said of his nineteen-year relationship with Sabine Stehle, describing it as a partnership in which specific spheres of authority are clearly defined. (In the interest of her family's privacy, Stehle preferred not to participate in this story.) "We live in a matriarchy here, so we will see what happens," he remarked on another occasion, concerning some issue with his teenage daughter.

Later, Reinhold's younger brother Hubert dropped by. Hubert had accompanied his famous brother on a number of the horizontal ventures, including the crossing of the Greenland ice cap, and in the summer of 2000, he had joined Reinhold and two friends on an expedition to Nanga Parbat; it was the thirtieth anniversary of Günther's death.

"We decided to climb Nanga Parbat on a completely new route, a very beautiful route," Hubert said. "I didn't go to the summit. I stopped on 7,300 meters. I stopped there because I felt not mentally strong." They ascended by way of the Diamir Face, and Reinhold pointed out the place where he thought Günther had died. "We had perhaps all these strong feelings, and it's difficult," Hubert lowered his voice, his words suddenly stumbling. "In the tent, he was calling me every time Günther."

.   .   .

The 2000 expedition to Nanga Parbat may have been the catalyst for Reinhold's decision, in October 2001, to reopen old wounds from the 1970 expedition. The public occasion he chose was a press conference hosted by the German Alpine Club to celebrate the publication of a biography of Karl Maria Herrligkoffer. Instead of making expected words of polite praise, Reinhold lashed out at the expedition members: "Some of them, older than me, wouldn't have minded if the two Messners hadn't returned."

The backlash against Reinhold was extreme. Two expedition members, Hans Saler and Max von Kienlin, the paying guest, published books making serious claims: Not only had the young Reinhold Messner always intended to make the historic traverse of Nanga Parbat, but he had also left Günther to die on the Rupal Face, while he crossed over and descended the Diamir Face. Several team members reported memories of Reinhold studying maps of both sides of the mountain: "He told me about the traverse in the evening by the fire in base camp," Jürgen Winkler recalled. A distinguished alpine photographer, he was one of the two 1970 expedition members present at the press conference when Reinhold shocked his audience. But would the young Reinhold Messner, ambitious as he was, really have been so reckless as to set out, on his first Himalayan expedition, to traverse an 8,000-meter mountain without a rope or bivvy bag and supplied with only a handful of nuts and raisins and a bottle of water?

"Reinhold Messner is *un homme extraordinaire*," Winkler said, by way of answer. "There is no second person in the world like Reinhold Messner."

Of his search for Günther's body, Reinhold told me, "I was hoping like a dream—maybe late in the year, when the sun has taken away part of the avalanche cone . . . maybe he would appear." In the warm summer of 2005, out of the fog of libel suits and acrimony, this dream materialized. As if relenting of all the damage it had wrought, Nanga Parbat gave up its dead. On July 17, at 4,300 meters in the Diamir Valley, three Pakistani climbers came upon the remains of Günther Messner, identified by a detail on his old, pre-1980 leather climbing boot. The identification was later confirmed by elaborate tests of both mitochondrial and Y-chromosome DNA of that rare Messner genome, conducted by the Institute of Legal Medicine, Innsbruck Medical University.

Back on Nanga Parbat, Reinhold, knowing that a member of the 1970 expedition had been on the Diamir Face making a docudrama about the mountain's tragic history, feared that his brother's body could be exploited or even relocated. After consultation with his family, Reinhold cremated Günther's remains on the mountain.

Speaking to Uschi, I asked if the discovery of Günther's body on the Diamir Face had at last lifted a burden from Reinhold. She stared at me: "No. He always knew Günther was there."

·   ·   ·

"I give all of myself, all of my energy, my time, my money, my enthusiasm," Reinhold said. He was not speaking about 8,000-meter expeditions but about his latest museum. Family and friends had remarked on the pressure he had put himself under, and the new intensity and frequency of his rages. As opening day drew closer, the undertaking seemed to strike him as increasingly epic, and he was reaching for metaphors to compare it to extreme climbing. It involved all the elements he had identified as essential to the "strong experiences" that test one's limits—difficulties, strenuous effort, exposure. But not the risk of death, as I reminded him. "I can do like Hemingway," he replied, glumly.

When complete, the chain of five Messner Mountain Museums will form a neat circuit in the South Tirol; eventually, they will run themselves. "This is a dream of mine, that they should go without me—like how it is in the family," he mused. When total self-sufficiency in all aspects of his life has been attained, he will be free to follow another long-discussed, never actualized dream, and retreat to a cave. "I would prefer somewhere in the Dolomites," he said. "There are so many good places . . . I would stay maybe a month there and write, or think, or enjoy the morning light, climb a mountain. That is a very strong daydream, that I am a free person." He paused. "I am not a free person anymore."

Why not just retire? "Reinhold doesn't really relax," Hansjörg said. "Do you know this saying he has on his website? 'I am what I do.' But I think he may also believe the opposite: 'If I cease to do, I will not be.'"

How far Reinhold has traveled, from Stage One to Stage Six, is demonstrated in a film taken when he was in his late twenties, showing him climbing a sheer rock face in the Geislerspitzen. Like water flowing upward, he ascends the tower; his fingertips scarcely press the surface. His expression is of otherworldly reverence. "There are moments in difficult situations, far away, that there is no more doubt," he told me. "There, the questions are gone. And I think these are the important moments. If the question is gone, I have not to answer. Myself living—I am the answer."

GQ

WINNER—FEATURE WRITING

Andrew Corsello offers a harrowing portrait of a country, Zimbabwe, torn apart by a madman, and of two men—a white farmer and a fiery black priest—who resist the hatred around them. Transformed by their faith, they overcome their own prejudices and achieve a forgiveness that is a model of goodness.

Andrew Corsello

The Other Side of Hate

Jim Steele was mad as hell. His blacks were messing with the farm, with the land, and the land was *always* personal. He'd been born on this farm. Like many Rhodesians, his parents had planted his umbilical cord in the ground so the boy's life and the good earth would nourish each other forever. This land held the blood of his dead brother, his soul mate, thirteen months younger, who at age nineteen had reached into the truck for the shotgun and accidentally tripped its hammers, taking both barrels in the stomach and crying "My God!" as he fell. *The blood of my brother in the ground.* Though Steele called himself a Christian, the earth itself was his real religion; and his good and proper use of it, a form of worship. Any abuse of the earth or the fruit it brought forth was an assault on his person.

The barn boys had been abusing that fruit, killing it with their neglect. A line had to be drawn. You could not show heel to the African. He'd take advantage every time. Everybody knew that. Lord, all that *work:* Two months ago, he'd patched the cavernous tobacco barn until it was airtight. A month ago, he'd begun harvesting the leaves and hanging them in the barn to dry. Now it was a matter of carefully controlling the humidity and temperature in the barn, keeping the iron furnace stoked day and night. And his blacks had gone lazy on him.

Every day at dawn, Steele drove down to the barn to check the leaves. And every day for the past two weeks, he'd walked into a cold barn.

"It's cold in this barn," he said on the first day.

"No, Oom Jim," said the barn boy on duty, using the Afrikaans word for "uncle." "Check the thermometer."

The thermometer read as it should have, 38 degrees Celsius, but Steele knew the boy had been sleeping on the job, letting the fire die—had heard the boss man's truck and stuck the thermometer atop the furnace for a few seconds before hanging it back among the leaves.

Steele looked at his barn boy. The boy looked back.

"Yes, Oom Jim?"

"Stoke the fire," he said, and left.

For two weeks the charade continued, until the morning that it didn't. Steele woke angry. It was still dark when he got into the truck, but he could see his own breath in the glow of the dashboard, and this made him angrier. As he drove the rutted dirt road to the barn, the head of his watch, worn on the inside of his wrist to preserve its life, rattled insistently against the steering wheel, and this, too, fed his anger. By the time he reached the barn he was teetering. He threw the barn door open, stepped forward, exhaled, watched the breath curl from his mouth.

"It's goddamn cold in here."

"No, Oom Jim. Look at the thermometer."

It was then, in 1964, at the age of twenty-seven, that Jim Steele—a man who, per his father's orders, hadn't shed a tear after his brother's death—lost control. Without another word he grabbed a cloth, gripped the handles to the furnace doors, and opened them. The fire had faded to embers, but it was still glowing. Then he turned, braced one of his thick, flat, dirty hands against the boy's chest while thrusting the other around and between his legs, lifted him off the ground, and shoved him face-first at the fire.

"Tell me," he roared. "Does *that* seem hot enough for you?"

The boy threw his palms against the furnace wall to prevent his face from entering. The farmer could hear the flesh burning but didn't pull the boy back until he could smell it. Patches of the boy's palms remained on the furnace wall, curling. The farmer continued to embrace the boy for a moment, one broad arm around the boy's back, the boy arching, squirming, his other forearm jammed against the boy's forehead.

"Is it hot enough?" he yelled again. "Is it?"

Something touched him then. It wasn't so much that he was throwing the boy to the ground as another force, like wind but *solid*, was casting the two of them in opposite directions. In an instant they were on the ground, facing each other. The boy held out his hands in supplication. Then, in a childlike voice, he began to weep. *Oom Jim, Oom Jim, oh, it is so hot, Oom Jim.*

An unreflective man, Jim Steele had only ever known himself by the things he had done. Now he had done this. For a few moments, he lost the feeling of his own body, of his presence in it. He had a queer sense of floating, of being given a glimpse for the first time in his life of what lay beyond the surface of himself. What he saw there was not bad. It was worse: It was nothing.

Before coming to his senses and going for help, Steele sat dumb on the floor of the barn, listening to the boy's mewling, smelling his burnt hands. He could not shake a growing conviction that he was somehow at the mercy of the boy, that the boy had in fact acquired great power over him—a power he would hold forever.

.   .   .

Paul Mufanebadza learned to hate women before he could speak, before he could even know what hate was. He was an ill infant, feverish and limp—poisoned by his own malice, it was later said. The poison *killed* him. Among his people, if a baby dies before it cuts its teeth, elderly women must bury it that very day, before sunset, in a wet place. When Paul stopped breathing, four village elders came, put their ears to the child's mouth to confirm it was dead, then carried it out to a riverbed. They dug a shallow grave in the mud and dropped the baby in. The instant they did, its eyes flashed and a careening blood scream issued from its mouth. When the boy was old enough to ask why people called him the Spooky Child, his mother told him he'd been hexed by women eager to steal his father from his family. So it was that Paul Mufanebadza learned to believe women were witches.

Two of these witches dwelled in his home. Paul Mufanebadza Sr. was a regimental sergeant major and one of the two highest-ranking black men in the Rhodesian army, which fought throughout the 1960s and 1970s to preserve the country's minority white rule. The sergeant major was a man of means, a man who could afford to live polygamously. Paul junior's mother was his first wife, the domestic queen. Paul senior brought the second and third of his five wives—and the children he sired by them—to live in the queen's home in the city of Masvingo.

The sergeant major didn't much care for his namesake. "Father," his boy would say, pointing to his tattered shoes, "the other children are laughing at me. May I have a new pair?" As was his custom when the Spooky Child asked for his help, the sergeant major would pull a thick sheaf of cash from his breast pocket and show it to the boy. "I've got the money here," he'd grin. "And I'm not giving it to you." The Spooky Child knew who was enjoying his father's money. Though he dreamed of killing them, he hated the witches too intensely to hurt them—hurting them would have meant touching them, and touching them would have compromised the purity of his hatred. In the teen years, as other boys chased girls, Paul Mufanebadza refused even to look at them. Instead he gazed inward, at the gleaming black obelisk, ever larger, ever harder, of his own spite.

At the nearly all-white British primary school to which his father sent him, the Spooky Child was compelled to take tea while the white wives of senior army officers corrected his poor manners. A bitter pill, but not enough. The white teachers unable to decipher his rural Shona accent, who yelled "Speak!" into his face, as if the sounds out of his mouth were not human language but the barking of some bush animal? Also a bitter pill, but still not enough. Even the worship they forced on him, of Jesus Christ, that meek little man who refused to stand up for himself: not enough.

No, it was the sergeant major's tears that finally caused all of the boy's hates to congeal into a single, self-defining thought.

"Father," he asked, "why are you crying?"

The sergeant major convened the wives and children and announced that he had just received a great honor. A senior officer, a white man, had named his dog after him. "He loves his dog very much," Paul senior explained. "His dog is like his child. So he has named his dog Paul."

The thought young Paul had at that moment felt cool and clear and nourishing.

I hate women. I hate Christianity. And I hate white people.

Soon after this, Paul and his half brother, Paul Wonder—a hale and beautiful boy four months older than the Spooky Child and beloved of the sergeant major—were required to bring their birth certificates to school. The sergeant major produced the documents. Paul Wonder's read "Paul Wonder Mufanebadza." The Spooky Child's read "Paul Neshangwe."

"Who is Paul Neshangwe?" asked the Spooky Child.

"Do you want that certificate?"

After a long while, the boy said, "No."

"Go find another father," said the sergeant major.

Paul Wonder's mother had decided that the Spooky Child should not share her son and husband's surname. The sergeant major had agreed; "Neshangwe" belonged to some distant ancestor. The children at school were greatly amused with their new classmate, Paul Neshangwe.

"You are nobody's son!" they sang. "Nobody's son!"

Throughout his youth, Paul Neshangwe's hate attained a kind of perfection, the way the country's roilings—the racial hatred, the war, the sense of Rhodesia as a sentient being tearing its own heart out—seemed to affirm his interior goings-on. By the time he was seventeen, living on liquor, tobacco, and marijuana, he had developed the habit of bashing his skull against the cinder-block wall of his house. It helped.

One night he turned to his older (full) brother and said, "I want to destroy something." His brother nodded. "I want to destroy a person."

They decided to open Paul Wonder with knives. They accosted him outside his home. Paul Wonder fled, screaming. His mother ran into the street.

"Let's kill them both!" Paul's brother said.

But Paul wasn't sure, so they gave up the chase. Still, Paul couldn't shake his urge to destroy something. Several days later, he noosed his neck, stepped onto a chair, knotted the rope around a pipe, and leapt into the air. The rope snapped. He tried and failed twice more in the next month, once again by hanging and once with antimalarial pills.

Then the Christians came to town, tacking up posters for a movie about the life of Jesus—a white guy, apparently. Paul and his friends began tearing the posters down to use as rolling paper. As a joke, they went to a screening, sat in the back smoking their Jesus joints and shouting *"Murungu!"*—the Shona word for "white man"—whenever the lead actor spoke. In the lobby afterward, a young man approached.

"You have been taking down our posters."

Not an accusation. Just a statement of fact.

"That's us," said one of Paul's friends, pulling a joint from his pocket and lighting up. "That Jesus, he is your 'Lord and Savior,' *jah?*"

The man nodded.

"Well, we've been smoking your Lord and Savior."

Someone cracked a joke about God forcing Himself upon the Virgin and making Joseph take the rap for knocking her up.

"We will pray for you," the Christian smiled.

Fuck them, Paul thought, walking away. *Fuck Jesus. Fuck the Holy Ghost. And fuck the Father.*

Fuck the Father most of all.

.   .   .

Jim Steele knew what was coming. Wars of racial independence had been rippling across the continent, black Africans from Ghana to Mozambique to Angola overthrowing the European colonials who'd kept them under thumb for centuries. Now it was Rhodesia's turn. In November 1965, prime minister Ian Smith declared independence from Britain, which had begun urging Rhodesia toward democratic rule. The revolution began five months later—in the city of Chinhoyi, ten miles from Steele's farm—when government forces gunned down seven armed rebels. For some fifteen years the war raged, killing 30,000 blacks and 1,500 whites and ending in black-majority rule. On April 18, 1980, at a ceremony in a Harare soccer stadium in which Bob Marley performed freedom songs, Rhodesia became Zimbabwe, with a black militiaman named Robert Mugabe as its prime minister.

What shocked Jim Steele—and all his countrymen, black and white—was the inauguration speech by Mugabe, who'd spent ten years in a Rhodesian prison for "subversion" and risen to political prominence on a platform of black power. "If yesterday you hated me," he told his defeated white countrymen, "today you cannot avoid the love that binds you to me and me to you. . . . The wrongs of the past must now stand forgiven and forgotten. . . . It could never be a correct justification that because the whites oppressed us yesterday when they had power, the blacks must oppress them today because they have power. An evil remains an evil, whether practiced by white against black or by black against white."

For ten years, Mugabe lived those beautiful words. By 1990, thanks to his embrace of the country's whites, the economy was humming, and Zimbabwe was known as "Africa's breadbasket." The prime minister (and after 1987, president) vastly improved education and health care and brought blacks into the economy.

Shona blacks, that is. When members of the country's minority Ndebele tribe, which had been shut out of the new government, mounted a protest in the early eighties, Mugabe dispatched a shadowy militia known as the Fifth Brigade to slaughter some 30,000 Ndebele men, women, and children and to terrorize those they spared. The brigade forced survivors to sing Shona songs praising Mugabe's political party while dancing on the fresh graves of their families, and shot or hacked to death those who grieved openly.

Such a strange, divided man, Robert Mugabe. A charismatic Roman Catholic with seven university degrees. A reconciler and poet who raised his country from the ashes of total race war. And a man without hesitation or limits. By the time, years later, Zimbabwe's whites learned along with the rest of the world of the Fifth Brigade's obscenities—learned that Robert Mugabe was not the precursor to Nelson Mandela but a psychotic in the mold of Idi Amin—it was too late.

Jim Steele, too, was a divided man during the war. Not long before the first shots were fired in Chinhoyi, he decided to stop growing tobacco. No crop paid better, but what it exacted— the price of always having his money and his blacks on his mind—was more than he could afford. After 1964, Jim Steele used the 3,700 acres his father had begun farming in 1913 outside Chinhoyi to raise cattle and maize. This decision brought him a peace that remained and continued, quietly and slowly, to unfurl; while all around him, year after year, Rhodesia devoured itself, Steele devoted his time to his church, becoming an elder and lay preacher.

Good, but not enough: One Sunday in June 1970, as he sat in his pew at Lomagundi Presbyterian Church in Chinhoyi, Steele felt a tiny tendril take root in his chest, a pinprick of bliss that soon thickened into rapture, then shock, then terrible longing. Slain, drunk, he stumbled to the altar, collapsed, and confessed.

"I have been full of pride! I must surrender!"

Surrender and commit: At a time when the rest of Rhodesia's white farmers barricaded their homes with razor wire and slept with their shotguns, Steele and his wife, Janette, traveled the country distributing Gideon Bibles.

"Church is an appointment with God," he said whenever his son, who lived next door on the farm, begged his parents to stay home on Sundays. "Such an appointment cannot be canceled."

Even before the war's end, Jim Steele became known throughout Chinhoyi among both blacks and whites as a man who feared God and was fair with his blacks, a demanding boss but a tireless worker himself, a man capable of anger, surely, but slow to it.

And yet, throughout the war, this peace within him lived side by side with its opposite. Steele could not keep the country's fear and fury from penetrating his surfaces. He *detested* the war that left his farm fallow, detested the whites who had provoked it and the blacks who waged it. Steele read his Old Testament. Vengeance was His. But leaving vengeance to God did nothing to cool his wrath. It was a physical thing, a rock in the belly. And it was frightening—not because he couldn't abolish it but because he couldn't afford to. Unfettered, rage had once prompted him to feed a human being to a furnace. But measured, kept on a low simmer, anger brought a certain keenness and clarity, tuned him into what he could and couldn't expect from those mysterious others, his blacks, without whom he and his land would be lost.

So was Steele, at heart, the same man at the end of the war that he'd been before it began? Steele thought not; thought that the man who had put that boy in the furnace had been vanquished, replaced. Yes, he was still a hard man, still enraged at what fifteen years of war had visited upon his country. But he had changed his ways, and this change has been rewarded with a new consciousness and, after 1980, a measure of prosperity, had it not? By the mid-1990s, Jim Steele was a man who prayed and even thought that he had atoned not only for himself, but also in some small way for the trickery and theft and murder with which white men had made this land their own. Was he not entitled to such a sentiment?

Jim Steele was a fool. His land and his god hadn't even begun to test him.

· · ·

And then Paul Neshangwe changed. It was the strangest thing, not only because it happened but because it didn't take long—just a few months to begin altering the chemical structure of all that hate, of all those *hates*.

It was the Christians. They were Presbyterians, and they were relentless, coming for him in packs like hyenas after a blood scent.

How did they find him?

Easily. After the movie, as Neshangwe and his friends smoked the Savior in the lobby, the Presbyterians politely asked them to write down who they were and where they lived. Paul's friends scribbled fake addresses. Paul . . . did not.

The Presbyterians gave chase for weeks on end. Whenever they rapped on his door, Neshangwe—a man temperamentally capable of murdering his own kin—was *seized with terror*, leapt

out the window and ran. He eventually *moved*. And still, somehow, six months later, they found him. He was broke, three days
without a meal, when they came knocking. He opened up, and
there they were. Some black kids, Jesus boys, acolytes, whatever,
and a *murungu* in a white collar. The *murungu* spoke a bit about
the Man. Then he pulled the oldest evangelical's trick in the
book.

"Salvation is a free gift. Do you know what that means?" Paul
said nothing. The *murungu* fished a Zim dollar from his pocket,
clasped its edges, and snapped it taut.

"Like salvation. A free gift. Take it."

The year was 1987. The Zim dollar was powerful. Paul bought
bread, milk, paraffin. As he ate, an incomplete thought, thirteen
words, played and replayed itself.

My own father, who has never in his life given me a dollar . . .

Not a lightning strike. He wasn't *smote*. But he started coming to church, just to see.

Still, the anger in this man, this *boy*, unnerved. After graduating high school, he interviewed for the ministry. "What Paul
Neshangwe considers his calling is instead a confusion of rage,"
his evaluator wrote. He was ordered to complete university
training in South Africa. Bitterly, he submitted.

The first time he preached at the university chapel, a commerce student named Lydia Chituku watched from her pew,
trying to decide whether she believed the boy in the pulpit.
She'd heard about the ministry student from Zimbabwe. Everyone had. An aspiring man of God who yelled down classmates
and professors, smashed his head against walls, and didn't like
women. Now here he was, preaching about . . . that very
madness—his rage at women and white people and his father
and Jesus and the church officials who'd questioned his call to
the ministry. His voice was low and fierce. His eyes were hooded,
half shut, as if to scorn the sight of the sanctuary. Yet he made
himself so naked. He omitted nothing, spared himself nothing.

He did not even claim to have shed his rage, though he did say that he was reborn and that he was learning to forgive those who had wronged him, to release them and himself.

"It's not that you hate the people and things you say you hate," she said a few weeks after they began dating. "It's that you just don't know what to do with them."

Though everyone who'd ever known Paul Neshangwe told him that his hate was a cancer, no one had ever suggested *this*—that what he comprehended as the core of his identity wasn't at all what he thought it was.

Lydia became the first woman Paul Neshangwe ever loved physically and, after they married, the last. Later, after AIDS began to take his siblings—a brother, then another brother, then another brother, then a sister, then another sister, *five* of them—and Paul and Lydia began raising their orphaned nieces and nephews—nine through their home over the years, on a preacher's salary, including the children of yet another brother, who died of cerebral malaria—some began to ask whether Paul's refusal of all women before Lydia was part of God's plan, His mysterious way of sparing Paul the plague in order to preserve him for his work as a pastor. Paul always deflected the question. Even considering it made him feel unclean.

·   ·   ·

It was the oldest story in the world: A strongman becomes mesmerized by power for its own sake, transmogrifies, grows paranoid, intellectually unsupple, allergic to dissent; starts rigging elections, micromanaging the economy, imprisoning journalists he finds "offensive." By the mid-1990s, Robert Mugabe had begun turning Zimbabwe into a police state ruled by fear, censorship, and his omniscient Central Intelligence Organization. The first real threat to his regime came in 1997, when the country's war veterans—the only group capable of mounting a coup d'état—demanded giveaways. The unbudgeted $4 billion Zim-dollar (roughly $250 million U.S.) payoff Mugabe ordered pulverized the economy, but the vets pressed for still more. With no cash reserves, Mugabe began laying the groundwork for land confiscations, dubbing all whites "imperialists" and "colonial agents." Once this rhetoric became reality, it did not matter that virtually all the war veterans who took over white lands were uninterested in farming—that government-backed land invasions *guaranteed* economic ruin, if not famine. What mattered was Mugabe's continued hold on power.

The Steeles knew their land would be taken. It was inevitable. Upon waking each morning, they took tea, then walked together to the balcony overlooking the fields to see if it had begun. They knew the invasion would be violating and psychologically violent, just as they knew it would begin in silence, with a stranger strolling onto their land and pushing stakes into the soft soil to mark his claim. *Not yours. Mine.* Yet even before the settlers came, Jim Steele pitied them. He knew, as they did not, that they were cannon fodder, dispatched by the government to intimidate him into fleeing his farm without a fight. This was the way of land invasions. Once the whites fled (if not from the settlers, then from the soldiers who followed), the settlers would be driven back into the bush so a war veteran or regime crony could claim his prize. Jim and Janette Steele therefore decided more than a year before the settlers appeared that they would accept their presence. It was the practical thing to do: If they made a stand, the army would take not only their farmland but their house and perhaps their lives. But it was also the Christian thing to do, a turning of the other cheek.

It began in March of 2000. One family at first, then two, then ten, twenty, forty, wordlessly forming their low circular mud huts and wood-stick chicken pens. The Steeles responded, as planned, with silence and peace.

Yet there was no peace. On his balcony each morning, teacup in hand, beholding the distant huts and pens and stick-figure humans etched against the dawn, Jim Steele felt all the old terror and rage he thought he'd shed two decades before, when the war ended. All he had ever wanted in his life was to work this land, be its steward, bring order to its natural state of chaos. Now the settlers were here with their primitive, piecemeal agriculture. In a year or two, the soldiers would kick them back where they came from, and Steele would have to watch his farm backslide into the sullen scrubland it had been before his father emigrated from Scotland to civilize it at the dawn of the past century. The farm had gone half feral in the war years. But Steele knew then that the war would end, that he would once again bring order to the land. This was different. This was far more *personal*. And this was forever. In a decade or two, he would go to his grave, and not a trace of what he and his father had worked for would remain to speak for him. He was old, afraid, angry, and now, he realized, trapped. Jim Steele stood each morning watching the strangers grow ever more numerous, ever closer, and said aloud to himself, "My God, what am I to do?"

·   ·   ·

By 1999, when he began substitute preaching in Chinhoyi, Paul Neshangwe, too, had a decision to make about the farm invasions and the devastation he knew they would bring upon his country. Robert Mugabe frequently linked Christian churches to the white "enemy." ("[When they] came to our land, they brought us the Bible and they taught us to pray. When we opened our eyes, we had the Bible and they had the land.") The CIO was even sending spies into churches to track sermonizing that was "slanderous" to the president. Most of the country's clergy decided it was not worth losing one's parish and perhaps even one's freedom to preach what everyone already knew to be true.

In July of that year, Neshangwe was invited to conduct a service at a local Methodist church. At the appointed time, he stepped up to the pulpit, closed his eyes, and prayed that his words would make him an instrument of his Father's will. Upon opening his eyes, he was surprised to find himself not with Jesus but with Moses: the wrathful Moses who killed an Egyptian because that man had abused a Jew; and the rueful Moses who subsequently witnessed a Jew beating another Jew and realized that oppressors could be Egyptian or Jewish. Then Neshangwe said it: "Oppressors can be white. Or oppressors can be black." The congregation gasped. The fear in the sanctuary was palpable, but so was the exhilaration.

Once Paul Neshangwe started, he could not stop. Could not stop preaching . . . the truth. Could not stop preaching that Zimbabwe's troubles were man-made and not "God's will." Word came one day that he was required to perform funeral rites for a deputy minister for justice. The service was held outside Chinhoyi on a stately farm, until recently owned by a white family, that President Mugabe had bequeathed to the deputy.

"You will speak first," an official told Neshangwe when he arrived.

"No," Neshangwe said, smiling. "I will speak last." Nobody spoke this way to regime officials. The man stared. Neshangwe continued. "God will have the last word. Not even our pompous and blustering minister of justice will be allowed to speak after God."

God, indeed, got the last word. His servant Paul began the eulogy thusly: "My mother has begged me not to say anything today that will get me killed. So I will endeavor not to say anything too inflammatory." He then gestured to the grandeur of the farm, the rolling red hills, the elegant homestead. "It is not for me to say whether this man was right to accept the free farm that came his way"—the pastor then pointed to the casket—"because this man now stands before the ultimate court, before the ultimate judge, in whose hands his case now rests."

The minister of justice stormed out. Neshangwe knew he was fortunate Robert Mugabe had been unable to attend. If he had, the president might well have rewarded the pastor with a death warrant.

Neshangwe frequently substituted at a Presbyterian church that had been without a permanent pastor for several years. Lomagundi Presbyterian was its official name, but around Chinhoyi it was known simply as the "white man's church." An elder, a white farmer in his sixties named Jim Steele, had been holding it together. A quiet man. Serious. All business. Not the most affable fellow, and yet Paul felt immediately and powerfully drawn to the old man, his ruminative, plainspoken tone, the way he did nothing with fanfare but just . . . did it. Steele in turn found himself fascinated with, even bewildered by, Neshangwe, a serious man of God who was nevertheless an *imp*, whose piety seemed to draw its power less from humility than from laughter. Moreover, despite the thirty years and color line separating them, Steele and Neshangwe each recognized the other as an increasingly rare breed of Zimbabwean: an authority figure with no patience for the politics of race allegiance. Steele saw in Neshangwe a man willing to state from the pulpit truths most white people wouldn't dare utter outside their living rooms; Neshangwe saw in Steele a man who recognized and even embraced the fact that as whites fled the country, Lomagundi Presbyterian would become either a "black man's church" or an empty building.

Steele eventually told the other elders he wanted to offer the pastorship to Neshangwe.

"A *black* pastor?"

"This is not a white church," he snapped. "This is God's church."

But . . . Paul Neshangwe? Not just a black man but a provocateur? At a time when racial animosity was government *policy*?

When Steele himself was on the brink of losing his land? Did the old man actually think the regime wouldn't take an active interest in such a church?

"So," Neshangwe smiled when Steele made the offer, "the white man's church wants a black pastor?"

Steele failed to see the humor.

"It's *God's* church!"

Neshangwe consulted his wife.

"My husband," said Lydia, tapping his forearm lightly as she always did when she needed to calm him or herself, "I do not wish to be a widow. Not just yet."

A whole year passed as Neshangwe mulled the offer. In the meantime, he worked as the church's full-time "interim" pastor. He was still mulling the offer during the first wave of the Chinhoyi farm invasions, when the settlers came to Jim Steele's land, and even during the second wave, when Mugabe's men came for Jim Steele.

.   .   .

Excepting Sabbaths, Jim Steele hadn't known an idle day in his life. Now, as the settlers took over more and more of his land, he had time on his hands. He found himself driving into town, to Paul Neshangwe's home. The men would eat *sadza* and beans, and talk. Neshangwe had never known a white farmer, so Steele told him about his life prior to the invasion, what running a farm took and what it gave back, what it was like to be a white African. Neshangwe in turn told Steele about his life in the ministry, what his white collar and black skin meant to him and to those he'd met.

One Sunday, hours before church was to begin, Steele appeared at his priest's door. Despite his abiding rage at the settlers, the farmer had begun to wonder: Was his acceptance of these people the Christian thing to do? Was he even *doing* anything?

Like Jesus, who saw little value in answering spiritual questions directly, Paul responded with a parable—his own. He told the old man about the place of hate he had come from, and about the people and moments of grace that had renewed him, expanded his sense of what was humanly possible. Jim didn't know what to believe about his priest's story—its alarming proposition that a man could be one thing and then, almost at once, its opposite. The men arrived at no conclusion together. They simply talked for a time and then went to the service. Jim returned early the next week, though, and the next, and so on, so the two men could reflect on the Gospels, on the color of their skin, on each other's lives, and on their country.

"Paul, what do you *want*?" Jim asked one day. With the church, in other words. Paul felt he wasn't being asked so much as dared. He told Jim he wanted to provide food, medicine, and spiritual support to AIDS victims; to procure tallow and sewing machines so jobless parishioners could make black-market soap and school uniforms; to pay the school fees of penniless children; to extend the church where the need was greatest—in other words, to become what others would surely call a "black church."

Jim knew the instant Paul began to speak that he'd expected his priest to respond the way he had. Had *wanted* him to. So that he could say yes. So he could be a part of Paul's plans. The farmer began to walk with the priest on his visits to parishioners in the city, holding hands and praying with urban Shona men, women, and children on the dirt floors of their cinder-block abodes, bringing milk to women too depleted by AIDS to breast-feed their infants, delivering the tallow and sewing machines in his truck.

The tract that no longer belonged to Jim Steele was vast. With time on his hands, he spent hours covering it by foot, just to see the cattle and the maize rows. Sometimes his workers walked with him. Sometimes his priest came out to the country to walk with him. Most of the settlers seemed not to notice the walkers. A few looked back blankly before returning to their work. Then one afternoon, because it seemed odd not to, Jim turned to Paul and said, "Come, let's talk to them."

In the weeks that followed, Jim Steele got to know the people who had come to take everything he had ever worked for. He spoke directly to those who knew English and, through his priest or his workers, to those who spoke only Shona. He learned their names, where they'd come from, how many children they had. With each, he found himself asking the same question he had asked Neshangwe. *What do you want?* Often his tone carried bitter reproach, sometimes mere curiosity, sometimes even concern. Regardless, the answer was always the same.

"To live, sir."

Steele had been around Shona from the day of his birth, worked side by side with them, learned to trust and be trusted by them. But as he spoke with the settlers, with the urban poor to whom Paul tended, with Paul himself, a realization dawned: He had never known a Shona man, woman, or child personally. It had never occurred to him to do so. Now it did. As soon as he replaced the old narrow questions ("Does he show up on time? Can he do the job?") with the single broad one ("What's he like?"), he began to see . . . every little thing. The way, for instance, a Shona's life was filled with "brothers" and "sisters" and "cousins" but no "friends," since to call someone a "friend" was to call him something less than immediate family, to denigrate him. Or the way a Shona and her "sisters" often broke into song—in four-part harmony!—not for any *reason* but because they drew no distinction between speaking and singing and breathing; understood the three as a single substance whose form, solid or liquid or ethereal, was determined by a person's spiritual temperature. Or the way a visit with a Shona never ended, because a Shona always walked out the door with him and Paul, accompanied them to the next home, sat a while and talked, somehow remained present after physically departing.

How had Steele failed to discern all this *fluidity*? Where before he had seen an impenetrable sameness, a *mood,* he now saw the many ways in which Shona's lives and thoughts and egos bled into one another. Their very speech, as they glided within a single sentence from Shona to English and back again, was edgeless, the native tongue glistening and ebulliently inefficient as it pushed and caressed but never cut the air. Even their understanding of time and distance was fluid: If Steele asked a settler on his land how far it was to Chinhoyi, the answer depended on where the sun sat in the sky at that moment. In the morning, it was "not far." If the sun was low in the west, it was "too far"—since (of course) one was on foot and had to consider what might emerge from the bush after dark.

"White men keep watches," Paul laughed when Jim asked. "Shona keep time."

A funny thing about Paul: The more time Jim spent with him and other Shona, the less incredible the priest's stories of himself—smoking Christ at seventeen; serving Him at twenty—seemed. Steele had always thought people were what they were, the same at sixty as they'd been at six, only *more*. Now he wondered: In a land where the concept of property, of *boundaries*, was (like Christianity) barely a hundred years old, why couldn't a person also be a flowing, shape-shifting thing, rather than a sedimentary accretion? Why couldn't a person have a *change of mind*—not just a change of opinion, but the kind of irrational, self-shattering change of mind that Paul's namesake, the great apostle, underwent on the road to Damascus?

Neither Jim nor Paul knew exactly what was happening between them. Each felt God was speaking to him through the other, teaching him, raising him up, offering answers to questions he hadn't even been aware he was asking. Only later was it clear that both men had sensed what was to befall the older man, and together were preparing him for it.

•   •   •

One night, Jim Steele woke with a start. A whispering in the garden, then in the room, then in him. He felt as he always felt when visited in this way: blissfully repentant. Janette woke.

"*Emmanuel*," he told her. "God is with us."

They prayed. *Show us what you want us to do.* By dawn they had their answer: It was not enough merely to accept what had befallen them.

Word eventually circulated among the settlers that the *murungu*'s offer of free medicine was genuine. Not just over-the-counter remedies but inoculations, as well as sulfaguanidine for salmonella. Within a year, Jim and Janette Steele had cured more than a hundred malaria cases among the settlers, many of whom would have died without treatment.

Soon there was talk among Chinhoyi's farmers that Jim Steele was giving his settlers diesel and maize free of charge, even plowing (their? his?) fields with his tractor. Could any of it be true? White farmers either fled or shut themselves in their homes, then dreamed of retribution and reparation. They did not abet their own disenfranchisement.

But once Jim Steele started, he could not stop. He and his workers began refitting some of his unused farm buildings into a school for the settlers' children. There were one hundred pupils at first. But once word reached beyond the farm that the school was actually . . . a *school*, with paid teachers and books, chalk and boards, pencils and paper, 300 children from eight surrounding farms began attending. Was *this* enough? Was it enough for Jim Steele to give medicine and farming aid and cash loans and education to the people who had taken his inheritance?

His boss told him it was not.

"My wife and I would be honored if you would come to our church with us on Sundays," he told the settlers. Most didn't. Some did, and continued to go, underwent baptism, took Communion, accepted Jim's embrace at the offering of the peace, even as other whites in the pews refused to shake their hands or even look at them. "The commandment tells me to love my neighbor," Steele shrugged when confronted. "It does not tell me that I get to choose my neighbor."

There was more. Worshipping alongside the settlers, Steele came to feel a connection to the land they had taken from him—a connection he had not felt when it was his. A connection to the *dirt*, actually. He'd always noticed the way bare feet on dirt was not just an everyday but an every-moment-of-every-day fact of life for those many Shona who survived on what they grew themselves. Now he thought of how that fact would shape a person, how physically and urgently aware that person would be of the miracles—*all of life itself!*—made possible by that dirt. Such a person would accept the supernatural as a matter of course. Such a person would draw no distinction between his body and the world. His own mortality would feel dreadful to him, as ever, but also, in some small way, sweet. He would comprehend death not as an ending but as a point on an unending continuum.

So it came to be with Jim Steele. The dirt that settled on his skin when he was in the fields (making his white skin scuffed and lined and giving blue-black Shona skin, at high noon, an orange adobe glow), the fine red dust that in the hot months papered his nose and throat: With every breath he was communing with it, taking it—and a part of everyone and everything that had ever lived and died on it and in it, his mother and his father and his beloved brother and the numberless, nameless Shona—into his body. *Dust to dust.* The land was no longer personal; it was his very person.

Jim Steele would always be a white farmer. He would always believe that he had rightfully owned his land and that it had been wrongfully taken. But now, when he considered the famous words supposedly spoken to Cecil Rhodes by a Shona chieftain ("Buy land? Why not also buy the wind?"), he found them instructive rather than amusingly naive. The underlying notion—that people belonged to the land and not the other way around—was disturbing, but also strangely beautiful.

•   •   •

On August 6, 2001, some eighteen months after the first mud huts appeared on Jim Steele's land, a band of settlers laid siege to the home of a neighboring farmer—in retaliation, they claimed, for an attack by a posse of white farmers. Police immediately arrested the besieged man, along with twenty-one of Chinhoyi's other white farmers, including Jim Steele. In fact, both the siege and the "posse" tale were orchestrated; the arrests gave the regime a symbolic victory in the days preceding Heroes' Day, the annual celebration of the seven martyred freedom fighters of Chinhoyi, who'd begun the war for independence in 1966.

Crowds gathered outside the police station the morning after the arrests to jeer and throw garbage at the white women who came to ask after their husbands. The war veterans on duty encouraged the fun, though they motioned the crowd to relent for a black visitor.

Paul Neshangwe, who was still acting as the "interim" minister of Lomagundi Presbyterian, announced that he had come for Jim Steele. The veteran in charge eyed Neshangwe's collar with puzzlement.

"Are you his lawyer?"

"I am his priest."

The veteran stared.

"Are you here to preach to the black prisoners?"

"I am here for Mr. Steele."

Now the veteran understood—a joke.

"So tell me, *priest*," he said, playing along. "How much have these *varungu* [white men] paid you?"

It was exactly then, in the face of the veterans' mocking laughter, that Neshangwe realized he could no longer ask God to be good to people he did not love enough to serve; he would be saying yes to Steele's job offer.

"I am his priest," he said again.

The veteran, now aware that the man was serious, rose and stepped close.

"Leave," he said.

On the third day, the police transferred the farmers to Chinhoyi's remand prison for accused criminals awaiting trial, where they were thrown in with the all-black general population. The decision not to isolate the white men during Heroes' weekend, which even in less inflammatory times was a holiday whites were wise to spend at home, spoke for itself: *The varungu are fair game.*

The guards stripped Steele naked, provided prison pajamas. No shoes. Within minutes his skin burned and itched—lice. Twelve-by-eighteen-foot cells, thirty-six men in each, six blankets. It was August, wintertime in Zimbabwe, bitter cold. At lights-out, the men lay, sardine-style, on the concrete floor. The first night was quiet. Steele had toiled alongside black men before, smelled their sweat, but this was different. The thirty-six bodies were pressed together, *locked* together, so that when one man turned over every other man was required to do the same. He could hear and smell the breath of the men on either side of him. Did he smell different to them? he wondered.

They woke at five, ate, went into the yard. The farmers convened. Steele was the oldest. They addressed their question to him.

Oom Jim, what will happen to us?

Steele didn't know. How could he? He told them so. Yet still they asked, again and again, in the yard, in the mess, through the walls separating the cells, as if the constant repetition carried a warding power. *Oom Jim, what will happen to us?*

On the second night, just after lights-out, Steele was praying silently, asking for guidance—*Show me what you want me to do,*

Lord—when a voice from another cell, quiet, unfamiliar, Shona, repeated the question that had been ringing in the air.

"Oom Jim, what will happen to us?"

A sarcastic little barb?

"Yes, Oom Jim." Another Shona. "What will happen to us?"

These men were in earnest. Steele knew then what he was being shown to do. His first prison sermon, delivered while he was prone and pressed between the bodies of strangers, was short and simple, more a sentiment than a sermon.

"God says we must live one day at a time," he said to the dark. "Whether we are here four days, until the end of Heroes' weekend, or whether we are here four weeks or four years, we must ask every day for His protection and peace."

That was all. No one else spoke, and the men went to sleep.

He preached the next morning in the yard. He was surrounded at first only by the other white men, who clumped together as a defensive measure when not locked in their cells. He preached about Jesus in the wilderness, alone and beset. As always, his voice and his manner were quiet and convincing. He spoke without fear and without reproach, as if he and the other farmers were in no danger at all. The Spirit moved him to preach at length, almost thirty minutes, and when he was done there were as many black inmates as white gathered around him.

Afterward, two black prisoners introduced themselves.

"We would like to sing you a song," they said.

They were Malawian, a bass and a tenor. They sang beautifully, in harmony, in their own language. Jim couldn't understand the words but knew without having to ask that it was a Christian song.

No one planned what happened that night. No one said, "We will do it this way." It just happened, and every subsequent night the farmers were in prison—eleven more in all. At eight the lights were extinguished. For a time there was silence. Then the Malawians began to sing. A few of the hymns were familiar.

Most were not. All were sung in their native language, and the way the rest of the prisoners knew what was being sung at the same time that they had no idea what was being sung made the music even more rich and strange. Time lost its purchase when the Malawians sang, so it was hard to know if they were singing for thirty minutes or an hour or two hours. They simply sang until they stopped, and when they stopped there was an observed silence. The first night this occurred, after the singing had come to an end, Jim Steele had no idea what to do. He felt called to preach, but he also felt the Malawians had brought the spirit of God upon them all, and that it was not his place to break such a silence. Indeed, it was not. Quietly, one at a time, the prisoners began to speak into the dark. As they did, one of the men against whom Steele's body was pressed, an accused thief named Simon, translated the words of those who spoke in Shona. Some offered prayers. Some offered testimonies—who they were, what they did for a living, what they wished for. Others offered confessions. The prison was divided into two classes of inmate, violent and nonviolent, and though the men on this ward had been accused of nonviolent or mildly violent crimes, many of the voices issuing from the dark told of terrible acts. Some of the confessions lasted ten minutes. Some lasted ten seconds. A heavy silence separated each.

I raped a young girl.
I stole from my neighbor.
I killed my wife.
I cursed God.
I hurt my child.

The men told their stories knowing they were being listened to. Most asked for forgiveness. Some claimed they were beyond it. Jim waited until every man who wanted to had spoken, then began to preach. He spoke a sentence or two at a time, then waited as Simon called out his words in Shona. When Steele finished, there was an amen, then sleep.

On the first Saturday morning, the guards announced that the farmers' heads would be shaved. The lice, they explained. The younger farmers raged: This was about ridicule, not lice; they would not submit. Steele motioned them to be still. The yelling— it was just what the guards wanted, so they could later claim the whites had "rioted" to justify whatever violence they were planning.

"What should we do, Oom Jim?"

"As a sheep before his shearers, as a lamb before the slaughter . . . ," he quoted to the farmers. Then to the guards: "I will be first."

There was a problem. Though the guards were prepared to beat the farmers, they hadn't actually prepared to shave them: There were no clippers in the prison. Clippers were delivered four hours later. Another problem: Since every inmate carried lice, and not just the white farmers, and since the shavings had been publicly announced, the guards were compelled to shave every head in the prison to save face. Most of the black inmates found this episode highly amusing.

That night, after the bald Malawians sang their songs, and anonymous bald inmates offered their confessions to the night, and bald Jim Steele preached his sermon and said his amen, a bald man from another cell whispered into the dark. A Shona accent.

"Oom Jim, do you really see the light at the end of the tunnel?"

"Yes, my friend," Steele said solemnly. "The truth will set you free."

A minute passed. Then, once more, the whisper.

"Oom Jim, do you think you could turn that light up a little?"

As the laughter of the prisoners faded, another voice.

"Very good."

Jim knew the voice was the warden's but couldn't read its tone.

The next day, as the prison's nonviolent inmates mingled in the yard, the warden, flanked by a dozen guards, appeared and ordered the men to sit. Then, in violation of prison policy, he ordered the so-called D inmates—the men charged with murder and arson and rape—into the yard.

This is it, Steele thought. The openness of it all surprised him. One would have thought the matter of doing in the whites would be a semi-discreet affair.

The warden ordered the D prisoners to sit. Then he pointed at Steele.

"You," he said. "Stand."

Steele stood.

"Preach."

Was this some form of mockery? Steele decided he didn't care. His job was to bear witness. He gestured to Simon. Simon stood. Then, with Simon translating, he began to preach.

"Some of you are guilty of the crimes you have been charged with. I have heard you confessing at night. Some of you are not guilty of the crimes you have been charged with. But whether you are guilty or not, you, me, all of us, are sinners. You have all done something you are ashamed of. I have done something I am ashamed of. We all need to be changed." He spoke about Daniel in the lions' den. "God was there, and God is *here*, in our midst. Do not be afraid," he said, smiling. "Do not be afraid. Because when you leave this place, the lions of the earth will be everywhere. *Do not be afraid!*"

Some of the D prisoners came to him when he was done, asking about his religion, offering confessions, thanking him. Two others—they happened to be nonviolents—wished to discuss something else.

"You are an old man," one said.

"Yes?"

The man pointed to Jim's eyes. "You do not see well."

"I see well enough."

"But you wear glasses?"

"They were taken when I arrived."

"No glasses," the man said, shaking his head. "Take off your tunic."

What?

"Your lice."

The men were offering to do for Jim what he, with his sixty-four-year-old's eyes, could not do for himself: pick the lice from his prison pajamas. Then and every day thereafter, the two Shona, an accused thief and a vandal, meticulously picked the lice from Jim Steele's prison pajamas while the old man sat beside them in the cold air of the prison yard, naked and peaceful.

After seventeen days, when it became clear that the whites were not going to end up getting hurt, that their presence in the prison was in fact creating a most unpalatable racial harmony, that even the warden was developing worrisome tendencies, the order came down: Give the whites their bail.

They were freed with the stipulation that they leave their farms, and Chinhoyi altogether, for one month. On the day Jim and Janette Steele returned, they stopped in town for supplies. The tension was alive in the air—the sense of eyes, of suspended rules, of Chinhoyi having declared open season on whites.

Jim Steele and Paul Neshangwe said nothing when they spotted each other across the street. Just began walking. For several minutes, while the people of Chinhoyi looked on, the two men held one another.

"You are my pastor," Jim finally said. "You are my pastor."

"And you," Paul said, "are a father to me."

·   ·   ·

And still there is anger. At his government. At his losses. Even at the settlers he has provided for. Can it be reconciled with his forgiveness? Is he a changed man?

Jim Steele scorns such questions.

"Repent," he says early one Sunday morning. "*Repent.*" His tone is harsh, his knuckles white as he skins a broken extension cord with a knife. "The word itself means 'to turn around.' There can be no forgiveness without repentance, without a turning around. Remorse is not enough. Judas had remorse. But did he repent? Did he ask Jesus Christ for forgiveness and vow to change his ways? No, he went off and hung himself. Remorse is *not* repentance. It is just an emotion. Like anger—just an emotion. Repentance is a process. It involves asking, 'Lord, how shall I proceed?' and then *acting*. It is an act of will. It is not for the weak."

Jim Steele is filled with grace, but he will never forget what has been done to him. Forgiveness is not a forgetting. Jim Steele is quite aware that he has lost many of his friends and most of his money, that paint peels from the walls of his living room, that he and his wife often go days without electricity, that their phone hasn't worked in years. He will never believe that the presence of settlers on his land is just. Justice is another issue for another day. Such is Jim Steele's forgiveness: While it creates peace, it is not an absolution or an excusing. It is, like his dirty farmer's hands, rugged and unpretty and functional, a thing he will be working with until the day he dies.

But then, after the sharp words, Steele smiles at his wife and says, "Let us go." The ride to church, in an old station wagon packed with settlers, is upbeat and chatty. Every few minutes, though, the car goes silent as those inside look out at the country Robert Mugabe has killed. Such a sad nation, Zimbabwe. The return to ancient slash-and-burn agriculture has turned the verdant earth into a moonscape of baked-black dirt and the air into an acrid broth. Mugabe's misrule has driven inflation to quadruple digits while AIDS has lowered the national life expectancy to thirty-nine. After this morning's service, many parishioners will return to squalid boxes—sticks stabbed into the dirt and covered with rusted tin sheets—because their homes were bulldozed last summer as part of Operation Drive Out the Trash, a "civic beautification" project that serves to scatter into the rural areas those poor urban blacks most likely to coalesce into a force of opposition.

Zimbabwe, once lovely and flowing, is now frozen. No one can move; petrol is impossibly rare and expensive. No one can speak; CIO agents are everywhere. Those not demoralized to the point of paralysis leave if they can. Few dream of resistance. "Take up arms?" Zimbabweans say, time and again. "There is nothing left worth fighting for." Even the president has succumbed to some odd, whole-body petrification. At the dawn of Zimbabwe, Mugabe was a joyful and athletic orator. Now, at eighty-two, the man appears embalmed, face locked in an inscrutable wooden stare, arms set as straight as oars down the sides, voice imprisoned in a narcoleptic two-note range.

The station wagon pulls up to the church an hour early, and as they have every Sunday for more than five years, Jim Steele and Paul Neshangwe reflect on their country, then choose which Bible lessons speak best to its plight. There is no acknowledgment of how radical this linking of the worldly and the otherworldly is. The growing number of black faces in what was once Chinhoyi's white-man's church speaks for itself. As does the occasional presence in the pews of CIO spies sent to report on Neshangwe's sermons. As does the charred hull of the church's parish office—firebombed during 2004's Heroes' weekend. ("Don't you think," one investigator coyly suggested, "that whoever destroyed your office is angry that you welcome both whites and blacks into your church?") Sometimes Steele's pragmatic nature prompts him to ask, "Is this too much?" Neshangwe's response is always the same: "Ah, Jim, the recklessness of faith!"

The service itself is joyously chaotic. There is no hymn list, and music doesn't occur, it *strikes*; seized by the Spirit, some guy in the back cries *Hi-ya! Hi-ya! Hi-ya!* in a piping high voice, and by the fourth *Hi-ya!* he's been joined in full harmony. As a white woman produces an acoustic guitar, two black men sprint, as if on fire, toward the altar and get to work on a bongo and a grotesquely out-of-tune upright piano.

In the middle of the madness is Jim Steele, with his old brown ill-fitting suit and his mussed hair. Is he a man who ever thinks to look in a mirror? It is not possible. Earlier, during the hour-long earthquake of Paul's sermon, he was fidgeting, flinty, tapping his watch, the disciplining father—prompting Paul to declare, without breaking the musical cadence of his sermon-speak, that "Brother Jim is tapping his watch, yes, yes . . ." But now, as he is enveloped in sung praise—in the voices of his brothers and sisters, whom he has loved and lifted and, in some cases, saved from death—the edginess, like the anger from earlier this morning, vanishes. Even the folds and shadows of his sun-baked farmer's face depart as he floats up on tiptoe, palms open and raised in supplication, eyes closed, a silly grin forming as he sings and prays. Is he still here?

He is not. He gave up his life years ago.

Discover

FINALIST—COLUMNS AND
COMMENTARY

*With humor and a keen sense
of history, Bruno Maddox tackles
the old, the new, and the odd in
science and technology. His
gracefully written "Blinded by
Science" columns provoke
and educate, dislocating
preconceptions and helping
readers make sense of challenging
ideas even while making them
laugh out loud.*

Bruno Maddox

Blinded by Science: When First We Clicked

I write to you this morning with tidings of a most somber and dispiriting nature. If the Business section of *The New York Times* is to be believed—and after everything they've been through of late, one would imagine that organ is taking extra care to be accurate—executives of Western Union announced yesterday that this nation's telegraph system has been retired after a century and a half of service. Apparently, the last telegrams were sent last week. The final dozen included messages of heartfelt condolence, some birthday greetings, and in a first for the system, missives from several people simply trying to be the last person ever to send a telegram.

The article was written by a member of the Associated Press who seemed unaware—at least he didn't mention it—that the very organization that puts food on his table and provides him with an office was itself an artifact of the telegraph. Once the telegraph had made it possible, in the mid-nineteenth century, to receive news from overseas in something approaching real time, New York newspapers formed the AP as a syndicate. Foreign correspondents back then were just as skilled at running up astronomical room-service bills as their modern counterparts. It seemed only logical, given that all the stringers would be delivering essentially the same news at the same time, that there be only one of them. Perhaps it was some lingering fraternal bitterness that led the AP to announce the death of the telegraph with such good humor. The article's headline was a sidesplitting tour de force: "Western Union—STOP—Ends Telegram Service." LOL, as we say these days.

Then again, it could just be the fact that nobody talks about the telegraph anymore if they can possibly help it. We are living through a media revolution, spelled I-n-t-e-r-n-e-t, which pundits never tire of reminding us is just as profound as the invention of the book, the camera, or even—sometimes—language itself. Yet we avoid the comparison with the media revolution that the Internet most resembles: the telegraph.

How similar is the Internet to the old Victorian telegraph system? On a superficial level, extremely. Just like the Internet, the telegraph was a global web of wire-linked nodes operated by people at desks tapping purpose-built clickers with their right index finger. Just like the Internet, the telegraph endured a period of feckless infancy when its usefulness seemed limited to the transmission between distant points of the message: "Check it out, I'm sending you a message!" Businessmen were influential early adopters in the case of both media—deriving comfort, prestige, and occasionally profit from a stream of real-time stock quotes piped directly into their offices. Both media had been in mainstream use for about a decade before someone figured out that the existing technology actually had far higher bandwidth than was initially realized (for the telegraph, the discovery of duplex and quadruplex transmission). And in the case of both revolutions, the pioneers were rewarded with unprecedented levels of wealth that would make their high school friends wake up in a pool of sweat at four every morning wondering what kind of sick, sadistic God would bestow such fortune on a pigeon-chested geek who couldn't even throw a football properly. Samuel Morse, for instance, inventor of the telegraph itself and the eponymous code, was eventually compensated for his intellectual property with the still nontrivial sum of

$80,000—this in an age when men holding court behind ice buckets in the corner booths of Manhattan nightclubs could comfortably brag about pulling in a cool $2,000 a year.

I could go on. Not indefinitely, perhaps, but at least for a while. Suffice it to say that the technology, ontogeny, and social impact of the Victorian telegraph are so eerily similar to those of the Internet, it's a wonder the founders of Google aren't mincing around in frock coats doing lines of snuff. At the very least, you would think the birth of the telegraph would occasionally be one of the historical advances that the Internet revolution is likened to. Yet it isn't.

Why not?

Because the comparison, ultimately, is not flattering.

For one thing, the construction of the global telegraph network required feats of physical heroism that no Mountain Dew–slurping genius from Northern California could even begin to emulate, no matter how many evenings a week he condescends to play Ultimate Frisbee with the interns from the marketing department. The Internet was born with an infrastructural silver spoon in its mouth in the form of a preexisting global telephone network; before the telegraph could happen, a nonmetaphorical web of electric cable had to be spun around the planet—literally. Establishing the basic telegraph connection between Europe and America, to take just one example, was an epic, decades-long process of trial and error that makes Tolstoy's *War and Peace* look like a fifteen-second Super Bowl commercial. Laying 2,500 miles of cable would have been an impressive, nay, herculean, achievement even without the troublesome presence, between the two continents, of a treacherous body of water. Terrible things happened. They'd be halfway across and the cable would snap or suddenly unspool into some undersea trench along with hundreds of thousands of dollars of hard-won seed capital. In one particularly heartbreaking attempt, two ships met mid-Atlantic, each having laid half the cable, only to find that they'd put down cable sheathing from different manufacturers and that the two halves of the link wouldn't, as we say, interface. Little wonder that when the line was finally finished in 1858, cannons boomed, church bells rang, and headlines proclaimed the dawn of a new era in human understanding—reflecting a sense of optimism that endured undimmed throughout the few short weeks before the linkup stopped working.

As an intellectual triumph, the telegraph eats the Internet's lunch. Whereas the Internet has grown by a series of incremental realizations—Hey, what's to stop me from viewing this Web page graphically?! What's to stop me from using my TV cable instead of my phone line?! What's to stop me from putting a Webcam in my shower?!—every step forward in the telegraph's development required that something else had to be invented first. In order to lay cables underwater, somebody needed first to discover the only kind of rubber—gutta-percha, from a tree native to Malaysia—that could waterproof the wire effectively, and somebody else needed to invent a machine that could apply gutta-percha evenly to inconceivable lengths of cable. Before messages could be sent and received from rural villages in British India, somebody had to invent a telegraph pole that wouldn't immediately be devoured by ravenous white ants. And perhaps most impressive of all, before the telegraph could even be considered a means of interpersonal communication, somebody—Samuel Morse—needed to think up a system by which the infinite variety of concrete, abstract, and usually self-serving statements that a human being might wish to share with a species-mate could be reduced to pulses of electricity.

Again, I could go on. But I shall choose the path of mercy. My point is merely this: We've been here before, and the apocalyptic awe with which we tend to appraise our situation is out of proportion to the scale of this revolution. It's beyond debate that the power of the Internet is transformative—this very morning I myself received a crate of foul-smelling omega-3 fish-oil capsules that I ordered only yesterday from a mom-and-pop wholesaler in deepest Massachusetts. But to hail this transformation as unprecedented is to do our mustachioed ancestors a disservice—an act of wanton disrespect made only more unseemly when one considers that they were born and lived and went to their graves without ever once waking up on a birthday morning, scraping the ice off their laptops, and receiving salutations from a distant land in the form of an abysmal, not-quite-functioning cartoon of chickens—one year it was elephants—either attempting, or pretending, to dance.

For shame.

The New Yorker

FINALIST—FEATURE
WRITING

What led a doted-on gifted child to commit suicide? By standing back and enabling the protagonists to do much of the talking, Eric Konigsberg tells the complex story of a seemingly inexplicable tragedy without exploitation or sensationalism.

Eric Konigsberg

Prairie Fire

Last May, Patti and Martin Bremmer promised each other that they would get through the second Sunday of the month without mentioning that it was Mother's Day. Brandenn, their son, had committed suicide in March, at the age of fourteen, and Patti was intent on treating the day like any other. To the Bremmers, who live on a farm in western Nebraska, in the village of Venango (population 165), and who have earned money over the years by raising organic grain and by breeding dogs, this meant getting up at five-thirty to feed the animals and pitch tumbleweed—the very chores, they could not help but be reminded, that Brandenn used to do.

"We're having a real hard time right now, because we didn't have any routines that didn't involve Brandenn," Martin said. It was a little before noon, and they were sitting down to eat. Their dining room has lavender walls and a large picture window overlooking the front porch. In the distance, they could see a cluster of outbuildings on their property: an old horse barn, a bunkhouse, a washhouse (where Martin's ancestors made soap and did their laundry), a kennel building, and a quonset hut they had long ago converted into a storage shed for grain and tractors. Patti had prepared a freshly killed chicken, baked potatoes, and a salad with red-orange Dorothy Lynch dressing. For dessert, there was a store-bought cherry pie. With Brandenn gone, she didn't have the energy for baking.

Their son had killed himself with a single shot to the head from a .22-calibre rifle. It was his own varmint gun, which he'd been using on intrusive skunks since he was ten years old. He had been shooting since he was six, an early age at which to become acquainted with a firearm, but almost from the time of his birth the Bremmers had known that he was exceptionally precocious. "He was born an adult, basically," Patti said. "He chose when he would wean himself. I wanted to nurse for a full year, but at eleven months he crawled into the kitchen and motioned for a cup." Though Brandenn didn't talk until fifteen months, Patti said, "he started right off speaking in complete sentences." He potty-trained himself at eighteen months and memorized an entire book of "Mother Goose" nursery rhymes when he was two and a half. At the age of four, he drove a tractor that had a hand-controlled throttle and gearshift, and once, when he was eight, he sat on his father's lap and drove the family car home from town.

Brandenn was known as a child prodigy by almost everybody in this part of Nebraska. When he was a little boy, his I.Q. was scored at 178, and his parents decided to make sure that he was adequately engaged and challenged. They homeschooled him, and when he was six years old they enrolled him in high school through a distance-learning course at the University of Nebraska. He was ten when he finished, in 2001, the youngest graduate in the history of the program.

"We never pushed him," said Patti, whose own experience with higher education, like her husband's, went only as far as some commuter-college credits. "All of his motivation came from within. We never could explain why it was, but one day when he was nine and a half he just decided to finish up, and we didn't want to stand in his way. So he did the last two years' worth of classes in seven months, going at it twelve hours a day, six days a week."

Brandenn went on to take piano lessons through Colorado State University, in Fort Collins, two hundred and fifty miles away. In 2004, he recorded and released a CD of his own compositions, New Age–style washes of chords and arpeggios, entitled *Elements.* In January 2005, he enrolled in an introductory biology class at Mid-Plains Community College, in North Platte, Nebraska, the first step on an intended path to medical school. He was planning to become an anesthesiologist.

Brandenn was handsome and gangly, with blue eyes and curly auburn hair that in the final year of his life he had allowed to grow past his shoulders. He liked the musician Yanni, medieval history, making jewelry, baking cheesecake, lifting weights, playing video games (especially SimCity, SimFarm, and the Command and Conquer series), and *Late Night with Conan O'Brien.* He was also interested in animals, gross-out humor, and science experiments that he devised at home.

Late in the afternoon on Mother's Day, Martin and Patti took me upstairs to Brandenn's bedroom. In opposite corners of the room, each of them curled up in the same position: arms around legs, knees to chin—a child's pose. Martin, who is tall and lean and sharp-featured, sat on the bed with his back against the wall. Patti-small and fair-skinned, with a Friesian mane of hair—was on the floor. For a while after the suicide, Martin stopped by Brandenn's room almost every day. "Now I don't come up," he said. His eyes were filled with tears.

Brandenn and his father had remodelled the room in a Middle Ages theme, gluing floor tiles resembling rough-cut stone to the walls and festooning them with brocaded tapestries. There were swords and shields that Brandenn had ordered from a theatrical-supply Web site, a carved chest full of his piano trophies, wrought-iron candle holders, figurines of dragons, colored crystals. Patti pointed out five perfume bottles that were for Brandenn's ashes; they were made of red glass and had pewter screw tops. "Brandenn always liked expensive," she said.

His suicide was a mystery to them. They had searched the house for clues, and found nothing. He had left no note, and they hadn't seen any warning signs. "Brandenn wasn't depressed," Patti said. "He was a happy, upbeat person. There weren't sudden changes in his behavior." Neither recalled him being particularly upset about anything in the preceding months. He hadn't suffered a break-up, or endured a personal rejection. He hadn't been giving away prized possessions. In fact, Patti said, he'd just added to what he called his "unfinished list": he was selling some old Nintendo games on eBay in order to buy a PlayStation 2 console. And they'd ruled out the possibility of an accident. "Brandenn knew way too much about guns for that," Martin said.

Patti led the way down to the basement so that we could watch videotapes of Brandenn on TV. "We didn't want him to feel like he had to hide his gifts," Patti explained. "But we were very careful to protect him from doing too much media." When he was four, he appeared on *Real Life*, a nationally syndicated show ("Meet the next Doogie Howser"). The segment depicted him adding four-digit numbers, and then, with another child prodigy, playing pool and fencing with a plastic sword.

"See? He was normal," Patti said. "He got along with everybody."

"It was almost like he was amphibious," Martin said. "He was good on water and he was good on land. Adults took to him and children took to him." Brandenn's personality seemed to invite such metaphors. "He was like a therapy dog at a nursing home, making people feel better just by being himself," Patti said. "He calmed a whole roomful of children as soon as he started playing the piano."

A segment on *Leeza* showed Brandenn at the age of five, wearing a thrift-store suit. The Bremmers had been flown to California for the taping. "Martin and Brandenn had never seen the ocean," Patti said. "The waves knocked Brandenn down and took his breath away."

Watching Brandenn on the tapes was difficult but enchanting. He had freckles and long, giraffe-like eyelashes, and when he opened his mouth he really did sound like a little man. He spoke fast and in complete sentences. He had strident elocution and charm-school intonation. We watched as, at the age of eight, he told a local reporter about his high-school correspondence work. "I thought it would be neat if I graduated from high school in the year 2000," he said with convincing modesty, "but if I don't—well, what the heck?"

"That was Brandenn's attitude," Martin said. "No pressure." Then he held his head in his hands. "The three of us ate and lived and worked together every single day," he said. "Each of us knew what the other two were feeling at all times. We would have known if something was wrong."

·　　·　　·

Martin's maternal forebears came to Nebraska from Illinois by covered wagon in the 1880s, and received free land from the government near Venango, in Perkins County, on the condition that they stay for five years. (About half of the people who came to Nebraska under the Homestead Act managed to stick it out.) The high plains of western Nebraska were particularly rough country, and, to hold on to what was theirs, Martin's ancestors survived a drought in 1892, a plague of grasshoppers in 1904, and a prairie fire in 1905. Eventually, the family prospered. The descendants in Martin's line still own some four hundred acres, half their original portion of the land.

Martin was born in 1966 and grew up in Denver, where his mother had moved as an adult. In junior high school, he was briefly placed in a pilot gifted program, but he didn't take to it or to the other children, and he was a C student through high school. He took classes in agronomy and business at a local college, but didn't get a degree. "I knew I wanted to be farming," he says. "I came to my grandparents' place for a summer and never went back."

He met Patti in 1989, when she asked him to audition for a bit part in a production of *Grease* that she was directing for a local community-theatre troupe. After two failed marriages, Patti was living with her daughters, aged eight and thirteen, in a small house on the Colorado border, next door to the dairy where Martin worked. "The first time I visited Martin's family's farm, this feeling came over me: I'm going to live here," Patti recalled. Six months later, she and Martin were married.

Like Martin, Patti was an expatriate from city life. She'd come to Perkins County from Omaha, three hundred miles to the east, a dozen years earlier, with her first husband, a horse trainer. Patti had been marked as gifted in elementary school, and was put on an accelerated schedule that allowed her to skip seventh grade (although she ended up repeating eighth grade). She attended a vocational college in Omaha, but dropped out and worked as an accountant. As a single mother, she had a business raising greyhounds and selling them to racetracks.

Martin's grandparents were happy to keep the land in the family, and sold him the house. Branden (he added the extra "n" on a computer when he was two years old) arrived within a year of Patti and Martin's marriage. His sisters' time at home did not coincide much with his childhood; both moved out and married young, and Brandenn later said that in many ways he felt like an only child.

"He was definitely the focus of my mom's attention," said Patti's younger daughter, Dawn, who dropped out of high school after ninth grade, homeschooled herself, earned her diploma, and now lives in California with her three children. "When she puts her attention to a project, she expects it to get her noticed. She's always working on a masterpiece."

In the past few years, Patti has tried her hand at writing mysteries, and set up a vanity press to publish four of them. She says that she decided early on not to seek a commercial publisher. "I don't want an editor telling me how to change what I write," she told me. "I don't follow all the conventions of mystery writing." Once, when she was thinking about turning one of her books into a screenplay, she asked a friend's advice. "He told me, 'You've got too many characters, and you don't have enough action at first.' Well, I *like* to let it build slowly." Patti also likes having control over the books' covers, which feature photographs by Brandenn or, more recently, Martin, who then does the layout on his computer. In 2004, for the cover of her third novel, *Death Foreshadowed*, Martin took a picture of Brandenn outside on a foggy morning, dressed as the Grim Reaper, with a hooded cloak and a scythe.

.   .   .

Even before Brandenn was born, Patti had definite ideas about her child. She and Martin knew that this was the one child they would have together—he had a vasectomy as soon as she gave birth—and Patti wanted a boy. She consulted the book *How to Choose the Sex of Your Baby*, which says that intercourse within twelve hours of ovulation is more likely to result in a male. "So we timed it," she recalled. As a baby, Brandenn was colicky and in constant need of stimulation. When books and pictures were held in front of him, he looked as if he were already reading or comprehending them. When he wasn't being challenged or engaged, he squalled.

One day when Brandenn was eighteen months old, the Bremmers say, he clamored vigorously for his mother's attention while she was doing some bookkeeping. Brandenn had been playing with a set of magnetized plastic letters, and she absent-mindedly tried to keep him occupied by telling him to bring her an "A." When she looked up, a few moments later, Brandenn was holding up the letter "A." When she asked for a "B," he retrieved a "B." And on he went through nearly the entire alphabet.

"I ran outside and told Martin," Patti said. "Martin wanted to see. So Brandenn did it again."

At the age of two, the Bremmers say, Brandenn read aloud all the Dr. Seuss books they could order from a book club. "It gave me goose bumps," Martin said. "His muscles were still working to verbalize the words, but he knew all of them, and what they meant. He never had to sound them out." By the time Brandenn was three, he had read everything in the curriculum for first-grade students at the public school in Grant, a nearby town, so his parents asked the kindergarten teacher to enroll him a year early. The teacher told them that this was a bad idea. "She said, 'Just take everything away from him and slow him down,'" Patti recalled. "She wanted us to let the other kids his age catch up to him for a couple of years."

Patti and Martin were outraged, but Brandenn was perfectly happy to spend his days around his parents. "The kids were so below him intellectually that he had no desire to be with them," Patti said. "The teacher was giving them paper cups with seeds in them to teach science." Brandenn's sister Jennifer says, "He preferred adults." He once told his mother that he wouldn't mind going to school if the teachers were there and all the kids stayed home. If the Bremmers had another family over for dinner, he insisted on sitting at the adults' table. "It was almost a phobia he had about doing things associated with children," Patti said. He comported himself as if he were a grownup, clipping on a necktie to leave the house and telling women at the grocery store, "Excuse me, Madam, but you're looking exceptionally lovely today."

In November, 1994, just before Brandenn turned four, the Bremmers drove to Denver to meet with Linda Silverman, a psychologist with a practice devoted almost entirely to gifted children and their families. They'd got her name from Brandenn's pediatrician. On the parent questionnaire that Patti had filled out in advance, she described their son as "very strong willed" and "exhausting." She also wrote, "He questions authority on a regular basis and is quick to pick up on how serious the situation is and how far he can push. He doesn't like to be asked questions. He often responds with 'Why don't I ask you a question?'"

He was given an I.Q. test consisting of verbal, mathematical, and pictorial questions and problem sets that began at a level deemed answerable by a typical child slightly older than Brandenn. Each correct response increased his "mental age" score, and was followed by a more difficult question. Since Brandenn was three years and eleven months, his mental age went up by one month for each correct answer to questions appropriate for children aged between four and five. For every correctly answered question aimed at children between six and eight years old, he received two months' credit.

Brandenn's orneriness made a precise I.Q. score difficult to ascertain. He scoffed at age-appropriate questions (when a tester asked him what eyes were for, he said, "To bug out"), and tried to leave the room whenever he didn't know the answer to a question. Although Brandenn, according to the evaluation form, grew "bored" and refused to answer enough questions for the tester to complete the assessment, he got as far as answering questions at the level of a nine-year-old. Using a scale that compares a child's mental age with his chronological age, Silverman's office recorded Brandenn's I.Q. as 146.

At Silverman's recommendation, the Bremmers had Brandenn retested a year later. This time, although his attitude toward the test-taking was playful—he answered math questions in Spanish, which he'd been learning from a computer program—his I.Q. was scored at 178.

The scale that Silverman used on Brandenn classifies people who score between 130 and 144 as "moderately gifted" (the range for average intelligence is from 85 to 115), those who score between 145 and 159 as "highly gifted," between 160 and 174 as "exceptionally gifted," and above 174 as "profoundly gifted." The probability of someone's having an I.Q. above 176, according to standard I.Q.-distribution theory, is roughly one in a million, which means that at any given time there ought to be fewer than three hundred people in the United States with an I.Q. as high as Brandenn's.

.   .   .

Since 1979, Silverman's testing facility and practice, the Gifted Development Center, has given nine hundred and eleven children I.Q. scores of 160 or above, including sixty-four in the 200s. Unless almost every young genius in the country is coming through her office, then, she is recording a far higher incidence of profoundly gifted children than the statistical distribution of I.Q. results should allow. The particular I.Q. test that Silverman, almost alone among her peers, relies on may have something to do with this. Although she begins each assessment with one of the more widely employed I.Q. tests, when a child scores extremely high Silverman goes to the Stanford-Binet Intelligence Scale, Form L-M.

The Stanford-Binet was first developed in 1916, and enjoyed the status of the most widely accepted I.Q. test through three iterations, up to and including the Form L-M. The Form L-M (after the first names of its authors, Lewis Terman and Maud Merrill) came out in 1960, was updated in 1972, and then was replaced in 1986, by the Stanford-Binet Intelligence Scale, Fourth Edition. The update was never well liked by psychometricians, and several more recently developed tests, such as the Stanford-Binet Fifth Edition and the current Woodcock-Johnson exam, are considered more comprehensive and reliable. Silverman uses the Form L-M because it's the only version that officially calculates scores above 160. "There's nothing else to use with kids this gifted," she told me. But some critics of the test say that it not only assesses higher scores; it tends to produce them. "The Form L-M uses children from several decades ago as its comparison group, so of course the scores are going to skew much higher if it's used on today's kids—every generation of children is more academically and environmentally advanced than the previous generation," Susan Assouline, the associate dean of the gifted-education program at the University of Iowa, said. "It's not a useful test in this day and age."

Modern-day I.Q. tests were designed primarily to assess learning difficulties—to find the children in a typical classroom who might be lagging behind and in need of remedial attention. "These tests are most reliable at scoring average children or determining whether a child falls somewhere outside of average, but they're not intended to assess various levels of extreme giftedness," Sidney Moon, a gifted-psychology expert at Purdue, said. And a number of Silverman's colleagues say that there's no practical reason for an I.Q. test to measure high levels of intelligence. "Many of us who are lifers in the field agree that there are the gifted, and then there are the rare few who are really superstars among the stars," said Tracy Cross, a professor of gifted studies at Ball State University, in Indiana, and the editor of the *Journal for the Education of the Gifted*. "It's hard to argue that those superstars don't exist." But, Cross said, "I don't believe there's much difference between a person with an I.Q. of 160 and one with 170, or 180."

Silverman disagrees strenuously. When I visited her at her house, an A-frame high in the hills above Golden, Colorado, she bristled at her peers' lack of interest in these distinctions—and at the standard public-school practice of placing exceptionally and profoundly gifted children in classes designed for merely advanced students. She described an effort, in the nineties, to eliminate gifted programs in public schools as "a form of discrimination that makes me think of Nazi Germany."

Silverman is a slight woman in her sixties, with dark, stiff hair set in a grandmotherly pouf, and a manner of severe, white-knuckled resolve. She and her husband, Hilton, have reared two children of their own and have taken care of sixteen foster children. Their house was decorated with Jewish- and Christian-themed art, and dozens of photographs of gifted children. "The gifted are my passion," she said, noting that her own children "didn't come out technically gifted."

Even her adversaries in the field of gifted education say that they have yet to encounter a more ardent advocate for children than Silverman, and speak of her intimate and youthful manner around prodigies and their parents. But there was nothing about her that seemed the slightest bit playful, except perhaps the leopard-print blouse and costume jewelry she wore. When a telephone call came and went unanswered, and the woman on the other end introduced herself to the answering machine, Silverman cautioned Hilton not to pick it up, explaining to me that it was one of their foster children. "She's trying to sell us insurance," she said.

Silverman arrived in Boulder in 1972, after receiving a Ph.D. in educational psychology and special education from the University of Southern California, and taught at the University of Colorado. When her contract was not renewed after the first year, her family struggled for a time (they briefly went on food stamps). Meanwhile, she independently pursued her interest in gifted children, and her husband opened a day-care center in their house and a group home for wayward or abused kids. Over the years, she has published numerous books, including a widely used textbook, *Counselling the Gifted and Talented*, and she was a research consultant for the Stanford-Binet Fifth Edition. Though she has held college teaching posts since she left the University of Colorado, her work, unlike that of most of her gifted-education colleagues, isn't funded by a university.

Her reputation was damaged in 2001, after an eight-year-old boy whose I.Q. she had scored at "298-plus" (she said that he was "way beyond genius" and "probably unique in the world") threatened suicide and was later found to have been heavily coached on the Stanford-Binet test by his mother, who had obtained a copy in advance. The *Rocky Mountain News* revealed that Silverman had allowed the boy to take the test while sitting on his mother's lap, because he had an auditory-processing problem that sometimes made it difficult to understand his answers if his mother wasn't there to translate. Silverman appeared to be heavily invested in her appraisal of the boy's genius; he and his mother moved to Colorado from New York State, and she secured sponsors for them—they had been living in subsidized housing—and helped him enroll at a school for the gifted near Boulder. Even after his mother admitted that she had also forged his S.A.T. scores (800 math, 650 verbal), Silverman continued to insist that he was a prodigy: "Just memorizing the hardest I.Q. test would take an I.Q. of around 200!" she wrote in an e-mail to an acquaintance.

Silverman felt that the boy suffered from a culture that treats extremely bright children as freaks—that he was pressured not to achieve but to be average. "You would have appreciation for the difficulty for the parents of a seventeen-year-old trapped with a nine-year-old's mind," she told me. "But what about a seventeen-year-old trapped in a nine-year-old's body?" It can make for a miserable childhood, she said. "These are the children who are often told by educators and even parents that they're too much—too driven, too perfectionist. It's the gifted kids who are beaten up in school. It's not safe to be gifted."

·   ·   ·

After a second meeting with Silverman, Patti and Martin gave some thought to moving to the Denver area, which had eight or ten very strong gifted schools and programs, and where Brandenn had grandparents and cousins. But Silverman encouraged them to homeschool their son. They were initially skeptical. "We had always considered homeschooling something for religious freaks, and both of us were hard-core anti–organized religion," Martin said. "But Dr. Silverman told us that, even in the gifted programs, out of twenty kids maybe three would be able to keep up with Brandenn."

"All of these schools have had mixed success up in Brandenn's range," Silverman told me. "Their programs are aimed at the 130-ish kids—that's three standard deviations from him." On an I.Q. distribution chart, she counted three standard deviations down from 100, the average I.Q., and landed at 55. "Putting Brandenn with them would be like putting an average kid in school with the 55-I.Q. kids. A kid who has an I.Q. of 55, do you know how developmentally delayed that kid is?"

Besides, moving to Denver would have meant giving up the farm in Venango. "Martin's family had had the land for generations," Silverman, who once spent a weekend at the Bremmers' house, told me. "They had an idyllic lifestyle and the most beautiful family relationship. Brandenn had trees to climb and animals to be around. It meant so much to his parents that he was on that farm."

When Brandenn was four, his parents started him on the Perkins County elementary-school coursework, and within two years he'd finished the fourth-grade curriculum. Their routine varied from day to day. Typically, Brandenn was in charge. "We'd say, 'O.K., it's nine o'clock. What do you want to learn about?'" Patti recalled. "If he was passionate about reading that month, we'd do that. If he said, 'I want to learn about a dairy,' we talked about how cows work, making milk, all that. His goldfish died one day, so we dissected the fish under the microscope."

"It was kind of like the Biosphere Project," Martin said. "He had everything he needed: a greenhouse, books, land. It was like the ultimate school. He got to see birth, death, to see seasons in their entirety."

Along the way, the Bremmers became advocates for other parents in their situation. When they had started out, the state of Nebraska allowed homeschooling only on the ground of "sincerely held religious beliefs," but they persuaded a state senator to get a bill passed that broadened the exemption. They also started a charitable organization that raised and disbursed money to help needy parents of gifted children pay for tutors and tuition. For their part, the Bremmers realized that they were spending thousands of dollars a year on school materials that were typically free, and because Brandenn was absorbing information so rapidly anyway they decided to save money by skipping grades five through eight and going straight to the high-school curriculum. "Dr. Silverman said he was ready; we just had to follow his lead," Patti said. "She told us he was having every stage of a normal childhood—he just did it faster. He'd done the terrible twos in a few weeks."

The high-school correspondence program run by the University of Nebraska was designed for children who live far from the nearest school. Although it has a self-paced format that makes it a popular option for parents of gifted children, the program is more commonly used as a supplemental measure—for those who, according to a school catalogue, "find themselves short a few credits close to graduation" and still want to graduate on time, as well as for N.C.A.A. aspirants looking to boost their grade-point averages and students who want to take courses that may not be offered in small rural high schools.

There was no homework and few papers to write. Exams were administered in town and monitored by a neighbor who was registered with the program as a proctor. At first, the Bremmers limited Brandenn to two classes per year. "We were dragging it out, because we didn't know what else to do when he got through it all," Martin said. Eventually, Brandenn went on his tear. His transcript for the final two months looked like this:

4.03.2001: Personal Finance, B+
4.04.2001: World Geography 1, A

4.04.2001: Multicult Literature, B
4.10.2001: Small Engine Repair, B+
4.10.2001: Career Planning, A
4.19.2001: General Math 2, B+
4.19.2001: World Geography 2, A
5.15.2001: American Government, B+
5.18.2001: Ninth Grade English 1, B
5.19.2001: First Year Spanish, A
5.29.2001: American History 1, A
5.31.2001: American History 2, A
5.31.2001: Health Sciences 1, A
5.31.2001: Ninth Grade English 2, B+

He took only one year of a foreign language and no advanced math, and had his fair share of gut classes—nutrition, career planning, personal finance, and driver ed (which he completed when he was nine years old). And it was strange that Brandenn, who intended to go to college, followed the curriculum that, according to the catalogue, was recommended for "students whose immediate after-graduation plans include vocation or technical school, a job, or other noncollege situation."

Still, Silverman assured the Bremmers that what he studied was irrelevant. "He was so smart he didn't need to follow anybody's curriculum," Silverman told me. "It didn't even matter if he read books or not. He could already read at an adult level at the age of six." When it came time for college, she said, he would be able to adapt.

As Brandenn was finishing his last round of courses, Patti and Martin asked him if there was anything he wanted to do to celebrate. They offered to have a set of "senior pictures" taken, and Brandenn was delighted. He was photographed in a coat and tie, and then in a Harry Potter costume. He'd always liked the idea of graduating in a traditional cap-and-gown ceremony, so he persuaded the principal of the program to hold one, for the first time in the program's history. Only five other kids, all of them seventeen or eighteen years old, took part, out of a hundred and ninety students in Brandenn's class. (Among the qualifying graduates was Britney Spears, though she has no connection to the state of Nebraska.) Local news reporters were invited to film Brandenn at the event. From a lectern he could scarcely see over, he gave a very brief address—a stock commencement speech that he had found on the Internet, he said—and then ran through the auditorium playing tag with his nieces and nephews.

For the next three years, Brandenn focused on the piano. With his parents' encouragement, he traveled across Nebraska for Lions' Club competitions—"He always took first place," Martin said—and put out his first CD. ("All music on this CD is original and composed by Brandenn Bremmer," the album cover says. "Produced by Brandenn Bremmer: Age—13.")

Beverly Dismukes, a kindly woman in North Platte who taught Brandenn music theory and gave him piano lessons for two years, said that, despite what his parents thought, she didn't consider him one of her musical prodigies. "But you could play something once, and he would play it back to you—that's unusual," she said. "He was gifted in that he could do that." On a "fact sheet" that Patti and Martin had printed and distributed to the media, they listed, along with Brandenn's high-school grade-point average of 3.8, the items "His music has made it to Japan"; "Writes a song sometimes in less than an hour"; and "He holds all of his music in his head, never writes it out."

"He was what they call globally gifted: intellectually, physically, emotionally, musically," Martin said. "Mozart had his mathematicality going, and Brandenn's talent was more on the emotional, spiritual side of the music." He said he had always assumed that when Brandenn was in his twenties and thirties someone might "write a little biographical book and look back at when he was fourteen and see that this was when he was learning the groundwork for what was going to make him famous in music."

      •   •   •

Every corner of the Bremmers' house reveals the extent to which their lives were built on his: a microphone dangling from the ceiling of the den, which served as his recording studio; a life-size plastic skeleton, for the study of anatomy, in the dining room; a grand piano on which Patti and Martin still have another year and a half of payments to make. For a time, Martin kept above his computer a black-and-white photograph of a smooth-faced woman in a Mission rocker, her hair pinned up in a Willa Cather bun. The woman, Leta Stetter Hollingworth, is known to many today as the godmother of gifted education: she was a founder of the first public school for the gifted, in New York City, and, while on the faculty at Columbia's Teachers College, she started the world's first long-term study of the extraordinarily gifted. Hollingworth became particularly interested in children with an I.Q. above 180, and from 1916 until her death, in 1939, she found only twelve of them. In a landmark, posthumously published work, *Children Above 180 IQ (Stanford-Binet): Origin and Development*, she presented case studies of these children, vast accumulations of detail pertaining to family histories ("A's great-grandfather . . . a tailor, devised and patented a union suit, said to have been the first union suit"), head circumferences, grip measurements, and prepubescent doodles.

Hollingworth's enduring legacy stems from the emphasis that she placed on understanding the social and emotional difficulties endemic to extreme giftedness. By studying peer relationships among children of differing levels of giftedness, she came to define the I.Q. range of 125 to 155 as socially "optimal," because those children were most likely to be outgoing and confident—not so smart that they couldn't win over their peers.

But children with an I.Q. above 170, she said, were so unlikely to find mates of like ability that they were demoralized. "To have the intelligence of an adult and the emotions of a child combined in a childish body is to encounter certain difficulties," she wrote.

Her findings about this profoundly gifted minority contradicted the work of the Stanford psychologist Lewis Terman, her contemporary, who, in his famous longitudinal study tracking some fifteen hundred high-I.Q. children, asserted that his subjects were as socially well adjusted as anyone else, and that as adults they tended to be more emotionally stable than average. Hollingworth brought her personal history to the issue as well. She had grown up, like Brandenn Bremmer a century later, on a pioneer farmstead in the westernmost part of Nebraska, and she spent most of her childhood in self-imposed solitude. According to her biographer, Ann G. Klein, the ten-year-old Leta, beset by a string of family tragedies, willed herself to become an adult overnight. As Hollingworth later described the moment in a letter to her future husband, "I decided to grow up then and there, solemnly renouncing the rest of childhood."

Hollingworth's work fell into obscurity after her death, and was rediscovered only decades later. In 1980, a seventeen-year-old prodigy named Dallas Egbert III committed suicide. Egbert was from Dayton, Ohio, and had entered college at fifteen. "Before his death, almost nobody had thought to look at the social or emotional components for these kids," Elizabeth Meckstroth, who is now a consultant for families of gifted children, told me. The next year, she was moved to help start a support group for parents of gifted children, and later she wrote, with James Webb and Stephanie Tolan, *Guiding the Gifted Child*. "The National Association for Gifted Children conference until then had been all about finding tutoring, improving the math curriculum at schools, and so on," she said. "But Dallas Egbert's suicide was a call to arms."

Many articles have been published during the past two decades on the subject of suicide among gifted children, and, although there is no good evidence for it, some people think that their rate of suicide may be higher than average. Among the factors cited, besides the risks of social and intellectual isolation, are the attendant pressures of perfectionism (described by one psychologist as "an emotional need to develop themselves and master the world") and the possibility that the gifted have heightened sensitivity: even if they treat success and failure as equals, they take them both hard.

"The way these kids' minds work has to do with more than just being quick and right," said Meckstroth, who got to know the Bremmers over the years at various functions for gifted children and their families. "It's an ability to make connections between all kinds of things and sense meaning in the abstract: everything matters to them." If an average child's mind is like a pair of rabbit ears that picks up four basic TV channels, Meckstroth said, the minds of profoundly gifted children are like satellite dishes, receiving hundreds of signals at once. "It can be overwhelming," she said. "An ordinary four-year-old might dig a hole in the ground for the pleasure of digging the hole. And one of these children might be digging and thinking of all the animals he'll encounter underground, and the children in China he could help."

Linda Silverman believes that there is a higher incidence of a compassionate streak among gifted children, and told me of several ten-year-old peace activists she has encountered. "A lot of gifted kids are angels who are on this earth with responsibilities to help others," she said. "There's no other way to explain it."

.   .   .

Between homeschooling and the self-containment of a rural existence that didn't involve much dependence on, or obligation to, fellow-townspeople, Brandenn was seldom in the company of children his age. A major exception was the week or two each year that he and his parents spent at retreats and conferences for the highly gifted. The first gathering they went to, when Brandenn was eight, was the Davidson Institute's inaugural Young Scholars program, at Lake Tahoe. The program was filled with activities, like a public-speaking workshop, in which participants designed advertisements, and a class for future archeologists, in which participants dissected owl pellets.

"Brandenn and I became good friends right away," a boy from Long Island who met him at the Lake Tahoe retreat said. "I think we both figured anybody who'd been willing to go this far was willing to make the best of it. The whole thing was fun—a group of kids like me, you know? Although I had some friends back home who were pretty bright, this was different. Everybody was just very engaged."

The boy, who has asked that I call him Duncan, was about Brandenn's age, and the two stayed in touch over the years. When I met him this summer, at his home, he told me that he was helping a physics professor in a study of fluid dynamics and organizing a Wiffle-ball league with his friends. He and Brandenn shared a goofy sense of humor. In the summer of 2004, he visited Brandenn, and they made a short documentary film about Venango. It began with a shot of the single block that constitutes downtown, and then the camera rested on a street sign that said, "Slow Children," as Duncan walked in front of it and, in slow motion, pretended to trip and fall. They filmed a vending machine outside the laundromat and made note of the bullet holes in its coin-operating mechanism. "We can safely say that this vending machine is past its prime," Duncan said. "Let us have a moment of silence for this vending machine." Then Duncan lowered his head, and Brandenn, who was holding the video camera, followed, tilting the lens down and filming his own feet.

Patti and Martin drove Brandenn to Denver that summer for a four-day retreat hosted by the Gifted Development Center, Linda Silverman's organization. Brandenn hit it off immediately with K., a pretty girl from the West Coast. They were together constantly that week, K. said, and added that she and Brandenn weren't quite boyfriend and girlfriend, though she wasn't sure how to characterize the relationship. "What would you call someone who makes you a ring and a necklace on Valentine's Day, and a bracelet on your birthday?" she asked. "And the person who, when you decide to make him a scarf for Christmas, you spend three hours picking out the wool?"

In Denver, Brandenn, Duncan, K., and a few other kids spent most of the time together in their hotel, watching movies on TV (*Groundhog Day*, *Spaceballs*) and sitting around talking. "The thing about being gifted is the way you can be totally consumed by passionate interests," said K., who, at fourteen, is enrolled full time as a college student, plays three musical instruments, competes on a high-school gymnastics team, and cantors at her synagogue. "Lots of normal thirteen- and fourteen-year-olds find us off-putting. By 'normal,' I mean kids who are basically able to move from school to hobbies to their social lives, from subject to subject, without having to get obsessed about things. So for four days it was nice to pretend we were normal teen-agers."

K. described Brandenn as "a true gentleman." One night, there was a dinner dance to celebrate the twenty-fifth anniversary of the Gifted Development Center, and Brandenn performed "Spirit's Dream," a piano piece that he'd named for Silverman's Doberman pinscher. Later that night, he asked K. to dance, but she told him that she would have to take a rain check. She found Brandenn formidable, she recalled, which made her nervous around him: "He wasn't just a musician—he was a performer." A few days later, as the kids prepared to depart, they made plans to stay in touch and reconvene at the next summer's retreat. K. helped Brandenn carry his bags to his parents' car and told him, "You owe me a dance."

Patti and Martin enjoyed meeting other parents on the summer gifted circuit—who often refer to themselves as POGOs, for "parents of gifted off-spring"—but say that a high I.Q. was the only thing that Brandenn had in common with many of the kids. "A lot of them were the stereotypical gifted kids, with emotional deficiencies, manipulating their parents like a trainer would be leading a horse," Martin told me. "Some of the kids had real frailties—they wouldn't let different foods on a plate touch each other. One kid had a rat tail hanging down his back-hair that was ten years old. He said to cut it would be like cutting off a part of him." It frustrated Brandenn to be around kids like these, Martin recalled. "Brandenn wasn't a geek, he wasn't overweight, he wasn't pimply-faced."

"Which is why his suicide rocked their world," Patti said. "Many of these kids across the country are in counseling now because of Brandenn." She smiled a wistful smile. I thought Patti was referring to K., but when I mentioned her the Bremmers were dismissive.

"All the girls were madly in love with him," Patti said. "They were all planning to marry him. None of them knew about each other."

His parents were in no hurry for Brandenn to start dating. "I went all the way through high school without doing the girlfriend thing," Martin said. "The temporary girlfriend—what a waste of time."

Even though the Bremmers seemed to want to protect Brandenn from an immature adolescence, their description of the kind of mate and marriage he hoped to find someday sounded a lot like a young boy's idea of adulthood.

"He wanted someone who would share his interest in computer games and in music," Martin said. "Someone who liked to cook, who was good with raising kids, who wasn't dependent on him to make decisions for her. He wanted a house in Lincoln and one in Omaha for medical school"—the two cities are only forty-five minutes apart. "He wanted to trade in his old Ford Escort for a stylish new car. And then he would pursue a relationship." When he met the right girl, he would buy her an engagement ring that should probably, he figured, cost three hundred thousand dollars, because that was what he'd heard doctors earned in a year.

•   •   •

In the fall of 2004, Brandenn settled back into his routine at home, which included a piano tutorial he'd been taking for a year with David Wohl, a member of the music department at Colorado State. When Brandenn first performed for Wohl, he played a New Age piece he had written—"a lot of pedal, a lot of floating textures," Wohl told me. "It's like water music, basically. It doesn't require tremendous technique. I said, 'I'll take you on, but you're going to learn how to read music and you are going to learn the "Moonlight" Sonata and Bach.'" In return, Wohl taught Brandenn how to improvise more thoughtfully, manipulating harmony and using different chord spacings. Brandenn abruptly terminated his lessons in December, although he continued to compose and work in his music studio on his own. "It was odd," Wohl recalled. "I thought, Why stop now, just as he's getting into it? He'd been making a lot of progress, especially toward the end." Brandenn explained to Wohl that he was quitting lessons because he wanted to become a doctor, and after the holidays he was going to begin taking premed classes. "I guess I'm not going to make a career in music," he said.

"He had it all stepped out," Patti recalled. Brandenn planned to start with a couple of classes at Mid-Plains Community College, in North Platte, ninety miles from Venango. When he turned fifteen, he would get the rest of his premeds out of the way at the University of Nebraska in Lincoln, where his oldest sister, Jennifer, is a surgical nurse. When he turned sixteen, he would start medical school.

"He liked the challenge and he liked the income," Martin said, referring to Brandenn's talk of becoming an anesthesiologist. "I think he also liked the idea of not having to see patients all day long. He didn't want to be dealing with a lot of hypochondriacs coming in."

"He wanted to ease people's pain," Patti said.

He began in January, with an introductory college biology course. "He was a quiet boy who seemed at ease for the most part," his instructor, Sara Morris, told me. "The other students didn't know how young he was. One time during lunch break, his parents came and brought him a sandwich. Sometimes he ate in the cafeteria with the other kids."

There were a lot of new academic challenges. "He was kind of feeling his way along," Morris said. "I'd assigned a term paper on natural history. I knew from talking to him that he'd never done anything like that, and of course he had to learn how to do the citations. And he was nervous. We talked about doing some typing of his notes and how that might help him. It was an adjustment for him, but he was going to do just fine."

Brandenn spoke frequently on the phone with Duncan. "His biology course—he said he wasn't trying all that hard at it," Duncan recalled. "He just was never excited about it. He said, 'Basically, O.K., there's this living stuff and we call it organisms.' He found it incredibly abstract." It wasn't such a big deal to be disenchanted with a class, Duncan understood, but he was surprised to hear Brandenn sounding so listless. "He always went with such rapid fire at stuff he liked. But, with the bio, he was kind of detached from it."

At the time of his suicide, Brandenn had been graded on only a single exam, the course midterm. "It was either a B-minus or a C-plus, I can't remember," Patti said. "But it was scaled, so he was carrying a high B. He wasn't happy with it. But he always finished all his classes super. He sometimes got a C on a test in high school, and he'd always bring it up. It was like burning a piece of toast: 'I'll just put in another one.'"

• • •

Brandenn's sister Dawn didn't come home for Christmas in 2004, but she called from California. He was making cookies, he told her, and he was bored.

"Well, that sucks," Dawn said.

"Yeah, it does," Brandenn said.

Dawn wasn't speaking to Patti at the time. "My mom and I have fought my whole life," she told me. "I was the complicated sibling. I moved out when I was young." As Dawn saw it, her mother and Martin had created a life for their family that cut them off from the rest of the world. "They liked being that isolated, that whole all-we-need-is-each-other thing," she said. "I always called it Bremmer Island."

Brandenn talked with K. in intermittent bursts through the fall and winter. "There was probably a month when he called me every night," she said. "It always sounded like he was hiding, going outside the house to make calls, or only calling when his parents weren't there. He'd say, 'Oh, I gotta go—my mom's home from the grocery store.'"

He told her that he hoped to move to New York for medical school. "I want to go to school where there are people," he said. They talked about how much they missed each other, and began counting the days until Silverman's summer retreat in Denver. "He said he wanted to be there, but his parents might have something else for him this year," she said.

K.'s mother wrote Patti an e-mail in December. "I said our kids have created this nice relationship, albeit long distance," she recalled. "I just wanted to let her know how much Brandenn meant to my daughter. Patti wrote back that Brandenn had mentioned her, but his private world was all his own. She said she wasn't sure he was going to go to the POGO retreat, because of summer school."

Something else was going to change for Brandenn. Because the commute to the Mid-Plains campus was so long, Patti and Martin had made arrangements for Brandenn to start boarding in North Platte during the week, at the home of a Venango neighbor's grandmother. "He wasn't worried about being lonely, because he was happy with himself," Patti said. "He didn't need to have someone around all the time. He thought about it for a couple of days and then he said, 'No, I want to make the move.' We let him know he didn't have to. We kept telling him he could stay home and wait until he was in his twenties."

Over the holidays, K. received a text message from Brandenn. His mother had taken him to the library in Ogallala, where she was signing copies of her latest novel, *Victim Wanted*, and at the moment he had little interest in being there. "Save me," he wrote, and later, in an e-mail, "IT'S HER FAULT I WAS BORED OUT OF MY MIND." He had complained in the fall that Patti had put him up to delivering a speech to a group of children at the library, and wrote, "I'm still kind of mad at my mom, since I wasn't asked for my opinion on doing this thing at all, it was just a 'Hey Brandenn, your going to give a talk at the end of the month to a bunch of kids.'" Still, he had said he wasn't that upset: "It was alright, and we ate at a Subway that day, so hey you can't go wrong with that (I'm a healthy eater so Subway is my favorite place to eat out). So yeah, I'm content with my life right now."

K. wrote to ask how Brandenn's Christmas had been. She said that she and her parents had spent the day at the movies. A couple of hours later, Brandenn responded that, aside from watching *Shrek 2*, the Bremmers had done "nothing, as a family anyway." He explained in another e-mail, "Yeah, that's kind of what it's like here, I mean, we're a close family. . . . we just don't spend much. . . . time. . . . being. . . . that. . . . way. . . . Yeah."

In the middle of their exchange, a gift for Brandenn arrived in the Bremmers' mailbox. It was the scarf that K. had knitted, in marled gray alpaca, with suede fringes. He wrote to thank her:

> Your timing couldn't have been better, for the past week or so I've been depressed beyond all reason, so this was just what I needed, thank you very much.

She wrote back:

> Now, what's this about you being depressed all week? Talk to me, I want to hear about it. Because trust me, I've been there, done that and all I got was this lame t-shirt. ;) Just let me know okay? I want to help if I can, and it's really important to me that you're happy and all that jazz.

Brandenn replied:

> Thanks . . . I'm glad there's someone who cares. I don't know why I'm so depressed, before it was just every now and then, and you know, it was just "bummed out" depressed. But now it's constant and it's just, "What's the point of living anymore?" I don't know, maybe I just don't spend enough time around good friends like you. But like I can. Not out there in the middle of nowhere. At least there's this family kind of near by that aren't "Cowboys," or else just plain idiots, that I can spend time with. But even still, that's only like once every other week at the most. Oh well. Well I should probably go, thanks for being such a good friend.

Brandenn phoned K. that night. "He just said he was feeling down about everything," she recalled. "What teenager doesn't go through unhappiness, you know? I told him to talk to his parents. He said, 'Yeah, I'll think about it,' but he never mentioned them again." The two of them fell out of correspondence for a while, "not for any good reason," K. said. "We were both probably just too busy." On Sunday night, March 13, Brandenn called her to say hello, but she was out.

Two days later, on March 15, Brandenn finished recording a second CD of piano music, which he planned to call *Dimensions*. He listened to it with his parents at around noon, then went upstairs to sew up a hole in one of his favorite shirts. Martin came up to discuss Brandenn's design for the CD cover; it was an Escher-like tableau of three-dimensional geometric shapes assembled in a desert before a reflecting pool. A bit later, Patti and Martin drove to the town of Grant, thirty minutes away, to run errands. They stopped first at the public library to pick up a stack of unsold copies of Patti's novel, and then bought groceries.

At five-forty-five, when they pulled up to the house, Patti heard what sounded like choking noises coming from inside. She ran upstairs to Brandenn's room and saw his body crumpled on the floor. He had shot himself in the head. He was unconscious but breathing shallowly. She screamed for Martin.

"I knew right away what had happened," Martin said. "Seeing him like that was like stepping into a room and none of your five senses work. It was like seeing the snow falling upward."

Martin carried Brandenn in his arms to the car, called 911, and began driving him toward town until they were met by an ambulance. The hospital doctors in Grant tried unsuccessfully to revive Brandenn, and told them that he was not going to make it. A hospital employee asked the Bremmers whether they were willing to allow their son's vital organs to be harvested. They immediately said yes. Back in December, when Brandenn turned fourteen and obtained a rural student's driving permit, he had checked off the organ-donor box. The subject came up at supper that night, and Brandenn had told his parents that he was all for it.

While a helicopter airlifted Brandenn's body from Grant to Children's Hospital, in Denver, Patti and Martin drove through the night in order to get there. A neurologist performed a CT scan and a radiograph and rushed Brandenn to the I.C.U., again in vain. Martin cut a lock of his son's hair to save, and gently removed the stud earring that Brandenn wore. He got his own ear pierced right away, so that he could wear the earring himself.

The harvesting of Brandenn's organs took place over the next two and a half days. Despite extensive damage to his brain, the rest of his body was functioning. "They used everything—organs, veins, arteries," Patti said. "The hospital said his epidermal tissues will help fifty people. They said they were fortunate to get a body in such good shape."

·　　·　　·

The next afternoon, Patti sent an e-mail to more than seventy people, including friends, family, reporters, and POGOS:

> The latest from the hospital a few minutes ago was that Brandenn's kidneys were a "Perfect Match" there were only 6 perfect matches in the US and the chances of those 6 getting kidneys were almost impossible. Once again Brandenn did the impossible. His liver went to a 22 month old baby that would have . . . died within days without it. His heart is now beating in the chest of an 11 year old boy who was down to hours. He was flown to Children's as a last ditch effort in a holding pattern counting the minutes for someone in the United States to find a match. His heart was on a man-made machine to keep him alive until they could find a donor. . . . Brandenn was in the next operating room they thought what are the chances and he was a perfect match . . . .

I am trembling and crying as I write this but I want to share with you and the rest of the world that knows him.

The Bremmers had no health insurance, and to pay the local hospital and ambulance bills they sold the CDs that Brandenn had recorded and the Bernese-mountain-dog puppies he'd raised. After the suicide sank in, Patti says, she became taken with the idea that perhaps he'd actually killed himself so that his organs could be put to use in those who needed them.

"Brandenn was so spiritually aware that if he sensed that people needed his help he would have helped," she told me once.

"So you're saying he had the ability to sense that people needed something from him and that's why he did what he did?" Martin put in, elaborating on the thought.

"Yes," Patti said. "I'm ambivalent about Christianity, but a lot of people have said he reminded them of Jesus. You know: 'He came, he taught, he left.'"

Patti told me that she thought Brandenn might have been an "Indigo Child," a concept that she learned about after his death, and that was described in a book by the New Age authors Lee Carroll and Jan Tober. *The Indigo Children: The New Kids Have Arrived* includes essays by psychologists and doctors, and suggests that a new breed of children born in recent decades possess not only great cognitive ability but supernatural insight. While these children are often misdiagnosed as having attention-deficit or hyperactivity disorder, they may actually be old souls reincarnated. Linda Silverman told Patti she believed that Brandenn was spiritually gifted, and that his mission to assist others in this lifetime may have been fulfilled by his death.

The idea that gifted children have supernatural abilities has gained some currency in the past few years. They have some origin in observation: intelligent children often pick up what's going on around them so well that they're able to intuit others' emotions; they can be extremely aware of themselves and their environment. "It's not so much of a leap to see that if all kids sense their mother or father's bad mood, a more intelligent kid can sense his mother's bad mood with less data," Sal Mendaglio, a psychologist and professor at the University of Calgary, told me. "And a child who sees more is more likely to experience anxiety himself when his mother is anxious. So that child's ability for greater empathy, his interest in doing altruistic things, then, is not so mysterious, either." Some people like to interpret this behavior, Mendaglio explained, as evidence of psychic ability or a divine mission.

"It wouldn't surprise me, the way he was, if he was so connected that he knew his organs were needed," Silverman told me. "There was always something otherworldly about Brandenn. He had a kind of ancient wisdom that was beyond anybody I'd ever seen."

During one of my visits to Silverman's house, just after she invited me to stay for lunch, she said, "Patti and Martin had contacts with him after he'd left his body. There was none for forty-eight hours. Martin cried the entire time. But then they both felt a sense of peacefulness. And he took the memory away from them of finding him." In effect, she said, Brandenn was healing his parents.

"With a suicide, especially of a child, the assumption we make in this society is that somebody is to blame for it," she went on. "I was extremely undone the night I found out that Brandenn had been lost. You couldn't help but examine the possibility of something going wrong. I asked him for guidance, because I could have missed something." And when she woke up the next morning, she said, "I had this overwhelming sense of peace, and just the feeling that he'd gone home."

Hilton Silverman, who had been in the kitchen, brought a platter of Reuben sandwiches to the table. Hilton has a gray beard, a wrestler's posture, and a heavily lined forehead. He wore fleece pants, a zippered skiing turtleneck, and flip-flops with socks.

"Well, I can tell you what the spirits are saying," he said. "He was an angel."

Silverman turned to face me. "I'm not sure how much you know about my husband. Hilton is a psychic and a healer. He has cured people of cancer."

"It kind of runs in my family: my grandfather was a kabbalist rabbi in Brooklyn, and my father used to heal sick babies with kosher salt," Hilton said. "Brandenn was an angel who came down to experience the physical realm for a short period of time."

I asked Hilton how he knew this. He paused, and for a moment I wondered if he was pulling my leg and trying to think up something even more outlandish to say next. "I'm talking to him right now," he said. "He's become a teacher. He says right now he's actually being taught how to help these people who experience suicides for much messier reasons. Before Brandenn was born, this was planned. And he did it the way he did so that others would have use for his body. Everything worked out in the end."

"I'll tell you who else is an angel," Linda Silverman said. "I think Martin's an angel."

"Oh, Martin, for sure," Hilton said. "He has a positive spiritual alignment. He and Brandenn meet a lot when he's asleep."

Linda looked at me helpfully. "You see, we don't know how to explain these kids—not scientifically."

"Scientifically!" Hilton scoffed.

.　　　.　　　.

Silverman seemed to hold fast to her interpretation of events, even after she saw the unhappy e-mail messages that Brandenn had written. She doubted they were representative, and suspected that they'd been taken out of context, or even manipulated.

At first, K. struggled to make sense of the e-mails. She worried that perhaps she ought to have prevented Brandenn's suicide. "I think I'm cycling through all stages of grief at once," she told her parents. They brought her to Vancouver to see a psychologist, and had her talk on the phone with another. K.'s mother shared the e-mails with Duncan and his family, and—through a coincidence of mutual acquaintanceship in Dawn's home town—ended up sharing them with Dawn, too.

All of them found something like relief in the e-mails. At the very least, the suicide appeared now to be something they had the vocabulary to understand. Brandenn hadn't been under a strange influence that told him he'd be doing something good for others by killing himself; it didn't seem that there was some awful secret behind his death. His friends and his sister agreed that he had probably felt alone or sad or frustrated or some combination of those things, and was momentarily helpless to find a way out. And, unfortunately, he had been in a position to act on a suicidal impulse. Perhaps if the gun hadn't been in his room just then, he wouldn't have gone through with it.

When Dawn tried to discuss the e-mails with her mother, she says, Patti dismissed them immediately, saying, "'Depressed' is a word we use all the time around here. It's just a figure of speech. It meant he was having a bad day." K.'s mother, she added, "is probably just into doom and gloom."

Patti told me that she thought it was K. who might have been unhappy. "Maybe Brandenn wanted her to feel better, so he wrote that he was miserable, too," she said. "That was Brandenn: if one of his sisters was struggling in school and said, 'I'm so dumb,' he'd say, 'Well, I'm *really* dumb.' He never sent any e-mails like that to anyone else."

Brandenn's sisters doubted that if he was feeling low he would ever have shared it with his parents. "He wasn't the sort of kid who'd have ever complained to us," Jennifer said. Dawn said, "I still feel a lot of guilt, like I should have done something to help—talk to him or let him know that life gets better when you're older. I'm sure my mom and Martin feel guilty, too. But with Brandenn it really would have been hard to see it coming."

.   .   .

One afternoon when I was with the Bremmers, the sky darkened over their front porch. It had been hot and dry for weeks, and finally a severe thunderstorm was rolling in from central Kansas. "We used to watch how Brandenn walked from the sidewalk to his biology class," Patti said. "In the past year, he became such a graceful young man."

"He glided," Martin told me earlier. "Until then, he walked like any other kid does, like Shaggy from *Scooby-Doo*, you know? Like he has no bones in his body." Patti had added, "Oh, and he had a six-pack. His stomach was rock hard. I'd punch his stomach and make a joke about how it hurt my hand."

On the porch, Martin took off his glasses and wiped them with his undershirt. "It's hard to convince yourself right now that we were good parents," he said. He felt embarrassed that, all these years, he and Patti had offered their services as advisers to parents of gifted children. "What right did I have to tell them how to raise their kid if this is my track record? I thought I had it all figured out, and then he kills himself. Now I think I must be a total failure as a person, because the one thing I devoted my life to was raising Brandenn."

"We did everything right," Patti said, wrapping her arms around her husband.

Martin said, "I see moms who smoked all through gestation, or moms who yell at their kids at the grocery store, and I look at the kids and they're just so beaten down. Then I think, Why is that family getting by?"

It started raining, gently for perhaps a minute, and then hard and fast. The Bremmers' Bernese mountain dogs—two mothers and a litter of new puppies—scampered from their pen into the kennel, a converted milk barn. When Brandenn was thirteen and taking time off from music class, Patti recalled, Martin had taught him construction. They'd gutted the barn, put in insulation and sheeting, and reinforced the walls with two-by-sixes. Over a single weekend, Brandenn learned woodworking and how to pour concrete, and he put up most of the aluminum siding himself.

This memory brought to mind a horticulture project that Brandenn had done when he was eight, in which he developed a sprinkling method—one that actually worked in their yard. "It's too windy here, and our pool sprinkler sprayed so hard it wasted a lot of seeds," Martin said. Brandenn found a misting hose and kept it going lightly twenty-four hours a day. The land remained soaked, even on ninety-five-degree days, and the grass seed finally took. "He changed all the rules," Martin said. "It was the first year we had a real lawn.

The Georgia Review

WINNER—ESSAYS

A Brooklyn man rescues a box of papers from his landlady's home after she dies. Inside he finds her late husband's letters, drawings, and other scraps, from which he pieces together a stunning portrait of the man's desires, dreams, and disappointments. We all die twice, author Michael Donahue says, first in body and second when no one remains alive who knew us. In this extraordinary essay, two ordinary people come heartbreakingly back to life.

Michael Donohue

Russell and Mary

1.

A few years ago, as sometimes happens to young people paying cheap rent in Brooklyn, I found myself suddenly driven from my apartment and furiously looking for a new one. This was February 2000, and rents were rising fast. After two weeks of panicked searching, I nearly settled in the windowless attic of an antique store on Atlantic Avenue, under the care of a ponytailed landlord who wanted me to address him as "Captain Dennis."

Luck intervened. Out of the blue, a place found *me*: a bright one-bedroom floor-through apartment in Park Slope, priced at $950 a month—about two-thirds its market value. Even better, there was no credit check and no realtor's fee. The landlady, a ninety-year-old widow who lived on the house's first two floors, didn't even know my last name until she saw it on the lease.

Of the two apartments that Mary rented out—on the third and fourth floors of her maroon brick row house—one was occupied by Ben Seigle, a history teacher who was then a colleague of mine. He's the one who saved me from Captain Dennis. When he introduced me to my prospective landlady one Saturday afternoon, she came waddling out of her ground-level door like an ill-tempered duck, well under five feet tall and weighing perhaps eighty pounds. A yellow pallor glazed her teeth and cheeks, and she wore a droopy, tattered housedress. With eyes made huge by the lenses of her horn-rimmed glasses, she looked me up and down forbiddingly until Ben finally informed her, "This is the man I told you about, Mary. For the apartment?" She motioned us to come inside.

Dogs were barking. Paint was peeling. A pungent blend of odors hung in the air: unwashed dog, stagnant broccoli water, scorched marinara. We walked down a dim hallway. Flypapers dangled from the ceiling. At the kitchen, Mary stopped in her tracks and stared all around the room. We halted behind her.

"Where'd they go?" she shouted. "*Where'd* they *go*?"

She lifted her hands in frustration. "We're right behind you," I offered.

She turned around, looked at me sternly, and said, "Well—sit down."

We signed a two-year lease.

2.

Seventeen months later, on a Wednesday morning in late August 2001, a few minutes after nine o'clock, I looked out the window of my third-floor apartment and saw that a moving truck had pulled up in front of Mary's house.

I was the building's last surviving resident: Ben had moved to Chicago, and Mary was four months dead. The men spilling out of the enormous truck and horsing around on the sidewalk had no interest in me. They'd come because Mary had died without a single living relative, and now her things—her lifetime's collection—had to be taken to a government-owned warehouse downtown.

The man in charge of the operation, a heavyset official from the Public Administrator's Office, which deals with Brooklyn's uninherited property, explained to me that this would be the first of two rounds. Today they were taking only "the nice stuff," the pieces that could be sold at auction: appliances, mirrors, chairs, and other things that family members, had they existed, might have wanted.

Two hours later, when most of those pieces had been loaded into the truck, the official said I could go back through Mary's two floors and take any books that I liked, since they would only be thrown away. So I found myself in her living room, rummaging through boxes and kicked-over lamps. Scattered throughout the debris were dozens of books which, it would turn out, belonged not to Mary but to her husband, Russell, who had died many years before.

I was skimming through titles like *A History of Sacerdotal Celibacy* and *Sex Today in Wedded Life* when I came across a large cardboard box stuffed with litter. Its original contents had been a microwave oven, as shown in the faded color photograph along the side, but now the box held newspapers, envelopes, and some pamphlets. At the top there was a stack of yellowed newspaper clippings, mainly from the 1950s, and I dipped into them. The first headline I saw read,

SLAYS PARTNER OF 30 YEARS, AND THEN HE KILLS HIMSELF

and was followed by these:

POURS BENZINE ON SELF, LIGHTS IT, DIES OF BURNS
LEAPS OFF SPAN AS 2 FRIENDS WATCH IN CAR
DAD SENDS BOY ON ERRAND, SHOOTS WIFE AND HIMSELF
EXEC'S SOCIALITE WIFE PLUNGES TO HER DEATH
SLASHES WIFE, KILLS SELF WITH BREAD KNIFE
WIPES OUT HIS FAMILY OF 4 WITH A BOY SCOUT HATCHET

The box held about a hundred of these articles, all neatly scissored out of newspapers.

Beneath the clippings I found a pile of personal letters, all signed by or addressed to Russell. Buried even farther down in the box was a piece of white cardboard with a cartoon sketched on it in colored pencil. The cartoon showed a woman bending over, her buttocks bulky and tinted pink, her labia sagging, as a man with a superfluously large penis penetrated her. "Keep fuckin' it," read the caption. "Hard. Faster. Way up in me. I'm gonna go right now. Oh, you sweet fuckin' son of a bitch."

"Hey," somebody said behind me. It was one of the moving men. My heart rate tripled. I shoved the cartoon back into the box.

The man passed through, and I stood there in a room full of trash, unsure of what to do. Here, in one microwave box, was the collection of a dead man's papers—not only pornography, suicide notices, and personal letters, but legal documents, poems, to-do lists, dream narratives, journal entries, published articles, whole and fragmented manuscripts, original drawings, photographs, hotel receipts, and magazine clippings.

I could have ignored it—left it alone, to be carried out later and stuffed into a dumpster. But that seemed like a brutal choice, given the care with which the collection had been compiled. So when no one was looking I bearhugged the box and lumbered up the stairs to my apartment. The movers left around one o'clock, and I spent the rest of the afternoon sitting on my living room floor, organizing Russell's mementos into piles, beginning the long process of piecing together the story of his life.

3.

When I moved into the building, in March 2000, I learned within days why the rent was so low. To get to my apartment, I had to pass through Mary's space, and despite her slowness she often managed to be standing there in the hallway, by the stairwell, to greet me with a long and unintelligible tirade. Or I would hear her shout from another room, "Who's there?"—as though it were an awful surprise to find somebody else on the premises. "Hi, Mary,"

I would call out as benignly as I could. "Oh," she would say slowly and quietly as she finally reached the hallway and saw that I was merely her tenant, not a killer. Whether it was three in the afternoon or ten at night, the conversation would end with her saying kindly, and too loudly, "OK, good luck! Have a good night!"

Then there was the matter of the smell. As the weather turned warm that spring, the unpleasant odor that I had noticed from the very beginning took a terrifying turn for the worse. It seemed that Mary was losing control of her dogs, and the dogs were losing control of themselves. Turds cropped up near the staircase. Puddles of urine oozed their way under the radiator in the corridor. My friends were repulsed as they entered the building; some refused to come inside.

At night, in the long silences before falling asleep, I could hear every now and then all of the house's stray noises coming up the stairwell. Mary's television was sometimes turned up too loud. She would scold her dogs. They would bark endlessly. A door would bang shut, again and again. Her microwave would signal its finished job with a ding.

4.

One of the things I learned early on, while going through Mary and Russell's stuff, was that he had died late in 1965—a date I gleaned from a condolence letter Mary had stuck inside a French dictionary. Since the microwave oven didn't become a common household appliance until the late seventies, well after Russell's death, it might well have been Mary rather than Russell who put those contents in that box.

It took a long time to get through Russell's pornographic cartoons. There were dozens of them, they were skillfully drawn, and they had a certain perverse appeal: the women with their reddened, oversized nipples and their bright smiles said things that, for all their lasciviousness, often sounded as if they had been written by someone who was disarmingly naive: "I'm not kiddin', I want to be fucked!" and "Oh, brother, I've got some lovely things to suck—want to try 'em?" and "Oh you big-peckered son of a bitch—Oh it feels good—fuck—fuck—fuck me forever—wear my piss-hole out."

Some, though, were genuinely disturbing—for example, the father-daughter scenes. These showed tiny girls in pigtails handling huge paternal penises, letting out remarks like, "When will I have big-woman orgasms, Poppa?" The father-daughter combo was common throughout the stash; in the rarer mother-son drawings, the boy was always a scrawny eight- or nine-year-old, the mother a voluptuous redhead, and a typical exchange had the boy proposing, "I'll do the best I can for you, Momma," and the mother assuring him, "You always do, Son."

Contrasting with these drawings was Russell's more "mainstream" work—the majority of the cartoons in the box—in which he focused on radically more acceptable themes such as Faith, Peace, and Temperance. A typical cartoon, titled "Where It Rests," showed a large planet Earth sitting on a book. Russell labeled the globe THE FATE OF OUR WORLD, and the foundation it rests on DYNAMIC, INTELLIGENT, CHRISTIAN FAITH.

5.

Mary's decline was swift. By the autumn of 2000, her life had been taken over by a nonprofit guardian agency. Apparently a neighbor had reported her to the city as someone who had lost control of her own affairs, and a judge appointed the official caretaker. (I worried that one of the pieces of evidence given for her senility had been the outrageously low rent she was charging Ben and me.) The agency took control of her money and provided her with a daytime home attendant.

Late one night in March 2001, almost a year after I'd moved into the building, a sharp new smell entered the air. It was gas, and thinking there might be a leak, I called KeySpan. Two enormous uniformed men showed up and ordered me to lead them downstairs. In the kitchen we found Mary awake—at one in the morning—standing and staring at a roaring television. A stove burner was turned on, flameless, shooting gas into the room. Her dogs were going bonkers, barking maniacally, and I had to shout over them, "Mary, you left your burner on!"—to which she cried out joyously, "That's my dog!"

She was unable to string together a single sentence. I felt for her, but I was also furious: this one senile gaffe could have blown up the building. Three nights later, smelling gas again, I stormed downstairs and found *another* burner turned on without a flame. This time ten seconds passed before she knew I was standing in the same room.

It was the only time I ever raised my voice with her: "If you do this again, we could die, Mary. We could die! Do you understand what I'm saying to you? *Do you understand?*"

She said, "OK. Good luck. Have a good night."

6.

"One of the first things I learned to do at school was masturbation," Russell wrote. "They showed me just how to do it. At Williams one day we all played with ourselves. I went home with Mahlon Kaiser and that's what we did before we slept. The intricacies were discussed and the ways it felt best." I found these words in Russell's seven-page memoir about his childhood in Indiana—an unfinished, lightly annotated typescript that was well preserved in the box. Here I learned that Russell was born in 1901 and that at a young age he wanted to leave the family farm to make a career as an artist. "I could draw better than most kids of my age," he wrote, "and probably was told often 'You ought to be an artist.' I had such important things to do that I had no time to waste on the farm."

Mostly the memoir consisted of small, childlike impressions full of non sequiturs and with a special keenness for the sexual:

> Someone told of a man they knew who had a penis about a foot long, or more. I tried to make mine so near that as possible. The first time sperm came I was frightened and thought I was diseased or something. I was in a wagon at the time waiting for dad.
>
> I didn't like Jake White. He did the most unreasonable things with his penis. One day I finally got mad enough at him to keep hitting him. The rabbit whose leg I tore off, I was sorry about this and worried for some time.
>
> Once with one or two other boys at Potter's Bridge I smoked part of a cigar. It made me sick and I was afraid I was going to die.

7.

Three weeks after the gas scare, on a Saturday morning in April 2001, I woke to the sound of the downstairs buzzer. Somebody outside was crying Mary's name. When I got down to the stoop, the weekend home attendant—a middle-aged Caribbean woman—greeted me with a desperate shout. I let her in, and when we went down to the first floor we found Mary at the foot of her bed, crumpled up and unable to move. She could only answer our questions with groans.

There was no telling how long she'd been lying there—she could have fallen anytime after five o'clock the previous day, when Friday's home attendant had left the house.

We grabbed an arm apiece and lifted Mary onto the bed; she was heavier than I expected. Later that day, she was taken to Methodist Hospital with a fractured leg. She would never see the house again.

8.

Looking back at his days on the farm, Russell thought he could pinpoint the one moment—his single tragic mistake—that had ruined everything. It happened one Sunday afternoon in 1918.

He was seventeen, still in high school, and he had gone nosing through his uncle's private possessions. There, Russell later wrote, "I found a book on sex aimed at young men—a 'horror book' such as those written in the previous century, as this one probably was. I borrowed it, read part of it, and took it quite seriously. This brought on great conflict between religion and sex, which in turn produced a distressing symptom, great difficulty in getting my breath. It was also a frightening symptom, because when at its worst, it made me feel certain I was going to die."

For several months after the event in his uncle's room, Russell suffered from what we would now call panic attacks—harrowing moments when he literally believed he was on the verge of death. However, he didn't seek medical help (perhaps because he thought he'd have to come clean about reading the sex book), and since he was still in high school, his grades dropped off sharply.

Then, quite suddenly, the panic attacks stopped. There was no explanation. Russell thought he was cured.

9.

When Mary was taken to the hospital, the only ones affected in any serious way were her dogs: Sherry, the black poodle who sniffed legs; and Judy, my favorite, the long-eared golden spaniel, still a puppy. (Judy had replaced a dog—also named Judy—who had died the previous summer.) A guardian agency official informed me that I was now in charge of these animals.

What I found downstairs was authentically shocking. The dogs were starving, emaciated. Judy's ribs poked prominently out; Sherry, tied to the basement doorknob, stared at her paws and refused to get up from her soiled pallet. Dried excrement stuck to their backsides in clumps. That first night they devoured three cans of wet food in three minutes, then lapped hotly at my legs; Judy, in her excitement, stepped on her water bowl and sent it crashing into the radiator.

Once when Ben and I went down to feed the dogs (and clean the floor, which they never failed to desecrate with the most amazing quantities of turds), we saw that the kitchen had been ransacked. Sherry and Judy had gotten loose from their leashes and mauled a basket full of photographs, strewing them all over the floor. Cleaning it all up, we came across some eerie pictures of Mary as a young woman—dwarfish, broad faced, and never smiling.

A week after Mary went into the hospital, Ben and I walked over there to try to visit her. Just as we got to the room, we found a nurse preparing Mary to be moved for an X-ray, and the little inert body looked pitiful under the white blanket. She was barely conscious, but there was agony in her face, and as the nurse wheeled her out of the room, I saw through Mary's yellow teeth that her mouth, tongue, and throat were black.

On 3 May 2001, a Thursday, I went down to feed the dogs and found a note from the home attendant written on a piece of pink scrap paper.

"Hi Mike," it read. "Mary died this morning at 9:15."

10.

A couple of years after Russell's sex-book incident, in the summer of 1920, a chautauqua passed through his part of Indiana.

Named after the upstate New York lake upon whose shore the first such program began as a religious retreat in the 1870s, the chautauqua evolved into a traveling edification circus: rather than clown cars, merry-go-rounds, and bearded ladies, it offered religion and history lectures, art exhibits, and musical revues.

At the Indiana show Mr. Pitt Parker, a "chalk talker"—an entertainer who drew cartoons as he spoke—caught young Russell's eye. According to the *Indianapolis Times*—in an article written in 1934, when Russell was the paper's political cartoonist—he "got the 'bug' badly," and after graduating from high school he spent several academic years at Wittenberg College in Ohio (without ever getting his degree) and the summers as a "tent man" on the chautauqua circuit.

He was an artist now, a performer. This was his boyhood dream. With the rest of the chautauqua crew he roamed all over the country, and not once did the specter of those panic attacks appear—not even when his mother died early in the twenties. Russell had untangled himself from the farm.

When he went back to his home county, it wasn't to rejoin the family but to propose marriage. My landlady's predecessor was a pretty local girl named Helen, and Russell married her on 1 July 1928.

11.

A week after Mary's death, when I got home from work and went downstairs to feed the dogs, I found that they'd been taken away. The agency that had managed Mary's affairs now withdrew from the scene; their duty, they said, had only been to manage Mary's final days. Now the city would take over the property, because there were no relatives and no friends. The agency had paid for the burial with Mary's own money.

The fridge had not been opened for a month. The milk was solid as tofu and had to be flushed down the toilet, the potato salad was navy blue, and some pasta in a Tupperware container looked surprisingly edible. All got triple bagged.

12.

Russell had joined the *Indianapolis Times* in about 1931, starting out as the "lodge page editor" and rising quickly to the post of cartoonist. It was amazing good fortune. The only problem was that at about the same time his panic attacks began again.

In the peppy 1934 *Indianapolis Times* profile, Russell

> strides down the street each morning on his way to the *Times* office in deep reverie. He does his thinking while he's taking his morning constitutional and should some brazen passerby let loose with one of those piercing whistles to attract some friend, up comes his head with a jerk. He is almost a young Puritan, but his thoughts at that precious moment are far from Puritanical. For people who whistle on the street are his pet peeve—his only one, in fact.

> [Russell] at one time expected to become a minister, but instead, has drifted to the other extreme. He has become a newspaper cartoonist, and now he strives for effect in his cartoons on the Times' editorial page instead of driving home his point from the pulpit.

Also from this period was a letter written from Spelman College on the stationery of the NAACP journal the *Crisis*: the letter requested that Russell finish up a particular cartoon and then give the journal permission to run it; the signature on the letter was that of W. E. B. Du Bois.

Clearly, Russell and Helen never should have left Indiana. They seem to have been happy there. Russell was a local star whose opinions were being heard. Kiwanis and Rotary clubs asked him to speak at their luncheons.

But Russell was too ambitious to stay put. His idol Rollin Kirby, who in 1922 had won the first Pulitzer Prize given for editorial cartooning, drew for the *New York Post*; Russell must have figured that to hit it big, he would have to head east. He moved to Connecticut, alone at first, to put himself within striking distance of Manhattan. Helen remained temporarily in Indiana, and in July 1937 she got a postcard from her husband that noted, "One of my cartoons was carried in a Camden, NJ paper. Gotta go to NY tomorrow. We'll get there yet."

13.

At the end of June 2001, shortly after Mary's death, Ben moved to Chicago, leaving me alone in the house. There was still no indication of when anyone was going to step forward and do anything. No relatives arrived. No city officials either. I paid no rent. The place was mine. That summer, on vacation from teaching, I spent many afternoons in Mary's backyard—reading the paper, basking in the sun, and stretching my legs out among the weeds.

I dreamed of taking over the place—maybe a judge would just *sign over* the house to me, bowing to my rights as sole tenant; maybe I would retire from teaching and become a landlord, if not a full-fledged real estate mogul. Maybe I had become Mary and Russell's heir—by default.

In the end it was the gas company that ruined my little paradise. I went out of town for three weeks, and when I came back in early August there was a piece of paper posted to the front door, warning that gas service in the whole building was about to be cut off. The unpaid bill was for more than thirteen hundred dollars.

I called Mary's former guardian agency to alert them to the bill, and a person there told me to call the Public Administrator's Office of Kings County. Even now, it is a complete mystery to me why they had not told me to do this immediately after Mary's death—or why they had not done it themselves.

"Be sure you have the date of death," I was told. "They're really disorganized in that office."

14.

When Russell and Helen moved to Manhattan in 1938, life must have seemed full of promise. Russell's idol Kirby even wrote him a personal invitation to stop by the *Post* for advice. But one thing kept getting in the way: at any moment, without warning, Russell might lose his breath and be seized by the fear of death.

"I went from one doctor to another," Russell wrote of this time, "who did not understand the cause of my breathlessness. I experimented with eating very light meals five times a day, fletchering [that is, chewing his food very slowly], fasting, eliminating meat from my diet, drinking hot water, holding a hot water bottle on my stomach, and for months I wore an abdominal belt because one doctor said I had 'fallen stomach.'" He went to a chiropractor and an osteopath, tried deep breathing and exercise, and sought relief in cod liver oil, yeast, and a myriad of antacids. His condition only got worse.

Crippled by intermittent terror, he discovered that a young doctor lived in his building, and one night, in the midst of an especially hideous episode, with Helen weeping by his side, Russell summoned his neighbor and begged for help.

It came in the form of a grain-and-a-half capsule of Seconal—an extremely addictive barbiturate that in those days was sometimes prescribed to treat anxiety. When the drug kicked in, Russell was at last able to catch his breath; but he would take the drug every day for the next twenty-five years.

Near the end of his life, when he claimed to have put his addiction to rest, Russell wrote a memoir—seven pages in typescript, with extensive revisions in pen—titled "I Was a Barbiturate Addict." This explained to me why Russell's box had such a scant record of the early 1940s: during that time, he had gradually stopped cartooning and begun working in hotels—because hotels had resident physicians who could write Russell prescriptions. Seconal, it turned out, was even more harmful to his cartooning career than the panic attacks had been.

No evidence remains of what Helen did during Russell's unraveling. Somewhere, there must have been a pivotal moment, maybe a public breakdown. All I know is that in the spring of 1945, Russell landed in the Pilgrim psychiatric hospital in West Brentwood, Long Island.

15.

"That guardian agency does not have a very organized office," grumbled Mr. Hill, the Public Administrator investigator I reached on the phone. "They didn't give me the heads-up on this." He was cranky when I told him what had happened, and he audibly scoffed at any mention of the guardian agency. I had called the right place.

Mr. Hill and his partner, Mr. Sultan—both gray haired and mustachioed—first visited the house during a mid-August heat wave, waving their badges and taking Polaroids of all the rooms. They were amiable, brusque, fact-loving men who held clipboards and wrote things down with fat felt pens. Mr. Sultan took a Polaroid of me standing next to Mr. Hill.

I learned that in cases like this, when a property owner dies without heirs, Mr. Hill and Mr. Sultan show up and set things in order. They comb the premises, searching for anything that might help the government take over the estate—a will (if they're lucky), the traces of living relatives, keys to safety-deposit boxes, bank account numbers. Mr. Hill explained that he would make a full inventory of all the items in the house—except mine, of course; then everything would be cleared out and anything of value sold. Finally, the house itself would be auctioned off. "What about me?" I asked.

"You don't worry about you," said Mr. Hill, dad-like. "*You* have a lease—right? You are gonna be OK."

"Do you guys do this all day?"

"Yep," said Mr. Sultan proudly. "For all of Brooklyn."

16.

From the time span of Russell's stay at the mental institution, I found thirteen letters from him and eight from Helen, who remained in New York and visited him on Sundays. Helen's letters try to soothe and reassure her husband, while Russell's try to convince his wife that he is soothed and reassured. Helen refers to her visits—"I couldn't believe it when the nurse said it was time to leave"—and sometimes makes gentle jokes: "Yesterday I went to the doctor. He thinks I'll live—and I'm afraid so too." But her typical tone is serious: "Please don't worry or feel too alone out there. I can take care of things and I have the very best guidance."

Being separated strained their marriage. "I'm hoping we'll find some other way to live than we were before I came in here," Russell wrote her. "Can't we figure out a better way than we're doing now?" By the time of this letter, he had received (according to his own count) twelve shock treatments and was facing another eight before his time was up.

At last, Russell's tone gets frantic: "I certainly hope the treatment here gets me fixed up, partly because I want our status settled. I want you but if I don't get well I don't like the idea of being a burden to you any longer. Meanwhile I have more memories of your sweetness than you realize. The rest is—just life."

17.

Mr. Hill and Mr. Sultan pasted seals over the doors to Mary's second-floor rooms, but not over the door at the bottom of the stairs that led to her kitchen and bedroom. I was curious to see what they had done—and, to tell the truth, I was starting to feel that the house was my personal domain—so one Sunday afternoon in late August, I went down there to take a look.

Back in May, the dogs had done a decent job of wrecking the kitchen, chewing up papers and spreading photographs all over the floor. But that was paltry compared to what Hill and Sultan had done. The men had mutilated the place. The kitchen was carpeted wall-to-wall in speckled white paper, and boxes of knickknacks had been sprinkled on top. A barefoot person might not have escaped alive. Cracked-glass picture frames cast spider webs over smiling faces; they'd probably been knocked over when the mattress was hurled against the wall. I noticed a framed picture of young Queen Elizabeth II, resting on a Certificate of Appreciation dated 20 September 1994, from Feed America, thanking Mary for her assistance to "America's disaster victims and homeless." There, too, was her Claimant's Insurance Book from 1956, noting her departure from Gracette Lingerie on Madison Avenue and documenting her twenty years' experience as a seamstress. There was a booklet entitled *The Truth About Constipation* by Victor H. Lindlahr. Soiled rubber gloves, the calling card of the Public Administrator, were scattered about. A lone, massive fly flew desperately from room to room.

Mixed in with the rubber gloves and the ripped envelopes were dozens of photographs. One showed Mary, maybe thirty years old, posing with neatly folded hands in front of a brownstone stoop. She wore a fresh floral-print dress and a morose expression.

The photo that interested me the most was a small, black-and-white portrait of a man. Appearing to be in his sixties, he wore a dark suit and black-framed glasses. With a visage of almost poignant benevolence, he was holding up a stick with a parakeet perched on it. He was looking the parakeet straight in the eye, and smiling.

This was my first glimpse of Russell.

That photo was the only thing I removed from the wreck. The following Wednesday, the Public Administrator's moving men pulled up to the house for the first round of cleanup.

18.

Among the relics of Russell's hospital stay I also came across something of more prurient interest: a sheet of notebook paper covered on both sides in pencil-scrawl. At the top he had written, "Why should strict and uncompromising monogamy be socially useful? Why—if the wife agrees—should a husband not have intercourse with a widow or a divorced woman? Why should not a wife—if the husband consents—have intercourse with a husband who is unfortunate enough to have a crippled or hopelessly sick wife? What is the virtue in denying for denial's sake?"

Below this paragraph is a list of questions. "How serious were you when you mentioned it? What did you expect me to say?" "How would you feel if I did the same?" "What would you do if I got out in a month? You are not planning to quit. I would be willing that you go to him even on nights when I was out. I would not only not interfere. I would help wherever I could. Would you be willing that I do the same? And would you feel our marriage was over if I did?" At one point, he simply lists ten women's names—perhaps his preferred partners, should this arrangement be implemented.

Whichever path they chose, there was no doubt that the marriage deteriorated rapidly during and after his time in the hospital. Nothing in the box testified to how Russell got out, but there was clear evidence that by 1947, he was in Mexico, alone, still hooked on Seconal but hoping the warm weather might soothe his anxiety. Helen had stayed in New York, and Russell's father had died of a heart attack while feeding livestock, leaving his son $2,735.86—this according to a letter from Russell's brother on 1 March 1947. Russell did not return to Indiana for his father's funeral.

There's a poem in the folder that probably addresses Helen:

I gave you your chance at life, my love,
I gave you the best I knew,
And now that you've chosen the ancient groove,
There's nothing for me to do.
But I hoped for you—for I loved you much.
Now I know that it could not be.
With a chasm of centuries in between
You could not take the path with me.

Helen's last letter in the box went to Russell in Mexico and is dated 16 March 1947. Helen's old mollifying tone has vanished; she begins, "Gug! It's been a helluva long time since I got around to writing you. Missed me?" She's angry. She relays the advice of an accountant regarding Russell's tax situation: "Uncle Sam would let you alone as long as you felt Mexico was better." The letter ends: "It snowed here again last night. It's cold and sunny today. Some people would say it's a nice day. For me I'll take the snow and blow and rain. It's alive."

In a postscript, she mentions coolly, "Jim was in town one night last week. I had cocktails and dinner with him. We always laugh as though things were funny." And that's the end of Helen.

19.

Late in the afternoon of 18 September 2001, after getting home from work, I spent several hours watching a crew of men load a dumpster with the refuse of Mary's house—the second wave of cleanup. One of the mattresses still had a price tag on it, $79.50; an old man passing by stopped and thought about taking it. The woman in charge of the garbage operation—a wrinkled, chain-smoking blond—begged me to take some pots and pans.

Heading out that evening, around nine o'clock, I caught one of the workers peeing on the front of the house.

20.

In another of Russell's many unpublished memoirs, this one called "My Emotional Escape to Mexico," he says he went down south to recover from his shortness of breath—leaving out any mention of the barbiturate addiction, the ineffectual hospital stay, or the dissolving marriage. The memoir is a long-winded description of Mexico, with special emphasis on the citizens' sexual attitudes and practices.

The most bizarre piece of evidence from Russell's Mexican adventure is a document dated 24 September 1948 and marked "Requirements for Marriage License in Arkansas." It is an application for marriage between him, "age 47," and one Maria Luisa Contrera-Romo, of Nuevo Leon, "age 34." So it's possible, though hard to believe, that Mary was actually Russell's third wife. Poor Señorita Contrera-Romo did not turn up anywhere else in the microwave oven box.

21.

Finally, gutted of everything but me, the house was ready for auction. The next Saturday and Sunday, a soft-spoken court officer opened up the building, and about seventy sets of people had a look. They had learned about my house from an ad the Public Administrator had put in the newspaper.

Many were frightened by the urine-logged carpets, the sagging ceilings, and the comically unstable staircase. A few were probably turned off by my presence, since a tenant can slow down renovation. But for the most part the mood was convivial: people moved through Mary's empty rooms, flushed her toilets, ran her faucets, chuckled at her flypaper. They pointed out details in the fireplaces and ceilings; they argued with one another about the building's dimensions; they speculated on the place's value and on how much repair was needed.

I talked to dozens of people. Many were feeling me out, maybe to see if I was a reasonable tenant; my lease wouldn't run out until the following March, and whoever bought the house would be stuck with me until then. Neighbors came to see the inside for the first time. "What a tough cookie Mary was!" somebody said. "Look, she put the radiator right in front of the fireplace." "What's going to happen to *you*, Sweetie?"

It seemed that whenever I found myself alone in a room with one of these strangers, before long I was listening to a confession of the most personal information. One man, probably in his late sixties, told me about his childhood in Poland, his family's flight to Siberia during World War II, and his return home to find everything destroyed. Then he suddenly frowned, said "I never talk about this," and left.

A hardware store owner explained to me his new philosophy of life. "I'm starting over, Mike. I have a new woman, and a new life, and I think this house—this house is *it*."

22.

Mexico was a bust. When Russell returned to New York in 1949, he moved into the Hotel Chesterfield on West Forty-ninth Street, where the McGraw-Hill building now stands. His marriage finished, he briefly aspired to go abroad; I have a letter from the government of India's Ministry of Education, dated 19 July 1949, informing Russell that "it is regretted that there is at present no suitable post to be offered to you." (Mrs. Asghar, education officer, kindly tells him, "We are glad to know that you have a special interest in India.") Probably living off what was left of his small inheritance, he began to draw cartoons again, took a class on magazine writing at City College, and wrote "My Emotional Escape to Mexico."

A letter from a professor at the University of Chicago, written in May 1951, begins, "In answer to yours of the 25th, I think the most authentic statement on the chances of going insane is to be found in . . ."

23.

The morning of the auction I called in sick, then showed up early and took my seat in Room 319 of the Supreme Court building, that drab edifice on Cadman Plaza in downtown Brooklyn. I wasn't there to buy the house, of course; I was there to stay on top of things, to defend my interests, to know who my new landlords were at the very moment they assumed the role.

The courtroom was standard looking, except that instead of a judge up front there was a wide panel of clerks and accountants. About two hundred people trickled in and lined up to register for the neon-green cards that would let them bid on any of the nineteen lots for sale. I recognized many people from the open house, including a pair of siblings named Suzann and George, the bidders I liked the best; the hardware store owner; a tall guy with a baby; a couple of chipper newlyweds; and a duo of obese Hasidim in black suits.

The hardware store owner, eyes closed, was praying by the back wall, moving his lips visibly.

24.

The last verifiable artifact from Russell's pre-Mary era was a note-to-self scrawled on a sheet of lined paper—maybe a page torn from a diary. "I have nothing left," he wrote. "No job, no wife, no home, no friends, no education, no religion, no money. I don't even have clothes. . . . Today I have been worried, wondering whether the relatively good days will ever return. Will I ever be able to think again?"

The good days would return soon enough. Sometime in the winter or spring of 1952, Russell—fifty-one years old and broke—met a short, severe-looking forty-two-year-old seam-stress named Mary. She had grown up in Brooklyn and, accord-ing to the custom for unmarried Italian women, still lived with her parents. I don't know how the two first got acquainted, the microwave box providing no record of the event. But in June of that year Mary wrote Russell two letters that ended up in my hands. Her stationery was pink, her spelling erratic.

The first letter, written Sunday night, 15 June 1952, begins, "Darling: This is my first letter from me. This is a confession. You did not know how serious it was for me to be in love with you." She says that Russell is "7 or 8 miles away"—he must have found summer employment outside the city. "I'm willing to drop out of existence, + find myself in your arms next Sunday instead, giving you my love. I can easily give you my life, + you know it, will you ever find it out, you took me so innocently. *Please* don't run away from my life. I love you so much more now that you are away. Write as often as you can, + remember darling, I love you, I wor-ship you—I idolize you + you know it. I send many many kisses. Don't forget me darling." She signs off cryptically, "Enclosed you find my picture. You know the reason."

I don't know if he ever wrote her back—of about a hundred letters in the box, not a single one was from Russell to Mary.

25.

My house was first on the list to be sold, and the upset price, where bidding begins, was set at $500,000. The auctioneer, a middle-aged man in a sharp double-breasted suit, said, "Do we have five hundred?" and after a few seconds of hesitation, the first card went up—Suzann. Then the tall guy, the hardware store owner, the chipper newlyweds. Neon-green cards were popping up all over the room—*everybody* wanted Russell and Mary's house.

Bidding moved swiftly through the five hundred thousands and into the sixes, driven up by amateurs too eager to restrain themselves. You could spot the experienced bidders, because they entered the fray late and would only raise their cards when the house was almost in someone else's hands.

By the high sixes only three bidders remained—the tall guy, the Hasidic duo, and a stranger with a menacing real-estate-mogul expression. Naturally I rooted for the only amateur standing, but alas, he was done in by the menacing stranger's bid of $700,000. There was then a moment of quiet; the crowd glanced at the Hasidic duo, then at the menacing stranger, then back at the duo. With a second's hesitation that I suspect was only for dramatic effect, one of the Hasidic men bid five thousand more, and his rival crumbled.

"Sold!" cried the auctioneer.

26.

By October 1953 at the latest—the date of a congratulations card I found in the box—Russell and Mary were married, and by the following year they had moved into the Park Slope house.

These middle-aged newlyweds kept a distance from their neighbors: the ones who were still around in 2001 couldn't tell me much about either of them. In the twelve years of their marriage, Mary kept working as a seamstress, while her husband stayed home to draw cartoons, care for his pet parakeets, and write articles for tiny Christian publications. He did not, apparently, contribute to the purchase of the house.

In fact it isn't clear how Russell made a living during these years, if he did at all. He had, in the past, been a full-time cartoonist; now he was an armchair intellectual—an amateur psychologist, ornithologist, and poet. In the tranquil realm of his second-floor living room, he must have regularly perused his heavy tomes on abnormal sexuality and psychology. He wrote letters to public figures, including one to Jawaharlal Nehru of India congratulating him on "keeping the peace." He pitched articles to national magazines. He sent a letter suggesting ways to improve the shuttle bus service at Idlewild Airport. He wrote to prominent scholars asking them complicated questions, the renowned geographer Ellsworth Huntington of Yale University writing back to refer Russell to part 3 of his *Mainsprings of Civilization* and its explanation of climate's influence on North American robustness.

He also wrote verse:

> I strolled this afternoon beneath the old and rugged pine
> Where one sweet evening years ago I asked you to be mine
> I think I found the very spot where we were sitting then
> And ah but it was good to sit and reminisce again!

Meanwhile, Mary brought home the bacon. In 1951 Russell was a drug addict with no prospects; by 1954 Mary had transformed him into a drug addict with a spacious Park Slope house and no need to work. He had his books, his wife, his parakeets, and of course his pills.

Mary gave Russell shelter—which, unfortunately, leaves him open to cynical evaluations. He was a fairly desperate man when they met. Did he really fall in love with this homely old maid, or was it that he found himself conveniently in the arms of a woman with a house to share? (There was almost nothing in Russell's box to provide information on Mary's parents, but documents from Mary's destroyed kitchen showed that the house, purchased circa 1953, belonged only to people with Mary's maiden name.)

There's a love poem in the box which, in my kinder moments, I like to think is Russell writing to Mary. It's a first draft written messily in pencil.

> I lived a lifetime in one glorious week
> That lifetime started when I first kissed you
> And I had such love as all men seek

> How could such a fragile lovely
> little thing as you
> Become a lighthouse, strong and high
> to shed its beams
> Upon the turmoiled waters of my life?

After two illegible lines, the poem ends:

> I'd trade the rest of my life dear
> for one more night with you

It *could* be referring to Mary. There was no doubt, even to me, that
Mary had rescued Russell. But the poem's tone seems a little inappropriate for such a thoroughly attainable object of desire as Mary
must have been.

This mattered to me. I wanted Mary to be Russell's savior. He
may have been an awful poet, but I wanted him to be a good
man. I wanted him and Mary to have been happy. And how
could they not have been? Russell, who had recently been wandering the East Forties high on Seconal and dreaming of India,
and Mary, who had never lived apart from her parents and had
toiled as a seamstress for two decades without finding a
husband—they had found each other, they had joined together
in a life of shared solitude.

And, according to a poem written late in Russell's life—in
typescript, with corrections in red pencil—they had conceived a
child:

> It was dusk when we began our long journey homeward,
> And I noticed Mary leaned a little more
> On my arm than when we started from the village,
> And she walked a little slower than before.
>
> As the years go by we both are growing older,
> And I know we haven't very long to stay.

Then we'll tread the path that Bobbie took before us
And we'll meet him in some other world some day.

And I think perhaps the Lord will let us have him
As our little boy, our little man again.
And we'll have him with us there again forever,
In a land devoid of sorrow, tears, and pain.

Mawkish lines, I know, but they made me put aside my suspicions and my cynical conclusions. They made me ready to believe in Russell and Mary's marriage, in their persistent, childless, weary love. He had washed up, nearly drowned, on her shores, and she had been there, as he said, like a lighthouse, shedding her beams on him. Bad metaphor, maybe, but this was still a love story—though Russell spoiled the mood by vandalizing his poem. At the top he angrily scrawled BAD, and then at the bottom under the last line, AMATEURISH, in red pencil. Whether he was disavowing the poem's form or its meaning, I will of course never know.

The box had not a single other trace of Bobbie, Russell and Mary's "little man."

27.

I imagine it this way: When Russell died in 1965, Mary discovered the collection of relics from his first life, the one she was never part of. She found that in the place where Russell kept his precious possessions, much more space was reserved for Helen than for herself. She found that in his free time her husband was drawing cartoons depicting grown men having sex with children and that all along he had been watching the suicides of the world with a fascination that bordered on envy. No wonder she was a mean old woman.

"Mary was a terrible bitch—forgive me, I know she's dead, but it's true," said an elderly man named Tom, who lived a few doors down and who approached me once as I sat on the stoop of the house during the Public Administrator's cleanup. "Mary's husband was a very nice man," he went on. "He kept birds in the house." But Mary was mean. She screamed at tenants. She harassed passersby. She never cooperated with the block association. "Look here," he said, pointing to the thirty-foot-high tree in front of the house. "She didn't even want this tree to be planted. She screamed and screamed when we planted it!"

One time, he recalled, when one of Mary's tenants needed some plumbing repairs and Tom volunteered to look at the problem, she saw him in the house and shrieked, "Get the hell out! I don't want no Greeks in this house!"

I said to Tom, "Well, isn't it still sad that her stuff is being carted out like this, and that she had no family or friends?"

"But you have to be good!" he shouted. "You have to be good in life! You can't be a bad person!" His face was turning red.

28.

When I got home from the auction, I looked at my desk. It was covered in Russell's stuff.

His porn was discreetly concealed in its folder; his letters were overflowing theirs. Photographs of him, with and without parakeets, lay scattered here and there—under a dictionary, leaning against my telephone. His books were stacked on my dresser: Theodor Reik's *Psychology of Sex Relations*, Wilhelm Stekel's two-volume *Impotence in the Male*, the unexpurgated *Lady Chatterley's Lover* with its forlorn midway bookmark. And I know it may sound odd, but for the first time during all of this, I felt embarrassed. These things didn't belong to me. They didn't even belong to Mary. They were the remains of someone I had never met—the secret registry of all his feelings, his ambitions, and his terrors. Did anyone else, anywhere, know about these things? It felt unseemly—it was unjust—for me to know things about Russell that no one else had known.

I had begun to let myself believe that when I'd finished studying all the scraps of paper, I would *know* Russell. I had started to believe my own theories about him, and he had taken form in my mind as a gentle, even meek man, talented and upright, but given to panic and eager to withdraw into a reclusive space where he cared for tropical birds and dabbled in perversion.

In truth, I knew nothing. Russell had died nine years before I was born. He could have been saving the suicide clippings for an article he was writing, could have been drawing pornography just to pay the bills. His love for Mary could have been totally free of financial motive. I could have had him all wrong. There's no way I *couldn't* have had him all wrong.

It was right then, as I surveyed Russell's stuff laid out on the desk, that I decided to go look through my own closet and drawers, my files and boxes. I had a chastening couple of hours, pretending to be some young man rummaging through my things in the 2070s. There were so many buffoonish photographs, inexplicable ticket stubs, letters girls wrote me when I was in high school. ("I love airplanes! Can you believe they really stay in the sky?") There were dozens of callow, petty poems, differing from Russell's only in their lack of rhyme. It was easy to laugh at Russell, with his cartoons and his strange ideas, but at the end of that laughter lay a grim realization: any life, examined this way, looks ludicrous. We put ourselves at the mercy of whoever survives us, and I hope I am luckier than Russell.

And yet, was he really unlucky? If I hadn't gone down there and stolen his stuff, it would have ended up in a dumpster—rained on, ripped up, or strewn in the street. Neighborhood kids might have made off with the sketches of naked women, but the remnants of Russell's mind would have been snuffed out forever, his little electrical current grounded. As it happened, he crossed somebody else's mind.

I had postponed Russell's *second* death—the one that occurs as soon as none of the minds in the world still harbor you. Russell got remembered—and that, a hundred years after his birth, was not such a bad end.

29.

A few months later, I left Mary's house. I spent a year and a half in Cobble Hill, living in a garden apartment owned by good friends who charged me less than the place was worth. Then I got married and moved into an apartment in Boerum Hill, where my landlords were brusque neighborhood butchers. Finally, about a year ago, my wife and I moved back to my old neighborhood in Park Slope, just around the corner from Mary's old house. Walking by at night, I can see that the place has been completely renovated, the insides gutted and replaced.

I still have Russell's box. It sat in a corner of my bedroom in Cobble Hill, then in the bottom of my closet in Boerum Hill, and now it occupies a space in our basement storage bin. A fresh new plastic storage container holds the withering old cardboard microwave oven box. I really ought to throw the thing away; it's taking up more than its fair share of space, and I'm a little concerned that its contents might one day be mistaken for my own belongings. But I can't quite bring myself to get rid of the thing.

Inside the box, on the surfaces of papers, people are still talking to each other, and to themselves. The parakeet man is still annotating his margins. Wives are still writing their husbands. Editors are still rejecting articles. Poems are still rhyming. Seconal is still being prescribed. Men and women, in all the colors of pastel, are still making love in the midst of the most outrageous exclamations.

Whenever I take out the box—and I do take it out every now and then—I find their voices lingering there, interrupting each other and blending together:

I seem to hear you knocking at the door and you're not there.

I have slept little the last 2 nights being exerted with sexual thoughts.

I am sorry to hear that you have not had the best of financial luck but of course that is the way it's always been with artists.

More trouble with their phallic parts for a longer period than any other group in history!

I feel I will be able to cut down a lot on the seconal.

I'm comin'! I'm comin'! Stick it in as far as it will go!

We danced a lot last night. The girls were over for around 3 hours. Miss Scotty was on. I have been helping Miss Bigelow in the grain room.

Oh darling, it feels as though it was almost touching my heart.

My dream. I was somewhere in Mexico.

It's really swell having you in the family.

But there is a great deal of hope in this. I feel a new and freer life is opening up.

Rolling Stone

FINALIST—REPORTING

Through a nine-month investigation highlighted by interviews with both embittered former Scientologists and current high-ranking church members, Janet Reitman provides a balanced—if ultimately damning—look at an organization that not only has never before opened its doors to the press but has typically used intimidation and coercion to keep its practices hidden from scrutiny, yielding a rare, uncensored view into one of the world's most secretive faiths.

Janet Reitman

Inside Scientology

The faded little downtown area of Clearwater, Florida, has a beauty salon, a pizza parlor, and one or two run-down bars, as well as a bunch of withered bungalows and some old storefronts that look as if they haven't seen customers in years. There are few cars and almost no pedestrians. There are, however, buses—a fleet of gleaming white and blue ones that slowly crawl through town, stopping at regular intervals to discharge a small army of tightly organized, young, almost exclusively white men and women, all clad in uniform preppy attire: khaki, black, or navy-blue trousers and crisp white, blue, or yellow dress shirts. Some wear pagers on their belts; others carry briefcases. The men have short hair, and the women keep theirs pulled back or tucked under headbands that match their outfits. No one crosses against the light, and everybody calls everybody else "sir"—even when the "sir" is a woman. They move throughout the center of Clearwater in tight clusters, from corner to corner, building to building.

This regimented mass represents the "Sea Organization," the most dedicated and elite members of the Church of Scientology. For the past thirty years, Scientology has made the city of Clearwater its worldwide spiritual headquarters—its Mecca, or its Temple Square. There are 8,300 or so Scientologists living and working in Clearwater—more than in any other city in the world outside of Los Angeles. Scientologists own more than 200 businesses in Clearwater. Members of the church run schools and private tutoring programs, day-care centers, and a drug-rehab clinic. They sit on the boards of the Rotary Club, the Chamber of Commerce, and the Boy Scouts.

In July 2004, *The St. Petersburg Times* dubbed Clearwater, a community of 108,000 people, "Scientology's Town." On the newspaper's front page was a photograph of Scientology's newest building, a vast, white, Mediterranean Revival–style edifice known within Scientology circles as the "Super Power" building. Occupying a full square block of downtown, this structure, which has been under construction since 1998, is billed as the single largest Scientology church in the world. When it is finally completed—presumably in late 2006, at an estimated final cost of $50 million—it will have 889 rooms on six floors, an indoor sculpture garden and a large Scientology museum. The crowning touch will be a two-story, illuminated Scientology cross that, perched atop the building's highest tower, will shine over the city of Clearwater like a beacon.

·　　·　　·

Scientology—the term means "the study of truth," in the words of its founder and spiritual messiah, the late science-fiction writer L. Ron Hubbard—calls itself "the world's fastest-growing religion." Born in 1954, the group now claims 10 million members in 159 countries and more than 6,000 Scientology churches, missions, and outreach groups across the globe. Its holdings, which include real estate on several continents, are widely assumed to value in the billions of dollars. Its missionaries—known as "volunteer ministers"—take part in "cavalcades" throughout the developing world and have been found, en masse, at the site of disasters ranging from 9/11 to the Asian tsunami to Hurricane Katrina. Within the field of comparative religions, some academics see Scientology as one of the most significant new religious movements of the past century.

Scientology is also America's most controversial religion: widely derided, but little understood. It is rooted in elements of Buddhism, Hinduism, and a number of Western philosophies, including aspects of Christianity. The French sociologist Régis Dericquebourg, an expert in comparative religions, explains Scientology's belief system as one of "regressive utopia," in which man seeks to return to a once-perfect state through a variety of meticulous, and rigorous, processes intended to put him in touch with his primordial spirit. These processes are highly controlled, and, at the advanced levels, highly secretive. Critics of the church point out that Scientology, unique among religions, withholds key aspects of its central theology from all but its most exalted followers. To those in the mainstream, this would be akin to the Catholic Church refusing to tell all but a select number of the faithful that Jesus Christ died for their sins.

In June of last year, I set out to discover Scientology, an undertaking that would take nearly nine months. A closed faith that has often been hostile to journalistic inquiry, the church initially offered no help on this story; most of my research was done without its assistance and involved dozens of interviews with both current and former Scientologists, as well as academic researchers who have studied the group. Ultimately, however, the church decided to cooperate and gave me unprecedented access to its officials, social programs, and key religious headquarters. What I found was a faith that is at once mainstream and marginal—a religious community known for its Hollywood members but run by a uniformed sect of believers who rarely, if ever, appear in the public eye. It is an insular society—one that exists, to a large degree, as something of a parallel universe to the secular world, with its own nomenclature and ethical code, and, most daunting to those who break its rules, its own rigorously enforced justice system.

Scientologists, much like Mormons or Christian evangelicals, consider themselves to be on a mission. They frequently speak of "helping people," and this mission is stressed in a number of church testaments. "Scientologists see themselves as possessors of doctrines and skills that can save the world, if not the galaxy," says Stephen Kent, a professor of sociology at the University of Alberta, in Canada, who has extensively studied the group.

Church officials boast that Scientology has grown more in the past five years than in the previous fifty. Some evidence, however, suggests otherwise. In 2001, a survey conducted by the City University of New York found only 55,000 people in the United States who claimed to be Scientologists. Worldwide, some observers believe a reasonable estimate of Scientology's core practicing membership ranges between 100,000 and 200,000, mostly in the U.S., Europe, South Africa, and Australia. According to the church's own course-completion lists—many of which are available in a church publication and on the Internet—only 6,126 people signed up for religious services at the Clearwater organization in 2004, down from a peak of 11,210 in 1989. According to Kristi Wachter, a San Francisco activist who maintains an online database devoted to Scientology's numbers, this pattern is replicated at nearly all of Scientology's key organizations and churches. To some observers, this suggests that Scientology may, in fact, be shrinking.

But discerning what is true about the Church of Scientology is no easy task. Tax-exempt since 1993 (status granted by the IRS after a long legal battle), Scientology releases no information about its membership or its finances. Nor does it welcome analysis of its writings or practices. The church has a storied reputation for squelching its critics through litigation, and according to some reports, intimidation (a trait that may explain why the creators of *South Park* jokingly attributed every credit on its November 2005 send-up of Scientology to the fictional John and Jane Smith; Paramount, reportedly under pressure, has agreed not to rerun the episode here or to air it in England). Nevertheless, Scientology's critics comprise a sizable network of ex-members (or "apostates," in church parlance), academics, and independent free-speech and human-rights activists like Wachter, who have declared war on the group by posting a significant amount of previously unknown information on the Internet. This includes scans of controversial memos, photographs, and legal briefs, as well as testimonials from disillusioned former members, including some high-ranking members of its Sea Organization. All paint the church in a negative, even abusive, light.

When asked what, if anything, posted by the apostates is true, Mike Rinder, the fifty-year-old director of the Church of Scientology International's legal and public-relations wing, known as the Office of Special Affairs, says bluntly, "It's all bullshit, pretty much."

But he admits that Scientology has been on a campaign to raise its public profile. More than 23 million people visited the Scientology Web site last year, says Rinder, one of the highest-ranking officials in the church. In addition, the church claims that Scientology received 289,000 minutes of radio and TV coverage in 2005, many of them devoted to the actions of Tom Cruise, the most famous Scientologist in the world, who spent much of the spring and summer of 2005 promoting Scientology and its beliefs to interviewers ranging from Oprah Winfrey to Matt Lauer.

Shortly after *Rolling Stone* decided to embark on this story, Cruise called our offices to say that he would not participate. Several weeks later, the magazine was visited by Cruise's sister, Lee Anne DeVette, an upper-level Scientologist who until recently also served as Cruise's publicist, along with Mike Rinder. Both expressed their dissatisfaction with previous coverage of Scientology by major media outlets, and they warned against what they perceived to be the unreliability of the faith's critics—"the wackos," as Rinder described them. He then invited *Rolling Stone* to Los Angeles to show us "the real Scientology"—a trip that took five months to set up.

A number of people who have spoken for the purposes of this article have done so for the very first time. Several, in speaking of their lives spent in the church, requested that their identities be protected through the change of names and other characteristics. Others insisted that not even a gender be attached to their comments.

There will always be schisms in any religious group, as well as people who, upon leaving their faith, decide to "purge" themselves of their experiences. This is particularly true in the case of members of so-called new religions, which often demand total commitment from their members. Scientology is one of these religions. "We're not playing some minor game in Scientology," Hubbard wrote in a policy paper titled "Keeping Scientology Working," which is required reading for every member. "The whole agonized future of this planet, every man, woman and child on it, and your own destiny for the next endless trillions of years depend on what you do here and now with and in Scientology. This is a deadly serious activity."

•   •   •

It is impossible to go anywhere in downtown Clearwater without being watched by security cameras. There are about 100 of them, set up on all of Scientology's properties, which include several hotels, a former bank, and a number of administrative buildings. Cameras face in, toward the buildings themselves, as well as out at the street.

While some might find this disconcerting, Natalie Walet, seventeen, thinks it's normal. "It's just a point of security," she says over coffee one evening at the downtown Starbucks. She notes that Scientology's buildings have been marred with graffiti

311

Inside Scientology

and are routinely picketed, which she sees as a sign of religious bigotry. "You have a church that a lot of people don't like, and some people are assholes," she says. That said, Natalie adds, most people in Clearwater have "very high standards and morals—they're ethical people."

A pretty girl with a long black ponytail, Natalie was born and raised in Scientology. Both of her parents and her grandmother are church members, and her involvement in Scientology centers around Clearwater. But the church has other far-flung hubs, including the organizational headquarters in Los Angeles, home to the powerful Church of Scientology International; and *Freewinds*, the 440-foot cruise ship that docks in Curaçao and is used as a training facility, meeting hall, and vacation destination for elite Scientologists, including Cruise and John Travolta. There is also "Gold Base," the exclusive desert compound housing the Religious Technology Center, or RTC, the financial hub of the church, located about eighty miles southeast of Los Angeles, home to David Miscavige, the charismatic forty-five-year-old who heads up the international church.

Natalie's everyday reality is one of total immersion in all things Hubbard. Scientology kids are raised in a very different manner than mainstream kids. Most of them, like Natalie, have been educated by special tutors, and enrolled, as Natalie was when she was younger, in private schools run by Scientologists that use a Hubbard-approved study technique. Most kids are also put "on course"—enrolled in classes at the church that teach both children and adults self-control, focus, and communication skills. Natalie was put on course, upon her own insistence, when she was seven or eight years old. Between school and church, life was "kind of a bubble," she says.

It is a steamy night, and Natalie is dressed in a sleeveless black Empire-waist blouse and tight jeans; her short, bitten nails are painted red. She lights a Marlboro Menthol. Smoking is Natalie's only vice. She neither drinks nor takes drugs of any sort—"once in a grand while I'll take a Tylenol," she says. "But only if my headache is really bad." She admits this with embarrassment because Scientologists consider many illnesses to be psychosomatic and don't believe in treating them with medicine, even aspirin.

Like all Scientologists, Natalie considers her body to be simply a temporary vessel. She thinks of herself as an immortal being, or "thetan," which means that she has lived trillions of years, and will continue to be reborn, again and again. Many Eastern religions have similar beliefs, and Natalie is quick to note that Scientology is "actually a very basic religion. It has a lot of the same moral beliefs as others." What's special about Scientology, Natalie says, is that it "bears a workable applied technology that you can use in your everyday life."

"Technology," or "tech," is what Scientologists call the theories, methods, and principles espoused by L. Ron Hubbard—"LRH," as Natalie calls him. To the devout, he is part prophet, part teacher, part savior—some Scientologists rank Hubbard's importance as greater than Christ's—and Hubbard's word is considered *the word*. Hubbard was a prolific writer all his life; there are millions of words credited to him, roughly a quarter-million of them contained within *Dianetics*, the best-selling quasi-scientific self-help book that is the most famous Scientology text.

Published in 1950, *Dianetics* maintained that the source of mental and physical illness could be traced back to psychic scars called "engrams" that were rooted in early, even prenatal, experiences, and remained locked in a person's subconscious, or "reactive mind." To rid oneself of the reactive mind, a process known as going "Clear," Dianetics, and later Scientology, preached a regressive-therapy technique called auditing, which involves reexperiencing incidents in one's past life in order to erase their engrams.

Natalie is a fan of auditing, something she's been doing since she was a small child. Most auditing is done with a device called

the electropsychometer, or E-meter. Often compared to lie de-
tectors, E-meters measure the changes in small electrical currents in the body, in response to questions posed by an auditor.
Scientologists believe the meter registers thoughts of the reactive mind and can root out unconscious lies. As Natalie explains
it, the E-meter is "like a guide that helps the auditor to know
what questions to ask." Sometimes, she says, you might not remember certain events, and you might not know what is causing
your problems. "But they'll just dig it up until you go, 'Holy shit,
was *that* what was going on?'" She smiles. "And afterward, you
feel so much better."

Natalie has just begun her path to Scientology enlightenment, known as the Bridge to Total Freedom. There are specific
stages, or "grades," of the Bridge, and the key to progressing
"upward" is auditing: hundreds, if not thousands, of sessions
that Scientologists believe can not only help them resolve their
problems but also fix their ethical breaches, much as Catholics
might do in confessing their sins. The ultimate goal in every
auditing session is to have a "win," or moment of revelation,
which can take a few minutes, hours, or even weeks—Scientologists are not allowed to leave an auditing session until their auditor is satisfied.

So far, Natalie has gotten much of her auditing for free,
through her parents, who have both worked for the church. But
many Scientologists pay dearly for the service. Unique among
religious faiths, Scientology charges for virtually all of its religious services. Auditing is purchased in 12.5-hour blocks,
known as "intensives." Each intensive can cost anywhere from
$750 for introductory sessions to between $8,000 and $9,000 for
advanced sessions. When asked about money, church officials
can become defensive. "Do you want to know the real answer? If
we could offer everything for free, we would do it," says Rinder.
Another official offers, "We don't have 2,000 years of acquired wealth to fall back on." But Scientology isn't alone,

church leaders insist. Mormons, for example, expect members to tithe a tenth of their earnings.

Still, religious scholars note that this is an untraditional approach. "Among the things that have made this movement so controversial," says S. Scott Bartchy, director of the Center for the Study of Religion at UCLA, "are its claims that its forms of therapy are 'scientific' and that the 'truth' will only be revealed to those who have the money to purchase advancement to the various levels leading to 'being clear.' It is this unvarnished demand for money that has led many observers to opine that the entire operation looks more like a business than a religion." Clearing the stages along the Bridge to Total Freedom is a process that can take years and cost tens and often hundreds of thousands of dollars—one veteran Scientologist told me she "donated" $250,000 in a twenty-year period. Other Scientologists can wind up spending family inheritances and mortgaging homes to pay the fees. Many, like Natalie's parents, work for their local church so they can receive auditing and courses for free.

Both of Natalie's parents are Clear, she says. Her grandmother is what's called an "Operating Thetan," or "OT." So is Tom Cruise, who is near the top of Scientology's Bridge, at a level known as OT VII. OTs are Scientology's elite—enlightened beings who are said to have total "control" over themselves and their environment. OTs can allegedly move inanimate objects with their minds, leave their bodies at will, and telepathically communicate with, and control the behavior of, both animals and human beings. At the highest levels, they are allegedly liberated from the physical universe, to the point where they can psychically control what Scientologists call MEST: Matter, Energy, Space, and Time.

•   •   •

The most important, and highly anticipated, of the eight "OT levels" is OT III, also known as the Wall of Fire. It is here that

Scientologists are told the secrets of the universe, and, some believe, the creation story behind the entire religion. It is knowledge so dangerous, they are told, any Scientologist learning this material before he is ready could die. When I ask Mike Rinder about this, he casts the warning in less-dire terms, explaining that, before he reached OT III—he is now OT V—he was told that looking at the material early was "spiritually not good for you." But Hubbard, who told followers that he discovered these secrets while on a trip to North Africa in 1967, was more dramatic. "Somehow or other I brought it off, and obtained the material and was able to live through it," he wrote. "I am very sure that I was the first one that ever did live through any attempt to attain that material."

Scientologists must be "invited" to do OT III. Beforehand, they are put through an intensive auditing process to verify that they are ready. They sign a waiver promising never to reveal the secrets of OT III, nor to hold Scientology responsible for any trauma or damage one might endure at this stage of auditing. Finally, they are given a manila folder, which they must read in a private, locked room.

These materials, which the Church of Scientology has long struggled to keep secret, were published online by a former member in 1995 and have been widely circulated in the mainstream media, ranging from the *New York Times* to last year's *South Park* episode. They assert that 75 million years ago, an evil galactic warlord named Xenu controlled seventy-six planets in this corner of the galaxy, each of which was severely overpopulated. To solve this problem, Xenu rounded up 13.5 trillion beings and then flew them to Earth, where they were dumped into volcanoes around the globe and vaporized with bombs. This scattered their radioactive souls, or thetans, until they were caught in electronic traps set up around the atmosphere and "implanted" with a number of false ideas—including the concepts of God, Christ, and organized religion. Scientologists later learn that many of these entities attached themselves to human beings, where they remain to this day, creating not just the root of all of our emotional and physical problems but the root of all problems of the modern world.

"Hubbard thought it was important to have a story about how things got going, similar to the way both Jews and Christians did in the early chapters of Genesis," says UCLA's Bartchy. "All religion lives from the sense either that something in life is terribly wrong or is profoundly missing. For the most part, Christianity has claimed that people have rebelled against God with the result that they are 'sinners' in need of restoration and that the world is a very unjust place in need of healing. What Hubbard seems to be saying is that human beings are really something else—thetans trapped in bodies in the material world—and that Scientology can both wake them up and save them from this bad situation."

The church considers OT III confidential material. But there are numerous science-fiction references in Scientology texts available to members of all levels. The official "Glossary for Scientology and Dianetics" includes an entry for "space opera," a sci-fi genre that the glossary says "is not fiction and concerns actual incidents." Scientology's "Technical Dictionary" makes reference to a number of extraterrestrial "invader forces," including one, the "Marcab Confederacy," explained as a vast, interplanetary civilization more than 200,000 years old that "looks almost exact duplicate [*sic*] but is worse off than the current U. S. civilization." Indeed, as even Rinder himself points out, Hubbard presented a rough outline of the Xenu story to his followers in a 1967 taped lecture, "RJ 67," in which he noted that 75 million years ago a cataclysmic event happened in this sector of the galaxy that has caused negative effects for everyone since. This material is available to lower-level Scientologists. But the details of the story remain secret within Scientology.

Rinder has fielded questions on Scientology's beliefs for years. When I ask him whether there is any validity to the Xenu story, he gets red-faced, almost going into a tirade. "It is not a *story*, it is an auditing level," he says, neither confirming nor denying that this theology exists. He says that OT material—and specifically the material on OT III—comprises "a small percent" of what Scientology is all about. But it is carefully guarded. Scientologists on the OT levels often carry their materials in locked briefcases and are told to store them in special secure locations in their homes. They are also strictly forbidden from discussing any facet of the materials, even with their families. "I'm not explaining it to you, and I *could not* explain it to you," says Rinder heatedly. "You don't have a hope of understanding it."

Those who have experienced OT III report that getting through it can be a harrowing experience. Tory Christman, a former high-ranking Scientologist who during her tenure in the faith reached the near-pinnacle of enlightenment, OT VII, says it took more than ten years before she was finally invited onto OT III. Once there, Christman was shocked. "You've jumped through all these hoops just to get to it, and then you open that packet, and the first thing you think is, '*Come on*,'" she says. "You're surrounded by all these people who're going, 'Wow, isn't it amazing, just getting the data? I can tell it's really changed you.' After a while, enough people say it and you're like, 'Wow. You know, I really feel it.'"

Natalie has a long way to go before she reaches OT III. Although virtually everything about the OT levels is available on the Internet, "I don't look at that stuff," Natalie says. She believes it is mostly "entheta," which are lies, or negative information about Scientology meant to undermine the faith. "You know, sometimes in school, kids would hear I'm a Scientologist and be like, 'No way—are you an alien?'" Natalie says. "I don't get mad about it. I just go, 'OK, let me tell you what it really is.'"

Natalie's view of Scientology is the one church officials promote: that it is not a religion about "space aliens" but simply a set of beliefs that can help a person live a better life. And Natalie appears to be the poster child for Scientology as a formula for a well-adjusted adolescence. Articulate and poised, she is close to her family, has a wide circle of Scientologist and non-Scientologist friends and graduated from high school last spring as a straight-A student. "I'm not saying that everybody must be a Scientologist," she says. "But what I am saying is that I see it work. I've learned so much about myself. LRH says, 'What is true for you is what you observe to be true.' So I'm not here to tell you that Scientology is the way, or that these are the answers. *You* decide what is true."

· · ·

Truth is a relative concept when discussing the life of Lafayette Ronald Hubbard. He was born in 1911, and, according to his legend, lived a life of heroic acts and great scientific and spiritual accomplishment until his death, in 1986. Photos of Hubbard in robust middle age—often wearing an ascot—hang in every Scientology center. You can read Hubbard's official biography on the Scientology Web site, which portrays the man Scientologists call the "Founder" as a great thinker, teacher, scientist, adventurer, ethnographer, photographer, sailor, and war hero.

The reality of Hubbard's life is less exhilarating but in many ways more interesting. The son of a U.S. naval officer, he was by all accounts an unremarkable youth from Tilden, Nebraska, who flunked out of George Washington University after his sophomore year and later found moderate success as a penny-a-word writer of pulp fiction, publishing hundreds of stories in fantasy magazines like *Astounding Science Fiction*. As a lieutenant in the Navy, Hubbard served, briefly, in World War II, but never saw combat and was relieved of his command. He spent the last months of the war as an outpatient at a naval hospital in Oakland, California, where he received treatment for ulcers. Years later, Hubbard would claim to have been "crippled and blinded" in battle, and that, over a year or so of intense "scientific research," he'd cured himself using techniques that would later become part of Dianetics.

After the war, Hubbard made his way to Pasadena, California, a scientific boomtown of the 1940s, where he met John Whiteside Parsons, a society figure and a founder of CalTech's Jet Propulsion Laboratory. A sci-fi buff, Parsons was also a follower of the English occultist Aleister Crowley. Parsons befriended Hubbard and invited him to move onto his estate. In one of the stranger chapters in Hubbard's life, recorded in detail by several biographers, the soon-to-be founder of Dianetics became Parsons' assistant—helping him with a variety of black-magic and sex rituals, including one in which Parsons attempted to conjure a literal "whore of Babalon [*sic*]," with Hubbard serving as apprentice.

Charming and charismatic, Hubbard succeeded in wooing away Parsons's mistress, Sara Northrup, whom he would later marry. Soon afterward, he fell out with Parsons over a business venture. But having absorbed lessons learned at Parsons's "lodge," Hubbard set out to figure his next step. In his 1983 autobiography, *Over My Shoulder: Reflections on a Science Fiction Era*, the sci-fi writer Lloyd Eshbach describes meeting Hubbard in the late 1940s. "I'd like to start a religion," Eshbach recalls Hubbard saying. "That's where the money is."

Dianetics: The Modern Science of Mental Health was published in May 1950, and it soon became a runaway hit. Written as sort of a practical pop-psychology book, *Dianetics* promised that by practicing certain techniques, some of which seemed almost hypnotic, one could be free of sickness, anxiety, aggression, and antisocial tendencies, and develop perfect memory and astounding intelligence. Hailed by the newspaper

columnist Walter Winchell as a "new science" that "from all in-
dications will prove to be as revolutionary for humanity as the
first caveman's discovery and utilization of fire," *Dianetics* remained on the *New York Times* best-seller list for twenty-eight
consecutive weeks.

But a number of factors, including condemnation from the
American Psychological Association, hurt book sales. Public
support for Dianetics took a downturn, and by the end of 1952,
Hubbard was facing financial ruin.

Rather than admit defeat, Hubbard "improved" Dianetics
and unveiled what he claimed was an even more sophisticated
path to enlightenment: Scientology. This new technique was designed to restore, or enhance, the abilities of the individual, as
opposed to simply getting rid of the reactive mind. In 1954, the
first Church of Scientology was born, in Los Angeles. L. Ron
Hubbard was now the founder of his own religion.

From there, Hubbard set about spreading Scientology around
the world, opening churches in England, Australia, New Zealand, and elsewhere. In 1955, a policy known as "Project Celebrity" was launched with the aim of recruiting stars in the arts,
sports, business, and government—those dubbed "Prime
Communicators"—who could help disseminate the message. As
incentive, these celebrities were given free courses; those who
did outstanding work could be "awarded" an OT level, in honor
of their service to the organization. Special churches—known
as "celebrity centres"—were set up, allowing its members to
practice Scientology away from the public eye. The most lavish
of these is the neo-Gothic Celebrity Centre International, which
is housed in a former chateau on Franklin Avenue, at the foot of
the Hollywood Hills.

Among the high-profile types who dabbled in Scientology
was the writer William S. Burroughs, who would later attack the
organizational structure as suppressive of independent thought.
But other artists were less critical. John Travolta became a

Scientologist in 1975 after reading *Dianetics*. "My career imme-diately took off," he states in a personal "success story" pub-lished in the book *What Is Scientology?* "I landed a leading role on the TV show *Welcome Back, Kotter* and had a string of suc-cessful films." Indeed, Travolta says, "Scientology put me into the big time."

In addition to Travolta, Scientology attracted musicians Chick Corea and Isaac Hayes, actresses Mimi Rogers and Kirstie Alley, and the influential acting coach Milton Katselas, who brought in a number of others, including actresses Anne Archer and Kelly Preston, who later became Travolta's wife. And those celebrities begat others, including Tom Cruise, who was introduced by his then-wife, Rogers, and Jenna Elfman, introduced by her husband, actor Bodhi Elfman. Others, such as Juliette Lewis, Erika Christensen, and Beck, were born into Scientology.

But as Scientology raised its profile, so too did it find itself under increased scrutiny by the U.S. government, which raided Scientology's offices a number of times in the late 1950s and early 1960s. In 1963, the Food and Drug Administration confis-cated hundreds of E-meters from Scientology's Washington, D.C., offices (the FDA accused the church of making false claims about its healing powers). Soon afterward, Hubbard moved his base of operation from the U.S. to England, but continued to face condemnation from a variety of Western governments. To avoid such scrutiny, Hubbard purchased a small fleet of ships in 1967, and, dubbing himself "Commodore," headed for the high seas, which would serve as Scientology's official home and, some maintain, tax shelter until the mid-1970s.

Serving Hubbard at sea were a small group of devoted follow-ers who comprised a private navy of sorts. They were known, col-lectively, as the "Sea Organization," and dressed in full naval uniforms. Mike Rinder, who joined the Sea Org when he was eigh-teen, served on Hubbard's lead ship, the *Apollo*, as a deckhand.

He arrived in 1973, having endured years of discrimination in his native Australia (southeastern Australia banned Scientology from 1965 to 1982). "You couldn't own Scientology books," he says. "If you did, you had to hide them because if the police came and found them, they'd take them away."

On the *Apollo*, Rinder found Hubbard, a reputed recluse, to be totally accessible. He hosted weekly movie nights and often strolled across the ship talking with the crew. "What was most incredible about being with him was that he made you feel that you were important," Rinder recalls. "He didn't in any way promote himself or his own self-importance. He was very, very loving and had the widest range of knowledge and experience that you could possibly imagine—he'd studied everything." Rinder marvels at Hubbard's abilities: He knew how to cultivate plants, fix cars, shoot movies, mix music, fly an airplane, sail ships.

At sea, Hubbard, who had officially resigned his post as the head of the Church of Scientology (leaving the day-to-day management of the church to lesser officials), worked on his writings and "discoveries." Hubbard also began to obsess over the forces he saw opposing him, including journalists, whom Hubbard long distrusted and even banned from ever becoming Scientologists. Worse still were psychiatrists, a group that, coupled with the pharmaceutical-drug industry—in Hubbard's words, a "front group"—operated "straight out of the terrorist textbooks," as he wrote in a 1969 essay titled "Today's Terrorism." He accused psychiatrists of kidnapping, torturing, and murdering with impunity. "A psychiatrist," he wrote, "kills a young girl for sexual kicks, murders a dozen patients with an ice pick, castrates a hundred men."

To attack his enemies, Hubbard issued a policy known as "Fair Game," which maintained that all who opposed Scientology could be "tricked, sued or lied to and destroyed." This policy was enforced by Scientology's quasi-secret police force, known as the Guardian's Office. By the 1970s, among its tasks was

"Operation Snow White," a series of covert activities that included bugging the Justice Department and stealing documents from the IRS. (Scientology officials say Fair Game was canceled decades ago.)

The plan was discovered in FBI raids on Scientology's Los Angeles and Washington, D.C., offices in 1977, which yielded wiretap equipment, burglary tools, and about 90,000 pages of documents. Eleven Scientology officials, including Hubbard's third wife, Mary Sue, went to federal prison for their role in the plot, which led to a 1982 "sweep" of the church's upper management.

By then, Hubbard, who was cited as an "unindicted co-conspirator" in Operation Snow White, had vanished from the public eye. For the next several years, rumors of his whereabouts circulated freely—he was at sea; he was on an island. In fact, Hubbard was on his isolated ranch, Whispering Wind, near the town of Creston, in the California desert. He was attended by a small number of Scientology officials, and his physician, Dr. Eugene Denk, who treated him for a number of conditions, including chronic pancreatitis. On January 17, 1986, Hubbard suffered a crippling stroke. A week later, he died, in a 1982 Blue Bird motor home on his property. He was seventy-four years old.

Upon Hubbard's death, his ambitious twenty-five-year-old aide, David Miscavige, who would soon succeed him as leader of the church, announced that Scientology's founder had willingly "dropped" his healthy body and moved on to another dimension. In keeping with Hubbard's wishes, his body was cremated within twenty-four hours. There was no autopsy. But the coroner's report described the father of Scientology as in a state of decrepitude: unshaven, with long, thinning whitish-red hair and unkempt fingernails and toenails. In Hubbard's system was the anti-anxiety drug hydroxyzine (Vistaril), which several of his assistants would later attest was only one of many psychiatric and pain medications Hubbard ingested over the years.

These secrets were kept under wraps by Scientology officials. The church would later be named Hubbard's successor in accordance with his will, which had been amended and signed just a day before his death. In it, Hubbard ceded the copyrights to all of his works, as well as a significant portion of his estate, making Scientology, not Hubbard's wife and five children, his primary heir.

Today, every church or Scientology organization has an office reserved for Hubbard. Usually found on the church's ground floor, it is carefully maintained with books, desk, chair, pens, notepads, desk ornaments, and other accouterments, as if the Founder might walk in at any moment.

·　　　·　　　·

The imposing limestone-and-granite Church of Scientology in midtown Manhattan calls itself the "New York Org." A stately building on West Forty-sixth Street, northwest of Times Square, it is here that I come, on a hot July afternoon, to experience Scientology for myself.

The first Scientologist I meet here is a kid named Emmett: a clear-eyed and enthusiastic young man in his early twenties whose job is to be a "body-router," which means someone who brings people into the church. "Hi!" he says, accosting me as I stand near the center's entrance. "Do you have a minute?" He waves a postcard-size flier in my face. "We're showing a fifteen-minute film inside," he says. "It's about Dianetics. Ever heard of it?"

He ushers me through a set of glass doors and into the church's lobby, a glossy-marble space with the kind of lighting that bathes everything in a pinkish-golden glow. It is set up as a sort of museum, with a number of video-display panels, one of which offers an earnest testimonial by Tom Cruise. "The Aims of Scientology," a document written by Hubbard, also hangs in the lobby, and it declares Scientology's goals as "simple, but great," including "a civilization without insanity, without criminals and without war; where the able can prosper and honest beings can have rights, and where man is free to rise to greater heights."

The New York Org claims to receive more than 500 phone calls per day, and nearly as many visitors in a week. But aside from its staff, I find the place to be almost entirely empty. Seated alone in a small auditorium, I watch the film, which turns out to be an infomercial featuring a cast of "real" people talking about how Dianetics changed their lives, curing them of ailments ranging from cancer to depression. Scientology is not mentioned once in the film. Nor is Hubbard. And neither are mentioned afterward, during an hour or so conversation I have with a motherly woman in her early fifties named Laurie. She is what is known as a "greeter," and her role is to keep me in the church long enough for me to feel encouraged that, maybe, all of this is worth my time.

Self-betterment is a powerful concept to use as a sales technique, and Laurie begins her pitch in the gentlest of ways. "Tell me about yourself," she says. "What made you interested in Scientology?"

"I guess I was just curious," I tell Laurie.

"Good!" she says with a smile. "We like curious!"

In the next hour or so, Laurie asks me a number of questions: Am I married? Am I happy? What are my goals? Do I feel that I'm living up to my potential?

A failure to live up to potential is one of the things known in Scientology as one's "ruin." In trying to get at mine, Laurie is warm and nonaggressive. And, to my amazement, I begin to open up to her. While we chat, she delivers a soft sell for Scientology's "introductory package": a four-hour seminar and twelve hours of Dianetics auditing, which is done without the E-meter. The cost: just fifty dollars. "You don't have to do it," Laurie says.

"It's just something I get the feeling might help you." She pats my arm, squeezes it warmly.

Then she gets down to business and presents me with the $100 Dianetics "starter" kit, which includes a large-type copy of Hubbard's tome, a few CDs, and some workbooks to practice the stuff at home. "It's really such a good thing you came in," Laurie adds reassuringly. "You'll see."

On my next visit to the church, the following day, I see Laurie again. She spots me as soon as I walk in and rushes to greet me. "You're back!" She gives me a hug. "I am so glad you decided to give this a try." She then introduces me to a preppy-looking guy in his early thirties named Rurik, who, wasting no time on small talk, leads me to the church's second floor and installs me in a room for my introductory seminar. As with the previous day's film, I'm the only one there.

Rurik starts his lecture with the claim that the mind really isn't in the brain. "Close your eyes and think of a picture of a cat," he tells me. I do. "Now, open your eyes and point to where you saw that picture."

I point to my eyes.

Rurik grins. "See? When you're asked to use your mind, you don't point to the brain."

The brain, Rurik says, has absolutely no bearing on our thoughts or feelings. Nor, he adds, does the mind—its chief function is to serve as a memory bank of all we've experienced in trillions of years of lifetimes. Indeed, Scientology holds that the entire field of neurological and mental-health research—from Freud to the study of brain chemistry—is pseudoscience. In Scientology's overview text, *What Is Scientology?*, psychiatry is described as a "hodgepodge of unproven theories that have never produced any result—except an ability to make the unmanageable and mutinous more docile and quiet, and turn the troubled into apathetic souls beyond the point of caring."

Most of the dedicated Scientologists I meet echo this opinion, including Kirstie Alley, who has been a Scientologist for more than twenty years and is the international spokesperson for Narconon, the church-supported antidrug program. In an interview with Alley several weeks later, she calls Scientology the "antitherapy." "Therapy is based on some guy analyzing you, and what he thinks is going on with you," she says. "And when he can't quite figure it out, he makes up a disease and gets a drug for that. If that doesn't work, he shocks you. And then surgery . . ." Scientology employs a holistic detoxification program known as the "purification rundown," which involves heavy doses of vitamin supplements, primarily niacin, used in conjunction with exercise and long hours in a sauna. Though many doctors point out that none of this has ever been scientifically proven, and, indeed, might be harmful, Scientology claims that the "purif" cleanses the body of impurities. "I can get someone off heroin a hell of a lot faster than I can get somebody off a psych drug," says Alley. "The guy on heroin's not being told daily, 'This is what you need for your disease, and you're gonna have to take this the rest of your life.'"

A few days later I arrive for my free Dianetics auditing sessions. I am put in a large, glass-enclosed room with a student auditor named David, who asks me to "relive" a moment of physical pain. "Don't choose something that's *too* stressful," David suggests.

Try as I might, I cannot relive much of anything—indeed, I can barely focus, given that I am surrounded in the room by a number of other pairs who are all being asked to do the same thing. After fifteen minutes, I give up.

Jane, the registrar who is now handling my "case," then whisks me away and, taking a look at my Oxford Capacity Analysis—a 200-item questionnaire that I filled out on my first day—tells me that she thinks I need something more personal. "I really want you to have a win," she says.

What Jane recommends is called Life Repair, basic Scientology counseling that she explains will "get to the root of what's inhibiting you." It is conducted in a private room, and involves one, but most likely two, 12.5-hour auditing "intensives," using the E-meter, which will cost around $2,000. Coupled with the purif, which is recommended to anyone starting in Scientology, the total cost will be around $4,000. "And then you'll be on the Bridge," Jane says enthusiastically. "You'll see. It'll change your life."

At the intake level, Scientology comes across as good, practical self-help. Rather than playing on themes that might distance a potential member—the concept that I am a "thetan," for example—members hit on topics that have universal appeal. Instead of claiming some heightened degree of enlightenment, they come across as fellow travelers: people who smoke too much, who have had bad marriages, who have had addictions they couldn't handle but have somehow managed to land on their feet. Scientology, they explain, has been a form of "recovery." As one woman I meet puts it, "Scientology *works*."

There are, however, a few things that seem jarring. Like the cost: $4,000 is a lot to spend for what Jane suggests are "basic" sessions. But perhaps even more alarming is the keen interest they take in my boyfriend. While Laurie inquired sympathetically about the dynamic of our relationship, Jane is suspicious, concerned with his views of the church and his attitude toward my being here. "If he's not open," she says, "that could be a problem."

And then there are Scientology's rules. A fiercely doctrinaire religion, Scientology follows Hubbard's edicts to the letter. Dissent or opposition to any of Hubbard's views isn't tolerated. Nor is debating certain church tenets—a practice Scientologists view as "counterintentioned." Comporting oneself in any way that could be seen as contrary to church goals is considered subversive and is known as a "suppressive act." One text that sheds enlightenment on both the mind-set of the founder and the inner workings of the church is *Introduction to Scientology Ethics*, which every Scientologist owns. In this book, the list of suppressive acts is six pages long and includes crimes ranging from murder to "squirreling," or altering Hubbard's teachings.

Jane hands me a form and asks me to sign. The document absolves Scientology of liability if I am not wholly satisfied with its services, and also requires me to pledge that neither I nor my family has ever sued, attacked, or publicly criticized Scientology. It also asks me to pledge that I will never sue the church myself.

For the next several months, Jane and various other registrars call my cell phone, asking me to come back to the church and have a "win." I never do.

.   .   .

Somewhere in the vast California scrubland east of Los Angeles, west of Palm Springs, and near the town of Hemet, is Gold Base, the heart of the Scientology empire. It has been described in some news reports as a "top-secret" facility, monitored by security cameras and protected by electric fences. Most Scientologists have never been to Gold. Within church circles, it is often spoken of in whispers: as INT Base, Scientology's management headquarters and hangout for the likes of Tom Cruise and David Miscavige.

Gold, a former resort, was purchased by the church in the mid-eighties and sits at the foot of the San Jacinto Mountains. A simple metal gate announces its presence, behind which is a long driveway and, beyond that, a golf course. The 500-acre grounds include grassy meadows and a small lake where swans and ducks roam at will. There are no visible security cameras. But there are electric fences. "*Of course* we have fences," says Tommy Davis, a senior church official who, with Rinder, accompanies me on a tour of the compound. "We have $60 million worth of equipment here."

Gold is the central dissemination facility for the church. It is best known as the home of Golden Era Productions, Scientology's film, video, and sound facilities. Scientology produces myriad promotional and training films here, teaching parishioners everything from auditing techniques to what goes on during a marriage-counseling session. It also makes CDs, produces events, and prints its own packaging. Even its E-meters are made here, in a building where Scientologists work on a sort of corporate assembly line, producing roughly 200 of the devices per week.

There is a Disney-esque quality to Gold Base. The focal point of the complex is a beige estate house, known as the Castle, which houses the film wing. The Tavern, a nearby stone carriage-house building, is used for visiting VIPs and is decorated in a King Arthur motif, complete with a sizable round table. There are winding paths and walkways made out of what appears to be fake flagstone. All of the buildings, save the Castle, are white, with blue-tiled roofs.

Breaking up the uniformity is a startling sight: a three-mast rudderless clipper ship, the *Star of California*, built into a hill overlooking the campus. Some former Scientologists say this structure was built for Hubbard—though he'd "dropped his body" before it was finished—but Rinder explains it as just "an idea someone had to build a ship" as a place to house restrooms and a snack bar near the pool. It has a broad wooden deck, mermaid figurines, and, at its gangplank, a fishing net adorned with plastic crabs.

Despite these colorful landmarks, Gold is essentially an office park. Its buildings are furnished like a series of corporate suites, complete with bland gray or blue rugs. There's virtually no artwork save a few Scientology posters inscribed with the words of L. Ron Hubbard, and, in the sound studio, framed headshots of various Scientologist celebrities, including Tommy Davis's mother, Anne Archer.

Davis, thirty-three, helps run the Celebrity Centre in Hollywood and is the scion of one of California's real estate dynasties. He freely admits to being a Hollywood rich kid. He dresses in Italian suits, drives a BMW, and is addicted to his Blackberry. "I have enough money to never work a day in my life," he says.

But Davis, who calls L. Ron Hubbard "the coolest guy ever," works for the church as a nonuniformed member of the Sea Organization, the Church of Scientology's most powerful entity. Sea Org members staff all of the senior ecclesiastic positions in the church hierarchy, and the top members have exclusive authority over Scientology's funds. In a nod to the group's nautical beginnings, Sea Org members were required to wear naval-style uniforms, complete with epaulets for "officers," until several years ago. Today, for all but those who serve on the *Freewinds*, the epaulets have been retired. At Gold, whose entire population, save the actors and directors of Scientology films, are Sea Org members, men and women dress in the style of deckhands: short-sleeve dress shirts over dark T-shirts and chinos.

The church describes the Sea Org as a fraternal order—not a legal entity—requiring lifelong commitment. It is, in fact, an eternal commitment: Sea Org members sign contracts pledging 1 billion years of service to the church. Scientology's publicity materials portray the Sea Org as similar to the U.S. Marines: "The toughest, most dedicated team this planet has ever known," according to one recruiting brochure. "Against such a powerful team the opposition hasn't got a chance."

Kim Fries, who works in Gold's audiovisual editing department, has been in the Sea Org since she was fifteen. Now thirty-two, Fries says she couldn't imagine living any other way. "What else are you going to do with your life?" she says, with a flick of her dark, wavy hair.

The Sea Org has often been portrayed as isolated, almost monastic; members are rarely allowed to see films, watch TV, or read mainstream magazines. "Are we devoted? Yes. Sequestered?

No," says Fries, who married a fellow Sea Org member. "I go out into the world, I talk to people out in the world, I definitely live a very full life. This isn't a priesthood. I mean, if it were a priesthood, do you think I'd work here? It would just be so unhip."

Gold is seen as the place "every Sea Org member aspires to work," says Rinder. There are expansive grounds to wander, a crystal-blue pool in which to swim; the dining hall is large and features low-fat and vegetarian entrees. A tiny shop sells cigarettes, juice, soft drinks, and junk food.

In my ten or so hours at Gold, I am aware of being taken on an elaborately orchestrated junket, in which every step of my day has been plotted and planned. I don't blame the group for wanting to present its best face; at least half of my conversations with Rinder and Davis pertain in one way or another to what Scientology perceives as a smear campaign on the part of the mainstream media. A chief complaint is that reporters, eager for a story, take the words of lapsed members as gospel. Davis says Scientology gets little credit for the success of its social-betterment programs, which include Narconon and also literacy and educational programs. "Look around," says Davis. "People are out here busting their butt every day to make a difference. And one guy who leaves because he wants to go to the movies gets to characterize the whole organization? That sucks."

Scientologists do not look kindly on critics, particularly those who were once devout. Apostasy, which in Scientology means speaking out against the church in any public forum, is considered to be the highest form of treason. This is one of the most serious "suppressive acts," and those who apostatize are immediately branded as "Suppressive Persons," or SPs. Scientologists are taught that SPs are evil—Hitler was an SP, says Rinder. Indeed, Hubbard believed that a full 2.5 percent of the population was "suppressive." As he wrote in the *Dianetics and Scientology Technical Dictionary*, a suppressive person is someone who "goofs up or vilifies any effort to help anybody and particularly knife with violence anything calculated to make human beings more powerful or more intelligent."

Given this viewpoint, I wonder why anyone with connections to Scientology would critique them publicly. "Makes them famous," Rinder says. "They do it for their fifteen minutes."

Scientology has been extremely effective at attacking its defectors, often destroying their credibility entirely, a policy that observers call "dead agenting." Some of the church's highest-profile critics say they have been on the receiving end of this policy. In the past six years, Tory Christman claims, the church has spread lies about her on the Internet, filed suit against her for violating an injunction for picketing on church property, and attempted to get her fired from her job. Rinder dismisses Christman as a "wacko" and says her allegations are "absolute bullshit."

When Christman split from the church, her husband and most of her friends—all of them Scientologists—refused to talk to her again. Apostates are not just discredited from the church; they are also excommunicated, isolated from their loved ones who, under Scientology rules, must sever or "disconnect" from them. Scientology defines those associated with Suppressive People as "Potential Trouble Sources," or PTS.

Rinder says disconnection is a policy of last resort. "The first step is always to try to *handle* the situation," he says. A "handling" generally refers to persuading a wayward member to return to the church in order to maintain contact with his family. The parent of someone who's apostatized might call his child and ask him to "handle" a problem by essentially recanting. "They'll ask them to make some amends, show they can be trusted . . . something to make up the damage," says Davis. Those amends might range from volunteering in a literacy program to taking a public advocacy role—campaigning against psychiatry, for example.

But some people, the officials admit, refuse to be handled. What happens to them? "Then I guess not believing in Scientology means more to them than not seeing their family," Davis says.

Excommunication is nothing new in organized religion. A number of sects have similar policies to Scientology's: the Amish, the Mormon Fundamentalists, the Jehovah's Witnesses. All have a rationale. Scientology's rationale is very simple: "We are protecting the good of the religion and all the parishioners," says Rinder.

"It's for the good of the group," says Davis.

"How are you going to judge what is and isn't the worst tenets and violations of the Church of Scientology?" Rinder asks. "*You* aren't a Scientologist." Complaints about these policies, he adds, "come from people who aren't Scientologists [anymore]. What do they give a shit for anymore? They left!"

I spend a lot of time talking about the question of apostasy with Rinder and Davis. Both feel the church has been miscast. "Somewhere there is a concept that we hold strings over all these people and control them," says Rinder. But provided you don't denounce Scientology, it's perfectly fine to leave the church, he says. "Whatever. What's true for you is true for you." Nothing will happen to those who lose their faith, he says, unless they "tell bald-faced lies to malign and libel the organization—unless they make it seem like something it isn't."

•   •   •

Paul James is not this twenty-two-year-old man's real name. He is the son of established Scientologists, blond and blue-eyed, with the easy smile and chiseled good looks of a young Matt Damon. He has had no contact with the church since he was seventeen. "I honestly don't know how people can live psychotically happy all the time," Paul tells me over coffee one afternoon at his small, tidy house outside Los Angeles. "Or *thinking* that they're happy," he adds with a grin. "I'm talking about that fake-happiness thing that people make themselves believe."

Like Natalie, Paul was educated by Scientology tutors, sent to Scientologist-run private schools, and put "on course" at his church. Unlike her, he hated it. "I never found anything in Scientology that had to do with spiritual enlightenment," he says. "As soon as common sense started hitting me"—around the age of ten—"it creeped me out."

Though there are a significant number of second-generation Scientologists who, like Natalie, are devoted to the church, there are also kids like Paul. This, says the University of Alberta's Stephen Kent, is to be expected. One "unanticipated consequence" of the widespread conversions of young people to sects like Scientology in the 1960s and 1970s, Kent says, has been a "wave" of defections of these members' adult children.

A fundamental element of Scientology is that children are often regarded as small adults—"big thetans in little bodies," as some parents call them. Paul's parents worked eighteen-hour days for the church, he says, and generally left him and his older brother to their own devices. "My brother was babysitting me by himself when he was eleven years old," Paul says. When his brother went off with his friends, "I'd get home from school and be wandering around the [apartment] complex."

Paul's school was no more structured, he says. Students were encouraged to work at their own pace on subjects of their choosing, and, according to Paul, received little guidance from teachers, who are called "supervisors." I found this to be true at the Delphi Academy in Lake View Terrace, California, part of a network of elite schools that use Hubbard's study technology. Maggie Reinhart, Delphi's director, says that this technique forces a student to take an active role in his education. A number of Scientology kids have thrived in this environment. Others, like Paul, felt lost. "I just kind of roamed from classroom to classroom and nobody cared," he says. At Delphi, I saw teachers assisting certain students, but there was no generalized "teaching," no class discussions.

Discussion, as some academics like Kent note, isn't encouraged in Scientology, nor in Scientology-oriented schools. It is seen as running counter to the teachings of Scientology, which are absolute. Thus, debate is relegated to those in the world of "Wogs"—what Scientologists call non-Scientologists. Or, as Hubbard described them, "common, ordinary, run-of-the-mill, garden-variety humanoid[s]."

Paul met very few Wogs growing up, and those he did know often didn't understand him. Scientology has its own unique lexicon. "It's kind of like being a French Canadian," Paul explains. "You speak one thing out in the world and another thing at home."

Many kids who've grown up in Scientology describe it as Natalie did: "a bubble" that exists in tandem with the mainstream world. "It's impossible to understand it unless you've lived it," says Paul.

Even when you've lived it, as one young woman notes, it's hard to fully understand. This twenty-two-year-old, whom we'll call Sara, left Scientology in high school. After leaving, she and a friend who quit with her sat down with a dictionary. "We looked up all the words we used [because] we didn't know if we were speaking English or not," she says.

Hubbard created Scientology's language to be unique to its members. It includes words that are interpretations, or variations, of standard terms: "isness," for example, which Scientology's glossaries say, in essence, means "reality." But there are also words that are wholly made up, such as "obnosis," which means "observation of the obvious."

The chaotic world, as one might call it in the mainstream, is, in Scientology, "enturbulated," which means "agitated and disturbed." To correct, or solve, personal or societal problems requires the proper application of "ethics," which in Scientology refers to one's moral choices, as well as to a distinct moral system. Those who conduct themselves correctly have their ethics "in." Those who misbehave are "out-ethics." A person's harmful or negative acts are known as "overts." Covering them up is known as a "withhold."

All of these terms, and many more, are contained in a number of Scientology dictionaries, all written by Hubbard. Scientologists consider word comprehension and vocabulary skills to be essential parts of their faith.

The Hubbard Study Technology is administered in schools through an organization called "Applied Scholastics"; it emphasizes looking up any unknown or "misunderstood" word in a dictionary, and never skipping past a word you don't understand. This same study method is used in church, where adults of all ages and levels of advancement spend hours poring over dictionaries and course manuals.

One key word is "gradient," which is defined in the official Scientology and Dianetics glossary as "a gradual approach to something, taken step by step, level by level, each step or level being, of itself, easily surmountable so that, finally, quite complicated and difficult activities or high states of being can be achieved with relative ease." This principle, the glossary notes, "is applied to both Scientology processing and training."

Another key belief is "communication." One of Scientology's basic courses is "Success Through Communication," taught to young people and adults. It involves a series of drills, known as "training routines," or "TRs." One drill asks students to close their eyes and simply sit, sometimes for hours. Another asks them to stare at a partner, immobile. A third requires students to mock, joke with, or otherwise verbally engage their partner. The partner must passively receive these comments without moving or saying a word.

These drills, Scientologists say, help improve what they call their "confront," which in Scientology's lexicon means "the ability to be there comfortably and perceive." A fourth drill requires students to pose a series of questions to one another, such as "Do fish swim?" Their partner may respond in any way they like, with the question being asked repeatedly until the partner answers correctly. Sara's favorite drill involved an ashtray: "You tell it to stand up, sit down, and you 'move' the ashtray for hours. You're supposed to be beaming your intention into the ashtray, and the supervisor is going to tell you if you're intent enough."

At Delphi, students take a course called "Improving Conditions." "Conditions" refers to key Hubbard principles. Charted on a scale, they relate to one's relationship to oneself and to those within one's organization, school, or "group." A Scientologist's goal, it's often noted, is to "improve conditions."

From highest to lowest, the Conditions are: Power, Power Change, Affluence, Normal, Emergency, Danger, Non-Existence, Liability, Doubt, Enemy, Treason, and Confusion. Together, these conditions form the spine of the practical application of Scientology "ethics," which is, many say, the true heart of the faith. "Ethics," as a Scientological term, is defined as "rationality toward the greatest good for the greatest number of dynamics," as well as "reason and the contemplation of optimum survival."

To survive, Scientology applies its philosophy, or "ethics tech," across a broad social and societal scale. They do good works—indeed, as Rinder notes, "Scientologists are driven by a real concern for the well-being of others. They see the world around them and want to do something about it."

But the church's drug-treatment and literacy programs and anti-psychiatry campaigns do more than just evangelize through charity; in fact, they exist largely to help prepare people to become Scientologists. Once a person is drug-free, psychiatrist-free, and literate, he is qualified for auditing. And auditing is the centerpiece of Scientology. "It's all about going up the Bridge," says Paul.

Paul began auditing when he was four. Rebellious by nature, he says it did very little for him. By the age of eleven or twelve, he says, "I was so out of control, my parents had no idea what to do with me."

Scientologists run a number of boarding schools around the country, including the prestigious Delphian School, in the Willamette Valley of Oregon, which counts Earthlink founder Sky Dayton among its graduates. Scientologists' kids who caused trouble, or otherwise displeased their parents, have been sent to more restrictive private boarding schools. Paul was sent to Mace-Kingsley Ranch, located on 2,000 acres in New Mexico, which was closed in 2002.

Paul arrived at Mace-Kingsley when he was thirteen, and stayed for three and a half years. As he tells it, he underwent what sounds like a typical "boot camp" experience, complete with hard labor, bad food, tough supervision—all with a high price tag, roughly $30,000 per year. The school enforced a rigid Scientology focus that many former students now say served as both a mechanism of control and a form of religious indoctrination.

The process began for all new students with an IQ test and the Purification Rundown, which Paul says was given to kids as young as eight or nine years old. Then they were administered the Oxford Capacity Analysis, created by Scientologists in 1953. The test was designed to find out the student's "tone," or emotional state, in preparation for auditing. Students were audited daily at the ranch. By the age of sixteen, Paul says, he'd grown so used to the process, he'd figured out how to "trick" the E-meter: By remaining calm enough for no electrical charge to register, he was often able to hide most of his inner feelings from his auditors and his "case supervisor," who oversaw his progress.

But not always. "There are things they wanted to know, and they'd just keep asking until you finally told them," he says. "They'd get me to tell them about lies, or things that were bad, right down to my thoughts—some of which were overts." So were some of his deeds. Masturbation is an overt—strictly forbidden in Scientology, as Hubbard believed that it can slow one's process to enlightenment. "It's not evil, just out-ethics," says Paul. "They'll dig it up in session and tell you to stop because it's slowing you down."

Another overt is homosexuality, which Hubbard believed was a form of sexual "deviance" best treated by therapy, or institutionalization. This view was espoused by many psychiatrists of Hubbard's generation. Mainstream psychiatry has changed its view since the 1950s. Scientology as an institution takes no formal position on issues like gay marriage, but homosexuality, sexual promiscuity, or any other form of "perversion" ranks low on Scientology's "tone scale," a register of human behavior Hubbard described in his 1951 book *Science of Survival: Prediction of Human Behavior.*

This book, according to Mike Rinder, is perhaps the most important Scientology text after *Dianetics.* In it, Hubbard denounced virtually every sexual practice that doesn't directly relate to marriage and children. "Such people should be taken from the society as rapidly as possible . . . for here is the level of the contagion of immortality and the destruction of ethics," he wrote of homosexuals. "No social order will survive which does not remove these people from its midst."

In auditing, Scientologists are frequently asked about their sexual thoughts or practices, particularly in the special auditing sessions called "security checks." This process requires a church member to write down any break with the ethical code. Security checks are administered to every Scientologist on the Bridge, and particularly to all OTs, who must be checked every six months "to make sure they're using the tech correctly," as church officials explain. In September, I received, through a source, a faxed copy of the standard security-check sheet for adults. Its questions include "Have you ever been involved in an abortion?" "Have you ever practiced sex with animals?" "Have you ever practiced sodomy?" "Have you ever slept with a member of a race of another color?" as well as "Have you ever had any unkind thoughts about L. Ron Hubbard?"

Paul resisted his security checks—he says he sometimes fell asleep during the sessions. But Sara, who says she went through months of "sec checks" after deciding, at age fifteen, that she didn't want to be a Scientologist any longer, says she was highly disturbed by the process. At first, she says, counselors at her church tried to "clear" her. She was forced to repeatedly look up words in the dictionary to make sure she misunderstood nothing about Scientology. Then they gave her a security check. "For months I'm going to the church every night after school, and I'm in this fucking basement for four hours a night, on the E-meter," she says. "They're asking me questions about sex—every personal question known to man." If she tried to leave, Sara adds, the auditors would physically block her path and force her back in her chair. Officials say this forced auditing is for the subjects' own good, as it might be harmful if they were to leave a session before they were ready.

"Scientology has a plausible explanation for everything they do—that's the genius of it," says Sara. "But make no mistakes: Scientology is brainwashing."

•   •   •

Jeffrey Aylor was thirteen when he joined the Sea Organization. Raised in a Scientology family in Los Angeles, he was at church one day when a Sea Org recruiter approached him. "What are you doing with your life?" he asked the teen.

Jeffrey had no idea what to say. "I'm thirteen, I'm not doing anything with my life," Jeffrey said. The recruiter asked him if he wanted to "help" people. Jeffrey said, "Sure. What kid doesn't want to help people?"

Thus began Jeffrey's immersion into the tightly wound world of the Sea Org, where he would spend the next seven years of his life. In that time, he would see fewer than ten movies, would rarely listen to music, and never had sex. Though theoretically reading newspapers and magazines was allowed— *USA Today* is sold openly on Gold Base—in practice it was discouraged, along with surfing the Internet and watching TV. Indeed, all contact with the world at large was "entheta." "I never considered myself a Scientologist until I joined the Sea Org," Jeffrey says.

Jeffrey's indoctrination began with a boot camp known as the "Estates Project Force," or EPF. There, he learned to march, salute and perform manual labor. Physical work is a key training technique for new recruits. Jeffrey's sister, for instance, went through the EPF when she was twelve and was forced to crawl through ducts that were roach- and rat-infested. Like the TRs, this kind of work, Jeffrey explains, is meant to raise a person's "confront," enabling them to be more in control of their environment.

After the EPF, Jeffrey was given a blue shirt, blue tie, and dark-blue trousers, and sent to work as a receptionist at the American Saint Hill Organization for spiritual training, on Scientology's expansive Hollywood campus. He was paid fifty dollars per week and worked an average of fifteen hours per day, including an hour or two of auditing and other training. Home was a large barracks-style room in a building where Jeffrey lived with about twenty other boys and men. In seven years, Jeffrey says, he saw his family just a handful of times. His only free time was the few hours he received on Sunday mornings to do his laundry. Hubbard believed strongly in productivity, which he saw as highly ethical behavior. "We reward production and up-statistics and penalize nonproduction and down-statistics," he wrote in *Introduction to Scientology Ethics*.

Eventually, Jeffrey found himself on "PTS watch," monitoring Sea Org members who wanted to leave the order. According to church officials, Sea Org members can leave anytime they want. But in practice, the attitude is "the only reason you'd want to leave is because you've done something wrong," says Jeffrey. This would call for a round of "sec checks," which would continue throughout the "route out" process, which can take up to a year. During that time, former Sea Org members have asserted, they are subjected to so much pressure they often decide not to leave after all.

To make sure no one would leave before their route-out was complete, Jeffrey would shadow them: "I've been assigned to go and sleep outside somebody's door—all night, for as many nights as it takes—on the floor, against the door, so I could feel if they opened it. If they went to the bathroom, someone would stand right outside. Someone is always there."

Some wayward members have "disappeared" for long periods of time, sent to special Scientology facilities known as the "Rehabilitation Project Force." Created by Hubbard in 1974, the RPF is described by the church as a voluntary rehabilitation program offering a "second chance" to Sea Org members who have become unproductive or have strayed from the church's codes. It involves intensive physical labor (at church facilities) and auditing and study sessions to address the individual's personal problems. The process is given a positive spin in church writings. "Personnel 'burnout' is not new to organizations," a post on Scientology's official Web site reads, in relation to the RPF, "but the concept of complete rehabilitation is."

Former Sea Org members who've been through the program charge that it is a form of reindoctrination, in which hard physical labor and intense ideological study are used to break a subject's will. Chuck Beatty, a former Sea Org member, spent seven years in the RPF facilities in Southern California, from 1996 to 2003, after expressing a desire to speak out against the church. For this, he was accused of "disloyalty," a condition calling for rehabilitation. "My idea was to go to the RPF for six or eight months and then route out," says Beatty. "I thought that was the honorable thing to do." In the RPF he was given a "twin," or auditing partner, who was responsible for making sure he didn't escape. "It's a prison system," he says, explaining that all RPFers are watched twenty-four hours per day and prevented from having contact with the outside world. "It's a mind-bending situation where you feel like you're betraying the group if you try to leave."

Quiet and disciplined by nature, Jeffrey never minded the regimentation and order of the Sea Org. "I was wrapped up in work," he says. "And that's what I liked doing. And I thought I was helping people." But when he became ill, his perspective radically changed. For the first six years of his Sea Org service, Jeffrey had kept his asthma and other health issues in check. In the spring of 2004, he began to develop severe chest pains. By the summer, he was unable to work. By fall, he could barely get out of bed.

Scientologists believe that most illnesses are products of a person's own psychic traumas—they are brought upon themselves. Sea Org members are promised medical care for any illness, but Jeffrey says that he received little medical attention or money with which to seek outside medical care. Instead, he was sent to Ethics counseling. When that didn't cure him, it was suggested he return to the EPF to repeat his training.

Even while bedridden, "if I wasn't there pushing somebody to take me to a doctor . . . it didn't happen," he says. Lying in bed one night, Jeffrey listened to a taped lecture given by L. Ron Hubbard, in which he made his famous statement "If it isn't true for you, it isn't true." For Jeffrey, this began a questioning process that would eventually lead to his leaving Scientology altogether. "Nobody can force Scientology upon you, but that is exactly what was happening to me," he says.

And so, one day last February, he asked for some time off to see a doctor. Then he called his mother and asked her to come get him. When she arrived the next morning, Jeffrey left his keys and his Sea Organization ID card behind on his bed. Then, taking only his clothes, he left.

Now twenty-three, Jeffrey lives in a small mountain town more than four hours from Los Angeles. Since his "escape," as he calls it, from the Sea Org, he has not returned to the church. He has never spoken out about his experiences, which he still insists "weren't all that bad." But because he left the Sea Org without permission, he has been declared suppressive. Soon, he believes, his family still in the church will have nothing more to do with him.

The order of disconnection, called a "declare," is issued on a piece of gold-colored parchment known as a "goldenrod." This document proclaims the suppressive person's name, as well as his or her "crime." According to one friend of Jeffrey's mother who has read his declare, Jeffrey's crimes are vague, but every Scientologist who sees it will understand its point.

"This declare is a warning to Jeffrey's friends in the Sea Org," this woman, who is still a member of the church, explains. "It's saying to them, 'See this kid, he left without permission. This is what happened to him. Don't you make the same mistake.'"

·   ·   ·

During the time I was researching this piece, I received a number of e-mails from several of the Scientologists I had interviewed. Most were still technically members of the church in good standing; privately they had grown disillusioned and have spoken about their feelings for the first time in this article. All of the young people mentioned in this story, save Natalie, are considered by the church hierarchy to be Potential Trouble Sources. But many have begun to worry they will be declared Suppressive Persons.

Their e-mails expressed their second thoughts and their fears.

"PLEASE, let me know what you will be writing in the story," wrote one young woman. "I just want to make sure that people won't be able to read it and figure out who I am. I know my mom will be reading."

"The church is a big, scary deal," wrote another. "My [initial] attitude was if this information could save just one person the money, heartache and mind-bending control, then all would be worth it. [But] I'm frightened of what could happen."

"I'm about two seconds away from losing my whole family, and if that story comes out with my stuff in it, I will," wrote a third. "I'm terrified. Please, please, please . . . if it's not too late . . . help me keep my family."

One particularly frantic e-mail arrived shortly before this story was published. It came from a young Scientologist with whom I had corresponded several times in the course of three or four months. When we first met, she spoke passionately and angrily about the impact of the church on herself and those close to her.

"Please forgive me," she wrote. "The huge majority of things I told you were lies. Perhaps I don't like Scientology. True. But what I do know is that I was born with the family I was born with, and I love them. Don't ask me to tear down the foundation of their lives." Like almost every young person mentioned in this piece, this woman was given a pseudonym to protect her identity, and her family's. But it wasn't enough, she decided.

"This is my life. . . . Accept what I tell you now for fact: I will not corroborate or back up a single thing I said.

"I'm so sorry," she concluded. "I hope you understand that everyone I love is terribly important to me, and I am willing to look beyond their beliefs in order to keep them around. I will explain in further detail, perhaps, some other day."

Esquire

FINALIST—FEATURE
WRITING

Tom Junod investigates the only people who have been officially blamed in the aftermath of Hurricane Katrina. Using the persecution of nursing-home proprietors Sal and Mabel Mangano as an entry point, Junod shows the ripple effects of the disaster and pulls the reader into a vortex of issues that affect all of us: eldercare, litigiousness, and the need to assign blame.

Tom Junod

The Loved Ones

It was the right decision. Of course it was. Mamaw was killing herself taking care of Papaw. Papaw was killing himself taking care of Mamaw. You were killing yourself taking care of them both. They were going to burn the house down if they kept living in it. They were going to kill themselves or someone else if they kept driving. They couldn't see. They couldn't hear. They couldn't always remember your name. They were speaking gibberish. They were staring out into space. They fell asleep in the middle of conversations. They either weren't taking their pills or they were taking too many. They were found wandering around. They were falling. They were in wheelchairs. They were immobilized. They were sick. They were old. It was—and these were the words you heard yourself saying, the words you heard everybody saying, everybody except them—time.

It couldn't have been an easy decision, no. That it was a decision, and that you had to make it, was in itself a terrible burden. That you were the one called upon to do the final arithmetic seemed cosmically unfair. Your life and theirs, in a ledger. Well, not just your life—your spouse's, your kids'. You had to think of them, too. Did money play a part? Sure it did. But more important was the question of quality of life. Theirs. Yours. You were being *eaten alive* . . . and so in the end you did what you thought best. You made the Decision.

•   •   •

"Mr. Cobb, how are you doing?" I asked James Cobb, a lawyer in New Orleans, Louisiana.

"It depends on what you mean," Mr. Cobb answered. "If you mean how am I doing after losing my house and every fucking thing in it, and after being forced to live in a two-bedroom shithole with my wife and two kids and being told how *lucky* I am to get it, and after being *fucked*—and I mean absolutely fucked—by my insurance company and by the United States government (and by the way, just so you know, if anybody from New Orleans, Louisiana, tells you that they're not getting fucked by their insurance company and by the United States government, they're fucking *lying*, all right?) . . . if you mean, how am I doing after all that is factored in: Well, I guess the answer is that I'm doing fine. Now, how can I help you?"

Jim Cobb and I had never spoken before. These were the first words he spoke after my initial greeting. I was calling him because he represented—and represents—Sal and Mabel Mangano, the couple who operated St. Rita's nursing home in St. Bernard Parish, just southeast of New Orleans. They had not evacuated their residents when Hurricane Katrina was making its way to Louisiana—they had not evacuated in the face of what was said to be a mandatory evacuation order—and when the levees failed and St. Bernard was inundated with ten feet of water, thirty-five helpless people died. No: drowned. No: drowned screaming for someone to save them, at least according to the initial press accounts. No: "drowned like rats," in the words of a prosecutor in the office of Louisiana attorney general Charles Foti, who was charging the Manganos with nearly three dozen counts of negligent homicide. Now they were notorious—icons of abandonment whose mug shots after their arrest personified more than just the prevailing stereotype of unscrupulous nursing-home owners. An entire American city had been left to die, and sixty-five-year-old Sal and sixty-two-year-old Mabel Mangano had somehow become the public faces of a national disgrace.

I was calling Jim Cobb to talk to him about the decision the Manganos had made but also about something else, something at once more universal and more personal: the Decision. My own parents are elderly. I have not made the Decision, but there is not a day when I don't think about it and dread it, and in this I am not so different from many of my friends and millions of people from my generation. The horror of St. Rita's was a nightmarish realization of my dread, a brutal rejoinder to the hopeful voice that inoculates children from the emotional consequences of institutionalizing their parents: *It's for the best.* This was not for the best, nor could it ever be rationalized as such. This was tragic theater catching up with a social and moral issue that had already caught up with America, and in the aftermath of Katrina, I was haunted by reports that the St. Rita's staff had tied residents to their beds and left them to face the rising waters alone. I was transfixed by Jefferson Parish president Aaron Broussard breaking into tears when he said that the mother of one of his employees had telephoned for help from St. Rita's for five days and had died when no help came. I was even fascinated by the multiple rage-gasms of CNN's Nancy Grace, who brought herself off by urging the government to redeem itself by bringing Sal and Mabel Mangano to justice. And when I later found out that little of what I had seen or heard about St. Rita's was actually, you know, *true*, I began to wonder whether the Manganos, who had made the wrong decision, were paying the psychic price for all the millions who had either made or were making the Decision and had to be assured that it was right.

I offered some of this to Jim Cobb. He responded helpfully, translating it into the ungoverned language of his poor dying city. "Yeah," he said, "people need to look in the mirror. I've done a lot of nursing-home work. When a nursing home gets sued, it's because a resident died. And then the kids become avenging angels for Mamaw and Papaw. Well, where were you when Mamaw and Papaw were shitting all over themselves and we were cleaning up? You weren't avenging angels *then*. You want to talk about Sal and Mabel? Let's talk about Sal and Mabel. They cared as much as you did. They were wiping Mamaw and Papaw's ass while you were driving to Destin."

.   .   .

Take care of the old people. It's what people are supposed to do in that part of the world. It's what they learn to do when the storms come. And this time, the storm that was coming was supposed to be major, was supposed to be the one that could bring on the deluge that everyone feared. So Steve Gallodoro and his brother and his sister decided to evacuate their father, Tufanio. They decided to put him in a car and get him the hell out of St. Bernard Parish, which is low-lying and vulnerable to storms. It was Cheryl this time: She was the one who decided to take it on, since Steve himself was a fireman in St. Bernard and had to be around in the event of an emergency. "They were headed to Tennessee," Steve Gallodoro says. "Sixteen hours later, they were in Jackson, Mississippi, and my dad could physically go no farther. He could no longer sit up in the car. They were rescued by a man who saw them at a gas station and said, You look like you need help, we have a big house, you can stay. And so they stayed with him. We refer to him as an angel."

That was 2004. That was Hurricane Ivan, and though it was indeed major, it spent most of its force in the Florida Panhandle and brought damage, but not deluge, to Louisiana. It was, however, decisive in its way: It brought the Gallodoros to the Decision. "My father was eighty-two years old," Steve

Gallodoro says. "He had a couple of strokes, he was paralyzed on the left side, he was confined to a wheelchair. We were physically unable to care for him anymore. We tried the sitters, the aides, but it was too much." Fortunately there were four nursing homes in St. Bernard Parish, and one, St. Rita's, was just six or seven minutes away from where Tufanio Gallodoro's three children lived. It had been in business for twenty years and was a family operation, run by Sal and Mabel Mangano, whose own home was on the twenty-acre property, next door to the homes of their daughter Tammy and their son, Sal Jr., known as "Little Sal," and his wife, TJ. The Manganos, all of them, were in St. Rita's not just every day but night and day. Sal was known for eating breakfast with the St. Rita's residents and Little Sal for being in the building as late as midnight, fixing what needed to be fixed. One of the things Little Sal would say to families shopping for nursing homes—and says even now, as a piece of advice—was this: "Find one that's family run, because if something goes wrong, you know who to point your finger at."

Tufanio Gallodoro became a resident of St. Rita's almost a year before the next storm season. According to Steve Gallodoro, there was still some "emotional upset" in his family about putting Tufanio in a nursing home, but that was eased by the proximity of the place and by its policy of keeping its doors open to family members long after most other nursing homes locked up. "He was visited every day," Steve Gallodoro says. "We would come by and shave him. We would wash his hair. We would give him a haircut. We would feed him." Besides, Tufanio's nickname was TJ, just like Little Sal's wife. He liked TJ, who, during the birthday party the Manganos threw each month for their residents, would dance with the men and sometimes dance on the tables. TJ liked Tufanio, too, and that's the way it was, Little Sal says: "I used to tell families who were leaving a loved one there, 'You're not the only ones who have the right to love them. We have the right to love them, too.'"

•   •   •

"Hey, you ugly bitch!" Jim Cobb shouts through the open window of his big green BMW. He's driving down one of the alley-like streets in the business district of New Orleans, on his way to what's left of his home, and he's spotted a former client on the sidewalk, a tall black guy who's wearing a sheer black jersey and a black skullcap, white iPod plugs in his ears. He's got that New Orleans thing about him, the spindly hard glamour, the high cheekbones, the Asiatic cast to his eyes.

"Hey, bitch, I saw you on CNN defending those people," the client says. "You gon' go to *hell* for that shit."

"Fuck you, bitch," Cobb cackles, and closes the window before heading out to where his city is no more.

You know, you always hear what America is going to lose if it loses New Orleans, and it's always in terms of the jazz or the French Quarter or the red beans and rice or whatever. It's never in terms of *this*—its prickly racial proximities; its ongoing realization of its mulatto history; its men calling one another bitch as a matter of course; its citizenry still drinking, still cursing, still talking without undue deliberation of consequence. It's never in terms of the human artifacts of all those vestigial tendencies, like Jim Cobb. Cobb is fifty-three now. He's lived in New Orleans all his life, and with his trimmed gray beard, his textured face, and his wrinkle-centered, red-rimmed hound-dog eyes, he looks like one of those dissolute Confederate generals of legend who kept a flask on his hip but still managed to lead those boys up the hill. He loves his causes, and now that he's convinced that the cause he really represents by representing Sal and Mabel Mangano—the cause of his beloved New Orleans itself—is a lost one, well, the man will say *anything*.

"Did you see Bertucci's testimony?" he's saying as he's driving. "Was it good for my case? *Fuuuuuuuck.* It was awesome for my case. It was so good, I'm considering jerking off while reading it." For one of the civil lawsuits against the Manganos, Cobb has just taken the deposition of Dr. Bryan Bertucci, the elected coroner of St. Bernard Parish and the man Cobb regards as the state's star witness in its case against the Manganos. It was Bertucci, you see, who offered St. Rita's two school buses for use in an evacuation, and Bertucci who told the world of the nursing home's disastrous reply: No. "The state is trying to prove that Sal and Mabel were negligent," Cobb says. "That means willful, wanton, reckless disregard. So I ask him, 'Have you ever witnessed them treat their patients in a careless manner?' 'No.' 'In a negligent manner?' 'No.' 'In a reckless manner?' 'No.' I mean, I'm practically reading from the *statute,* man. But wait, it gets better. He says, 'No, as a matter of fact, in my opinion they ran the best nursing home in the parish.' All right? This is *their* freaking witness."

At the same time Cobb's saying all this, however, he's on the cell phone with one of his colleagues, talking about a doctor from his neighborhood whose house burned to the ground the night before. The neighborhood is Lakeview, and every house in it is striped by a piss-colored high-water stain that runs as high as the top of the front door. They're all still standing, though, except for the doctor's, which is now knee-high and smoldering. Still on his cell, Cobb parks along the curb and then gets out of his car and climbs on the blackened ruin, saying, "This lucky mother*fucker*—his house burned down. What? He's upset about it? Well, he's a doctor. He's too stupid to know that it's good. Are you telling him he should be breaking out the fucking champagne? His homeowner's goes into effect! He gets full value for his house! The only thing I get is flood insurance. I have to go back! He's free! Tell him congratulations. No, tell him I want to know the dago he hired to do this. I want to get some of that Italian lightning for my house."

And then he goes to his house, which, like all the other houses in Lakeview, is empty and dead. Lakeview is dead. The Ninth Ward of New Orleans is dead, too—famously dead, savagely and spectacularly dead, *vehemently* dead, as dead as Nagasaki in 1945. But Lakeview is different. It's gangrenously dead. It's a museum of itself, a museum that stretches for miles, with the only visible life-forms either grotesque, as in a grown man riding a Big Wheel alone down an uninhabited street, or predatory, as in the looters still plying their trade, with boxes yet. Or simple, as in mold. There's a lot of mold in Lakeview, indeed a lot of mold in Jim Cobb's house, scavenging black mold with the characteristics of fire, stoked in the foul remnants of flood. Floodwater still fills his pool, still fills his crawfish pots and his turkey fryer, and he's uncharacteristically quiet while he's in his house, until he goes outside and starts walking toward the lake, where the vista opens to the wartime view: the black helicopters hovering static over what passes for a levee, the X's spray-painted hastily on the doors of the houses, the occasional 1 or 2 mixed in with the zeros, noting how many bodies were found inside.

"You know who died in these houses?" Cobb says. "Old people. The storm wasn't a black thing or a white thing; it was an old thing. Sixty-five percent of those who died were over sixty-five. Forty percent were over seventy-five. It was a complete fucking catastrophe for old people. And what does the attorney general do about it? Who are the people he arrests? Two senior citizens, Sal and Mabel Mangano. He arrests *them* for neglect while Michael Brown and Ray Nagin and Kathleen Blanco and Michael Chertoff and George W. Bush get a pass? No fucking way, man. They'll have to kill me first."

•   •   •

They each had favorites, the Manganos did. Oh, sure, they treated everybody well: Mabel used to walk around with fifteen or twenty bucks' worth of change in her pocket, and it was for everybody. If a resident wanted a Coke, Mabel bought him a Coke. She'd cut his hair, too, even if the resident's family didn't give him any money. More than anyone else, the ones she doted on were the ones who never saw their families.

Still, her favorite was Janie. Definitely. Janie was a little slow, and Mabel loved her. Is it all right to say that? Because she did. Before Sal and Mabel bought the Hummer, they had a Lincoln, and as Little Sal says, "On some days I'd drive up to the nursing home and there they'd be, Janie driving my mom's Lincoln up and down the driveway, Mom sitting shotgun." Janie had never driven a car in her life—no one had ever thought to let her—and sometimes Mabel would tell her that one day they'd get in the Lincoln and she'd let Janie drive all the way to New York City. Of course, it wasn't going to happen. But it was Janie's dream.

You have to do that when you run a nursing home. You have to keep dreams alive. You have to give the residents something more to look forward to than the relief of death. The Manganos weren't sophisticated people; they weren't particularly educated people; but *that* they knew how to do. It's why they got into the business. Mabel's grandmother, Rita Serpas, was in a nursing home in St. Bernard Parish back in the old days. She was getting forgetful; she'd started going to the highway with dollar bills squeezed between her thumb and forefinger and hitching rides to Canal Street. The nursing home was the kind that gave nursing homes a bad name: three or four beds to a room and the owners free to do as they pleased, since the industry was less regulated back then. Mabel used to visit her grandmother and thought she—and her family—could do better. She and Sal had twenty acres of land in St. Bernard, and when a new highway came next to it, Mabel told Sal that she wanted to build a nursing home. He never thought that much about it, never thought much beyond "Let's do it." They'd run some businesses before— a small trucking business, a feed store—and Sal was always looking for ways to better himself. Mabel did all the paperwork, without a lawyer, and Sal, a mechanic, oversaw the construction of the sixty-room building. St. Rita's opened on September 23, 1985, with a full staff and one resident, because that was the rule: Before you could open for one resident, you had to be fully staffed. In a week, Sal and Mabel had seven or eight residents, and in a year they had enough to have a parade.

The parade was held the Sunday before Carnival, and it was a big deal, not only for the nursing home but also for the neighborhood. The Manganos wanted to make sure everyone in St. Bernard Parish knew about St. Rita's, so they helped the residents get dressed up in costumes and tuxedos, loaded them with beads, and put them on seven floats, along with family members. The residents who were in wheelchairs went on a flat-bed trailer, their chairs tied down by Sal himself, and there was a double amputee they named Carnival queen. After several years, the parade got *too* big, and so the one big event allowed by the Manganos' insurance policy became the feast of St. Joseph. Every March 19, the Manganos fed up to eight hundred people. They baked and gave away a few thousand cookies, made twelve or fifteen casseroles, and stuffed three hundred artichokes. They invited the parish council to eat with them, and the residents—well, the residents they dressed up as saints.

It was fun. They *had* fun, Sal and Mabel. They wanted people other than their residents to want to be there, and people came. People even came during hurricanes and waited out the storm with them. Not just their family—their whole *clan*: grandchildren, nephews, staff members who were working, staff members who weren't working, a few of their neighbors, and then just some people who didn't want to be alone for the storm. Hell, in addition to their residents, they'd have more than thirty people staying with them during big storms, and in the words of Little Sal, "Once you stayed with us the first time, you wouldn't even have to call the next year to feel welcome." Evacuate? They had an evacuation plan, sure; they were required by law to have one. But they never evacuated. Twenty years, hurricanes came buzz-sawing in off the Gulf, and Sal and Mabel Mangano stayed put. Why would they move? People came to *them*. They had faith in the levees, faith in their building, but, more than that, faith in themselves. They survived. Their clan survived. Their residents survived. And then, Little Sal says, after the storms would pass, "There was always an abundance. We'd have fried shrimp and softshell crabs and oysters and redfish and everything from peo-ple's refrigerators. People from the neighborhood would bring their food to us before it went bad. We had big barbecue grills going; it was an *event*."

.   .   .

Who's going to take care of old people? More to the point, what should you expect from the people who *do* take care of old peo-ple when their families can't or won't do it anymore? Even more to the point, what should you expect from the people who take money to take care of old people because *you* can't or won't do it anymore? Do you expect them to love your mother or father as much as you do? Do you expect them to love your mother or father *more* than you do? Do you expect their love to be abso-lute? And do you expect their love to be absolute because you found out that yours wasn't—because you made the Decision? Or do you expect their love to be absolute because they're get-ting paid for it, and their obligations are legal and contractual, whereas yours were strictly moral? Or, in Cobb's translation: "What is it we can expect from caregivers who are taking care of your parents for ninety-five bucks a day? That's the Medicaid rate, I believe. Ninety-five bucks a day, and for that a lot of peo-ple think nursing homes should be the Ritz-Carlton Naples."

These are the issues Charlie Foti has to hash out as attorney general of the state of Louisiana. Well, not really. He really has to decide how to enforce the law, which means that he has to decide whether, say, the prosecution of Sal and Mabel Mangano for thirty-four counts of negligent homicide is in the state's interest. (The thirty-fifth body was found after the Manganos were arrested.) But Charlie Foti is interested in old people. They mean a lot to him, personally and politically. They're his *constituency*, politically. When he was sheriff of Orleans Parish, he had a big dinner every Thanksgiving for old people who were too poor or too alone to have one for themselves. He didn't forget them, and when he ran for AG in 2003, *they* didn't forget him, helping make him the state's top lawyer. And personally— personally he just likes them. For many years, he took care of his aged father. His father died in 2004 at the age of ninety-three, but when the phone rang for the first year Foti was in office, it was as likely as not the old man, calling for reasons any son with an old father knows all about. And Foti always took the call, no matter how busy he was. It's not easy watching your parents get old, but from Charlie Foti's point of view, it's not half as difficult as watching them die.

And so, according to his spokeswoman, the attorney general has made "elderly issues his first priority" since he entered office. In fact, he and Fred Duhy, the lawyer in charge of his Medicaid-fraud unit, were just about to launch a major public-relations campaign about what Duhy calls the "plight" of the elderly before Katrina came along and provided all the awareness, and all the plight, they would ever need. "When you have elderly people and infirm people in your care, you have a greater standard of care, because you're talking about people who can't take care of themselves," Duhy says in his office one afternoon before he goes to see his boss. "We deal with cases every day where people in nursing homes threaten to withhold food and water from people who can't reach for it. We just arrested someone who flung food at someone's face." Is Duhy saying that the Manganos ran that kind of nursing home? No, he's not. What he's saying is that the case against them is similarly straightforward. He is saying that they knew—that they had to know—the extent of the storm coming their way. He is saying that they had an evacuation plan and did not follow it. He is alleging that Louisiana's governor issued a mandatory evacuation order on the Sunday afternoon before the storm hit in the early hours of Monday morning, and they ignored it. He is saying that the other three nursing homes in St. Bernard Parish all evacuated, and they lost one patient among them. "Here, read this," he says, and opens his copy of the Louisiana criminal code to the page on criminal negligence, which, in the language of the statute, "exists when, although neither specific nor general criminal intent is present, there is such disregard of the interest of others that the offender's conduct amounts to a gross deviation below the standard of care expected to be maintained by a reasonably careful man under like circumstances."

"When this results in a death," Duhy says, "you have negligent homicide. It's not a big mystery."

Then he goes into the conference room, where, taking a seat at the end of a long table, behind unkempt stacks of paper, is Charlie Foti. This is the other thing you have to love about this part of the world: People still have faces, and everybody seems to have the right one. Charlie Foti *looks* like the guy who ran the jail in New Orleans for thirty years. He's wearing a rumpled white shirt and a loosened tie, and he looks damp, man. He doesn't just sit down; he slumps in his chair, so that his eyes are about table level, and then he doesn't *move*. He doesn't blink, doesn't look at anyone asking him questions. What he does is belch, softly and without excuse, and then set about lovingly chewing an unlit cigar into cud. When he starts talking, it's with the intention of talking without interruption. He says, "Do you expect these nursing-home people to have the responsibility to protect their patients? . . . You might not ask for the responsibility, but you got it. . . . You just gotta do what you gotta do. . . . My poor brother evacuated my father when he was ninety-two. . . . St. Bernard Parish evacuated prisoners. . . . We evacuate criminals but not people who can't move? . . . If I make that decision and I die, woe is me. . . . If I make that decision for someone who can't walk . . ."

He is as patient and oblivious—and as seemingly drowsy—as a snapping turtle, and he just keeps sinking deeper into his chair until he is asked this: The fact that a lot of the most lurid details reported in the media didn't turn out to be true—how does that affect your case? That's when his head turns, quickly, and he snaps, "What didn't *happen*? They died in their beds. That will be horrendous enough." And he's right, of course. Sal and Mabel Mangano may not be guilty of the crimes conjured up by the media and the public's imagination. Negligent homicide may be notoriously difficult to prove. Charlie Foti for all we know may have, as Jim Cobb says, "the legal acumen of an unlit charcoal briquette—and that's being too hard on charcoal briquettes." But on his side of the ledger he has thirty-five helpless people, horribly and inexcusably dead. Cobb has only Sal and Mabel, and they are already guilty of staying alive.

·   ·   ·

Take care of the old people.

Jimmy Martinez came to St. Rita's to wait out Katrina with his wife, Peggy, who had Alzheimer's. Gene Alonzo came to wait out the storm with his brother Carlos, who was severely disabled from a boating accident. Nine families came before the storm and got their loved ones out of there. For Steve Gallodoro, however, there were no easy choices. He couldn't evacuate Tufanio because the last time anybody tried that, his father almost died. He couldn't stay with Tufanio because he was a fireman and had to work during big storms. So on Saturday he went to talk to the people who were taking care of his father. He went to St. Rita's, and he says, "The Manganos assured me they'd contracted with bus services, they had staff coming in, they had two facilities to transport the residents to if the call for evacuation was made. They said, We are the professionals, leave him with us, he's better off. My sister had some emotional struggles about leaving him, but I told her the Manganos had a plan in place, let's leave him with them.

"My family left the parish early Sunday morning," he says. "I was at the firehouse. I cleared up things that needed to be done, got in my unit, and went to St. Rita's. I walked up to Sal Mangano and asked what he needed. I said, However many men you need for the evacuation, I'll give them to you. He told me they were not evacuating. They decided they were going to stay. I left and ran into someone from the parish. I informed him of what St. Rita's had told me, and he said, We'll go back to the government center and have the coroner call them. So Dr. Bertucci called and advised them that they should leave and offered buses and manpower. The Manganos refused.

"Then we were in the middle of the storm. The next morning the water started coming up, and I couldn't get back to St. Rita's. I had no contact with the eastern end of the parish, but I heard that it was dry. That was inaccurate. But I thought that if something had happened, I would have gotten some word. So we got into boats on Monday and started rescuing. As soon as we left the complex, we could not travel any great distance without filling the boat with survivors. People were on rooftops, and to get to St. Rita's I would have had to pass people by. I didn't do that, and so I didn't get to St. Rita's until the next morning."

You know what came next. You know what Steve Gallodoro saw when he got into a boat on Tuesday morning and went to St. Rita's. And, given what you know: Does it matter what the Manganos have to say? Does it matter that they say they told everyone who asked—Steve Gallodoro included—that they were staying put for the storm? Does it matter that they say no government official called to inform them of a mandatory evacuation order? Does it matter that Dr. Bryan Bertucci, the one government official who did call with an offer of two school buses, has admitted in his deposition that he never pushed the issue: "No, I didn't say, 'You got to leave,' " Bertucci says. "That's not my job. But I was suggesting, obviously, I thought they should leave, or I wouldn't have offered them the buses."

It matters to them, of course. It matters to the Manganos because they have been charged with legal responsibility for the death of Tufanio Gallodoro and nearly three dozen others. To Steve Gallodoro, though, there is nothing they can say that changes anything, because there is nothing they can say that changes these facts: Tufanio Gallodoro couldn't swim. Tufanio Gallodoro was deathly afraid of the water. Tufanio Gallodoro drowned. For his son, the horror of St. Rita's will always be a moral horror, and he will never stop holding the Manganos morally responsible.

· · ·

"So you met with Charlie Foti," Jim Cobb says. "Did Charlie tell you that the first witness I'm going to call is Charlie Foti?"

Well, yes, he did. His employees did, anyway. Fred Duhy did. It's one of Cobb's more entertaining characteristics—making you privy to secrets he has told everyone under the sun. Back in the spring, when it became clear that the attorney general was going to move forward with the prosecution of the Manganos— that he wasn't, in Cobb's words, going to "stand down"—Cobb went to Baton Rouge for a meeting with Duhy and, for as long as Cobb succeeded in holding his attention, Charlie Foti. "He kept going in and out of the meeting," Cobb says. "You've heard of ADHD? Well, he's ADHDDDDDDDDDDDDDDDD." Cobb's intention was to *get* Foti to stand down by citing all the officials who to his mind had more legal responsibility than Sal and

Mabel Mangano for the thirty-five deaths at St. Rita's. According to Cobb, the meeting went like this: "Duhy leaned over and said, Is that some sort of veiled threat against the attorney general? I said, I don't think there's anything *veiled* about it." According to Duhy: "He told us point-blank that he intended to call the governor or whoever. I don't think there's anything to it. And I don't appreciate this 'stand down' business. I don't appreciate someone telling me how to do my job. I'm going to do my job the way I see fit, and I'm not going to be bullied."

Cobb has said he doesn't want to go to trial. Normally sparing with biblical references, he has even gone so far as to say, "Father, take this cup." At the same time, he has pursued a course of such single-minded provocation with Charlie Foti that you wonder if his intention is to make it impossible for Foti to let the prosecution go away so that he can put Foti on the stand.

Why Foti? Simple. Because Cobb wants a chance to ask him, *Why the Manganos?*, when on April 1, 2005 ("April Fool's Day," Cobb says), Louisiana governor Kathleen Blanco approved an emergency-evacuation plan that gave legal responsibility for the evacuation of nursing homes to Louisiana transportation secretary Johnny Bradberry.

And because in December 2005, Secretary Bradberry told Senate investigators that "we put no plans in place to do any of this."

And because, according to the *New York Times*, the state "even turned down an offer for patient-evacuation assistance from the federal government," in much the same way the Manganos were said to have turned down an offer of assistance from the St. Bernard Parish coroner.

And because St. Rita's wasn't the only nursing home in the area that didn't evacuate for Katrina. Indeed, only twenty-one of fifty-seven nursing homes did.

And because the thirty-five people who died at St. Rita's weren't the only people who died in unevacuated nursing homes and hospitals when the levees failed—more than two hundred did.

And because the storm itself left St. Rita's unscathed. It was the failure of the *levees* that sent the ten feet of water that swallowed up the one-story structure in less than an hour.

And because even the commander of the Army Corps of Engineers has admitted that blame for the failure of the levees lies with the Corps itself.

And because the same thing that killed thirty-five people at St. Rita's killed *more than fifteen hundred* people in the New Orleans area. "And guess what?" Cobb says. "It wasn't Sal and Mabel. It was a flood caused by the negligence of the Army Corps of Engineers and the levee boards. And so if Foti is going to charge someone, why not charge the motherfuckers who killed fifteen hundred people? Why charge Sal and Mabel? Why isn't he doing his *job*? Which is what I intend to ask him if he persists in fucking around with me and the Manganos. I don't want to, but I will. We're looking to try the ultimate responsibility for Katrina. Everybody talks about responsibility. The fact is, nobody wants it. That's what this whole prosecution is about. The state doesn't want to be responsible for its part in the whole fucking catastrophe. The attorney general thinks the case is about responsibility, too? Fine, let's go. You take Kathleen Blanco and the Army Corps of Engineers. I'll take Sal and Mabel. Let's get it on."

.   .   .

"Sal was making the rice for the red beans when the water came," Mabel says. "The beans was all ready. We figured the power would go out, so we made the beans the day before."

Yes, that's Sal and Mabel Mangano sitting in a conference room in Jim Cobb's office. Last seen as Sal and Mabel *M-a-n-g-a-n-o*, when Nancy Grace asked a guest to spell their surname so that all of America could identify them and hunt them down.

Last seen as the most vilified man and woman in the country, after Charles Foti announced their arrest to the national media. Sal and Mabel. They've been married forty-six years, after meeting at a dance in New Orleans. Now they live in a FEMA trailer like everyone else. They're sitting next to each other at the long table, occasionally holding hands. Mabel's got the soft voice, the blue blouse, the big hair, the cantilevered eyebrows, the handbag either on the table or in her lap, the tissues squeezed in her free hand. Sal's the blunt instrument. He's a squat man, a mechanic with thick fingers, his hair combed straight back off his forehead. In back of them, hovering around them, pacing, standing, always standing, never sitting down, is Sal Mangano Jr., Little Sal, an amalgam of both his parents, compact and muscled in a short-sleeved shirt, like his father, but with the same polished face as his mother, with the same perpetually amazed and amazing eyebrows, combined with black hair combed straight back from a widow's peak and a black Sharpie's mustache. He's forty-three. He does most of the talking while chewing the *shit* out of a black coffee straw, but when his father, out of nowhere, says, "Take that stick out of your mouth," he does as he's told without saying a word.

·   ·   ·

And so: Sal was making the rice for the red beans when the water came. It was ten-thirty in the morning on Monday, August 29. Katrina had hit in the wee hours, and the lights had gone out, but the generators had kicked in, and they had power for everything except the air conditioners. They had prepared in their usual way. They had water, they had diapers, they had generators, they had medicine, they had ice, they had the red beans already done. And, at ten-thirty in the morning, they told themselves they had made it; they told themselves they had survived the storm, just as they had for the last twenty years. Their clan was with them—the workers, the nonworkers, the children, the children's children: thirty-one people in all. And the residents: sixty-two of them. All that was left was to go outside and check the wind damage sustained by the one-story building that was long and low and straight as a piece of pipe.

Then the nursing home started filling up with water. *Woe-tah*: That's how the Manganos pronounce it. There has been some talk of a wall of water coming down the road with a rumble, but the Manganos just remember the water's incessant *rise*. "Even when it's two feet deep, you hope it's going to stop," Mabel says. "But it didn't. It just kept coming in." Or, as Little Sal puts it, "When I jumped outside onto the patio, the water was about two or three feet deep. My house is 150 feet away from the nursing home. My fence is five feet tall. By the time I got to my fence, I was able to swim over it." He was with his wife, TJ, and his son Tanner and Emmett Unbehagen, the husband of one of the nurses. They were trying to get to their boats, which had been parked on the lawn. Little Sal's boat was caught in an oak tree, and they rode the current of water coursing through his living room to get it, spark plugs and keys in Little Sal's mouth. Emmett's boat was chained to a trailer, and by the time they got to it, the chain was pulling it under the water. Tanner took a gun and shot the chain. Then they started the boats and went back to St. Rita's and all its drowning saints.

People were already hanging from the gutters when they got there. Well, Big Sal was on the roof, trying to keep the doors open. But Mabel was hanging from the gutters, holding on to Janie. Or Janie was holding on to her. When the home first began flooding, Mabel hooked Janie with one arm and held a resident floating on a mattress with the other. She was standing on a platform that was filled with flowers the residents grew. Then Janie, panicking as the water rose, began grabbing at Mabel with her legs, and Mabel was pulled under the water. She figured then that if she stayed inside, she was a goner, so she made her way outside with her human cargo. There had been life jackets stored away in a shed, and Tanner had gotten them when the flood first started. Mabel had one on, and so did some of the children. Very few of the workers could swim, and they were holding on to anything they could, anything that would float. The residents, the lucky ones, were on mattresses.

"You know, you hear that we tied people to mattresses," Little Sal says. "Actually, that wouldn't have been such a bad idea, because mattresses in nursing homes are in waterproof liners. They float." Indeed, according to the Manganos, that was the margin of life and death at St. Rita's. The residents who made it onto mattresses rose with the flood. The immobilized residents— the ones who couldn't get off their chairs or out of their wheelchairs—were gone, says Little Sal, "before we got the boats in the water."

The building started falling apart from the inside out. Walls were popping out, TJ says, "like dominoes." And yet, Mabel says, there was no screaming. No: "It was so quiet, it was almost eerie." Residents and nurses and staffers were praying in the dark. The only screaming, Little Sal says, was the back-and-forth hollering of the people forming a chain of rescue. Mabel's brother Tony Buffone was in the hallway, pulling residents out of the rooms. Little Sal was taking them from Tony and bringing them to Tanner, who was putting them in the boats. Emmett and TJ were driving the boats, and Tammy's son Johnny was pulling people from the boats to the roof, along with a worker named Wayne King. Big Sal was at the door. The wind, which had been calm when the flood first started, kicked in again, and whitecaps topped the water.

One end of the building became blocked with floating furniture and debris, and when they tried to get in through the patio door, water had sealed it shut. So Tanner found his gun again and shot out the glass. Water by this time had climbed above the doorjambs, and Uncle Tony had to dive into the rooms to find residents and take them back under the water to get them out. "Uncle Tony was hollering into the rooms," Little Sal says. "And I'd say, 'No, Uncle Tony, that one, he can't holler back. Go in.' We kept going down them hallways till Uncle Tony didn't bring anyone else out." They kept making their way down the hallways until water sealed the building like a tomb.

There was a place for the living, and it was the roof. More than fifty people, half of them elderly and incapacitated, were marooned there, until Little Sal and the rest of them started loading them in the two boats and taking them away. They went first to Tammy's house, which was on the property, about three hundred feet from St. Rita's. Then they went a little more than half a mile to the Beauregard Middle School. It was an old courthouse, three stories high, and Little Sal and Tanner began carrying the residents up the stairs, until they couldn't anymore, until they ran out of strength and started constructing beds out of desks and filing cabinets to keep the residents out of the water on the first floor. Sal Sr. and Emmett found some help and went back to the nursing home, where they cut a hole in the roof and found several people clinging to a floating ice machine, including the head of nursing and a nurse named Thelma Lee. Thelma was diabetic and had almost slipped into the water when her blood sugar dropped. The head of nursing had grabbed her by the hair, had held her by the shoulders, and then when a Tupperware container of bread came floating by, had fed her until Thelma regained enough strength to hang on.

They had been floating for six hours, and the five of them—three staffers and two residents—were the last people rescued from the building on Monday. Dark came, and it was black dark. While the Manganos stayed on Tammy's second floor and the residents and staff members stayed at Beauregard, the dead began their extended occupancy of St. Rita's. And in the morning Little Sal got in his boat with Tanner and his nephew and went back to see if there was anybody left *but* the dead. "And my nephew heard someone hollering, 'Little Sal, Little Sal, don't leave me.' It was Miss Janis. She was in her room when the water came. A dresser fell down, the door came open, she fell onto the door, and the dresser floated. The only person she was looking for was me, she didn't care about the moon and the sun, but that's the way it was all the time. She said, 'I knew you wouldn't leave me, Little Sal.'"

And that's it. That's the Manganos' story. Is there anything left to say? Well, yes, there is, and Little Sal is going to say it, because he's heard other accounts of the rescue, and they give credit to everyone except the Mangano family and the other workers at St. Rita's. The story that has been accepted in the press is the story of local people coming upon the nursing home in an impromptu flotilla and saving old people while the Manganos saved themselves. "They're saying what happened in my *yard*," Little Sal says, bouncing on the balls of his feet behind his parents. "How can they tell me what happened in my yard? I hear how we left, I hear how all those people came and saved people from that building. Well, it happened too fast for that. Okay, some boys came later on in the day to help us. But nobody saved anybody from that building but us. And if anybody tells you different, they *lying*. I hear about the bad choices we made. I think we made some pretty good choices, once the water came. We saved fifty-eight people with six people in two boats. If ever there's a flood, I'm the man you want next to you, because I'm going to save your life. I don't give a shit whether I like you or not."

· · ·

"It wasn't until Tuesday that I was able to get clear to go to the nursing home," Steve Gallodoro says. "I was with a friend from the parish council and some other guys. We saw no one around the facility, no movement whatsoever. I thought at the time that they must have at the last minute evacuated, but as we got closer to the front of the building, I saw the Hummer the Manganos owned and knew they hadn't evacuated.

"I swam into the water," Steve Gallodoro says. "I couldn't open the glass door, so I had them bring me to the patio area. I climbed up on the patio; it had three feet of water, one of them glass doors was broken, and as I was walking to the door, I came across a body. I moved the body around to see sort of who it was, and it was an elderly female. I walked into a doorway, and as soon as I stepped in the doorway, there was another body floating. It was another female. I was in the TV room of the lobby in the north wing, and I came across another body about ten feet later, another elderly female. There was four feet of water or so, beds floating, furniture floating. It would have been impossible for me to walk any farther down the hallways. I hollered, 'Fire Department, is anybody here, does anybody need help?' and it just echoed."

· · ·

The day after the flood, you could still take the roads through St. Bernard Parish, if you had an airboat. You could follow the asphalt, which was visible through the water. There were even stop signs, poking up through the surface at street corners. It was the same world, except that it was entirely underwater. Todd Baker, a biologist from Louisiana's Department of Wildlife and Fisheries, had been pressed into rescue operations, along with a few of his colleagues and a state trooper. The state trooper wanted to check out St. Rita's and knew how to get there. They took the airboat along the roads where the Manganos had held their parades.

"We get to St. Rita's," Baker says, "and I'll never forget it. There's a guy in a flatboat. He says, 'Don't go in there unless you want to see thirty dead bodies.' He says, 'I pulled out everyone I could.' He says, 'I took them over to the school.' Then he says, 'Thank God you showed up.' We were apparently the first search-and-rescue people he'd seen.

"The school was the most depressing stuff I've ever seen. People were hanging out of the windows because of the heat. All ages. When we pulled up to the back side, there was a guy cooking hamburgers, because people were emptying their food. And then we walked through the door and that's when it hit us—the smell. There were nursing-home patients lying everywhere. In the back they'd stacked filing cabinets or desks, and the people on them were pretty bad; one was a double amputee. Half of them looked like they were dead or about to die.

"What he said about the thirty dead bodies didn't register until we hit the school, and we thought, Oh, God, these are those who *survived*," Todd Baker says. "It's disgusting is what it was."

.   .   .

"People say we left people in that building," Sal Mangano says. "If anyone was still alive, we're taking them. But we had no place for the dead."

And so they helped with the living—on Tuesday, Emmett in his flatboat and Little Sal and the entire St. Rita's staff helped Baker and the others from Wildlife and Fisheries move the survivors to triage—and then, when they saw a dump truck making its way through the water, past Tammy's house, the Manganos did what everyone else did: They got on. They got out. They evacuated St. Bernard Parish. There were eleven of them, and the dump truck took them to the jail, and then they went to a shelter set up at a warehouse, and then they got on a bus and went to Algiers, and then they went to the New Orleans airport, and then they went to another shelter, in Terrell, Texas, and then Sal paid a bus driver $200 to take them all to a town near

Shreveport, where they got a hotel room and went to a Wal-Mart and changed their clothes for the first time since the flood.

The *bodies*, though: The bodies stayed behind in the nursing home. They hadn't been evacuated, and now they couldn't evacuate and nobody would evacuate them. TJ Mangano says that she would never have left if she hadn't been assured by the police that a recovery team was on its way, but no recovery team came. Steve Gallodoro says that he tried to initiate a recovery effort of his own but was told that the parish had no body bags and that even if he did start pulling bodies out of the water, "nobody would accept them." And so the bodies stayed. They stayed as the flood receded and the sun came out and the days got hot and the story of what had happened at St. Rita's started leaking out in the press, and a nation that had decided to put its elderly where they could not be seen now had its conscience inflamed by the grotesque spectacle of their abandonment. They stayed as the state of Louisiana and the federal government came to a stalemate over the recovery of the dead and, in the words of Robert Jensen, CEO of Kenyon International, the company that finally *did* the recovery for the state, "it became a job that everybody waited for someone else to do." They stayed until the federal mortuary team that attempted to do the job couldn't do the job because the job was so terrible. They stayed in the building for eleven days, until at last, on September 9, Kenyon came with its hazmat suits and took the bodies out in a hideous parade witnessed by Fred Duhy and other representatives of the attorney general. And though it was not just government that collapsed during Katrina, but rather the very *idea* of government as an entity that took care of its people and its dead, it isn't government that Duhy is angry at when he says that "by the time that last body came out, I was ready to spit nails."

It is Sal and Mabel.

.   .   .

In 1992, Tom Rodrigue went to visit his mother, Eva, in New Orleans. She lived alone, and he was used to knocking on a locked door. This time, though, he pushed on the door and the door swung open. His mother was gone. He went looking for her in his car and couldn't find her; he came back to the house and the phone rang. It was a nun from Charity Hospital, saying that his mother had been found wandering a vacant lot with a wad of cash. She went to St. Rita's and was there for a very long time: Miss Eva, the Manganos called her, and, as Rodrigue says, "she was kind of the mascot for the place." On the weekend of Katrina, Rodrigue called the nursing home several times, telling whoever picked up the phone what was coming in the Gulf. You see, Rodrigue was an emergency-operations manager for Jefferson Parish. He knew damned well what was coming, but he could never get the Manganos on the phone, and when he called his counterpart in St. Bernard Parish, he was told that the coroner had called St. Rita's and offered buses. "What else can I do?" his counterpart said.

On September 4, the president of Jefferson Parish, Aaron Broussard, went on *Meet the Press* and, with tears in his eyes, told this story about Rodrigue's experience: "The guy who runs this building I'm in, Emergency Management, he's responsible for everything," Aaron Broussard says. "His mother was trapped in St. Bernard nursing home, and every day she called him and said, 'Are you coming, son? Is somebody coming?' And he said, 'Yeah, Mama, somebody's coming to get you. Somebody's coming to get you on Tuesday. Somebody's coming to get you on Wednesday. Somebody's coming to get you on Thursday. Somebody's coming to get you on Friday.' And she drowned Friday night. She drowned Friday night."

This was, of course, untrue, and lavishly so. Miss Eva died on Monday, August 29, in the initial flooding. She never made it to the roof, much less had access to a telephone. Nevertheless, when Broussard went back on *Meet the Press* three weeks later and was asked to explain, this is what he told Tim Russert: "Listen, sir, somebody wants to nitpick a man's tragic loss of a mother because she was abandoned in a nursing home? Are you kidding? What kind of sick mind, what kind of black-hearted people want to nitpick a man's mother's death?"

Certainly, Miss Eva's death was horrible enough. What happened at St. Rita's was horrible enough. But St. Rita's became *something else* in the weeks following Hurricane Katrina. The story alchemized according to the laws of political expedience and media opportunism, and Sal and Mabel Mangano went from caregivers to fuckups to criminals to monsters. On September 8—the day before the recovery of the St. Rita's dead—Charlie Foti announced that Sal and Mabel were wanted for questioning. At this time, they were on a bus on their way to Lafayette, and when they heard they were wanted by the attorney general, they started looking for Jim Cobb, who with his family had been displaced to a hotel in Houston. On September 12, Nancy Grace was on CNN, quivering as she contemplated what they would be charged with: "I'm thinking negligent homicide. Especially if some jury in a parish down in Louisiana gets wind that these two owners row, row, rowed away, leaving all the elderlies to die in their wheelchairs. Oh, *yes*."

A day later, Cobb met with the Manganos and listened to their story. He called Fred Duhy and told him he would break the cardinal rule of defense attorneys: He would bring his clients in for a meeting with the prosecutor. "I told Duhy, 'I've talked to them, and I think you need to do that, too.' Duhy says, Deal. I go to a meeting with Sal and Mabel. I tell them, 'If you tell them what you told me, they can't arrest you.' She's all upbeat. On the fourteenth I get the call. It's Duhy. 'Jim, bad news. The meeting's off. I have an arrest warrant for your clients.' I ask him, 'What's the charge?' He says, 'Thirty-four counts of negligent homicide.' Thanks, Fred. Thanks for not piling on. Now I have to go back and tell Sal and Mabel. She falls into my arms, sobbing like a baby."

It's been war ever since, with Foti and Duhy attempting to funnel the faults of the state into the vessel of the individual, and Cobb attempting to funnel the faults of the individual into the vessel—capacious, in this case—of the state. And when Cobb is told that Foti and Duhy have claimed that the prosecution of the Manganos actually *saved lives*, because when Hurricane Rita hit a few weeks after Katrina, you can bet that every single nursing home in Louisiana and Texas knew to evacuate, here is what he has to say: "Have you ever heard of that nursing home in Bellaire? It's in a high-class neighborhood in Houston. The nursing home evacuated, the bus caught fire, and they fried twenty-three seniors on the interstate. I was in Houston when the Manganos called, so I went to the nursing home. It was *dry*. They shouldn't have evacuated. They made a *terrible mistake*. Is Charlie Foti taking credit for that? Congratulations, General. We drown ours, you fry yours."

· · ·

So why didn't they evacuate? That's the big question, isn't it? Fred Duhy says that governor Kathleen Blanco issued a mandatory evacuation order for St. Bernard Parish at 1:30 P.M., Sunday, August 29, 2005. He says that the Manganos ignored it for one reason, and for one reason only: money. "There's the contract with EMS. That's the initial expense. Then there's the cost of transportation itself. That's the second expense. Then when the new facility takes the residents in, the Manganos lose all that Medicaid would've paid. It's a very expensive proposition. . . ."

In fact, there is no record of a mandatory evacuation order being issued for St. Bernard Parish, either by the governor or the parish council. There is certainly no record of anyone calling St. Rita's and telling the Manganos that a mandatory order was in effect. The government's effort to evacuate St. Rita's nursing home amounted to this: Dr. Bertucci. Two school buses. And that's it.

And yet, as Charlie Foti says, "you don't need the government to tell you that a major storm was on the way." If the Manganos had evacuated, they would have saved lives.

So why didn't they? They say—well, they say a few things. They say that a resident died on Sunday morning, and they couldn't get an ambulance to take the body without Dr. Bertucci's intervention, so how in the world could they have gotten an ambulance service to evacuate their most at-risk patients on Sunday afternoon as Katrina bore down on them? They say they were afraid they would have lost at least five patients if they had put them on school buses. They say they never thought the levees would break. And they say they didn't leave because they had never left, that they stayed because they had always stayed. . . .

But maybe none of these explanations are sufficient, psychologically. Maybe the only psychological explanation that makes any sense is the unexpected offshoot of the Manganos' twenty years of running an institution and seeing people institutionalized: love. Maybe they stayed because they believed they loved their residents as much as anyone did, even their families. Maybe they stayed because they believed they knew their residents better than anyone did and knew what was best for them. Maybe they stayed because they weren't going to let the government decide the fates of their residents, their favorites, their saints. Maybe they stayed because they believed that to evacuate was to abandon people who had already been abandoned. "We stayed for these people," TJ Mangano says. "We wasn't about to leave them. If one of them wasn't going, we weren't going."

Indeed, even when Little Sal is talking about the thirty-five who died, he never simply says, "He died," or "She drowned." He says, "I didn't save him," or "I didn't rescue him." He says this not as an apology but rather as a reminder of his own role in who lived and who died—his power. The Manganos were not irresponsible; they were, if anything, too responsible, for they had only done what the families of the residents asked them to do.

Until, of course, they didn't die. That's where the contract between them and the families of the dead broke down—in the unforgivable fact of their survival.

And so there they are, in the conference room, Sal and Mabel, the Manganos. Mabel is squeezing a tissue, her face is shiny and wet, and there's a sense that she's not the person she was when she first sat down—that she's slipping away behind some scrim of personal devastation. Sal is holding her hand. Little Sal is pacing.

"I loved them, I loved these people," Mabel says. "I miss them, my heart aches."

"We loved them," Big Sal says. "We loved what we done. Sure, we done it for money, it was our livelihood. But we never even had a budget. . . ."

"Whether or not we saved your family or lost your family, we are sorry for the water that came in," Little Sal says. "But not for the decision to stay."

You know what's the worst thing for them? That they can't do it anymore. That they can't . . . care. They were really good at caring. They had it inside them. And so their dream, if they escape the criminal charges, if they have a dime left after the thirty-one lawsuits and Jim Cobb's legal bill, is to rebuild. Right there. On the property. St. Rita's. There are staff members who have told them they want to come back. There are people in St. Bernard who have said they are waiting for the day when they can live with Sal and Mabel. . . .

And that's the thing for Steve Gallodoro. That's one prospect he does not want to contemplate. "I don't need to see them go to jail. The only thing I want to see is that they are never given an opportunity to hold a license that would enable them to care for any elderly, handicapped, disabled, because they have shown they are not responsible, and I need to know they can never be responsible for the lives of other people again."

But it's not his decision anymore. It's yours. Would you ever put your loved ones in a nursing home run by Sal and Mabel Mangano? Would you ever put your loved ones in a nursing home at all? Would you make the Decision?

I would. But every day I pray that I won't have to.

Smithsonian

FINALIST—ESSAYS

In this insightful, iconoclastic, and wry essay, novelist Paul Theroux describes the delights and challenges of his ten years of living among geese. Theroux's observations—"I have come to the obvious conclusion that they live in a goose-centric world, with goose rules and goose urgencies."

Paul Theroux

Living with Geese

When I first began to raise geese, in Hawaii, my more literate friends asked me, "Have you read the E. B. White piece?" This apparently persuasive essay was all that they knew about geese other than the cliché, often repeated to me, "Geese are really aggressive! Worse than dogs!" or "They're everywhere!"—regarding them as an invasive species, spoiling golf courses. Received wisdom is not just unwise, it is usually wrong. But I was well disposed toward E. B. White. In his writing he is the kindest and most rational observer of the world. And a man who can write the line "Why is it . . . that an Englishman is unhappy until he has explained America?" is someone to cherish.

Though I had read much of White's work, I had not read his essay "The Geese." I avoided it for several reasons. The first was that I wanted to discover the behavior of these birds, their traits and inclinations, on my own, at least in the beginning. I loved the size of geese, their plumpness, their softness, the thick down, the big feet of fluffy just-born goslings, the alertness of geese—sounding an alarm as soon as the front gate opened; their appetites, their yawning, the social behavior in their flocking, their homing instinct, the warmth of their bodies, their physical strength, their big blue unblinking eyes. I marveled at their varieties of biting and pecking, the way out of sheer impatience a goose wishing to be fed quickly would peck at my toes, just a reminder to hurry up; the affectionate and harmless gesture of pecking if I got too close; the gander's hard nip on the legs, the wicked bite on my thigh, which left a bruise. I also marveled at their memory, their ingeniousness in finding the safest places to nest; their meddling curiosity, always sampling the greenery, discovering that orchid leaves are tasty and that the spiky stalks of pineapple plants are chewable and sweet.

But it was the second and more important reason that kept my hand from leaping to the shelf and plucking at the *Essays of E. B. White*. It was White's conceits, his irrepressible anthropomorphism, his naming of farm animals, making them domestic pets, dressing them in human clothes, and giving them lovable identities, his regarding them as partners (and sometime personal antagonists). Talking spiders, rats, mice, lambs, sheep, and pigs are all extensions of White's human world—more than that, they are in many cases more sensitive, more receptive, truer chums than many of White's human friends.

But here's the problem. White's is not just a grumpy partiality toward animals; rather, his frequent lapses into anthropomorphism produce a deficiency of observation. And this sets my teeth on edge, not for merely being cute in the tradition of children's books, but (also in the tradition of children's books) for being against nature.

Animal lovers often tend to be misanthropes or loners, and so they transfer their affection to the creature in their control. The classics of this type are single species obsessives, like Joy Adamson, the *Born Free* woman who raised Elsa the lioness and was celebrated in East Africa as a notorious scold; or Dian Fossey, the gorilla woman, who was a drinker and a recluse. "Grizzly man" Tim Treadwell was regarded, in some circles, as an authority on grizzlies, but Werner Herzog's documentary shows him to have been deeply disturbed, perhaps psychopathic and violent.

Assigning human personalities to animals is the chief trait of the pet owner—the doting dog-lover with his baby talk, the smug stay-at-home with a fat lump of fur on her lap who says, "Me, I'm a cat person," and the granny who puts her nose against the tin cage and makes kissing noises at her parakeet. Their affection is often tinged with a sense of superiority. Deer and duck hunters never talk this way about their prey, though big game hunters—Hemingway is the classic example—often sentimentalize the creatures they blow to bits and then lovingly stuff to hang on the wall. The lion in Hemingway's story "The Short Happy Life of Francis Macomber" is sketched as one of the characters, but that is perhaps predictable given Hemingway's tendency to romanticize what have come to be called charismatic megafauna. Moby-Dick is wicked and vengeful, and Jaws was not a hungry shark but a villain, its big teeth the very symbol of its evil. And goodness is embodied in the soulful eyes of a seal pup, so like a six-year-old that at seal culling season you find celebrities crawling across ice floes to cuddle them.

The literature of pets, or beloved animals, from *My Dog Tulip* to *Tarka the Otter*, is full of gushing anthropomorphists. The writers of nature films and wildlife documentaries are so seriously afflicted in this way they distort science. How many ant colonies have you seen on a TV screen while hearing, "Just putting that thing on his back and toiling with his little twig and thinking, I've just got to hang on a little while longer," speaking of the ant as though it's a Nepalese Sherpa.

Possibly the creepiest animals-presented-as-humans film was *March of the Penguins*, a hit movie for obviously the very reason that it presented these birds as tubby Christians marooned on a barren snowfield, examples to be emulated for their family values. When a bird of prey, unidentified but probably a giant petrel, appears in the film and dives to kill a chick, the carnage is not shown nor is the bird identified. The bird is not another creature struggling to exist in a snowfield but an opportunistic mugger from the polar wastes. We are enjoined to see the penguins as good and the giant petrel as wicked. With this travesty of science people try to put a human face on the animal world.

This is perhaps understandable. I've named most of my geese, if only to make sense of which one is which, and they grow into the name. I talk to them. They talk back to me. I have genuine affection for them. They make me laugh in their wrongheadedness as well as in the ironies of their often-unerring instincts. I also feel for them, and I understand their mortality in ways they cannot. But even in the pathos, which is part of pet owning, I try to avoid anthropomorphizing them, which is the greatest barrier to understanding their world.

But E. B. White patronizes his geese and invents feelings for them and obfuscates things. After years of goose rearing, I finally read his essays and, as I feared, was in the company of a fanciful author, not an observant gozzard, or goose rearer. Here was "a gander who was full of sorrows and suspicions." A few sentences later the gander was referred to as "a grief-crazed old fool." These are the sentimentalities you find in children's books. A goose in White's "classic" story about a spider, *Charlotte's Web*, says to Wilbur the pig, "I'm sitting-sitting on my eggs. Eight of them. Got to keep them toasty-oasty-oasty warm."

Edward Lear was also capable of writing in this whimsical vein, yet his paintings of birds rival Audubon's in dramatic accuracy. Lear could be soppy about his cat, but he was clear-sighted the rest of the time. E. B. White is never happier than when he is able to depict an animal by humanizing it as a friend. Yet what lies behind the animal's expression of friendship? It is an eagerness for easy food. Feed birds and they show up. Leave the lids off garbage cans in Maine and you've got bears—"beggar bears" as they're known. Deer love the suburbs—that's where the easiest meals are. Woodchucks prefer dahlias to dandelions. The daily imperative of most animals, wild and tame, is the quest for food, which is why, with some in your hand, you seem to have a pet, if not a grateful pal.

White's geese are not just contented but cheerful. They are also sorrowful. They are malicious, friendly, broken-spirited. They mourn. They are at times "grief-stricken." White is idiosyncratic in distinguishing male from female. He misunderstands the cumulative battles that result in a dominant gander—and this conflict is at the heart of his essay. He seems not to notice how at the margins of a flock they bond with each other—two old ganders, for example, keeping each other company. It seems to White that geese assume such unusual positions for sex that they've consulted "one of the modern sex manuals." Goslings are "innocent" and helpless. When I came across the gander White singled out as "a real dandy, full of pompous thoughts and surly gestures," I scribbled in the margin, "*oh, boy.*"

During ten years of living among geese and observing them closely, I have come to the obvious conclusion that they live in a goose-centric world, with goose rules and goose urgencies. More so than ducks, which I find passive and unsociable, geese have a well-known flocking instinct, a tendency to the gaggle. This is enjoyable to watch until you realize that if there is more than one gander in the flock, they will fight for dominance, often quite vocally.

Their sounds vary in pitch and urgency, according to the occasion, from wheedling murmurs of reedy ingratiation, along with the silent scissoring of the beak, as they step near knowing you might have food, to the triumphant squawk and wing-flapping of the gander after he has successfully put to flight one of his rivals. In between are the *ark-ark-ark* of recognition and alarm when the geese see or hear a stranger approach. Geese have remarkable powers of perception (famously, geese warned the Romans of the Gallic invasion in 390 B.C.); the hiss of warning, almost snake-like, the beak wide open, the agitated honk with an outstretched neck, and—among many other goose noises—the great joyous cry of the guarding gander after his mate has laid an egg and gotten off her nest. Ducks quack, loudly or softly, but geese are large eloquent vocalizers, and each distinct breed has its own repertoire of phrases.

· · ·

My first geese began as three wobbly goslings, scarcely a day old, two ganders and a goose. The goose became attached to one of the ganders—or perhaps the other way round; the superfluous gander became attached to me—indeed "imprinted" on me so deeply that even years later he will come when called, let his feathers be groomed, scratched, and smoothed, and will sit on my lap without stirring, in an astonishing show of security and affection. Konrad Lorenz describes this behavior as resulting from a gosling's first contact. Affection is of course the wrong word—mateship is more exact; my gander had found a partner in me because his mother was elsewhere and no other goose was available.

Every day of the year my geese range over six sunny Hawaiian acres. Penning or staking them, as some gozzards do in northern latitudes, is unthinkable. White mentions such captivity in his essay but makes no judgment: it is of course cruel confinement, maddening big birds, which need lots of space for browsing, rummaging, and often flying low. When it comes time to sex young geese, the process is quite simple: you tip the birds upside down and look at the vent in their nether parts—a gander has a penis, a goose doesn't. A little later—weeks rather than months—size and shape are the indicators; the gander is up to a third bigger than the goose.

White never mentions the breed of his geese, another unhelpful aspect of his essay, but if they were Embdens, the gander would be thirty pounds at maturity and the goose five to ten pounds lighter; English gray geese are bigger, China geese a bit smaller, and so forth, but always the gander heavier than his mate. I have raised Toulouse geese, China geese, Embdens, and English grays. Toulouse are usually overwhelmed by the Embdens, which seem to me to have the best memories and the largest range of sounds. Embdens are also the most teachable, the most patient. China geese are tenacious in battle, with a powerful beak, though a full-grown English gray gander can hold its ground and often overcome that tenacity.

Spring is egg-laying time. When there is a clutch of ten or a dozen eggs, the goose sits on them and stays there in a nest made of twigs and her own fluffy breast feathers. The goose must turn her eggs several times a day, to spread the heat evenly. Performing this operation hardly means withdrawing from the world, as White suggests. Though a sitting goose has a greatly reduced appetite, even the broodiest goose gets up from her nest now and then, covers her warm eggs with feathers and straw and goes for a meal and a drink. The gander stands vigil and, unusually possessive in his parental phase, fights off any other lurking ganders. When the goslings finally appear, they strike me as amazingly precocious—indeed the scientific word for their condition is precocial, which means they are covered with soft feathers and capable of independent activity almost from the moment of hatching. After a few days they show all the traits of adult behavior, adopting threat postures and hissing when they are fearful.

An established gander will carefully scrutinize new goslings introduced into his flock. It is simply a bewildered gander being a gander, acting out a protective, perhaps paternal possessive response. It is acting on instinct, gauging where the goslings fit in to his society. Their survival depends on it.

Geese develop little routines, favorite places to forage, though they range widely and nibble everything; they get to like certain shady spots, and through tactical fighting, using opportunities, they establish leadership; they stay together, they roam, and even the losers in the leadership battles remain as part of the flock. White's geese, which had to endure the hard Maine winters, were often confined to a barn or a pen, which are prisons producing perverse overreactive, defensive, aggressive behavior, as all prisons do.

The gander takes charge in normal surroundings: it is part of his dominance—keeping other ganders away. He rules by intimidation. He is protective, attentive, and aggressive in maintaining his superior position among all the other birds, and will attack any creature in sight, and that includes the FedEx deliveryman way up at the front gate. When young ganders grow up, they frequently challenge the older one. The victor dominates the flock, and the goslings have a new protector. The old gander has merely lost that skirmish and has withdrawn, because he is winded and tired and possibly injured. But win or lose they remain with the flock. Defeated ganders go off for a spell to nurse their wounds, but they always return. One of the most interesting aspects of a flock is the way it accommodates so many different geese—breeds, sexes, ages, sizes. Ganders go on contending, and often an old gander will triumph over the seemingly stronger young one. Only after numerous losing battles do they cease to compete, and then a nice thing happens: the older ganders pair up and ramble around together at the back of the flock, usually one protecting the other.

There is a clue to White's self-deception in this part of the essay: "I felt very deeply his sorrow and his defeat." White projects his own age and insecurity onto the gander. "As things go in the animal kingdom, he is about my age, and when he lowered himself to creep under the bar, I could feel in my own bones his pain at bending down so far." This essay was written in 1971, when White was a mere seventy-two, yet this is the key to the consistent anthropomorphism, his seeing the old gander as an extension of himself—a metonymical human, to use French anthropologist Claude Levi-Strauss's definition of such a pet. The essay is not strictly about geese: it is about E. B. White. He compares the defeated gander to "spent old males, motionless in the glare of the day" on a park bench in Florida. He had shuttled back and forth from Maine to Florida; his anxiety is real. He mentions summer sadness twice in his essay, a melancholy that may sadden a person precisely because the day is sunny.

What saddens me about this confident essay is that White misses so much. Because he locks up his geese at night, he never sees the weird sleeping patterns of geese. They hardly seem to sleep at all. They might crouch and curl their necks and tuck their beaks into their wings, but it is a nap that lasts only minutes. Do geese sleep? is a question that many people have attempted to answer, but always unsatisfactorily. If they are free to ramble at night, geese nap in the day. However domesticated a goose, its wakefulness and its atavistic alertness to danger has not been bred out of it.

Their alliances within a flock, their bouts of aggression and spells of passivity, their concentration, their impulsive, low, skidding flights when they have a whole meadow to use as a runway, the way they stand their ground against dogs or humans—these are all wonders. I find them so remarkable, I would not dream of eating a goose or selling a bird to anyone who would eat it, though I sometimes entertain the fantasy of a goose attacking a gourmet and eating his liver.

There are many more wonders: the way they recognize my voice from anyone else shouting and how they hurry near when called; or follow me because they know I have food in my bulging hand. They will follow me 300 yards, looking eager and hungry. I have mentioned their inexhaustible curiosity—sampling every plant that looks tasty, as well as pecking at objects as though to gauge their weight or their use. Their digestive system is a marvel—almost nonstop eating and they never grow fat (*Why Geese Don't Get Obese (And We Do)* is a recent book on animal physiology); their ability to drink nothing but muddy water with no obvious ill effects; and with this their conspicuous preference for clean water, especially when washing their heads and beaks, which they do routinely. Their calling out to a mate from a distance, and the mate rushing to their side; or if one becomes trapped under a steepness or enmeshed in a fence, and sounds the faint squawk of helplessness, the other will stay by, until it is released. Their capacity to heal seems to me phenomenal—from a dog bite, in the case of one gander I had that was at death's door for more than a month, or from the bite of another gander in one of their ritual battles for supremacy. Such conflicts often result in blood-smeared breast feathers. Their ability to overcome internal ailments is a wonder to behold.

I had an old, loud China gander that was displaced by a younger gander—his son, as a matter of fact, who ended up with the old goose we named Jocasta. From the time of Adam, we humans have had an urge to name the birds of the sky and the beasts of the field. The old gander may have been defeated by the son, but he remained feisty. Then he became ill, got weak, ate very little, couldn't walk, sat only in shade, and moaned. He was immobilized. I dissolved in water some erythromycin I got at the feed store and squirted it down his throat with a turkey baster, and added some more to his water.

Several weeks went by. He lost weight, but I could see that he was sipping from his dish. From time to time I carried him to the pond—he paddled and dipped his head and beak, but he was too weak to crawl out. Still he seemed to respond to this physiotherapy. After a month he began to eat. One morning, going out to give him more medicine, I saw that he was standing and able to walk. I brought him some food, and as I put the food in his dish he took a few steps toward me and bit me hard on the thigh, giving me a purple prune-size bruise. This is not an example of irony or ingratitude. It is goosishness. He was thankfully himself again.

The Atlantic Monthly

FINALIST—REVIEWS AND
CRITICISM

*With a sharp, bemused eye that
she turns as easily on herself as
on her subjects, Sandra Tsing Loh
has written a set of funny, incisive
articles in the* Atlantic *that
puncture and illuminate attitudes
about money, education, and the
plight of the affluent modern
woman.*

Sandra Tsing Loh

Rhymes with Rich

M ore and more these days, reading women's writing fills me with a vague, creeping, slightly nauseating feeling. Lying in bed the other night, cradling some seltzer water, my stomach gurgling, the word for my malaise suddenly came to me: "afflufemza," wherein the problems of affluence are recast as the struggles of feminism, and you find yourself in a dreamlike state of reading first-person essays about it, over and over again. We've always had rich mothers, of course; it's just that the boundaries between the privileged and the un- used to be clearer. Back in the eighties, for instance, I was among the many couch, or at least futon, potatoes who used to love *Dynasty*—the Mothra-versus-Godzilla grapplings of the Car- ringtons and the Colbys, of Joan Collins's deliciously nasty Alexis and Linda Evans's nurturing, oddly affectless Krystle. Alexis was the Execu-Bitch; Krystle, the Saintly Wife. It was the eternal female ur-struggle, ever campy, ever watchable, ever con- veniently framed for us—out there in the distance—by that swoopily hammy Bill Conti score, those soaring trumpets, those glittering Denver skyscrapers.

Twenty years later, gone are big hair, big diamonds, and big shoulder pads. In their place, among America's most affluent mothers, is a kind of gnawing, grinding anxiety—and a media- centric conviction that this fretfulness is somehow that of every woman. Or so it appears in the just-published *Mommy Wars: Stay-at-Home and Career Moms Face Off on Their Choices, Their Lives, Their Families*, edited by Leslie Morgan Steiner. The cover flap describes the angst thus:

> With motherhood comes one of the toughest decisions of a woman's life: Stay at home or pursue a career? The dilemma not only divides mothers into hostile, defensive camps but pits individual mothers against themselves. . . . Ranging in age from 25 to 72 and scattered across the country from New Hampshire to California, these mothers reflect the full spectrum of lifestyle choices.

OK, let's slow down for a minute and unpack this description of Everymother before, with iced mochaccino latte in hand, we hurriedly whisk on. There are, in fact, great varieties of American mothers left out of Steiner's anthology. They're women for whom work is not a "lifestyle choice" but a necessity—a financial one, gauchely enough, and not an emotional one. Why do they work? To keep the electricity on. Such women would include, oh, single-mother waitresses, hotel maids, factory workers, grocery-store cashiers, manicurists, even countless low-level white-collar functionaries, from bank clerks to receptionists to data processors. Imagine a nanny wondering about her lifestyle choice: *Why have I always had this burning dream to spend sixty hours a week taking care of other people's children? Is it because of unresolved communication issues from a lonely childhood? Would I experience more personal fulfillment—find more of my true "voice"—in department-store retail? Perhaps these are issues I should examine this week in therapy, before I put my call through to Po Bronson.*

But clearly no one at Random House thought to red-pencil this, because it's a given today, in non-zine, non-blog, hardcover-anthology women's writing, that "Everymother" implicitly means "every mother from the well-defined e-mail list of people like us"—media professionals who have now become their own class and tribe. A female member of the mediacracy can now seize the bully pulpit for all women without needing to give even lip service to those women whose lives, unglamorously enough, are more blue collar than blue state. (Actually, that's not entirely true: they do occasionally give lip service, in the most bizarre and self-aggrandizing ways. More on that in a bit.)

However, even when one excludes most American mothers, there's still plenty of material for a book. Life at the top may be privileged, but it is not simple. Take the mini-autobiography proffered by Steiner, a graduate of Harvard and Wharton, the general manager of *The Washington Post Magazine*, and the former Johnson & Johnson executive who was responsible for the international launch of Splenda. Her dilemma, she explains, was being married to an investment banker who kept getting ever more attractive jobs in ever new places. The crisis came when he was "offered the presidency of a hot Internet start-up," which would require a family move to Minneapolis. The pain of it had Steiner lying on the parquet floor in her beloved Upper West Side, fighting tears: "Within a ten-minute walk lay my son's favorite playground, my sister's apartment, my in-laws' condo, Gymboree, a pediatrician as kindly as Big Bird, five or six Starbucks, the Reebok gym, and at least a dozen museums." But no. "My husband calmly explained that we were very lucky and really had to go. Millions of dollars in stock options, he said."

(Again, for comparison, I don't want to go red state on you but a military wife might take the news of a move differently, perhaps even thinking something like, *Yes, moving is inconvenient, but sacrifice is part of the duty our family owes our country* . . . which in the "mommy wars" universe would be a strange notion full of foreign words.)

Steiner's female-empowering argument is that her only choice, as a mother, was to return to full-time work at a plum

Washington Post advertising job in order to gain the economic leverage needed to have a say in household decisions. It is a leverage that Steiner's own depressed, rum-and-Coke-swilling, stay-at-home—if brilliant, Radcliffe-educated—mother never had, since Steiner's cheerful lawyer father was the one who worked. And, well, what with the battling upper-class incomes and the pretty continual flap, almost as though in a wind tunnel, of Ivy League sheepskins, it was at this point that even I—a media professional who has the freedom to type, at my desk, about the waitresses who labor hourly for minimum wage—began, from my relatively privileged position in the cosmic sisterhood, to feel the cultural disconnect of the downwardly mobile.

Never mind that—with such *Mommy Wars* essayists as *Publishers Weekly* editor-in-chief Sara Nelson, ten-year Viking editor Dawn Drzal, *Washington Post Magazine* deputy editor Sydney Trent, and *Lizzie McGuire* creator Terri Minsky—it's conceivable that in the next wave of cultural rightsizing we could have a genre of women's literature written entirely by media executives; it's just that, even when the media moms quit work to raise their children, they're still able to spend a lot more than I do, on a daily basis.

It began with little things, like Georgetown mom Page Evans's frustrating day juggling three-year-old daughter Katherine's ballet class with six-year-old daughter Peyton's kiddie yoga class ($15 per session). There was stay-at-home mom Monica Buckley Price's resignation about her husband's having to work out of town, co-executive-producing *The Joan Cusack Show*, in order to cover her autistic son's expensive Santa Monica preschool and therapy bills of $700 a week. On the Upper West Side, Drzal's small son mistakenly consumed a brunch centerpiece of two pounds of Barney Greengrass eastern Gaspé smoked salmon. In yet another gastronomically sophisticated part of Manhattan, working-from-home mother Susan Cheever's baby literally hurled foie gras and made playthings with quenelles de brochet. (I wondered if there was any Random House editor for whom that image had given a moment's pause: "Baby hurling foie gras . . . Let them eat cake . . . Marie Antoin—hmm.")

Then came the onslaught of designer labels. Not since Daisy Buchanan wept over Gatsby's shirts have individual items of clothing been so emotionally fraught. There were the traditional "Armani success suits" (which one abandons when one leaves office life), "Merrell Jungle Slides" (as casual wear, worn to pick up the kids), a "new BCBG suit" (bought for speaking engagements, though the cost of it unfortunately offsets the honorariums), a favorite "forest-green wool Regina Rubens" (to cheer oneself up enough while returning to one's publishing job in Manhattan). The autism piece, while poignant in its descriptions of Price's son's condition, happens to be titled "Red Boots and Cole Haans," a reference to the mom's "funky new Anthropologie outfit" and Cole Haans, which loom touchingly large against the preschool children's tiny Stride Rites (the piece recounts a much happier day than at Gymboree, when the son soiled his "fabulous blue-and-white-striped Petit Bateau outfit"). No surprise, then, that the battle between stay-at-homes and career moms is described unfailingly in terms of outerwear and accessories. In "Sharks and Jets," Evans writes, "I imagine Jerome Robbins choreography. The stay-at-home moms in their park attire of rubber clogs, khakis, and T-shirts. The working moms in their pencil skirts, pressed blouses, and Ferragamos." Stay-at-home mom Catherine Clifford finds it difficult to retain her equanimity with "the mom who groused jealously that she couldn't afford not to work, then grabbed her Kate Spade bag and headed off in her new Mercedes SUV." (The image of Upper West Side—or, for geographic diversity, Georgetown—women hitting each other over the head with Kate Spade bags was hard to shake.)

·　　·　　·

All right, some might argue—so what? Affluent mothers have problems too—call it the Anxiety of the Mommytocracy, if you will. And people shelling out $25 for a hardbound book of essays are more likely to be intrigued by the lives of blue-coast elites than by those of poorly dressed office managers in Toledo, married to traveling salesmen, whose children eat pimiento-flavored Tuna Helper. Indeed, what's wrong—what's unfeminist, even—with celebrating not just the affluent but the powerful? What's honestly wrong with, to quote Naomi Wolf's glowing blurb for *Mommy Wars*, using "real women's voices to animate what is often a frenzied but ill-informed debate, thus bringing the texture, warmth, hope, and angst of real mommies—and real wars—to the table"? (Well, it could be argued that one of the problems is that Naomi Wolf feels this sampling is representative of real mommies.)

It's not like affluent moms don't have their "work" cut out for them too: "Every day at noon I would pack up the babysitter with tiny cartons of soy milk and cinnamon graham crackers, lest my son accept a forbidden cookie," Dawn Drzal reveals.

> Then I would go food shopping, setting out for a distant organic market or ethnic enclave to hunt down new prepared foods or a particular exotic ingredient for his meals (which my husband and I enjoyed as well). When the babysitter left at six, she would deposit him in his high chair, freshly bathed, and he would happily watch me sautéing onions or marinating tofu or cooking his favorite dinner, red lentils with garlic, onions, and ginger.

Calgon, take her away!

Further, to read these accounts, it's clear that even privileged women can suffer surprising emotional fragility. Conversations at cocktail parties are particular minefields. When high-powered career women shed their outer Armani layers to become stay-at-home moms, they suffer, over the fondue, risk of the dreaded "greet and turn," or "turn and pivot." Relatively high up on the pyramid of needs is a sense of "selfness," illustrated nicely here by Page Evans:

"So, what do you do, do you work?" a fifty-something gray-haired man in a black turtleneck and tweed jacket asks. We're standing in a claret-colored living room at a book party in Cleveland Park, and the bartender has just handed him a glass brimming with bourbon over ice.

"I'm basically a stay-at-home mom," I say.

"Oh, well, that's such an important job. Kids grow up so fast, don't they?"

"Yeah, they do," I say.

And that's the end of it. Turn and pivot.

But wait. Wait! Don't you want to know what I think about what's going on in the world? I want to scream out. I've spent the past seven years trying to improve my mind, to prove that I'm more than "just a mom." I see more plays, read more op-eds, take classes, visit museums. I'm in a book club. I write essays.

In another illustration of hard-fought (even, here, arguably hard-hearted) selfness, Terri Minsky describes having a demanding TV career that could put her in L.A. for months at a time, while her family remained in Manhattan. At one point, her two woeful children ask, "Mommy, do you love your television show more than us?" When she says "no," they counter with, "Mommy, then why are you with the show and not with us?" And what she thinks, but poignantly cannot say, is, "I want to do this. I need to do this. This is who I am, and it's taken a lot of therapy not to apologize for that." She then tells a roomful of network executives that her son eventually supported her need to self-actualize, and the moms among them burst out crying.

This would all be fine if proffered as the self-exploration of a consciously affluent class, or even as, heavens, *Dynasty*-style escapist literature (I'd love to hear Joan Collins deliver that Minsky line). But Steiner goes further, arguing that although stay-at-home moms do, in their own intimate way, add value to their communities, "without the money, the power, and the loudspeaker successful careers bring, women will never have the collective bargaining power to make the world better for ourselves, our children, and all the women who can't leave abusive husbands, the ones who wear veils, the moms who earn less than minimum wage cleaning houses and don't have choices about birth control or prenatal care or any other kind of care."

Again, to slow down and unpack (although it's almost enough just to note the delicious, vaguely hand-waving phrase "the ones who wear veils"): Steiner's enumeration of "money, power, loudspeaker" suggests that little good can ever be done by women suffering any combination of poverty, obscurity, or—most horrific of all—lack of media access. In Los Angeles, some of our most powerful community movers are the *promotoras*, Latina health workers, whose unusual access to, rapport with, and ability to get signatures from brown-skinned working-class families make them critical players in current demands for more accountability in failing inner-city schools. Again, I see that within the "mommy wars" universe, my previous sentence holds many strange and unfamiliar phrases.

Leaving that aside, the question remains: Once they have the proverbial loudspeaker, how much social good do affluent, successful, powerful women really do (other than treating their wonderful full-time nannies like members of the family)? I didn't notice any successful career women in the book mentioning specific campaigns they're waging on behalf of the less fortunate, nor did I catch to what women's or children's charities proceeds from the book will be given. (I would love to know the inner dynamics of this collective-bargaining arrangement of which Steiner speaks, whereby a turbo woman's pursuit of a glamorous career somehow makes the world better for her minimum-wage sisters.) These days, I suppose, it is feminist enough an action to edit a women's anthology, get on *Oprah*, sell a million copies, and make a pile of cash, all of which you keep, presumably so that your investment-banker husband can't move the family again. (One of our most famous and successful women, Oprah Winfrey, actually does have furthering the social good as part of her personal mandate. But that's a value many seem to forget. A colleague of mine, Rebecca Constantino, at Access Books, which creates and updates libraries for underserved children, received an Oprah Angel award for her work. Constantino noted wryly to me that her appearance on the show drew less than $500 in cash contributions, but 1,000 calls asking how to get on *Oprah*.)

Most troubling of all is not how little good is being done by affluent, successful, loudspeaker-bearing career women, but that they seem so unaware of who even needs help, even if those in need happen to live all around them. While our prominent female essayists are parsing fashions and feelings and moods—while they are probing, as Wolf puts it, the "angst of real mommies"—there are some elephants undealt with in the room. Consider the opening incident of the book, at a party at Washington, D.C.'s elegant Sulgrave Club, where Steiner is discussing her "mommy wars" book idea with a fellow publishing professional:

> Another neighbor, a stay-at-home mom whose kids go to school with mine, joined us. This woman is the head of the parent-teacher association at our public elementary school, as constant and welcoming a presence on the playground as a greeter at Wal-Mart. My friend, a former *Washington Post* reporter who makes her living posing provocative questions, asked our neighbor what she thought of my

book idea. Specifically, what she thought of moms who work. Without breathing, the stay-at-home mom answered, "Oh, I feel so sorry for them."

My cheeks flushed like a child with a fever.

I think it's worth noting (because apparently no one else will) that Washington, D.C., public schools are 96 percent minority and that Leslie Morgan Steiner is white—a racial juxtaposition not atypical for this anthology. Except for, most notably, two African American essayists who live in suburban Maryland (the one mentioning race citing it as less of a factor with her white in-laws than her turbo-powered career), the twenty-seven contributors to this anthology are almost all white women who live in major urban centers: Washington (whose public schools, to repeat, are 96 percent minority), New York (85 percent minority), and Los Angeles (91 percent minority). While these mothers tend to be, as indicated, top media professionals, the overwhelming preponderance of brown schoolchildren is something no one seems to particularly notice. The troubles of the poor and the brown don't seem to lap up much around the ankles of any of these mothers, whether they're shod in Chanel slingbacks or Cole Haan loafers. (Almost as though in an afterthought, there are a handful of exceptions in the back of the book.)

Of course, I suppose there's a chance that the Washington public school Steiner's kids attend is 4 percent white, and that she's just admirably color-blind. But it's more likely, given the increasingly Johannesburg-like patterns of American urban racial polarization, that the school she's referring to is enclaved—that is, that it's the quality elementary school, in the big brown city, where the kids of the white well-to-do go. ("Enclave" being my verb for the self-sorting occurring in our large urban areas.) I'm not singling Steiner out for unusual behavior here; anxious, educated (particularly Ivy League–educated), upper-middle-class parents generally, and understandably, want their children to go to the better schools (Steiner's stay-at-home neighbor is forced, in contrast, to send her children to what Steiner calls a "mediocre public high school"). I may even have things just half right: Steiner's kids' school may happen to be overwhelmingly minority and excellent, and the snotty PTA president may, in fact, be a colorful, headscarf-wearing immigrant from Zimbabwe.

But what is safe to say is that in the often embattled No Child Left Behind world of U.S. public schools—where the poorest inner-city children may deal with ever-changing arrays of substitute teachers, class sizes in the fifties, and textbooks published in the sixties—it's not the worst problem a mother can have if her over-involved PTA president, when pressed on a hot-button topic at a party, is a tad judgmental. Because, in point of fact, female PTA über-presidents tend to *be* judgmental. That's the alchemy of rabidly focused women. There's no one like an obsessive, hormonal female busybody to whip a school-wide gift-wrap drive to record-setting heights ("A new gym? No, Cheryl Ann—you didn't!"). At least that's how it is in our enclaved, high-achieving whiter schools in L.A., the ones upper-middle-class parents line up frantically before dawn to get their kids into. (This phenomenon was humorously described in the *Los Angeles Times* last year in a first-person essay by a *Times* staffer. As seems typical for today's journalists, this mother didn't feel it worth noting that the school the parents were knocking elbows to get into was the affluent, 79-percent-white one within a sea of poor browns.) Indeed, the most-whispered downsides about our enclaved L.A. schools these days are the overachieving parent associations (often, if not always, powered by a team of tennis-playing stay-at-home moms). I remember one such public elementary I visited, impossible to get into anyway, whose Booster Club required 500 volunteer hours per year per family! The parental pressure is such that the poor brown schools actually start to look like attractive alternatives. At one point I found myself thinking, *Sure, if we went to this "bad" school, most of my fellow parents would be Hispanic migrants who work three jobs . . . but at least I wouldn't have to deal with that crazy-ass Booster Club!*

•   •   •

But look—I don't wish to start another war. I don't want to sow festering seeds of class and racial discord. I come only to heal. And in that spirit, I have a modest proposal: mix it up, people. In Los Angeles, I'm happy to say, I myself have experienced zero mommy wars. (My daughter goes to a non-white-enclaved public magnet school, where she is the only blonde in her class of twenty-two.) It's not just because of the absence of Kate Spade bags or Ferragamo shoes (neither of which I could identify anyway without checking the label). I've never smarted at catty remarks from other moms, partly because those catty remarks, if made . . . *would have been in Armenian. Which I do not speak.* Or Spanish. Or Tagalog, Japanese, Russian, Arabic. Ours are the old-fashioned kind of Sharks and Jets. We have so much diversity in race, you don't really notice the diversity in shoe designers. I find it quite refreshing not to know what nanothoughts the other mothers are thinking at every nanosecond. For the moment, the highlights are enough—which seem to be, to gauge by my fellow parents' smiles and nods, that we are all quite delighted, as though we've won the lottery. After all, our L.A. public school has buildings, electricity, books, and teachers who actually seem to like what they're doing. Hurray!

I agree that mommy wars are not good for any mothers, that such wars are time and effort wasted. But what are these wars really about? Susan Cheever would have it that the catfighting is actually due to suppressed rage over the age-old inequities between women and men:

Women do the lion's share—perhaps it should be called the woman's share—of the child care and household work in this country. . . . What worsens our predicament is that women lack core representation in our government. . . . There isn't much support for women who work—support like office child care, flexible hours, and reasonable maternity leaves. There isn't much support for women who stay home—like tax breaks, financial protection in case of divorce, subsidized medical care, or even licensed child care.

For mothers who can afford full-time baby nurses and $20,000-a-year private schools? Who would no sooner partake of universal day care ("Women, unite! Universal day care!") than they would of their corner brown-skinned public elementary, where their nanny's children go? I don't think so. (Wealthy, powerful left-leaning women will never be able to admit that they have much more in common with wealthy, powerful men than they do with their poor, disenfranchised pseudo-sisters.) I do, however, like Cheever's notion that "working and stay-at-home moms today are like the famous psychology experiment in which too many rats are put in a cage with too little food." Although I think the cage is the three square miles around Seventy-sixth and Broadway, and the problem is too *much* food (if not actually Barney Greengrass eastern Gaspé smoked salmon).

More compelling for me is the take of Molly Jong-Fast, candidly self-described product of New York elite day schools, trips to Europe with the nanny, temporary withdrawal from Effexor, and, last but not least, Erica Jong and Howard Fast. (In a delightful bit of historical trivia, Jong-Fast notes that her mother was actually voted "Mother of the Year" in the early eighties. Fascinated, I had to look up whom else the Father's Day/Mother's Day Council has so honored. You might enjoy knowing that other Mothers of the Year have included Kathie Lee Gifford,

Joan Rivers, Sally Jessy Raphael, Ivana Trump, and Anna Wintour—causing me, still the hardcore *Dynasty* fan, to cry out, "What, no Leona Helmsley? It's an outrage!") Jong-Fast writes about trying to be in two places at once, at work and at home: "It's the schizophrenia of modern-day motherhood. It's the schizophrenia of affluence and more pointedly the schizophrenia of feminism. Why can't we admit that life is about sacrifices?" That seems the right pairing. "Affluenza," a term coined almost thirty years ago already, describes the vague depression brought on by the stress of overwork, a superfluity of material things, low self-esteem, and the grinding pressure of always having to keep up with the Joneses. Or in this case, the Janeses— thus giving rise to affluenza's modern-day postfeminist version: "afflufemza."

Sara Nelson of *Publishers Weekly* describes her mommy wars so:

> About half of the mothers of kids in Charley's class are working at least part-time. There's Maria, who designs handbags; Lauren, who works in advertising; Paulette, who writes children's books. The mother of Charley's friend Nick is an independent management consultant. And for the most part—and I gather this is unusual in the fiercely competitive world of New York private schools— there's little conflict between the employed mothers and the ones who stay home . . .
>
> Still, there is some tension bubbling under the surface. One morning one of the stay-at-home mothers referred to herself, quite pointedly, as a "full-time mom." Those three words made my blood boil. I've been a mother every second of every day for the past ten and a half years, whether I'm researching an article or pushing a swing. Would anyone dare to suggest that a woman who worked in a factory, or as a cop or a firefighter—a woman who worked at least

partly so that her children could have food and shoes and the occasional trip to Toys "R" Us—was any less a mother than my school acquaintance, who'd had the privilege to opt out of the workforce?

No, but apparently someone *would* dare to suggest that elective employment in the upper reaches of the publishing world is on a par with wage slavery and required-second-salary public-sector work. Which got me thinking how wonderfully refreshing it would be for Nelson to transfer Charley right away into a racially and socioeconomically mixed New York public school, with the children of mothers who actually are the factory workers and cops and firefighters she so admires. Even Steiner's snippy PTA über-mom at the Sulgrave Club would be invigorated by a relocation to one of the many poorer, browner Washington, D.C., schools, where she wouldn't have to rub elbows with those irritating Leslie Morgan Steiners. Then that PTA über-mom could really roll her sleeves up. Think what she could do: rebuild an entire school from the ground up—clearing out the asbestos and bringing in landscaping, violins, top-of-the-line computers. At her dogged persistence, the other parents would simply be amazed, awed, grateful. What a better world such demographic mixing would bring, for all women and children. And what a relief for the "mommy wars" moms to be finally liberated, into the wilds. Certainly all those catty remarks would be easier to restrain when the mommy close at hand is a Jamaican waitress taking the bus to her job, wearing not her forest-green Regina Rubens but the uniform of Howard Johnson.

Vanity Fair

WINNER—COLUMNS AND COMMENTARY

Whether describing terrors inflicted on Ugandan children, bearing witness to the lingering effects of Agent Orange, or noting the passing of a great political interviewer, Christopher Hitchens's incisive eloquence and expansive intellect puts his controversial subjects into context and reveals their larger meaning.

Christopher Hitchens

The Vietnam Syndrome

To be writing these words is, for me, to undergo the severest test of my core belief—that sentences can be more powerful than pictures. A writer can hope to do what a photographer cannot: convey how things smelled and sounded as well as how things looked. I seriously doubt my ability to perform this task on this occasion. Unless you see the landscape of ecocide, or meet the eyes of its victims, you will quite simply have no idea. I am content, just for once—and especially since it is the work of the brave and tough and undeterrable James Nachtwey—to be occupying the space between pictures.

The very title of our joint subject is, I must tell you, a sick joke to begin with. Perhaps you remember the jaunty names of the callous brutes in *Reservoir Dogs*: "Mr. Pink," "Mr. Blue," and so on? Well, the tradition of giving pretty names to ugly things is as old as warfare. In Vietnam, between 1961 and 1971, the high command of the United States decided that, since a guerrilla struggle was apparently being protected by tree cover, a useful first step might be to "defoliate" those same trees. Famous corporations such as Dow and Monsanto were given the task of attacking and withering the natural order of a country. The resulting chemical weaponry was euphemistically graded by color: Agent Pink, Agent Green (yes, it's true), Agent Purple, Agent

Blue, Agent White, and—spoken often in whispers—Agent Orange. This shady gang, or gang of shades, all deferred to its ruthless chief, who proudly bore the color of hectic madness. The key constituent of Agent Orange is dioxin: a horrifying chemical that makes total war not just on vegetation but also on the roots and essences of life itself. The orange, in other words, was clockwork from the start. If you wonder what the dioxin effect can look like, recall the ravaged features of Viktor Yushchenko—ironically, the leader of the Orange Revolution.

The full inventory of this historic atrocity is still being compiled: it's no exaggeration to say that about 12 million gallons of lethal toxin, in Orange form alone, were sprayed on Vietnam, on the Vietnamese, and on the American forces who were fighting in the same jungles. A prime use of the chemical was in the delta of the Mekong River, where the Swift Boats were vulnerable to attack from the luxuriant undergrowth at the water's edge. Very well, said Admiral Elmo Zumwalt Jr., we shall kill off this ambush-enabling greenery by poisoning it from the skies. Zumwalt believes his own son Elmo III, who was also serving in the delta, died from the effects of Agent Orange, leaving behind him a son with grave learning disabilities. The resulting three-generation memoir of the Zumwalt family—*My Father, My Son* (1986), written by the first and second Elmos about themselves and about the grandchild—is one of the most stoic and affecting family portraits in American history.

•　　　•　　　•

You have to go to Vietnam, though, to see such fallout at first hand. I had naïvely assumed that it would be relatively easy to speak to knowledgeable physicians and scientists, if only because a state that is still communist (if only in name) would be eager to justify itself by the crimes of American imperialism. The contrary proved to be the case, and for two main reasons.

The government is too poor to pay much compensation to victims, and prefers anyway to stress the heroic rather than the humiliating aspects of the war. And traditional Vietnamese culture has a tendency to frown on malformed children, whose existence is often attributed to the sins of a past life. Furthermore, Vietnamese in general set some store by pride and self-reliance, and do not like soliciting pity.

I am quite proud of what I did when I came to appreciate, in every sense of the word, these obstacles. The first time I ever gave blood was to a "Medical Aid for Vietnam" clinic, in 1967. That was also the moment when I discovered that I have a very rare blood type. So, decades later, seeing a small ad in a paper in Ho Chi Minh City (invariably still called Saigon in local conversation) that asked for blood donations for Agent Orange victims, I reported to the relevant address. I don't think they get many wheezing and perspiring Anglos at this joint, let alone wheezing and perspiring Anglos with such exclusive corpuscles; at any rate I was fussed over a good deal while two units were drawn off, was given a sustaining bowl of beef noodles and some sweet tea, and was then offered a tour of the facilities.

This privilege, after a while, I came almost to regret. In an earlier age the compassionate term for irredeemably deformed people was *lusus naturae*: "a sport of nature," or, if you prefer a more callous translation, a joke. It was bad enough, in that spare hospital, to meet the successful half of a Siamese-twin separation. This was a more or less functional human child, with some cognition and about half the usual complement of limbs and organs. But upstairs was the surplus half, which, I defy you not to have thought if you had been there, would have been more mercifully thrown away. It wasn't sufficient that this unsuccessful remnant had no real brain and was a thing of stumps and sutures. ("No ass!" murmured my stunned translator in that good-bad English that stays in your mind.) Extra torments had been thrown in. The little creature was not lying torpid and still.

It was jerking and writhing in blinded, crippled, permanent epilepsy, tethered by one stump to the bedpost and given no release from endless, pointless, twitching misery. What nature indulges in such sport? What creator designs it?

But all evil thoughts about euthanasia dissolve as soon as you meet, first, the other children and, second, those who care for them. In the office of Dr. Nguyen Thi Phuong Tan, a wonderful lady who is in charge of the equally impossible idea of "rehabilitation," I was taking notes when a lively, pretty, but armless ten-year-old girl ran in and sprang with great agility onto the table. Pham Thi Thuy Linh's grandfather had been in the South Vietnamese Air Force, had helped to vent Agent Orange on his communist foes, and had suddenly succumbed to leukemia at the age of forty-two. His curse has been transmitted down the generations, whether via the food chain or the chromosomes is unclear. While Pham Thi Thuy Linh deftly signed her name with her right foot—with which she also handled a biscuit from the fond nurses—I learned that she had been listed for some artificial arms, perhaps with modern synthetic flesh, from an organization in Japan. All this will take is a wait until she's fully grown, and some $300,000. Money well spent, I'd say. But there will be no "making whole" for these children—eerily combining complete innocence with the most sinister and frightening appearance, ridden and riddled with cleft palate and spina bifida. One should not run out of vocabulary to the point where one calls a child a monster, but the temptation is there. One sees, with an awful pang, why their terrified and shamed parents abandon them to this overworked clinic. One also realizes that it isn't nature, or a creator, that is to blame. If only. This was not a dreadful accident, or a tragedy. It was inflicted, on purpose, by sophisticated human beings.

•   •   •

I am not an epidemiologist. And there are professionals who will still tell you that there is no absolutely proven connection between the spraying of this poison and the incidence of terrifying illnesses in one generation, or the persistence of appalling birth defects in the next one or the next one. Let us submit this to the arbitration of evidence and reason: what else can possibly explain the systematic convergence? I left Ho Chi Minh City/Saigon and went down the road and along the river, by boat, to the delta town of Ben Tre. This is the very place where Peter Arnett heard the American soldier say in 1968 that "we had to destroy the town to save it." My ferry churned the big muddy waters that had once been cruised by the Swift Boats, and I stood out in the pre-monsoon rain to get a clear look at the riverbanks with vegetation that took so long to grow back. Ben Tre Province, then called Kien Hoa, was a kind of "ground zero" for this experiment on human beings and animals and trees.

Jungles can ostensibly rise again, but dioxin works its way down through the roots and into the soil and the water, where it can enter the food chain. The unforgivable truth is that nobody knew at the time they were spraying it how long it takes dioxin to leach out of the natural system. The muttered prayer of many Vietnamese villagers is that this generation will be the last to feel their grandparents' war in their bones and their blood and their epidermis, but the fact is that the town of Ben Tre is home to about 140,000 people, of whom, the Red Cross says, 58,000 are victims of Agent Orange. (I don't trust Vietnamese statistics, but these were supplied to me by a woman expert who is not uncritical of the communist regime, and whose family had been subjected to forced "reeducation" after the fall of Saigon.)

Once again, after a tour of some thatched hamlets and some local schools for the special cases, I experienced an urgent need to be elsewhere or alone. How many times can one pretend to "interview" the parents of a child born with bright-yellow skin? The cleft palates, the deafness, the muteness, the pretzel limbs and lolling heads . . . and the terrible expressions on the faces of the parents, who believe that this horror can sometimes skip a generation. There is just enough knowledge for agony and remorse, in other words, but not enough for any "healing process." No answer, above all, to the inescapable question: When will it stop? A rain from hell began falling about forty years ago. Unto how many unborn generations? At a school full of children who made sign language to one another or who couldn't sit still (or who couldn't move much at all), or who couldn't see or couldn't hear, I took the tour of the workshops where trades such as fishnet weaving or car repair are taught, and was then asked if I would like to say a few words, through an interpreter, to the assembly. I quite like a captive audience, but I didn't trust myself to say a fucking thing. Several of the children in the front row were so wizened and shrunken that they looked as if they could be my seniors. I swear to you that Jim Nachtwey has taken photographs, as one of his few rivals, Philip Jones Griffiths, also took photographs, that simply cannot be printed in this magazine, because they would poison your sleep, as they have poisoned mine.

.   .   .

"After such knowledge," as T. S. Eliot asked in "Gerontion," "what forgiveness?" That's easy. The question of forgiveness just doesn't come up. The world had barely assimilated the new term "genocide," which was coined only in the 1940s, before the United States government added the fresh hell of "ecocide," or mass destruction of the web of nature that connects human and animal and herbal life. I think we may owe the word's distinction to my friend Orville Schell, who wrote a near-faultless essay of coolheaded and warmhearted prose in the old *Look* magazine in March 1971. At that time, even in a picture magazine, there weren't enough photographs of the crime, so his terse, mordant words had to suffice, which makes me faintly proud to be in the same profession. And at some points, being naturally scrupulous about the evidence, he could only speculate: "There are even reports of women giving birth to monsters, though most occurrences are not reported because of nonexistent procedures for compiling statistics."

Well, we know now, or at least we know better. Out of a population of perhaps 84 million Vietnamese, itself reduced by several million during the war, there are as many as one million cases of Agent Orange affliction still on the books. Of these, the hardest to look at are the monstrous births. But we agree to forgive ourselves for this, and to watch real monsters such as Robert McNamara and Henry Kissinger, who calmly gave the orders and the instructions, as they posture on chat shows and cash in with their "memoirs." But, hey, forget it. Forget it if you can.

No more Latin after this, I promise, but there is an old tag from the poet Horace that says, *Mutato nomine de te fabula narratur.* "Change only the name and this story is also about you." The Vietnam War came home, and so did many men who had been exposed to Agent Orange, either from handling it and loading it or from being underneath it. If you desire even a faint idea of the distance between justice and a Vietnamese peasant family, take a look at how long it took for the American victims of this evil substance to get a hearing. The chemical assault on Vietnam began in 1961, in the early days of the Kennedy administration, and it kept on in spite of many protests for another ten years. The first effective legal proceeding brought in any American court was in 1984, in New York. This class action, settled out of court, was so broadly defined, in point of American victims and their stricken children, that almost nobody got more than $5,000 out of it, and there was a sharp (or do I mean blunt?) cutoff point beyond which no claim could be asserted. Six million acres of Vietnam had been exposed to the deadly stuff, and, as is the way with protracted litigation, the statistics began to improve and harden. It was established that there was a "match" between those who had been exposed and those who were subject, or whose offspring were subject, to alarming disorders. Admiral Zumwalt, who had first used the phrase "wrong war, wrong place, wrong time" in connection with Vietnam, took a hand in forwarding the legal cause and might have added that his grandson should not be (or do I mean should be?) the last one to suffer for a mistake. More than a mistake. A crime.

Long after both senior male Zumwalts had died—or in 2003, to be precise—the Supreme Court ruled that the issue had not been completely put to rest by the 1984 settlement. The way now lies open for a full accounting of this nightmarish affair. A report, written by Professor Jeanne Stellman, of Columbia University, as part of a U.S. government study, has concluded that nearly two million more gallons of herbicide were disseminated than has yet been admitted, and that the dioxin content of each gallon was much higher than had been officially confessed. (It has been calculated from tests on some Vietnamese that their dioxin levels are 200 times higher than "normal.") The implications are extraordinary, because it is now possible that thousands of Americans may join a million of their former, Vietnamese adversaries in having a standing to sue.

· · ·

"Doesn't it ever end? When will Agent Orange become history?" These were the words of Kenneth Feinberg, who figured as the court's "special master" in the 1984 suit, and who has more recently run the Victim Compensation Fund for the families of those who died in the attacks of September 11, 2001. One should not leave him to answer his own question all by himself. Agent Orange will "become history" in a different way from the trauma of September 11. Of that event, it's fairly safe to say, there will be no lapse of memory at least until everybody who lived through it has died. Of this Vietnam syndrome, some of us have sworn, there will likewise be no forgetting, let alone forgiving, while we can still draw breath. But some of the victims of Agent Orange haven't even been born yet, and if that reflection doesn't shake you, then my words have been feeble and not even the photographs will do.

The Nation

WINNER—REVIEWS AND CRITICISM

Stuart Klawans brings a fan's passion and a far-ranging intellect to his witty writing about film. From high culture to low, his reviews place what we see in context—and make us excited about the movies all over again.

Stuart Klawans

The Tracks
of My Tears

The first time I watched Penélope Cruz lip-sync "Volver," the old song that lends its sentiments and title to Pedro Almodóvar's new film, I wept—though why, I couldn't have said. The voice was dubbed; the musical idiom had been shifted, with Spanish imperiousness, from tango to flamenco; and the character's deepest motivations could only be guessed at, since Almodóvar was waiting for the final reel to reveal them. As perfect moments go, this one was odd and incomplete; and yet, when a plump droplet spilled across Cruz's eyelashes, tears came to me, too.

The next time, of course, I was prepared. Now every implication of the scene was known; every seam of Almodóvar's narrative stitchery had been exposed. I wept even more, as the title might have foretold. *Volver*: to return. All the emotions came back.

What else returns in this beautifully improbable movie? The list might begin with an actress, Carmen Maura, who is closely identified with Almodóvar but had long been absent from his films. Next comes the character Maura plays: a ghostly mother who reinserts herself into her family's affairs, while giving off (despite death) the flatulent scent of life. Then there's a repeated wrong. Years ago, Maura's character unwittingly harmed her daughter (Cruz), who now has done much the same to her own teenage child (the indelible Yohana Cobo). Like the wind-powered turbines you periodically see in this movie—the characters having come from a town of incessant gales, which are said to drive people crazy—the story keeps spinning back to these recurring elements, and more: a scuffed suitcase, a native landscape, a good deed, a corpse.

Memories of older films return as well, as they often do in Almodóvar's work. They are for him what biblical texts used to be for English poets: basic materials of thought. And so in *Volver* he imitates a bit of *Psycho* here, some *Mildred Pierce* there, to articulate his ideas. If I had to explain the themes in general terms, I'd say they concern the sin of not seeing what's before your eyes. *Volver* is about invisibility as a just punishment for this sin; about the false visibility, or self-exposure, promoted by a degraded form of show business; and about the revelations made possible, by contrast, through a true performance, which can be public and personal at the same time. Most of all, though, *Volver* is an exciting crime story, comedy, and tear-jerker about the ways these themes may loop back through generations of women.

Which just goes to show you: To explain *Volver* in general is to explain nothing at all. That's why Almodóvar needs his scriptures, including (most significantly) a clip from Visconti's *Bellissima*. A segment of that film, appearing late in *Volver*, encapsulates the events as no synopsis could. It also transforms Cruz retrospectively into another example of something that returns. Implicitly, the excerpt makes her a double of *Bellissima*'s star, Anna Magnani.

As types, the two are not much alike, except for their swarming heaps of dark hair. Cruz pokes skyward instead of pulling toward the earth; she lingers over her emotions, nestling them within, rather than hurling them out impatiently. Whereas Magnani instinctively, famously, shouted for help, Cruz is capable of suffering in silence. But as Almodóvar knows, his star can stride through a working-class district with all the authority of her predecessor. She, too, can seem to carry in her limbs the weight of a long day's labor. And if her body is too finely drawn to be entirely convincing in her present role—"These characters are always big-assed women," Almodóvar has written, "and Penélope is too slim"—a loving director knows how to show off what flesh there is. In an early shot that summarizes much in *Volver* and foreshadows more, Almodóvar photographs Cruz from directly above, so that the perspective lines run down the inner surface of her breasts into the profound shadows of a cleavage that the costumer keeps perpetually exposed. The character is standing at a kitchen sink, stoically washing the evening's dishes, while you gaze over this site of troubled, uncontainable sexuality, looking down toward the object at the vanishing point: a very large, very sharp knife, which will only temporarily remain clean.

Of course, any dramatist can bring out a knife in act one. But once the knife has been used, it takes an Almodóvar to blend realism instantaneously into melodrama, and melodrama into a moment of comic relief that's cutting in its own right. First Cruz's character feels the full moral gravity of her situation; then, though worn out by a day on the job, she has to set to work again with mop and rubber gloves. When interrupted at her grim task by a knock on the door, she next must hold off a friendly but inquisitive neighbor. "Did you hurt yourself?" he asks solicitously, having noticed a splash of blood on her neck. Fortunately, Cruz knows what makes men look away. With a dismissive wave of her hand, she explains, "Female trouble."

I give away this joke—and only this one, I promise—because it so neatly demonstrates the superiority of *Volver*'s women to its men. For a long while, in fact, you might imagine there aren't any men, but only one man here, another there. Taken singly, they're pretty bad, or weakly good. Viewed in a cluster—as they're seen, I think, only once—they can literally make a character gasp.

The women, by contrast, are almost always shown in a group: organizing meals, doing one another's hair, exchanging stories, giving or receiving aid. Much of the buoyancy and humor of *Volver* comes from this female conviviality—as when, for example, Cruz abruptly goes into the restaurant business and elicits impromptu help from half her neighborhood. Even the ghostly mother wants to be sociable—which is why she gets rid of her veil of loose white hair, so she will no longer look like one of Mizoguchi's spirits dressed in a cheap housecoat. Some of *Volver*'s biggest laughs come from Maura's down-to-earth manner, as she overcomes the indignities involved in rejoining human company. (When put in a tight spot, she can't just vanish, as a normal ghost would. She needs to duck under the bed, with the smile of a kid playing hide-and-seek.) At the end, though, when she once more returns to her solitude—or almost goes back to it—the sweetness of Maura's resignation gives the film its deepest pathos.

For that final return, Maura steps back into a region of timelessness—someplace that's separate from her daughter's world of bustle and worry ("I'm busy," Cruz continually complains) but is different as well from the conventional image of eternity. The film starts in a small-town cemetery, where women are busy cleaning the tombs. It concludes within the shadows of an old provincial house, where Maura will tend not a slab of marble but another woman's body and spirit. Sociability and hope win out in *Volver* over solitude and despair—tentatively, just a little—if only because "ghosts aren't supposed to cry."

The living may weep, though—which brings me back to that core scene in which Cruz performs the title song. I think "perform" is the right word, even though you hear someone else's voice, because Cruz makes her whole face sing: "Though time's passing, which wipes away the whole world / By now has killed off my oldest, dearest dreams / Still I hold within me, hidden like a treasure / Just the simple hope to come back home."

Why is she crying out these lines, and crying over them? On the public level, she is thanking the patrons of her restaurant, and maybe showing off a little for them. More privately, she sings because her mother, who's been lost, taught her "Volver" many years ago, and now she wants to give this song to her own daughter, who came close to being lost.

Cruz sings in two directions at once, to the past and the future, weeping for both. And if on first viewing you don't fully understand why she feels as she does, you weep for her anyway, just because she's there, in the present, alive. You, as her audience, help to make her so.

·　　　·　　　·

As many critics have pointed out, Clint Eastwood's *Flags of Our Fathers* is both a World War II epic and a pressing, critical commentary on today's events. Soon, I hope, I will have something to add to the discussion of this picture. For now, though, I feel it's more urgent that I tell you about James Longley's *Iraq in Fragments*, a nonfiction film that addresses contemporary reality without metaphor and yet is every bit as artful as Eastwood's movie.

It is practically handmade: produced, researched, and shot in Iraq from 2003 through 2005 by Longley himself, who recorded both image and sound. He also edited the material (with Billy McMillin and Fiona Otway) and composed his own *musique concrète* for the soundtrack. The result, as you see from the start, is perhaps less a document than an impression, conveyed through partial glances, stream-of-consciousness juxtapositions, unpredictable rhythms, a collage of sound. Without apology, Longley offers you his fractured, subjective view of Iraq under U.S. occupation. What justifies the film, and makes it compelling, is the corresponding subjectivity of its Iraqi narrators, who lend this movie not only their voices but their eyes and ears.

Part one, set in a poor Sunni quarter of Baghdad, focuses on a fatherless eleven-year-old, Mohammed Haithem, who was working in an auto-repair shop and flunking out of school for the third or fourth time. As Mohammed had come to fear his native city—which used to be beautiful, he said, but now was full of helicopters and tanks—so too did he cringe before his boss. "He loves me like a son," Mohammed insists on the soundtrack. "He doesn't swear at me or hit me." At which point, you see the perpetually simmering, impecunious "father" strike Mohammed while shouting abuse at him for his tears.

Part two looks at the Shiite south through the eyes of Sheik Aws al-Kafaji, a cleric in Muqtada al-Sadr's movement. But in this section, *Iraq in Fragments* also goes beyond the individual viewpoint and becomes a film of masses: flagellants in a procession, protesters at a rally, vigilantes carrying out a punitive raid against liquor sellers. The sporadic, personalized violence of part one gives way to something seething, generalized, apocalyptic.

Part three moves north into a Kurdish farming area, where you again listen to a young boy. Unlike his counterpart in the first section, he can dream of attending medical school; and his elders speak of independence. At last you hear a note of hope—and yet the smoke billowing from nearby brick kilns reminds you of smoke you saw earlier, rising from the explosions in Baghdad.

No truth about the war can be found in *Iraq in Fragments*. Longley discovers only truths—in individuals, in masses of people, in landscapes—that fit together provisionally, if at all. That is the heartbreaking lesson of *Iraq in Fragments*, and its indispensable art.

The New Yorker

FINALIST—REVIEWS AND
CRITICISM

Alex Ross's scholarly yet intimate portrait of a classical music artist gives us an appreciation of his work by exposing the creative processes that informed it. In this piece Ross unearths the pressures and influences that fueled Mozart's greatness.

Alex Ross

The Storm
of Style

Wolfgang Amadè Mozart, as he usually spelled his name, was a small man with a plain, pockmarked face, whose most striking feature was a pair of intense blue-gray eyes. When he was in a convivial mood, his gaze was said to be warm, even seductive. But he often gave the impression of being not entirely present, as if his mind were caught up in an invisible event. Portraits suggest a man aware of his separation from the world. In one, he wears a hard, distant look; in another, his face glows with sadness. In several pictures, his left eye droops a little, perhaps from fatigue. "As touchy as gunpowder," one friend called him. Nonetheless, he was generally well liked.

He was born in the archbishopric of Salzburg in 1756, and he died in the imperial capital of Vienna in 1791. He was an urban creature, and had almost nothing to say about the charms of nature. A product of the artisan classes—his ancestors were bookbinders, weavers, and masons—he adopted aristocratic fashions, going around Vienna in a gold-trimmed hat and a red coat with mother-of-pearl buttons. He was physically restless, quick-witted, sociable, flirtatious, and obscene; one of the more provocative items in his catalogue is a canon for six voices entitled "Leck mich im Arsch" (K. 231/382c). He frittered away money, not least on expensive apartments. He achieved

considerable success, although not as much as he knew he deserved. If audiences were occasionally perplexed by his creations,
listeners in high places recognized his worth. Emperor Joseph II
was a fan of Mozart's work, and, in 1787, to prevent "so rare a
genius" from going abroad, he gave the composer a well-paying
position that required little more than the writing of dances. In
a letter to his father, Leopold, Mozart had warned that "the Vi-
ennese gentry, and in particular the Emperor, must not imagine
that I am on this earth solely for the sake of Vienna."

As a child prodigy, Mozart was advertised in London as "the
most amazing Genius, that has appeared in any Age." Leopold
dubbed him "the miracle whom God allowed to be born in Salzburg." Prince Kaunitz, Joseph II's chief minister, said, "Such
people come into the world once in a hundred years." Praise at
this level, however justified, takes its toll on a man's humility.
Mozart, by his own admission, could be "as proud as a peacock,"
and the archbishop of Salzburg, whose service he quit in 1781,
was not the only person who considered him "dreadfully con-
ceited." Conceit edges easily into paranoia, and Mozart was not
immune. "I think that something is going on behind the scenes,
and that doubtless here too I have enemies," he wrote from
Paris, in 1778. "Where, indeed, have I not had them?" As he
traces conspiracies, mocks the French, and extols the Germans,
he sounds remarkably like Richard Wagner. Later, in Vienna,
Mozart clung to the idea that Antonio Salieri, the imperial Kapellmeister, was plotting against him. Whether or not such in-
trigues existed—John Rice's biography of the supposedly
dastardly Salieri portrays him as a likable character, and an
imaginative composer—Mozart himself was not above politick-
ing: when he applied for the job of second Kapellmeister, he
pointedly observed that "the very capable Kapellmeister Salieri
has never devoted himself to church music."

Playfulness was Mozart's saving grace. His counterpart in
modern times is perhaps George Gershwin, who was charming

and self-infatuated in equal measure. Latter-day attempts to find a dark, brooding layer in Mozart's psychology have been unconvincing. In his correspondence, he once or twice displays depressive symptoms—alluding to his "black thoughts," describing sensations of coldness and emptiness—but context is all-important: in the first instance, he is begging for money, and in the second he is telling his wife, the demanding Constanze, how much he misses her. Nor should too much be made of the fact that Mozart wrote to his dying father that death is the "true goal of our existence," the "best and truest friend of mankind." These sentiments were commonplace in a world where lives ended early and without warning. Of the seven children born to Leopold and Maria Anna Mozart, Wolfgang was one of two who survived infancy; only two of his own six children lived to adulthood. Against this backdrop, Mozart seems, if anything, indefatigably optimistic.

Leopold Mozart once said of his son, "Two opposing elements rule his nature, I mean, there is either too *much* or too *little*, never the golden mean." Often, an artist sets forth in his work what he cannot achieve in life, and Mozart's music is the empire of the golden mean. Nicholas Kenyon, in his excellent new *Faber Pocket Guide to Mozart*, writes, "Other great composers have expressed the extremes of life: affirmation, despair, sensual pleasure, bleak emptiness, but only in Mozart can all these emotions co-exist in the space of a short phrase." Mozart inhabits a middle world where beauty surges in and ebbs away, where everything is contingent and nothing pure, where, as Henry James's Madame Merle says, an envelope of circumstances encloses every human life. It is a place where genres meld; where concertos become operatic and arias symphonic; where comedy and tragedy, and the sensual and the sacred, are one. The golden mean runs through the Andante of the Sinfonia Concertante for Violin and Viola, from 1779–80. A beguiling four-bar melody appears twice, in E-flat major in the middle and in C minor at the end. The first time, the major mode is briefly shadowed by a turn into the relative minor. The second time, minor is flecked by major, creating the effect of a light in the night. The two passages are more or less the same, but the space between them could contain a novel.

The scholar Scott Burnham recently observed that Mozart offers the "sound of the loss of innocence, the ever renewable loss of innocence." There is no more potent subject for an artist, and it explains why Mozart remains so vivid a presence. As ever, the slow movement of the Piano Concerto No. 23 sends us into a wistful trance; the finale of the "Jupiter" Symphony wakes us up into a uniquely Mozartean kind of intelligent happiness; and the apocalyptic climax of *Don Giovanni* stirs our primal fear of being weighed in the balance and found wanting. The loss of innocence was Mozart's, too. Like the rest of us, he had to live outside the complex paradise that he created in sound.

·   ·   ·

Mozart was born two hundred and fifty years ago last January. As in past jubilee years—the most recent was 1991, the two-hundredth anniversary of his death—an onslaught of performances, recordings, and publications has threatened to put all rivals out of business. This summer, the Salzburg Festival is presenting all twenty-two Mozart operas and theatre works, from *Apollo et Hyacinthus* to *The Magic Flute*. At Tanglewood, James Levine will conduct *Don Giovanni*, with Mariusz Kwiecien in the title role; the same volatile masterwork will receive two important productions in Austria, one in Vienna, with the great Gerald Finley in the lead, and the other in Innsbruck, with the early-music maestro René Jacobs conducting. Here in New York, the Mostly Mozart Festival will present Peter Sellars's reconception of the youthful singspiel *Zaide* and a set of Mozart dances by Mark Morris. The festival has also commissioned an audiovisual installation by the Open-Ended Group, in which colorful abstract images generated by the coda of the "Jupiter" will be projected onto ten screens in front of Avery Fisher Hall. Every half hour, computer software will set about "learning" the music, pulling out melodic and harmonic patterns and playing them through speakers, until Mozart's sixty-four-bar coda is heard complete; then the computer's memory is erased, and the process starts again.

There are also piles of new Mozart books. You won't want to be seen at the beach without *Mozart: The Early Years, 1756–1781*, the satisfying first volume of a never-to-be-finished biography by the late Stanley Sadie (Norton; $35); David Cairns's enthusiastic and perceptive *Mozart and His Operas* (California; $29.95); Julian Rushton's crisp, learned *Mozart* (Oxford; $30); Jessica Waldo's probing *Recognition in Mozart's Operas* (Oxford; $45); Cli Eisen and Simon Keefe's *Cambridge Mozart Encyclopedia* ($175); and Lydia Goehr and Daniel Herwitz's anthology *The Don Giovanni Moment* (Columbia; $40). Coming from Yale in November is a sixteen-hundred-page translation of Hermann Abert's 1921 expansion of Otto Jahn's 1856 four-volume biography, for which adjectives are temporarily unavailable.

The thousands of books that have been written about Mozart present a bewildering variety of images. For a long time, well into the twentieth century, many people pictured Mozart as the "eternal child"—an antic boy-man who happened to write sublime music. This was a theme of Alfred Einstein's 1945 biography, long considered the standard work. Pushkin, in his play *Mozart and Salieri*, came up with an influential variant: Mozart as "idle hooligan." This led to the eternal adolescent of the play and movie *Amadeus*—the potty-mouthed punk who happened to write sublime music. Other commentators have made Mozart out to be a romantic in the making or a modernist before the fact—an aloof, tortured character, an agent of sexual subversion, or a clandestine social revolutionary.

Present-day scholars are picking away at the myths and fantasies that have encrusted the world's most famous composer. They describe him not as a naïve prodigy or a suffering outcast but as a hardworking, ambitious, successful musician—"Mozart as a Working Stiff," to borrow the title of a 1994 essay by Neal Zaslaw. One notable upshot has been the rehabilitation of Leopold Mozart, who has long loomed over his son's biography as an oppressive, even abusive, figure. Damning evidence against Leopold was presented in Maynard Solomon's powerful 1995 biography; he wrote of the father's "erotically tinged drive to dominate" his son. Leopold is said to have exploited Wolfgang in his early years, squirreling away profits from their European tours. When the gifted child became a problematic teenager, Leopold exhibited an unhealthy possessiveness, opposing his son's marriage plans and berating him for what he considered spendthrift behavior. His letters contain passages of world-class manipulation. "Your whole intent is to ruin me so you can build your castles in the air," Leopold wrote in 1778, not long after his wife died while accompanying her son to Paris. "I hope that, after your mother had to die in Paris, you will not also burden your conscience by expediting the death of your father."

Leopold was a bit of a monster, but the job of raising the Miracle of Salzburg would have taxed anyone's patience. Ruth Halliwell made the case for Leopold in her remarkably illuminating 1998 book, *The Mozart Family*. The father didn't so much exploit the son as make him possible. Those long European tours gave Mozart an incomparable education; he went to London, Paris, Vienna, Milan, and Munich, met the monarchs and princes of the day, and talked to most of the leading composers. Knowing that his son's musical gifts far exceeded his own, Leopold tutored him in the practical aspects of art and life, in which he was rather better versed. Who can deny the truth of Leopold's maxim "Where money is plentiful, everything is dear, and where living is cheap, money will be scarce"? Or: "The best way to make people feel ashamed of themselves is to be extremely *friendly and polite to those who are your enemies*"? Mozart's path would have been easier if he had absorbed a few of the bland but useful adages that his father mailed to him.

The letters between father and son take on a much more vibrant tone when music is the subject. On musical matters, the Mozarts are essentially of one mind; Leopold never seems to be reining in his son's imagination. In late 1780 and early 1781, Mozart was in Munich, preparing his first operatic masterpiece, *Idomeneo*, while Leopold was in Salzburg, supervising the opera's librettist. The young composer was unleashing every expressive device available to him: as Cairns observes in *Mozart and His Operas*, *Idomeneo* touches on "love, joy, physical and spiritual contentment, stoicism, heroic resolution; the ecstasy of self-sacrifice, the horrors of dementia, the agonizing dilemma of a ruler trapped in the consequences of his actions; mass hysteria, panic in the face of an unknown scourge, turning to awe before the yet more terrible fact; the strange peace that can follow intense grief; the infinite tenderness of a father's last farewell to his son." Leopold was mostly a bystander to Mozart's astonishing feat, but he did make one crucial contribution: for a pivotal scene in act 3, when the voice of Neptune's oracle rises from the depths, he requested "moving, terrifying, and altogether unusual" music, and went on to suggest a series of sudden crescendos and decrescendos in the brass and winds, bracketing the vocal phrases. Exactly this effect appears in the finished score.

Perhaps Leopold's greatest gift to his son was the instruction to write for both musical insiders and the general public. In a letter from 1782, Mozart takes that favorite phrase of his father's—"the golden mean"—and weaves around it a pragmatic philosophy that is even more relevant now than it was in the eighteenth century:

> These concertos [Nos. 11, 12, and 13] are a happy medium between what is too easy and too difficult; they are very brilliant, pleasing to the ear, and natural, without being vapid. There are passages here and there from which the connoisseurs alone can derive satisfaction; but these passages are written in such a way that the less learned cannot fail to be pleased, though without knowing why. . . . The golden mean of truth in all things is no longer either known or appreciated. In order to win applause one must write stuff which is so inane that a coachman could sing it, or so unintelligible that it pleases precisely because no sensible man can understand it.

One wonders what Mozart would have made of today's musical scene, when *American Idol* contestants cover Elvis hits and university composers write super-complex, mathematically recondite works, and the happy medium seems, on most days, deserted.

Scholars have also demolished the old idea that Mozart was an idiot savant, transcribing the music that played in his brain. Instead, he seems to have refined his ideas to an almost manic degree. Examination of Mozart's surviving sketches and drafts— Constanze threw many sketches away—reveals that the composer sometimes began a piece, set it aside, and resumed it months or years later; rewrote troubling sections several times in a row; started movements from scratch when a first attempt failed to satisfy; and waited to finish an aria until a singer had tried out the opening. Ulrich Konrad calls these stockpiles of material "departure points"—"a delineation of intellectual places to which Mozart could return as necessary." In other words, the music in Mozart's mind may have been like a huge map of half-explored territories; in a way, he was writing all his works all the time. The new image of him as a kind of improvising perfectionist is even more formidable than the previous one of God's stenographer. Ambitious parents who are currently playing the *Baby Mozart* video for their toddlers may be disappointed to learn that Mozart became Mozart by working furiously hard, and, if Constanze was right, by working himself to death.

· · ·

In 1991, the Philips label issued a deluxe, complete Mozart edition—180 CDs—employing such distinguished interpreters as Mitsuko Uchida, Alfred Brendel, and Colin Davis. The set has now been reissued in a handsome and surprisingly manageable array of seventeen boxes. During a slow week last winter, I transferred it to an iPod and discovered that Mozart requires 9.77 gigabytes.

On a computer, you can use search functions to create cross-sections of Mozart—a dreamworld of Adagios; a neo-Baroque swirl of fantasias and fugues; a nonet of Quintets (all major works). To listen to his twenty-seven settings of the "Kyrie" is to appreciate his inexhaustible invention: they range from the entrancingly sweet to the forbiddingly severe, each a convincing simulacrum of the power of the Lord. But the obvious challenge was to go through the whole megillah—to begin with the Andante in C Major (K. 1a), which Mozart wrote when he was five, and proceed to the bitter end, the Requiem (K. 626), which he left unfinished at his death, at thirty-five. It took me three months. I can't claim to have given every bar close attention; a patch of recitative in the early opera *La Finta Semplice*, for example, was disrupted by a protracted public-address announcement at Detroit Metro Airport, and most of the Contredanse No. 4 in F (K. 101) was drowned out by the crack drum corps Drumedies performing in the Times Square subway station. All recordings are fake events, and MP3 files heard on headphones are faker than most. But I got a rough aerial view of Mozart's achievement, and was more in awe than ever.

From the start, the music is astonishingly well made. (A caveat from the scholarly demythologizers: most of the earliest works were "corrected" by Leopold.) Young Mozart shows an uncanny ability to mimic the styles and forms of the day: Baroque sacred music, opera bua and opera seria, Gluckian reform opera, Haydn's classicism, the Mannheim symphonic school, Sturm und Drang agitation, and so on. Quite a bit of the music is reassuringly routine; Hermann Abert writes, in his massive biography, that Mozart "evolved along sound lines, without any supernatural leaps and bounds." But very early there are flashes of individuality. Some of the first come in the London Sketchbook, which dates from Mozart's London sojourn of 1764 and 1765 (and which Leopold did not touch). A piece in G minor (K. 15p) features stormy chromatic harmony of a kind that will appear to momentous effect in Mozart's minor-key symphonies and concertos. A piece in E-flat major (K. 15kk) has hypnotically murmuring chords and mournful slips into the minor, forecasting time-suspending Andantes and Adagios to come.

Hearing so many premonitions of future masterpieces, I got the feeling that Mozart's brain contained an array of musical archetypes that were connected to particular dramatic situations or emotional states-figures connoting vengeance, reconciliation, longing, and so on. One example appears in *La Finta Semplice*, the merry little opera bua that Mozart wrote when he was twelve. In the finale, when all misunderstandings are resolved, there is a passage marked "un poco Adagio," in which Giacinta and her maid Ninetta ask forgiveness for an elaborate ruse that they have pulled on Giacinta's brothers. "Perdono," they sing—"Forgive." Not just the words but the music prefigures the tremendous final scene of *The Marriage of Figaro*, in which the wayward Count asks the Countess's forgiveness— "Contessa, perdono!"—and she grants it, in a half-hopeful, half-heartbroken phrase. I looked at the New Mozart Edition scores side by side, and noticed that the two passages not only waver between the same happy-sad chords (G major and E minor) but pivot on the same rising bass line (B-C-D-E). It is unlikely that Mozart thought back to *La Finta Semplice* when he composed *Figaro*, but the idea of forgiveness apparently triggered certain sounds in his mind.

As Mozart grows toward adulthood, there is a palpable thrill of emergence. The routine becomes rare, the extraordinary ordinary. Having proved himself as an able technician of theatrical and sacred music (*Lucio Silla*, of 1772, and the Sacramental Litany, of 1776, are high-water marks of his youth), Mozart now imports exterior drama and interior reflection to instrumental genres: the fiercely concentrated Symphony No. 25 in G Minor, the swashbuckling violin concertos of 1775, the spacious String Quintet No. 1 in B-Flat, and, most strikingly, the Piano Concerto No. 9, which is a three-act instrumental opera of energetic play, melancholy withdrawal, and happy return. Whether any of these forward leaps can be connected with events in Mozart's life remains a matter of debate. Did the traumas of 1778—the failure of his venture to Paris, the death of his mother, Leopold's scathing criticism—create in Mozart a new musical maturity? During that Paris summer, Mozart wrote his darkly eloquent Piano Sonata in A Minor, another landmark in his development. The trouble is that we don't know whether it was written before or after Maria Anna's death, and, in the absence of other information, we have to assume that one day Mozart banged an A-minor triad like a wedge into the middle range of the piano and liked the way it sounded. Stanley Sadie concludes unsentimentally, "There is no real reason to imagine that [Mozart] used his music as a vehicle for the expression of his own personal feelings."

Then again, it's hard not to see some connection between the life and the art in the period from 1781 to 1786, when a series of independent acts—Mozart's escape from Salzburg to Vienna, his marriage to Constanze, his defiant response to Leopold's objections to the above—coincides with a staggering outpouring of inspiration: the six string quartets dedicated to Haydn, fifteen concertos for piano and orchestra, the "Haner" and "Linz" and "Prague" Symphonies, the Mass in C Minor, the operas *The Abduction from the Seraglio* and *The Marriage of Figaro*, and a dozen other pieces without which classical programming would grind to a halt. The instrumental works, with their architecturally imposing first movements and their slow movements that open up multiple inner worlds, are the most expansive of their time, looking forward to Beethoven only insofar as Beethoven looked back at them. Yet the futuristic broadening of scope is made possible by a study of the past; Mozart immerses himself in the art of Bach, prompted by a fad for old music in aristocratic circles. (The emperor liked fugues.) Counterpoint is used to elaborate and intensify the thematic argument of sonata form. Also, in the slow movements spasms of dissonance are used to offset the surplus of beauty; Scott Burnham notes that the famous Andante of the Concerto No. 21 contains a quietly shuddering five-note collection that is not so much a chord as a cluster. Counterpoint and dissonance are the cables on which Mozart's bridges to paradise hang.

Mozart's operas, meanwhile, abandon artifice in favor of moment-to-moment psychological realism. In *The Abduction from the Seraglio*, Belmonte ventures into the Ottoman Empire in search of his kidnapped love, Constanze. Having learned that she is nearby, he sings of the anxious beating of his heart ("O wie ängstlich, o wie feurig"). The heartbeat is indicated in a soft but insistent pattern of falling thirds, in which, Mozart wrote proudly to his father, "you see the trembling, the faltering." A fluttering, innocent-sounding kind of worry is suggested by rapid runs of flute and muted violins. Toward the end of the aria, the "throbbing" figure comes back in the minor mode, and it is reinforced by winds in unison. It ends up sounding obsessive and fearful—a lover's paranoia creeping in. This insistent deepening of an ostensibly comic situation would become Mozart's signature in the next several years; *The Marriage of Figaro, Don Giovanni,* and *Così Fan Tutte,* the three operas that he created in tandem with his ideal librettist, the Italian Jewish polymath Lorenzo Da Ponte, sprawl across the boundary between the comic and the tragic, defining life as what happens in between.

After 1786, the storm of style abates slightly. In this period, Mozart was no longer attracting sufficient numbers of subscribers to his public concerts, in part because of an expensive war with Turkey. So the production of piano concertos tapers off, and there are no more symphonies after the colossal "Jupiter," of 1788. Instead, there are frequent groups of minuets, contredanses, and other popular dances, the result of Mozart's new, revenue-enhancing job as Emperor Joseph II's Kammermusicus. They are exasperating to listen to in large quantity, but they are full of lively, even zany details, and serve as a reminder that eighteenth-century composers were expected to be adept at producing both "popular" and "serious" music, and that there was no categorical difference between the two. Popular dance styles are deployed to dramatic effect in the ballroom scene in *Don Giovanni,* in which an aristocratic minuet, a popular contredanse, and a working-class Deutscher are played simultaneously, in three different meters. The episode demonstrates Mozart's ability to move as a free agent through the social and cultural hierarchies of his time.

The works of Mozart's last three years have long caused puzzlement. Less prolific than before, he seems to be groping his way toward a new style, more concise in form and more melodically compressed. Schubert knew that there was something potent in the String Quintet in D, from 1790: he copied it almost note for note in passages of his "Trout" Quintet and his String Quintet. Charles Rosen, in *The Classical Style,* isolates a riveting passage in the Quintet's Adagio, in which "four completely different kinds of rhythm [are] superimposed in a contrapuntal texture at once complex and deeply touching": one violin moving up by steps, another stepping haltingly down, the violas sighing on repeated seconds and thirds, and the cello undermining the harmony with a jazzy pizzicato figure that plunges down an octave and a half. Right afterward comes a radiant little theme of rising-and-falling phrases, which brings back one of the oldest recurring motifs in Mozart's language—an archetype of love or longing. There is something elegiac in this gesture toward the past; Mozart, near the end, goes back to his beginnings. Yet it is hazardous to connect the elusive emotions of the late works with the fact of the composer's approaching death. Julian Rushton wryly notes that critics used to detect "feelings of impending doom" in the Clarinet Concerto and the Piano Concerto No. 27, which appeared in Mozart's final year; it turns out that the first movement of each was sketched several years earlier.

What Mozart might have done next is no one's guess. The pieces that emerged from the suddenly productive year 1791— *The Magic Flute*, the ultimate Leopoldian synthesis of high and low; *La Clemenza di Tito*, a robust revival of the aging art of opera seria; the silken lyricism of the Clarinet Concerto; the Requiem, at once cerebral and raw—form a garden of forking paths. Mozart was still a young man, discovering what he could do. In the unimaginable alternate universe in which he lived to the age of seventy, an anniversary-year essay might have contained a sentence such as this: "Opera houses focus on the great works of Mozart's maturity—*The Tempest*, *Hamlet*, the two-part *Faust*—but it would be a good thing if we occasionally heard that flawed yet lively work of his youth, *Don Giovanni*."

•　　　•　　　•

In a jubilee year, when all the old Mozart myths come rising out of the ground where scholars have tried to bury them, the usefulness of *Don Giovanni* is that it puts a stake through the heart of the chocolate-box Mozart, the car-radio Mozart, the Mozart-makes-you-smarter Mozart. If the opera were played in bus stations or dentists' waiting rooms, it would spread fear. It would probably cause perversion in infants. No matter how many times you hear the punitive D-minor chord with which the opera begins, or the glowering diminished seventh that heralds the arrival of the stone statue of the Commendatore ("Don Giovanni, you invited me to dinner, and I have come"), it generates a certain mental panic. Mozart's harmonies of disaster are all the more terrifying because they break through the frame of what purports to be a saucy comedy about an aristocratic seducer—a successor to *Figaro*. The fact that *Figaro* is actually quoted in the score—"Non più andrai" is one of the airs that the Don enjoys at dinner, just before the Commendatore arrives—suggests that Mozart is consciously subverting his reputation as a supplier of ambient musical pleasure.

The new anthology *The Don Giovanni Moment* is the book for readers who have had enough of the discussion of who Mozart really was, and who want to understand the music's impact on the intellect and, more widely, its influence on Western culture. That influence is huge; if you wanted to locate the moment at which the Enlightenment gave way to the romantic age, you might well settle on "Don Giovanni." As the essayists in *The Don Giovanni Moment* recount, Goethe set to work in earnest on his *Faust* after seeing a performance of *Don Giovanni*, in 1797; Kierkegaard was excited by the "sensuous genius" of Mozart's music, and by the Don's chase after erotic pleasure; the ambivalent liberal Pushkin was torn between the Don's swagger and the Commendatore's rectitude; George Bernard Shaw riffed on the opera in *Man and Superman*, letting the Don end up in Heaven. Wagner was deeply under the opera's spell; when the tragic god Wotan sings the words "*Das Ende!*" in the *Ring*, he traverses the same intervals with which the Commendatore intones Don Giovanni's name.

The leading romantic rhapsodist of *Don Giovanni* was the novelist, storyteller, critic, and composer E. T. A. Hoffmann, whose mesmerizing 1813 story-essay "Don Juan" is analyzed by Richard Eldridge in the anthology. For Hoffmann, the character of the Don is uninteresting on paper—"a *bon vivant* who loves wine and girls immoderately, who arrogantly invites the stone man, who portrays the old father whom he cut down in self-defense, to join him at his festive table." Mozart's music transforms him into a radical sensualist, a seeker of extremes. But he is a romantic gone to seed: restless longing devolves into sexual compulsion, a contempt for the ordinary curdles into cynicism. On the other side stand the Commendatore and his daughter Donna Anna, who, Hoffmann's narrator speculates, actually succumbed to the Don's advances, and swears vengeance to cover up her shame. Hoffmann is right in hearing something weirdly violent in Donna Anna's utterances, especially the aria "Or sai chi l'onore" and the wild recitative that introduces it. There is a blackness at the heart of her righteousness, just as there is a life force in the Don's malice. Mozart's quest for middle ground takes him into the risky space between good and evil. Both the terms and the outcome of this "conflict between godly and demonic powers," as Hoffmann called it, are murky.

When the Don finally goes down to Hell, you are not sure whether you are hearing infernal legions celebrating his arrival or the armies of Heaven rather too enthusiastically enjoying their capacity for destruction—or, perhaps, some unholy concert of the two. The scene is structured around a staggered sequence of upward-creeping lines, sometimes in the bass and sometimes in the treble. Twice, the strings embroider that pattern with furious up-and-down scales, and the fact that each scale is a half-step higher than the previous one gives the impression that the music is obliterating everything in its path, like a death machine in a medieval etching. Toward the end, a thumping four-note figure comes to the fore; it recalls the Commendatore knocking at the door but ends up sounding like the stomping of feet. (Tellingly, that four-note stomp reappears in the finale of Schubert's Ninth Symphony, where it connotes a young artist asserting his power.) At the same time, as Michel Noiray observes in the *Cambridge Mozart Encyclopedia*, the scene has an archaic, religious aspect, echoing Renaissance and Baroque sacred music. The unsettling device of an upward chromatic bass line—the downward, "lamenting" bass is more common—is used several times in Mozart's early settings of the Mass to underpin the word "*Crucifixus*."

The Don's almost existential fate, his crucifixion without resurrection, is a singular event in Mozart's world. Most of his operas end in a great scene of reconciliation, in keeping with the ideals of the Enlightenment. In *Figaro*, the Countess pardons the Count; in *Idomeneo*, Neptune's oracle, in whose music Leopold Mozart took such an interest, proclaims the power of love; in *The Abduction from the Seraglio*, Pasha Selim forgives his enemy's son; and in *The Magic Flute* and *La Clemenza di Tito*, both Sarastro and the Emperor rise above vengeance. (*Così Fan Tutte* is the other problem case; its reuniting of lovers is troubled by the fact that Fiordiligi has expressed high passion for the wrong man.) Jessica Waldo's book *Recognition in Mozart's Operas* connects these scenes to Aristotle's concept of anagnorisis, or recognition, the "change from ignorance to knowledge." In *Don Giovanni*, Waldo points out, the moment of recognition is withheld: the Don remains "unflinching, unreflecting." That is why the romantics revered him: he does not stray from the extreme path that he has chosen. In a way, he is more Faustian than Goethe's Faust—who does, in the end, repent.

A final twist awaits. In a cosmically laughing epilogue, the remaining principals gather to proclaim, in bouncy, up-tempo music, that evildoers always meet the same bad end. The romantics had such difficulty accepting this seeming anticlimax that they routinely cut it from the opera. Richard Strauss was one of the first to recognize its ironic intelligence, and to restore it in performance. In *The Don Giovanni Moment*, Philip Kitcher and Richard Schacht write that the ending imagines "life without awe," a truly human existence beginning on the other side of tragedy. The world may be a duller place without the Don and his occult nemesis, but it is still suffused with Mozartean pleasure. We can live without extremists, however much they may stimulate our faculties of lust and rage.

Don Giovanni, which is many people's choice for the greatest opera ever written, ends with something like a humble gesture: it dissolves its own aura of greatness. Having marched us to the brink of Heaven and Hell, Mozart abruptly pulls us back, implying that, in the manner of Shakespeare's epilogues, all is show, a pageant melting into air. "I'm just the composer, I don't have any answers," he seems to say. "Life goes on!" And he walks away at a rapid pace, his red coat flapping behind him.

McSweeney's

WINNER—FICTION

Rajesh Parameswaran uses clear, direct prose to tell the story of a make-believe medic playing a chilling game of doctor in a Southern strip mall. This tale grabs hold of the reader with an unabashed love of storytelling that at once charms and chastens.

Rajesh Parameswaran

The Strange
Career of Doctor
Raju Gopalarajan

Nore of us were surprised when we heard Gopi Kumar
had been fired from his job at CompUSA. We imagine he came home and bragged to his wife that at any
minute his manager would realize what a mistake she'd made
and beg him to take his job back. Manju would have breathed
out hard and told him, "Go to the unemployment office anyway and fill out the forms" (as Gopi eventually did). But what
Manju didn't know—what none of us understood—was that
Gopi had already decided to make his living by impersonating a
doctor.

In fact, within three weeks of that day, Gopi had signed the
lease on a small office in Manvel, a good hour and a half from
where he lived, a place where he hoped none of us would run
into him. He told his wife he was looking for a job, and later he
said he had found one, as a television salesman. But he would
come home those days carrying as many books about medicine
and surgery as the Doakum County Public Library System possessed. Every evening he pored through them, making margin
marks with his pencil, consulting the internet for clarification
on difficult points; and Manju would have stood in the doorway
and watched, in her weary way.

"You're not supposed to write in library books," she would
say. Manju was a secretary in an insurance agency, and it seemed

to us she was shy in public, a little insecure—the sort of woman who always wore saris, and who would respond in Tamil when you spoke to her in English. But we also noticed she had grown to be bold at home with him, because when you are married to a man like Gopi, a man who is always going to be a bit oblivious to those around him, you can be a little loud and say what you think and still not risk offending.

"Why not? My taxes pay for them," Gopi might reply.

"As if you pay all your taxes. What are you reading, anyway?"

And then he would turn to her and say, "Mind your own business," or, "Don't you have enough work to do that you don't have to stand there and bother me?" or, "You should try reading yourself one day, you might learn something."

"And you're such a genius yourself," Manju would answer. Or she might instead hold her tongue, deciding it wasn't important enough to continue provoking him.

Of course, when Gopi went to sleep or stepped into the bathroom, Manju would peep into the books herself to see what was engrossing her husband, and this is why some people say that she must have known and chosen not to stop him—that she was just as responsible as he was for all that happened later. After all, Manju herself told the story of the day in India when Gopi had gotten so fed up with the traffic outside of their house that he had assembled a police uniform using his father's old air-force khakis and gone out into the road. He had issued homemade tickets, ripping them up in exchange for boisterously negotiated bribes, stopping only after Manju pretended to call and report *him* to the police. Obviously, they say, Manju knew her husband had a history as a charlatan, and when she looked in those library books, she should have reached the logical conclusion.

But the people who say this don't understand that there was more than one logical conclusion. During their twenty-one years of marriage, as everybody knows, Manju had been unable to have a child, and seeing the books her husband brought home, with their graphic photographs of women's parts, of glistening uteruses and palsied vaginas, of dead, blue-green fetuses and rash-covered nipples, she might just as well have thought her husband was feeling the loneliness of being childless and almost old, and was seeking again a cure for a problem they had long ago decided would have to be left to the whims and the graces of God.

We liked Manju so much, and we miss her. She had a beautiful voice, and always we asked her to sing at our functions. She would sit down with crossed legs and clear her throat and the room would quiet and parents would hush their children. Then the voice would come out of her, low and quavering and full of awe and sadness, singing of beautiful, dark-skinned young Krishna and how she loved him and longed for him, how she lay alone and burned for him but never could be with him. And when she sang like that we would notice a hollow space in our own chests, and we would feel that space filled with a sweet longing we couldn't understand, and our eyes would grow hot and wet. When people talk about Manju and her husband and what they did and what happened to them, they should try to remember that people have depths.

.   .   .

The office space Gopi rented with his and Manju's small savings had previously housed a veterinary clinic, and Gopi would have liked it because it seemed to require little work to convert to a proper medical office. It was a small storefront in a low-rent strip mall on a quiet country highway, separated from other businesses by a grassy field where a dozen long-dead oil pumps stood like big-beaked birds, a field where in the summer grazed cheaply fed hamburger cows.

It was the sort of place where in the mornings young men wearing baseball caps and Stetsons gathered in the parking lot and stood there until the sun grew hot, then move into the thin shade that rimmed the building. Gopi would have seen them when he arrived in the mornings to clean and prepare, their hats bobbing outside his office window as they waited for the pickup trucks that arrived by ones or twos, and for the men inside the trucks to point out the ones they wanted.

One day, Gopi offered one of these waiting men thirty dollars to help clear trash out of the closets and wash the walls. The man seemed happy to do it. His name, as everyone knows by now, was Vicente, and he had a big smile and looked to be about twenty-three. Gopi asked him where he was from, and Vicente answered, "Puebla, Mexico. You?"

"Madras, India," said Gopi.

We picture Gopi and young Vicente sweeping the little poops and pet foods that lay scattered on the floor. They tossed out the rusty small-animal cages stacked here and there and scrubbed the strange stains on the small metal examining table that stuck out from one wall. They followed without luck in the walls and dark closet corners the knocks and noises that Gopi was convinced were the scamperings and squeals of someone's lost and forgotten pet; and when they were finished, the place still smelled stubbornly of urine, but Gopi was pleased.

To make the office seem complete, Gopi ordered over the internet a phone, a scalpel, forceps, scissors, gauze and cotton, rubbing alcohol, bandages of various sizes, rubber gloves, a microwave oven, and, from a friend who worked in a hospital in India, a small supply of prescription drugs.

After two weeks of preparation, Gopi was open for business. At a copy store he had made a small sign advertising the alias he had decided on: DR. RAJU GOPALARAJAN, MD; WOMEN'S DIFFICULTIES AND ALL OTHER MATTERS. Now he would have taped this sign in his window. We imagine he wore a white lab coat from the local uniform-supply store, and the stethoscope that had arrived in the mail that morning, and now he put it on his ears and listened to his own heart. The sound was clear and strong, and Gopi felt overjoyed at how well he had done. Then he danced, just for a minute. Afterward, sitting down behind his desk, he grinned his little-boy grin.

Then there was quiet. No strange creatures stirred in the walls, no one rang on the telephone. And in the quiet and the stillness, the sound of Gopi's own beating heart returned to him, and for a brief moment, the poor man saw himself as if from a distance. He saw himself as we see him, sitting alone in an office on an empty country highway. A doctor? He wondered if he should have started in a smaller way, working from a room of his house, prescribing medicines for his friends, writing doctor's notes for their children. But even that prospect now seemed absurd. His face grew warm with the dawning realization that he had made a ridiculous, a gigantic mistake.

As a tension began to form in his left shoulder and the base of his skull, Gopi tried to remind himself that he had to do this in the biggest possible way, so that people would feel that he *was* a doctor. But the panic remained, and Gopi felt desperately a need for the company of people, so he walked outside and stood among the men on the sidewalk.

"Good morning, fellows," he said to them. His hands were thrust into the pockets of his lab coat, and his stethoscope draped over his neck.

"Good morning," they said back. Gopi recognized Vicente and some of the other men, and when they saw him now in a doctor's white coat (he would have looked quite smart) one man said something in Spanish, and another said, "You're the doctor?"

Vicente added, "We didn't know you're the doctor. We thought you were making up the office for somebody else."

"I'm the doctor," Gopi said.

"Good morning, Doctor," Vicente smiled, and Gopi's tension disappeared.

Then Vicente's friend rolled up the cuff of his jeans and showed Gopi a rash of ugly white-and-black bumps on his shin, and all the men gathered around to look. And this is how Gopi Kumar, a.k.a. Dr. Raju Gopalarajan, got his first patients.

.   .   .

Like many of us, Gopi had wanted to be a doctor his whole life. Those of us who knew him back home remember how he thought himself a martyr for having abjured the field early on, after seeing the families of friends thrown into crisis by the necessity of paying enormous bribes to the medical school admissions committee. When his friends asked how he had done on the qualifying exams, Gopi, who had done abysmally, felt an indignant pride in telling them his score was irrelevant because he would never subject his father to the burden and indignity of groveling before those goondas.

He quit college and worked for a time as an orderly in a hospital in Madras. It wasn't work fit for a Brahmin, some people said, but he loved hospitals. He found them exciting. He'd had to lie to his father about what his actual duties were: picking up bloody dressings from the floor, handling the warm, wet test tubes of other people's urine. The doctors never liked him much—he didn't cringe and salaam, like the other orderlies, and they hesitated to give him the most menial chores, yet resented any slight resistance he offered when they did.

He met Manju around this time. At lunchtime and after work, Gopi had taken to sitting in the commissary of the college he had once attended, where he still had some friends, and talking to the girls there. He made headway with his imitations of various professors and his intimacy with the ins and outs of the college bureaucracy. And he bragged about the jobs he would one day get, the car and motorcycle and house he would eventually own, and about the life he would find one day in America.

He said he had visited America once: the floors there were covered in soft carpets, and cool air and warm air was pumped from the walls, and anyone could become American, it was in the laws, and he knew it, and he would do it. And when he talked like this, in his confident manner, Manju thought he seemed, in a way, magical. It was weeks into their romance before Manju realized that Gopi wasn't a student—he was an orderly in a hospital who came to the campus only to meet gullible girls. But by then, she told herself, it was too late. Manju was in love.

Her mother, of course, would be scandalized. Even some of her friends back then were scandalized. Manju had always been a shy and proper girl, they say; the last person who should have gone in for a love match.

But her friends' surprise was based on a misunderstanding. If they had looked more closely, they would have seen that Manju's shyness was the mask of an intensely interested observer of the opposite sex. She noticed the unnoticeable, skinny, silly-looking boys who sat in her classrooms, and she surprised herself by wanting them. She knew that the answer to her mind's and body's questions could be found in these greasy-haired creatures, because it was they who had made her realize the questions were there. She searched the faces of her married cousins for some sign of difference, of the calm confidence of transcendent knowledge, of satisfaction.

And so she married Gopi, and they moved in with his parents, and Gopi took a job as a salesman so he could save money; and four years later, just as he had promised, they moved to America. And that is also roughly how long it had taken, after the move, for him to lose interest in her, and for her to lose faith in him—four years.

Gopi had jumped from job to job to job, full of schemes. He approached us once for funds to start a Big Boy franchise. If we gave at all, it was out of friendship for Manju; but what became of the project, we never heard. Even Manju couldn't tell us—Gopi refused to share the details of his business ventures with her.

Incredible enthusiasm, followed by wild and ridiculous efforts, followed by boredom and abandonment: it was the pattern he followed in all his endeavors, Manju realized; and it was the pattern he had followed with regard to her.

This, she thought, was the great ocean of the middle of marriage. The home shore had disappeared from sight, and what had appeared as infinite promise became instead a terrifying endlessness, a lonely, crushing isolation of two selves in the world.

For Gopi, of course, lost in his own head, the promise was still there, always on the verge of fulfillment. There was opportunity all around in platefuls, and one only had to take his helping.

.   .   .

Gopi told the man with the rash on his shin that he would take care of him the next day. Then Gopi would have gone home and consulted his library books (which he renewed every two weeks, as he planned to do indefinitely), concluding finally that the rash was either a bacterial infection or a reaction to the sun. He forged a prescription for topical antibiotic, and recommended as well an over-the-counter anti-itch ointment and sunscreen. He charged the fellow thirty-five dollars for the advice, stressing that this price was a discount because this man was the clinic's first patient. Gopi figured the sum was less than half what a regular doctor would charge someone without insurance. Within five days, the rash disappeared.

Soon, Gopi was consulting with the workers on a whole catalogue of minor ailments, and they began also to refer their families and their friends to him. He recruited additional patients in bus stops or at the mall, preferring immigrants who looked newly arrived, Indians if we appeared trusting and un-Americanized. He would strike up a conversation to get a sense of the person and then hand out one of the business cards he'd printed up. In this way, Gopi generated business with surprising speed. People with very serious-sounding problems—old men with severe chest pains, for example—Gopi reluctantly turned away, but those with more minor ailments he gamely treated, or tried to, and after two-and-a-half months he was able to cover his monthly expenses.

Those first months were giddy ones for Gopi. In the evenings, over dinner, he might tell Manju, "I sold seven televisions today."

"Very nice," she might answer. "Bring one home for us one day, that would be something."

"Soon, my dear," he would tell her. "Soon we will have big-screen televisions and nice vacations, too," and he would grin in his unaccountable way, so pleased with himself. "Don't you trust me? It'll happen, Manju, why not, I say? Why not for us?"

Manju had become by this point more or less a sensible woman, but she would find something in Gopi's manner so infectious, so suddenly appealing—almost like the Gopi of old—that she would get up and take her dirty plate to the sink just so he wouldn't see the smile rising irrepressibly to her face.

At night, he would push up against her and bite her playfully on the neck.

"Ouch!" she would yell, and give him a push on the nose. "Don't be stupid."

"Why not? One good reason," Gopi would ask.

And Manju would answer, "What would be the point?"

"The point?" Gopi would laugh. "Now you see the point?" And Manju would finally relent, thinking, "Okay, why not?"

Of course, when Gopi squeezed himself between Manju's pudding thighs, in his mind he saw pictures of Deepika Shenoy, our doctor-acquaintance Dilip's wife; or of his old favorite, Dolly Parton.

"Whose key is in ignition?" he might even blurt, in his exuberance, "Gopi the physician!" And Manju would have snorted a laugh and asked him what he meant, if she could have, but on those first nights, at least, she was too distracted by the discovery that having his warmth inside her should feel so good and familiar, even though so much time had passed.

After he fell asleep, though, Manju would experience an aftertaste of unplaceable resentment. His behavior had the effect, in other words, of sharpening her long-dormant appetite for happiness, without satisfying it. She sensed Gopi's newfound sense of purpose, but didn't understand it. She saw the outline of a different life together, but the content was missing. And in this state of directed longing, of contoured emptiness, Manju began to suspect that she was pregnant.

It was entirely plausible. Manju had confided in some of us years ago that the doctors had only ever said it would be difficult, not impossible. And now, she thought, perhaps a child had finally arrived to pull Gopi back and create the love they had never properly had. Manju could scarcely believe it, but something Gopi had said kept echoing in her mind: Why not? Why not for us?

When she made the doctor's appointment, Manju decided not to tell Gopi, or any of us, until she had gotten an answer for sure. The doctor was kind to Manju, and patient, and interested in listening, and so Manju would have told her all about her body's changes, and the discomfort, and the intermittent sickness. And the doctor examined Manju and took her blood, and a week later called her back for more tests, and after this second visit, she was drawn and pale from the strain of spending long hours in cold rooms, half naked, stared at, pricked, pried open, and fingered by more people than she could clearly remember.

She drove home that day hoping that her husband at least would have done something about dinner. But when she opened the front door Gopi was hunched over a torn sofa cushion, its foam stuffing strewn over the floor.

"What in the world are you doing?" she asked.

"Nothing," Gopi yelled in alarm. "What do you think? Only fixing the cushion." Gopi had sliced it open with a knife and removed its innards, and now he was stuffing them back in and trying to stitch it all up as cleanly as possible. He was practicing. The following day, he was scheduled to perform his first surgery.

Vicente was the patient. Gopi had noticed that the young man had a lump on his forearm the size of a kumquat. Vicente said he'd had it for years, that a doctor had told him it was harmless—simply a fat deposit—and that it would cost nine hundred dollars just to remove it. Gopi said it was an ugly thing and ought to be gotten rid of, and that he would do it for a very reasonable price. Somehow, the boy agreed.

Vicente arrived at the office with a young lady whom Gopi recognized as the woman who always rode in Vicente's car. She was short and thin and wore loose blue jeans, a white T-shirt, and sneakers. Vicente introduced her as Sandra, and Gopi smiled and shook her hand; from the way he behaved, you could not have known how nervous he was. "Mucho gusto," said the woman, and Gopi corrected her. "I'm not Spanish, I'm Indian," he said. "But that's okay. Se habla Español. Right, Vicente?"

Sandra made a noise that sounded to Gopi like "Hmph."

"Do you want to watch?" Gopi asked her, indicating the examining room. Sandra looked to Vicente, who translated the question for her. She laughed and shook her head. "Oh, no," she said. She sat down in the waiting room.

As they walked into the examining room, Gopi asked Vicente. "She your wife?" Vicente grinned, embarrassed. "Not yet, Doctor. Can't afford to get married yet."

If any of us had seen him then, we might for a moment have doubted that this was the Gopi we knew, and not a surgeon long used to taking knives to human flesh. He smiled and spoke so calmly that Vicente himself was not at all nervous when Gopi told him to sit in a chair and roll up his sleeve and lay his arm on the examining table.

The novocaine had come in the mail from India months previously, but Gopi had not had occasion to use it until now. He opened the box and found his hypodermic, then filled the syringe with the drug, eyeballing the measurement. He injected Vicente in three places around the lump and stared gravely, waiting for the arm to numb.

After eight or ten minutes, Gopi poked the arm with his finger.

"Can you feel that?" he asked.

"Only a little," Vicente replied.

Gopi didn't want to take any chances. He refilled the hypodermic and injected the young man again. After a few minutes, he directed Vicente to close his eyes.

"Am I touching you or not?" Gopi asked him.

"Don't think so," said Vicente.

"Now?"

"Uh uh."

Finally, Gopi touched Vicente's arm. "How about now?"

"Nope."

Now Gopi couldn't help himself. He giggled. Then he thwacked Vicente with three of his fingers. "Did you feel that?" he asked.

"I heard it," said Vicente. "But I didn't really feel it."

"Okay then." Gopi squirmed his fingers into latex gloves and swabbed Vicente's arm with iodine. He had sterilized the scalpel by putting it into a bowl of water that had been microwaved on "high" for fifteen minutes, and now without hesitating and without giving himself time to grow afraid, he sank the blade into Vicente's skin.

The blade sank softly. Gopi sliced a thin line along the center of Vicente's lump. Blood welled slowly from the line, and Gopi wiped it with cotton gauze. Vicente didn't appear to feel anything. It was magical, Gopi thought; it was impossible. Gopi cut smaller, horizontal lines at each end of the vertical one, and then he took a breath and with his gloved fingers pried up a flap of skin. The lump was loosely anchored, and Gopi unmoored it with tentative scalpel cuts until it slipped out, slick and rubbery, into the palm of his hand. Gopi showed it to Vicente, who took one look and slumped down in his chair.

Gopi tried to catch Vicente up as he fainted, but in doing so he dropped the lump. It slid along the floor, and Gopi dropped Vicente to stop it with one foot. He picked up the lump and put it in the sink, making a mental note to flush it in the toilet later. Then he lifted poor Vicente off the chair as best he could and shoved his limp body onto the metal examining table, which seemed designed to hold, at most, a large dog. Vicente's legs dangled off awkwardly above the knees.

"Needle and thread, please, nurse," Gopi chuckled to himself, and then he picked up the surgical needle that he had laid out earlier on a tray, already strung with clear catgut medical suture.

Vicente woke up halfway through the stitching, and Gopi talked to him reassuringly. "Feeling better?" he asked. "Don't look. Almost done." Gopi tied a little knot and appraised his handiwork. The sutures were cragged and haphazard, but Gopi marveled that a man whose mother and wife had never let him so much as stitch a button on his own shirt could have done such a relatively clean job. Gopi covered the wound with a bandage. He washed his hands and took Vicente's cash, and advised him to go home and take lots of Tylenol. Then he gave Vicente a firm handshake, making the poor man wince.

"See me back in a month?" Gopi said.

When the two men came into the lobby, Sandra stood up. Her face was blanched.

"Qué pasó?" she asked.

She and Vicente spoke to each other in quick overlapping sentences, and Gopi interrupted. "Why is she excited? What happened?"

Vicente turned to Gopi. "She heard the commotion in there," he said. "She thought something bad happened. That's all."

"Nothing wrong," Gopi said in English. He took Sandra's hand in his. "He's a good boy. Take care of him."

Sandra frowned. As she and Vicente turned around to leave, Sandra cried out again: the back of Vicente's shirt was covered with Gopi's bloody fingerprints.

After they left, Gopi sat down. We see him as the adrenaline slowly ebbed, and he began to realize what he had just done. He had used a knife to cut into another man's body, and the man had been helped, not harmed. He had performed a surgery, and what's more, while doing so he had not had a self-conscious thought. He had become a doctor, unselfconscious, and at this realization, Gopi floated with elation. He floated above himself and understood that he was enjoying a delicious and slightly terrifying dream. And in this state of queasy exhilaration, Gopi walked outside, eager for the calming society of the men in the parking lot. But they had left already, so he visited the dry cleaner next door, hoping to make conversation with the teenaged-looking girl who worked there ("Where do you get so many hangers?"). She had gone to lunch, so Gopi walked in the gravel by the side of the long road until he reached the field of grazing cows. He talked out loud to the dumb, death-destined animals, and somehow this calmed Gopi down.

When he went home that night, before making love to his wife, he asked her, "How is it we came to be here, you and me, all alone in this country? Isn't it strange? That we thought certain thoughts that led to certain actions, and a lot of other things happened just by chance, and the net result is me lying here on top of you?"

"It is strange indeed," replied Manju, who, we would learn, had gotten some news from her doctor that day, and unbeknownst to Gopi, was experiencing her own private wonder.

.   .   .

At temple, on the festival of Krishna's birthday, Dr. Dilip Shenoy surprised Gopi by beckoning him over to sit at his table in the lunch hall.

"Sit with me, Gopi," Dilip said, with uncharacteristic friendliness, and Gopi wondered if this was a sign of the uncanny success of his deception—the unfriendly doctor now instinctively recognized Gopi as one of his own.

Dilip poised his thin fingers against his styrofoam lunch plate. "How are you, Gopi?" Dilip said. He had a long, serious face, and his gray hair plumed up softly. "Let's talk. What's going on?"

"Just the usual," Gopi said.

"Really? Nothing new?"

Dilip's intent stare, his tone, began now to strike Gopi as odd. "But how are *you*, Dilip?" Gopi asked.

"Let us not talk about *me*," Dilip replied. He smiled, just a little. "Because, Gopi, it seems that you are the much more interesting fellow."

Inside the temple, Manju was looking at the boy Krishna in the altar, the black stone Krishna with wide gold eyes and a wise grin, blowing with his blood red lips into the flute he held there. A lovely, playful Krishna; a mischievous, hilarious Krishna; and all at once, Manju thought, a terrible, mocking Krishna, grinning at all the capricious misery he had spun.

"Krishna, Guruvayoorappa," Manju prayed. She clasped her hands and clenched her eyelids and moaned the words quietly, trying in vain to muster the fever of trust and abandon to which she could sometimes move herself at this spot.

Manju looked around at all the other people in the temple, she looked at us chatting and praying, and thought how strange it was for us to behave as if all this were so normal. Her doctors would have given her months, maybe weeks, and now she looked at us as though we were a million miles away.

We didn't know what she was going through—she never once mentioned the word cancer—nor did she have a husband she could trust or tell, who could share the weight of her dying and make her less alone. She was by herself, floating far above us, and when she turned back to lord Krishna it was with grief but also with this lonely, exhilarating anger. "Is there really no hope?" she asked him in silence. "All my life you have given me only what you have wanted to give me and not what I have asked for. But that's another way of saying you have not been there and that you have never listened to me. Is there any sign to show that you are still with me, or that you ever have been? That after loving you so much my whole pointless life, you haven't abandoned me to die?"

It was Deepika Shenoy, finally, who had the presence of mind to walk softly up to Manju and put her arm around her, and to whisper in her ear and dab the tears discreetly with a corner of Deepika's own green silk sari. She took Manju out to the lunch line in the dining hall and made sure she got a little bit of everything, and brought her to sit down with their husbands, and by then Manju was looking reasonably calm.

We ask ourselves at what point it became inevitable, and perhaps it was then. Gopi looked up from his food and was grateful for the new company. He greeted Deepika and complimented her on her sari. She had always been Gopi's triple-deluxe dream; it was embarrassingly obvious. Looking at this dream Deepika, Gopi wished Manju would eat better, smile more, wear some jewelry. Deepika laughed at something someone said and put her hand on her shaking bosom. It was a gesture that normally would have made Gopi giddy with pleasure, but now he managed only a wan smile.

Then Manju tried in her way to make small talk, but her husband interrupted her as usual.

"Not now, Manju," Gopi said, because Dilip had reached his hand into his shirt pocket and pulled out a business card, and was talking now, oblivious of the women.

"My nephew was driving to our place last weekend from College Station," Dilip was saying. "You see, he studies hard, just like I did. People like us slog for years. Don't you find us silly? He was driving home and he stopped at a gas station, where someone gave him this business card." Dilip paused now to stare intently at his acquaintance; but Gopi's eyes stayed fixed on his plate. "Someone who looked very familiar gave him *this card*," Dilip repeated, extending the business card, clipped between two bony fingers, toward Gopi.

Gopi refused to touch it. And Manju looked at her husband and looked at the card. And at last, she herself took it from Dilip's hand.

"*Doctor Raju Gopalarajan, MD*," Manju read slowly. "*Medical Doctor Specializing in all things specially Women's Health Matters.*"

Dilip finally turned, exultant, to Manju. "But you already know Doctor Gopalarajan, don't you?"

Manju shook her head no.

"You don't?" Dilip gave her a mordant smile. "But he's the great doctor specializing in Women's Health Matters. One of the most difficult specialities in the world, and he is an absolute master."

"Aha?"

Dilip raised his finger in mock severity. "If something cannot be cured," said Dilip, who had always been more insinuation than action, and who, after scaring Gopi, was content to leave things there at that. "If something cannot be cured," Dilip said again, turning back toward Gopi, "then ask Gopalarajan, and Gopalarajan will find the cure!" Was there any hope for poor Manju, for either of them, after that?

•   •   •

The next morning, when Gopi's office phone rang—it's hard to believe, but in a way it isn't—he didn't even recognize his own wife's voice, at first.

"Who's calling, please?" he asked, and she spelled her name as he had heard her spell it so many times to others.

"M like Mary A-N like Nancy J-U-K-U-M like Mary A-R."

Gopi had not prepared for this moment, but for a few seconds his quick wits came to his aid. He drew in his breath and almost without thinking asked, "Something wrong with you, madam?" He spoke in a gruff tone he hoped his wife wouldn't recognize.

"Yes," Manju said. "That's why people call doctors, isn't it? Can I make an appointment, please?"

Gopi was surprised to find that Manju's voice, transmitted over the anonymizing phone, had an authority he had never appreciated in real life, and Gopi felt suddenly uncertain of his ability to bluff through the situation.

"Hello?" Manju asked.

The silence grew, and now Gopi panicked. He hung up, and when the phone rang again, he ignored it.

He had only a few minutes to wonder what in fact was wrong with his wife when he was interrupted again, this time by Vicente and Sandra walking in through the door. They held each other's hands stiffly.

The look in their faces struck Gopi with alarm. "Sorry to bother you, doctor," Vicente said. "But seems like, maybe, there's a problem."

"I did everything well," Gopi said. "What problem? Everything is fine." Sandra's face turned red, and Vicente looked at her, then at Gopi. And then Vicente began to cry.

"He has pain," Sandra tried to explain, as she and Gopi waited for Vicente to compose himself.

Gopi saw that the young man had tied a white cloth around his forearm, and the cloth was soaked through with some dark fluid, and his hand and fingers below were plumply swollen.

When he unwrapped the bandage in the examining room a few minutes later, the smell hit Gopi so hard he staggered to the door and leaned out of it for a few moments. When he came back, he tried to breathe through his mouth. He already knew from his reading what had to be done, and that there was no time to waste. As Sandra stood anxiously at the far end of the room, Gopi anesthetized Vicente's arm and began to cut away the blackening flesh. He cut and he threw the sloppy matter into the trash can and closed the lid, but still the stench didn't go away, so Gopi cut more. Blood oozed from the cavity in Vicente's arm, filling the hole and spilling to the floor. Gopi spooned out the blood with a plastic cup and cut quickly before the hole filled again. Sandra held her hand to her mouth and cried, and Gopi told Vicente, "Tell her to stop moaning, won't you?" but Vicente's eyes were half closed and his head was nodding backward and he didn't say anything. Gopi cut more and became very frightened when finally he encountered a length of white bone.

After he and Sandra laid Vicente in the back of his car, Gopi watched Sandra drive away (on her way, we know now, to the Manvel General Emergency Room). Then he stood on the pavement, damp and terrified, and let his head slump down to see the footprint-spattered trail of red leading from inside the examining room all the way to the parking lot, to terminate there, at Gopi's feet. Inside, minutes later, he didn't notice the sound of the front door opening, or hear the footsteps leading to the examining room door, or see his wife walk in until she was two feet away from him.

Manju and Gopi stared at each other in silence. She studied her husband's bewildered eyes and looked at the lab coat he was wearing. She saw the gore-caked instruments, and she remembered

Dilip Shenoy's odd expression at the temple the day before, and the voice on the phone when she had tried to make an appointment. She clutched harder the library book she held in her arms, and remembered Gopi's strange jokes in the bedroom, and the increasingly implausible stories about his advancements in television sales. And she remembered the lies Gopi had told everyone all his life.

And Gopi—exhausted, for once guileless—quietly pried the book from her trembling hands, bookmarked and dog-eared, and stared dumbly at the picture it showed: a woman's ovaries, bloated and blistering, laid out on a dissecting table, with a label that read INOPERABLE. The dull fear in his eyes was obvious to Manju.

"What's the matter?" Manju asked. She wiped her nose with the back of her hand. "You're such a famous doctor. Can't you help me? Hm?"

Gopi was unsure, for a moment, if his wife was credulous or mocking, but something in her tone seemed to demand an answer. "I can try," he said simply.

There are those who will never accept what must have happened next. They don't understand what Manju saw in Gopi, for a few moments, here at the dying-ember end of our story. But there is a reassuring certainty to some unlucky lives, which is to say that fear has no place for persons already doomed; and a kind of calmness descended on Manju, seeing her husband covered in some other man's blood, seeing him drained and frightened. And isn't it possible that Manju herself found in Gopi's examining room the iodine and the novocaine, the knife and the needles? Manju herself lay down on the examining table, just as the Manvel General doctors, having gotten the details from Sandra, were phoning the police station.

Gopi was still nervous, no doubt. It took him some time to fathom the hopeless clarity of the situation. But Manju's calmness would have calmed him, and soon he understood there was no help for either of them outside of that room. The news stations had even somehow picked up the story—didn't some of us hear the name on the radio and wonder who this doctor was, and if maybe we had met him at a function somewhere? And on his own, without asking, Gopi picked up the scalpel, knowing the red and blue lights would soon be shimmering through the cracks in the window blinds. We are with them as he picked up the scalpel and looked in Manju's eyes, knowing what the police would have no choice but to do when they came through the door and saw him doing what he was about to do.

But now those anxious police officers were still miles away along the highway. Vicente's friends had left for work already. The dry cleaner's clerk was late as usual. Only the skinny cows in their dirt-patch field could know what noises came from that desolate office building, and so there are some who will always have doubts—who will cling to their versions with the same shiftless confidence with which those cows stood waiting under the midday sun, dulled to their own fate or anyone else's—and who will never believe what happened when Manju looked down, and followed the sure movements of Dr. Gopalarajan's fingers, and smiled.

2007 National Magazine Award Finalists

NOTE: All nominated issues are dated 2006 unless otherwise specified. The editor whose name appears in connection with finalists for 2007 held that position, or was listed on the masthead, at the time the issue was published in 2006. In some cases, another editor is now in that position.

General Excellence

This category recognizes overall excellence in magazines in six circulation categories. It honors the effectiveness with which writing, reporting, editing, and design all come together to command readers' attention and fulfill the magazine's unique editorial mission.

Under 100,000 circulation

Bulletin of the Atomic Scientists: Mark Strauss, editor, for May/June, July/August, September/October issues.

I.D.: Julie Lasky, editor-in-chief, for March/April, May, June issues.

Metropolis: Susan S. Szenasy, editor-in-chief, for June, September, November issues.

Print: Joyce Rutter Kaye, editor-in-chief, for March/April, July/August, September/October issues.

The Virginia Quarterly Review: Ted Genoways, editor, for Spring, Summer, Fall issues.

100,000 to 250,000 circulation

Foreign Policy: Moisés Naím, editor-in-chief, for May/June, September/October, November/December issues.

Mother Jones: Russ Rymer, editor-in-chief, for March/April, September/October, issues; Monika Bauerlein and Clara Jeffery, editors-in-chief, for November/December issue.

Philadelphia Magazine: Larry Platt, editor, for September, November, December issues.

Salt Water Sportsman: Sid Evans, editorial director; David DiBenedetto, editor, for February, October, November issues.

Seed: Adam Bly, editor-in-chief, for June/July, November, December/January issues.

250,000 to 500,000 circulation

The Atlantic Monthly: Cullen Murphy, managing editor, for January/February, James Bennet, editor, for September, December issues.

Audubon: David Seideman, editor-in-chief, for March/April, May/June, September/October issues.

Cookie Magazine: Pilar Guzmán, editor-in-chief, for September, October/November, December/January issues.

New York Magazine: Adam Moss, editor-in-chief, for May 22, July 17, September 18 issues.

Texas Monthly: Evan Smith, editor, for March, September, October issues.

500,000 to 1,000,000 circulation

Condé Nast Traveler: Klara Glowczewska, editor-in-chief, for September, October, November issues.

The Economist: John Micklethwait, editor, for September 9, October 28, December 23 issues.

Esquire: David Granger, editor-in-chief, for July, September, November issues.

Gourmet: Ruth Reichl, editor-in-chief, for April, August, December issues.

GQ: Jim Nelson, editor-in-chief, for March, September, October issues.

Wired: Chris Anderson, editor-in-chief, for August, November, December issues.

1,000,000 to 2,000,000 circulation

Entertainment Weekly: Rick Tetzeli, managing editor, for June 30/July 7, September 22, December 29/January 5 issues.

Field & Stream: Sid Evans, editor-in-chief, for May, October, December-January issues.

More Magazine: Peggy Northrop, editor-in-chief, for February, June, October issues.

The New Yorker: David Remnick, editor, for February 13 & 20, March 27, October 9 issues.

Rolling Stone: Jann S. Wenner, editor and publisher; Will Dana, managing editor for May 4, May 18-June 1, November 16 issues.

Over 2,000,000 circulation

Glamour: Cynthia Leive, editor-in-chief, for May, September, December issues.

Martha Stewart Living: Martha Stewart, founder; Margaret Roach, editorial director, for March, July, December issues.

National Geographic: Chris Johns, editor-in-chief, for May, November, December issues.

O, The Oprah Magazine: Oprah Winfrey, founder and editorial director; Amy Gross, editor-in-chief, for February, July, November issues.

Time: James Kelly, managing editor, for June 12 issue; Richard Stengel, managing editor, for August 7, August 14 issues.

Personal Service

This category recognizes excellence in service journalism. The advice or instruction presented should help readers improve the quality of their personal lives.

Bicycling: Stephen Madden, vice president and editor-in-chief, for "Project Jeremy," by Selene Yeager, October.

Field & Stream: Sid Evans, editor-in-chief, for a four-part package, "How they Survived: A Taste of Death," by Keith McCafferty, "Lightning Rod," by Dave Hurteau, "Surprise Attack," by Hal Herring, "How Sportsmen Really Die," by Keith McCafferty, July.

Glamour: Cynthia Leive, editor-in-chief, for "What No One Ever Tells You About Breast Implants," by Liz Welch, November.

Redbook: Stacy Morrison, editor-in-chief, for "You can save a woman's life—just by asking her how she's doing," by Denise Dowling, October.

Wondertime: Lisa Stiepock, editor, for "Argue with Me!" by Jay Heinrichs, Winter.

Leisure Interests

This category recognizes excellent service journalism about leisure-time pursuits. The practical advice or instruction presented should help readers enjoy hobbies or other recreational interests.

Esquire: David Granger, editor-in-chief, for "Esquire's Best Bars in America," June.

Golf Digest Magazine: Jerry Tarde, chairman and editor-in-chief, for "Total Improvement Issue," May.

Men's Health: David Zinczenko, senior vice president and editor-in-chief, for a three-part series, "Your Perfect Summer": "Part One—A New Path to Change," by Jim Thornton; "Part Two—Your Breakthrough Season"; "Part Three—The Men Who Live Forever," by Christopher McDougall, July/August.

O, The Oprah Magazine: Oprah Winfrey, founder and editorial director; Amy Gross, editor-in-chief, for "Reading: A Love Story," July.

Wired: Chris Anderson, editor-in-chief, for "Second Life," October.

Reporting

This category recognizes excellence in reporting. It honors the enterprise, exclusive reporting and intelligent analysis that a magazine exhibits in covering an event, a situation or a problem of contemporary interest and significance.

Esquire: David Granger, editor-in-chief, for "The School," by C. J. Chivers, June.

Fortune: Eric Pooley, managing editor, for "The Law Firm of Hubris Hypocrisy & Greed," by Peter Elkind, November 13.

IEEE Spectrum: Susan Hassler, editor-in-chief, for "Re-engineering Iraq," by Glenn Zorpette, February.

Rolling Stone: Jann S. Wenner, editor and publisher; Will Dana, managing editor, for "Inside Scientology," by Janet Reitman, March 9.

Time: James Kelly, managing editor, for "One Morning in Haditha," by Tim McGirk, March 27; "The Shame of Kilo Company," by Michael Duffy, June 5; "The Ghosts of Haditha," by Michael Duffy, Tim McGirk and Aparisim Ghosh, June 12.

Public Interest

This category recognizes journalism that sheds new light on an issue of public importance and has the potential to affect national or local debate policy.

The Atlantic Monthly: James Bennet, editor, for "Declaring Victory," by James Fallows, September.

Best Life: David Zinczenko, editorial director; Stephen Perrine, editor-in-chief, for "Our Oceans Are Turning Into Plastic . . . Are We?" by Susan Casey, November.

New York Magazine: Adam Moss, editor-in-chief, for "On the Rabbi's Knee," by Robert Kolker, May 22.

The New Yorker: David Remnick, editor, for three articles by Seymour M. Hersh, "The Iran Plans," April 17; "Last Stand," July 10 & 17; "The Next Act," November 27.

Vanity Fair: Graydon Carter, editor, for "Rules of Engagement," by William Langewiesche, November.

Feature Writing

This category recognizes excellence in feature writing. It honors the stylishness, flair and originality with which the author treats his or her subject.

Esquire: David Granger, editor-in-chief, for "Sgt. Wells's New Skull," by Brian Mockenhaupt, April.

Esquire: David Granger, editor-in-chief, for "The Loved Ones," by Tom Junod, September.

GQ: Jim Nelson, editor-in-chief, for "The Other Side of Hate," by Andrew Corsello, July.

The New Yorker: David Remnick, editor, for "Prairie Fire," by Eric Konigsberg, January 16.

The Paris Review: Philip Gourevitch, editor, for "In the Sandbox," by Glyn Vincent, Spring.

Profile Writing

This category recognizes excellence in profile writing. It honors the vividness and perceptiveness with which the writer brings his or her subject to life.

Cincinnati Magazine: Jay Stowe, editor, for "Is Bill Cunningham a Great American?" by Kathy Y. Wilson, November.

National Geographic: Chris Johns, editor-in-chief, for "Murdering the Impossible," by Caroline Alexander, November.

New York Magazine: Adam Moss, editor-in-chief, for "Karl Lagerfeld, Boy Prince of Fashion," by Vanessa Grigoriadis, February 13.

The New Yorker: David Remnick, editor, for "He Knew He Was Right," by Ian Parker, October 16.

Vanity Fair: Graydon Carter, editor, for "A Face Only a President Could Love," by Todd Purdum, June.

Essays

This category recognizes excellence in essay writing on topics ranging from the personal to the political. Whatever the subject, it honors the author's eloquence, perspective, fresh thinking, and unique voice.

Foreign Policy: Moisés Naím, editor-in-chief, for "The First Law of Petropolitics," by Thomas L. Friedman, May/June.

The Georgia Review: Stephen Corey, acting editor, for "Russell and Mary," by Michael Donohue, Fall/Winter.

New Letters: Robert Stewart, editor-in-chief, for "The Beautiful City of Tirzah," by Harrison Fletcher, Winter.

The New Yorker: David Remnick, editor, for "Alice, Off the Page," by Calvin Trillin, March 27.

Smithsonian: Carey Winfrey, editor-in-chief, for "Living with Geese," by Paul Theroux, December.

Columns and Commentary

This category recognizes excellence in short-form political, social, economic, or humorous commentary. The award honors the eloquence, force of argument, and succinctness with which the writer presents his or her views.

Discover: Corey Powell, executive editor, for three columns by Bruno Maddox, "Blinded by Science: When First We Clicked," April; "Blinded by Science: Who's Freaky Now?" October; "Blinded by Science: How Birding in Central Park in an Age of Terror Makes the Man," December.

Field & Stream: Sid Evans, editor-in-chief, for three columns by Bill Heavey, "A Sportsman's Life: Why Knot?" June; "Sportsman's Life: Death and Fishing," August; "A Sportsman's Life: Dog Years," November.

Newsweek: Jon Meacham, editor, for three columns by Fareed Zakaria, "Iraq's Dark Day of Reckoning," October 16; "There's One Last Thing to Try," October 30; "Don't Punt on the Troops Issue," November 20.

The New Yorker: David Remnick, editor, for three columns by James Surowiecki, "Printing Money," April 3; "Through the Roof," May 8; "The Fatal-Flaw Myth," July 31.

Vanity Fair: Graydon Carter, editor, for three columns by Christopher Hitchens, "Childhood's End," January; "The Vietnam Syndrome," August; "Oriana Fallaci and the Art of Interview," December.

Reviews and Criticism

This category recognizes excellence in criticism of art, books, movies, television, theater, music, dance, food, dining, fashion, products and the like.

It honors the knowledge, persuasiveness and original voice that the critic brings to his or her reviews.

The Atlantic Monthly: James Bennet, editor, for three book reviews by Sandra Tsing Loh, "Rhymes With Rich," May; "Cheap Thrills," July/August; "The Drama of the Gifted Parent," October.

GQ: Jim Nelson, editor-in-chief, for three columns by Alan Richman, "2nd City No More," June; "Meals of Fortune," September; "Yes, We're Open," November.

Harper's Magazine: Lewis H. Lapham, editor, for "Blood and Time," by Roger D. Hodge, February.

The Nation: Katrina vanden Heuvel, editor and publisher, for three reviews by Stuart Klawans, "Down These Mean Streets," October 23; "The Tracks of My Tears," November 20; "Coming to America!" December 4.

The New Yorker: David Remnick, editor, for three reviews by Alex Ross, "American Sublime," June 19; "The Storm of Style," July 24; "Fervor," September 25.

Magazine Section

This category recognizes excellence of a regular department or editorial section of a magazine, either front- or back-of-book and composed of a variety of elements, both text and visual. Finalists are selected based on the section's voice, originality, design, and packaging.

Condé Nast Traveler: Klara Glowczewska, editor-in-chief, for its front-of book section "Word of Mouth," May, August, October.

Esquire: David Granger, editor-in-chief, for its "This Way In" section, June, November, December.

Esquire: David Granger, editor-in-chief, for its front-of-book section "Man at His Best," October, November, December.

Field & Stream: Sid Evans, editor-in-chief, for its section "Sportsman's Notebook," September, November, December.

New York Magazine: Adam Moss, editor-in-chief, for its "Strategist" section, June 12, July 24, December 11.

Single-Topic Issue

This category recognizes magazines that have devoted an issue to an in-depth examination of one topic. It honors the ambition, comprehensiveness and imagination with which a magazine treats its subject.

Backpacker: Jonathan Dorn, editor-in-chief, for "The Survival Issue," October.

The Believer: Heidi Julavits, Ed Park, Vendela Vida, founding editors; Andrew Leland, managing editor, for "The 2006 Music Issue," June/July.

Columbia Journalism Review: Mike Hoyt, executive editor, for "Into the Abyss: Reporting Iraq 2003–2006," November/December.

Departures: Richard David Story, editor-in-chief, for "The Latin Issue: South America 2006," October.

Newsweek: Mark Whitaker, editor, for "AIDS at 25," May 15.

Design

This category recognizes excellence in magazine design. It honors the effectiveness of overall design, artwork, graphics, and typography in enhancing a magazine's unique mission and personality.

The Believer: Heidi Julavits, Ed Park, Vendela Vida, founding editors; Andrew Leland, managing editor, for June/July, September, December/January issues.

Gourmet: Ruth Reichl, editor-in-chief; Richard Ferretti, creative director; Erika Oliveira, art director; for September, October, December issues.

GQ: Jim Nelson, editor-in-chief; Fred Woodward, design director, for March, April, July issues.

New York Magazine: Adam Moss, editor-in-chief; Luke Hayman, design director, for April 3, April 17, November 6 issues.

Outside: Hal Espen, editor; Hannah McCaughey, creative director, for January issue; Christopher Keyes, editor; Hannah McCaughey, creative director, for July, November issues.

Seed: Adam Bly, founder and editor-in-chief; Adam Billyeald, deputy art director, for June/July, November, December/January issues.

Photography

This category recognizes excellence in magazine photography. It honors the effectiveness of photography, photojournalism, and photo illustration in enhancing a magazine's unique mission and personality.

Country Home: Carol Sheehan, editor-in-chief; Mary Emmerling, creative director; Shelley Caldwell, art director, for February, April, June issues.

Gourmet: Ruth Reichl, editor-in-chief; Richard Ferretti, creative director; Erika Oliveira, art director; Amy Koblenzer, photo editor, for September, October, December issues.

Martha Stewart Living: Martha Stewart, founder; Margaret Roach, editorial director; Eric A. Pike, creative director; James Dunlinson and Joele Cuyler, art directors; Heloise Goodman, photography director, for January, July, December issues.

National Geographic: Chris Johns, editor-in-chief; David Griffin, senior editor, photography; Susan A. Smith, deputy director, photography, for May, November, December issues.

W: Patrick McCarthy, chairman and editorial director; Dennis Freedman, creative director; Edward Leida, group design director; Bridget Foley, executive editor; Julie L. Belcove, deputy editor; Nathalie Kirsheh, art director; Nadia Vellam, photo editor, for June, September, November issues.

Photojournalism

This category recognizes the informative photographic documentation of an event or subject in real-time. Although photo essays accompanied by text will be eligible, they will be judged primarily on the strength of the photographs.

Aperture: Melissa Harris, editor-in-chief; Yolanda Cuomo, art director, for "Silhouettes: Muslim Women of the Middle East and Afghanistan," by Caroline Mangez, photographs by Alexandra Boulat, Winter.

National Geographic: Chris Johns, editor-in-chief; David Griffin, senior editor, photography; Susan A. Smith, deputy director, photography, for "The Heros, The Healing," by Neil Shea, photographs by James Nachtwey, December.

The New Yorker: David Remnick, editor; Elisabeth Biondi, director of photography, for "The Waste Land," by Robert Polidori, January 9.

The Paris Review: Philip Gourevitch, editor, for "Kibera," by Jonas Bendiksen, Winter.

Vanity Fair: Graydon Carter, editor; David Harris, design director; Susan White, photography director, for "The Vietnam Syndrome," by Christopher Hitchens, photographs by James Nachtwey, August.

Photo Portfolio

This category honors creative photography and photo illustration. Although photo essays accompanied by text will be eligible, they will be judged primarily on the strength of the photographs.

City: John McDonald, editorial director and publisher; Fabrice G. Frere, creative director and COO; Adriana Jacoud, art director; Sarah Greenfield, photo editor, for "Penitentiary," photographed by Kenji Toma, March.

City: John McDonald, editorial director and publisher; Fabrice G. Frere, creative director and COO; Adriana Jacoud, art director; Sarah Greenfield, photo editor, for "White Heat," photographed by Horacio Salinas, April.

Details: Daniel Peres, editor-in-chief; Rockwell Harwood, creative director; Liane Radel, photography director, for "How TV Became Hollywood's Leading Man," photographed by Michael Thompson, August.

Vogue: Anna Wintour, editor-in-chief; Grace Coddington, creative director; Charles Churchward, design director; Danko Steiner, art director; Ivan Shaw, photo director, for "Teen Queen," photographed by Annie Leibovitz, September.

W: Patrick McCarthy, chairman and editorial director; Dennis Freedman, creative director; Edward Leida, group design director; Bridget Foley, executive editor; Julie L. Belcove, deputy editor; Nathalie Kirsheh, art director; Nadia Vellam, photo editor, for "Welcome to the Motor City," by Bruce Weber, September.

Fiction

This category recognizes excellence in magazine fiction writing. It honors the quality of a publication's literary selections.

McSweeney's: Dave Eggers, editor, for "Wild Child," by T.C. Boyle, April; "To Sit, Unmoving," by Susan Steinberg, July; "The Strange Career of Dr. Raju Gopalarajan," by Rajesh Parameswaran, September.

The New Yorker: David Remnick, editor, for "Once in a Lifetime," by Jhumpa Lahiri, May 8; "My Parents' Bedroom," by Uwem Akpan June 12; "Something That Needs Nothing," by Miranda July, September 18.

Playboy: Hugh M. Hefner, editor-in-chief; Christopher Napolitano, editorial director, for "Suicide Watch," by Joyce Carol Oates, May; "The Bad News," by Margaret Atwood, July; "Willa," by Stephen King, December.

The Virginia Quarterly Review: Ted Genoways, editor, for "Ships in High Transit," by Binyavanga Wainaina, Winter; "Wake, by Kevin A. González," Spring; "Shepherdess," by Dan Chaon, Fall.

Zoetrope: All-Story: Adrienne Brodeur, Francis Ford Coppola, founding editors; Michael Ray, editor, for "The Boys at the Lab," by Margaret Atwood, Fall; "El Ojo de Agua," by Susan Straight, Spring; "Our Lady of Paris," by Daniyal Mueenuddin, Fall.

General Excellence Online

This category recognizes outstanding magazine Internet sites, as well as online-only magazines that have a significant amount of original content. Sites must also convey a distinct editorial identity and create a unique magazine environment on the Web.

Beliefnet.com (www.beliefnet.com): Steven Waldman, cofounder and editor-in-chief.

BusinessWeek.com (www.businessweek.com): Stephen J. Adler, editor-in-chief.

ESPN.com (www.espn.com): John Papanek, senior vice president and editor-in-chief, ESPN New Media.

People.com (http://www.people.com): Mark Golin, editor.

Slate (http://www.slate.com): Jacob Weisberg, editor.

Interactive Service

This category recognizes an outstanding service feature on the Web. The practical advice or instruction presented should either help users improve the quality of their personal lives or should help them enjoy recreational interests. The category honors a site's creative use of multimedia technology, user involvement, personalization, or community tools, and must go beyond the simple display of text or images on a screen.

BusinessWeek.com B-School Channel (www.businessweek.com/bschools): Stephen J. Adler, editor-in-chief.

The Chronicle of Higher Education Careers (http://chronicle.com/jobs): Phil Semas, editor-in-chief.

Epicurious.com—Epi to Go 2.0 (http://www.epicurious.com): Tanya Steel, editor-in-chief.

NYmag.com—Grub Street (http://nymag.com): Adam Moss, editor-in-chief, New York; Ben Williams and Kelly Maloni, coeditors, nymag.com

Slate—*Slate Green Challenge* (http://www.slate.com/id/2151579/): Jacob Weisberg, editor.

Interactive Feature

This category recognizes an outstanding editorial Web feature focusing on news, entertainment, and other subjects that do not offer practical instruction. The category honors a site's creative use of multimedia technology, user involvement, personalization, or community tools, and must go beyond the simple display of text or images on a screen.

Mother Jones "Lie by Lie" (www.motherjones.com/bush_war_timeline/): Monika Bauerlein and Clara Jeffery, editors-in-chief.

National Geographic Interactive Edition—Antarctica (http://www7.nationalgeographic.com/ngm/antarctica/index.html): Chris Johns, editor-in-chief.

Nerve Film Lounge (www.nerve.com/filmlounge): Michael Martin, editor-in-chief.

Nymag.com—"Show & Talk" fashion week blog (http://nymag.com/): Adam Moss, editor-in-chief, *New York*; Ben Williams and Kelly Maloni, coeditors, nymag.com.

Newsweek.com—"The Boomer Files" (http://www.msnbc.msn.com/id/9925747/site/newsweek/): Deidre Depke, editor.

National Magazine Award Winners, 1966–2007

Best Interactive Design

2001	*SmartMoney.com*

Columns and Commentary

2002	*New York*
2003	*The Nation*
2004	*New York*
2005	*National Journal*
2006	*The New Yorker*
2007	*Vanity Fair*

Design

1980	*Geo*
1981	*Attenzione*
1982	*Nautical Quarterly*
1983	*New York*
1984	*House & Garden*
1985	*Forbes*
1986	*Time*
1987	*Elle*
1988	*Life*
1989	*Rolling Stone*
1990	*Esquire*
1991	*Condé Nast Traveler*
1992	*Vanity Fair*
1993	*Harper's Bazaar*
1994	*Allure*
1995	*Martha Stewart Living*
1996	*Wired*
1997	*I.D.*
1998	*Entertainment Weekly*
1999	*ESPN The Magazine*
2000	*Fast Company*

2001	*Nest*
2002	*Details*
2003	*Details*
2004	*Esquire*
2005	*Kids: Fun Stuff to Do Together*
2006	*New York*
2007	*New York*

Essays

2000	*The Sciences*
2001	*The New Yorker*
2002	*The New Yorker*
2003	*The American Scholar*
2004	*The New Yorker*
2005	*National Geographic*
2006	*Vanity Fair*
2007	*The Georgia Review*

Essays and Criticism

1978	*Esquire*
1979	*Life*
1980	*Natural History*
1981	*Time*
1982	*The Atlantic*
1983	*The American Lawyer*
1984	*The New Republic*
1985	*Boston Magazine*
1986	*The Sciences*
1987	*Outside*
1988	*Harper's Magazine*
1989	*Harper's Magazine*
1990	*Vanity Fair*

1991	*The Sciences*
1992	*The Nation*
1993	*The American Lawyer*
1994	*Harper's Magazine*
1995	*Harper's Magazine*
1996	*The New Yorker*
1997	*The New Yorker*
1998	*The New Yorker*
1999	*The Atlantic Monthly*

Feature Writing

1988	*The Atlantic*
1989	*Esquire*
1990	*The Washingtonian*
1991	*U.S. News & World Report*
1992	*Sports Illustrated*
1993	*The New Yorker*
1994	*Harper's Magazine*
1995	*GQ*
1996	*GQ*
1997	*Sports Illustrated*
1998	*Harper's Magazine*
1999	*The American Scholar*
2000	*Sports Illustrated*
2001	*Rolling Stone*
2002	*The Atlantic Monthly*
2003	*Harper's Magazine*
2004	*The New Yorker*
2005	*Esquire*
2006	*The American Scholar*
2007	*GQ*

Fiction

1978	*The New Yorker*
1979	*The Atlantic Monthly*
1980	*Antaeus*
1981	*The North American Review*

1982	*The New Yorker*
1983	*The North American Review*
1984	*Seventeen*
1985	*Playboy*
1986	*The Georgia Review*
1987	*Esquire*
1988	*The Atlantic*
1989	*The New Yorker*
1990	*The New Yorker*
1991	*Esquire*
1992	*Story*
1993	*The New Yorker*
1994	*Harper's Magazine*
1995	*Story*
1996	*Harper's Magazine*
1997	*The New Yorker*
1998	*The New Yorker*
1999	*Harper's Magazine*
2000	*The New Yorker*
2001	*Zoetrope: All-Story*
2002	*The New Yorker*
2003	*The New Yorker*
2004	*Esquire*
2005	*The Atlantic Monthly*
2006	*The Virginia Quarterly Review*
2007	*McSweeney's*

Fiction and Belles Lettres

1970	*Redbook*
1971	*Esquire*
1972	*Mademoiselle*
1973	*The Atlantic Monthly*
1974	*The New Yorker*
1975	*Redbook*
1976	*Essence*
1977	*Mother Jones*

485

National Magazine Award Winners, 1966–2007

General Excellence

1973	*BusinessWeek*	1990	*Metropolitan Home*
1981	*ARTnews*		*7 Days*
	Audubon		*Sports Illustrated*
	BusinessWeek		*Texas Monthly*
	Glamour	1991	*Condé Nast Traveler*
1982	*Camera Arts*		*Glamour*
	Newsweek		*Interview*
	Rocky Mountain		*The New Republic*
	Magazine	1992	*Mirabella*
	Science81		*National Geographic*
1983	*Harper's Magazine*		*The New Republic*
	Life		*Texas Monthly*
	Louisiana Life	1993	*American Photo*
	Science82		*The Atlantic Monthly*
1984	*The American Lawyer*		*Lingua Franca*
	House & Garden		*Newsweek*
	National Geographic	1994	*BusinessWeek*
	Outside		*Health*
1985	*American Health*		*Print*
	American Heritage		*Wired*
	Manhattan, inc.	1995	*Entertainment Weekly*
	Time		*I.D. Magazine*
1986	*Discover*		*Men's Journal*
	Money		*The New Yorker*
	New England Monthly	1996	*BusinessWeek*
	3-2-1 Contact		*Civilization*
1987	*Common Cause*		*Outside*
	Elle		*The Sciences*
	New England Monthly	1997	*I.D. Magazine*
	People Weekly		*Outside*
1988	*Fortune*		*Vanity Fair*
	Hippocrates		*Wired*
	Parents	1998	*DoubleTake*
	The Sciences		*Outside*
1989	*American Heritage*		*Preservation*
	Sports Illustrated		*Rolling Stone*
	The Sciences	1999	*Condé Nast Traveler*
	Vanity Fair		*Fast Company*

I.D. Magazine
Vanity Fair
2000 National Geographic
Nest
The New Yorker
Saveur
2001 The American Scholar
Mother Jones
The New Yorker
Teen People
2002 Entertainment Weekly
National Geographic
Adventure
Newsweek
Print
Vibe
2003 Architectural Record
The Atlantic Monthly
ESPN The Magazine
Foreign Policy
Parenting
Texas Monthly
2004 Aperture
Budget Living
Chicago Magazine
Gourmet
Newsweek
Popular Science
2005 Dwell
Glamour
Martha Stewart
  Weddings
The New Yorker
Print
Wired
2006 ESPN The Magazine
Esquire
Harper's Magazine
New York

Time
The Virginia Quarterly
  Review
2007 Bulletin of the Atomic
  Scientists
Foreign Policy
National Geographic
New York
Rolling Stone
Wired

General Excellence in New Media

1997 Money
1998 The Sporting News Online
1999 Cigar Aficionado
2000 BusinessWeek Online

General Excellence Online (formerly General Excellence in New Media)

2001 U.S. News Online
2002 National Geographic
    Online
2003 Slate
2004 CNET News.com
2005 Style.com
2006 National Geographic Online
2007 Beliefnet.com

Interactive Feature

2007 nymag.com

Interactive Service

2007 BusinessWeek.com

Leisure Interests (formerly Special Interests)

2002	*Vogue*
2003	*National Geographic Adventure*
2004	*Consumer Reports*
2005	*Sports Illustrated*
2006	*Golf*
2007	*O, The Oprah Magazine*

Magazine Section

2005	*Popular Science*
2006	*Backpacker*
2007	*New York*

Personal Service

1986	*Farm Journal*
1987	*Consumer Reports*
1988	*Money*
1989	*Good Housekeeping*
1990	*Consumer Reports*
1991	*New York*
1992	*Creative Classroom*
1993	*Good Housekeeping*
1994	*Fortune*
1995	*SmartMoney*
1996	*SmartMoney*
1997	*Glamour*
1998	*Men's Journal*
1999	*Good Housekeeping*
2000	*PC Computing*
2001	*National Geographic Adventure*
2002	*National Geographic Adventure*
2003	*Outside*
2004	*Men's Health*

2005	*BabyTalk*
2006	*Self*
2007	*Glamour*

Photography

1985	*Life*
1986	*Vogue*
1987	*National Geographic*
1988	*Rolling Stone*
1989	*National Geographic*
1990	*Texas Monthly*
1991	*National Geographic*
1992	*National Geographic*
1993	*Harper's Bazaar*
1994	*Martha Stewart Living*
1995	*Rolling Stone*
1996	*Saveur*
1997	*National Geographic*
1998	*W*
1999	*Martha Stewart Living*
2000	*Vanity Fair*
2001	*National Geographic*
2002	*Vanity Fair*
2003	*Condé Nast Traveler*
2004	*City*
2005	*Gourmet*
2006	*W*
2007	*National Geographic*

Photojournalism

2007	*The Paris Review*

Photo Portoflio

2007	*City*

Photo Portoflio/Photo Essay

2004	*W*
2005	*Time*
2006	*Rolling Stone*

Profile Writing

2000	*Sports Illustrated*
2001	*The New Yorker*
2002	*The New Yorker*
2003	*Sports Illustrated*
2004	*Esquire*
2005	*The New Yorker*
2006	*Esquire*
2007	*New York*

Public Interest (formerly Public Service)

1986	*Science85*
1987	*Money*
1988	*The Atlantic*
1989	*California*
1990	*Southern Exposure*
1991	*Family Circle*
1992	*Glamour*
1993	*The Family Therapy Networker*
1994	*Philadelphia*
1995	*The New Republic*
1996	*Texas Monthly*
1997	*Fortune*
1998	*The Atlantic Monthly*
1999	*Time*
2000	*The New Yorker*
2001	*Time*
2002	*The Atlantic Monthly*
2003	*The Atlantic Monthly*
2004	*The New Yorker*

2005	*The New Yorker*
2006	*The New Yorker*
2007	*Vanity Fair*

Public Service

1970	*Life*
1971	*The Nation*
1972	*Philadelphia*
1974	*Scientific American*
1975	*Consumer Reports*
1976	*BusinessWeek*
1977	*Philadelphia*
1978	*Mother Jones*
1979	*New West*
1980	*Texas Monthly*
1981	*Reader's Digest*
1982	*The Atlantic*
1983	*Foreign Affairs*
1984	*The New Yorker*
1985	*The Washingtonian*

Reporting

1970	*The New Yorker*
1971	*The Atlantic Monthly*
1972	*The Atlantic Monthly*
1973	*New York*
1974	*The New Yorker*
1975	*The New Yorker*
1976	*Audubon*
1977	*Audubon*
1978	*The New Yorker*
1979	*Texas Monthly*
1980	*Mother Jones*
1981	*National Journal*
1982	*The Washingtonian*
1983	*Institutional Investor*
1984	*Vanity Fair*
1985	*Texas Monthly*

1986	*Rolling Stone*
1987	*Life*
1988	*The Washingtonian and Baltimore Magazine*
1989	*The New Yorker*
1990	*The New Yorker*
1991	*The New Yorker*
1992	*The New Republic*
1993	*IEEE Spectrum*
1994	*The New Yorker*
1995	*The Atlantic Monthly*
1996	*The New Yorker*
1997	*Outside*
1998	*Rolling Stone*
1999	*Newsweek*
2000	*Vanity Fair*
2001	*Esquire*
2002	*The Atlantic Monthly*
2003	*The New Yorker*
2004	*Rolling Stone*
2005	*The New Yorker*
2006	*Rolling Stone*
2007	*Esquire*

Reviews and Criticism

2000	*Esquire*
2001	*The New Yorker*
2002	*Harper's Magazine*
2003	*Vanity Fair*
2004	*Esquire*
2005	*The New Yorker*
2006	*Harper's Magazine*
2007	*The Nation*

Service to the Individual

1974	*Sports Illustrated*
1975	*Esquire*
1976	*Modern Medicine*

1977	*Harper's Magazine*
1978	*Newsweek*
1979	*The American Journal of Nursing*
1980	*Saturday Review*
1982	*Philadelphia*
1983	*Sunset*
1984	*New York*
1985	*The Washingtonian*

Single Awards

1966	*Look*
1967	*Life*
1968	*Newsweek*
1969	*American Machinist*

Single-Topic Issue

1979	*Progressive Architecture*
1980	*Scientific American*
1981	*BusinessWeek*
1982	*Newsweek*
1983	*IEEE Spectrum*
1984	*Esquire*
1985	*American Heritage*
1986	*IEEE Spectrum*
1987	*Bulletin of the Atomic Scientists*
1988	*Life*
1989	*Hippocrates*
1990	*National Geographic*
1991	*The American Lawyer*
1992	*BusinessWeek*
1993	*Newsweek*
1994	*Health*
1995	*Discover*
1996	*Bon Appétit*
1997	*Scientific American*
1998	*The Sciences*

1999	*The Oxford American*
2002	*Time*
2003	*Scientific American*
2004	*The Oxford American*
2005	*Newsweek*
2006	*Time*
2007	*Departures*

Special Awards

| 1976 | *Time* |
| 1989 | *Robert E. Kenyon, Jr.* |

Special Interests

1986	*Popular Mechanics*
1987	*Sports Afield*
1988	*Condé Nast Traveler*
1989	*Condé Nast Traveler*
1990	*Art & Antiques*
1991	*New York*
1992	*Sports Afield*
1993	*Philadelphia*
1994	*Outside*
1995	*GQ*
1996	*Saveur*
1997	*Smithsonian*
1998	*Entertainment Weekly*
1999	*PC Computing*

| 2000 | *I.D. Magazine* |
| 2001 | *The New Yorker* |

Specialized Journalism

1970	*Philadelphia*
1971	*Rolling Stone*
1972	*Architectural Record*
1973	*Psychology Today*
1974	*Texas Monthly*
1975	*Medical Economics*
1976	*United Mine Workers Journal*
1977	*Architectural Record*
1978	*Scientific American*
1979	*National Journal*
1980	*IEEE Spectrum*

Visual Excellence

1970	*Look*
1971	*Vogue*
1972	*Esquire*
1973	*Horizon*
1974	*Newsweek*
1975	*Country Journal*
	National Lampoon
1976	*Horticulture*
1977	*Rolling Stone*
1978	*Architectural Digest*
1979	*Audubon*

American Society of Magazine Editors
Mission Statement

ASME is the nonprofit professional organization for editors of print and online magazines that are edited, published, and distributed in the United States. Established in 1963, ASME currently has about 900 members nationwide.

ASME's mission is to:

- Uphold editorial integrity

- Encourage and reward outstanding and innovative achievement in the creation of magazines and their content

- Bring magazine editors together for networking

- Disseminate useful information on magazine editing to magazine staff members and others

- Attract talented young people to magazine editorial work

- Speak out on public policy issues, particularly those pertaining to the First Amendment, and acquaint the general public with the work of magazine editors and the special character of magazines as a channel of communication

Permissions

Contributors

CAROLINE ALEXANDER has been published in *Smithsonian*, *National Geographic*, the *New Yorker*, and *Outside* magazine. She is also the author of several books, including two *New York Times* bestsellers. One of these, *The Bounty: The True Story of the Mutiny on the Bounty*, was a 2003 National Book Critics Circle Award finalist. She is currently a contributing writer for *National Geographic*.

SUSAN CASEY is the author of *The Devil's Teeth: A True Story of Obsession and Survival Among America's Great White Sharks* (Henry Holt, June 2005). From 2003 through 2006, she was the development editor of Time Inc., where she had previously been the editor of *Sports Illustrated Women* and an editor at large. She also served as the creative director of *Outside* magazine. Her writing has appeared in *Sports Illustrated*, *Esquire*, *Time*, *Fortune*, the *New York Times*, *Best Life*, and *Outside*.

C.J. CHIVERS is the Moscow correspondent for the *New York Times* and a regular contributor to *Esquire*. He began his writing career at the *Providence Journal* and in 1996 won the Livingston Award for international reporting. In 1999 Chivers joined the *Times* as a metro reporter. His personal essay on the September 11, 2001, attacks on the World Trade Center appeared in the September 2002 issue of *Esquire*. Since that time, Chivers has covered the American-led wars in Afgfhanistan and Iraq for the *Times*, as well as, after becoming Moscow correspondent in 2004, the ongoing wars between Russia and its separatist southern states. It was in this capacity that he witnessed the siege of the Beslan school.

ANDREW CORSELLO joined *GQ* as a correspondent in 1995. His first feature for the magazine, "My Body Stopped Speaking to

Me," a chronicle of his near death by liver failure, was nominated for a National Magazine Award—as were his essay "The Vulgarian in the Choir Loft," which was included in *The Best American Magazine Writing 2004* (HarperCollins), and his feature "The Wronged Man," the story of a man wrongfully convicted of raping a child and exonerated by DNA evidence twenty two years later. Two of his *GQ* articles have been optioned for motion pictures. Before coming to *GQ*, Corsello was a staff writer for three years at *Philadelphia Magazine*. His last story there, "Murky Waters," won the Society of Professional Journalists Sigma Delta Chi Award for Best Magazine Story.

MICHAEL DONOHUE was born in Tampa, Florida, and graduated from Princeton. A teacher at Saint Ann's School in Brooklyn, New York, he is currently on leave and working as a freelance writer in Beijing. "Russell and Mary," published in *The Georgia Review*, was his first major essay.

VANESSA GRIGORIADIS is a contributing editor at *New York* magazine and *Rolling Stone*. She has been with *New York* on and off since she graduated from Wesleyan University in 1995, first as an editorial assistant, then promoted to contributing editor in 1998. She was also a writer on the Style Desk at the *New York Times* in 2003. Prior to that, she spent a year studying the sociology of religion at Harvard University. She currently lives off the grid in Hawaii.

CHRISTOPHER HITCHENS joined *Vanity Fair* as a contributing editor in September 1992. He is also a regular contributor to the *Atlantic Monthly*. Hitchens began his career as a staff writer with the *New Statesman* and then worked as an editorial writer for the *Evening Standard*. He served as a foreign correspondent for *London's Daily Express* from 1977 to 1979 and then returned to the *New Statesman* as foreign editor from 1979 to 1981. Hitchens wrote a biweekly column for the *Nation* from 1982 to 2002. Hitchens has also served as Washington editor for *Harper's* and U.S. correspondent for the *Spectator* and the *Times Literary Supplement.* He was the book critic at *New York Newsday* from 1986 to 1992. Hitchens has appeared on *The Daily Show, Charlie Rose,* and *Real Time* with Bill Maher, among others. He was named one of the world's "Top 100 Public Intellectuals" by *Foreign Policy* and Britain's *Prospect.* He is the author of dozens of books including *Letters to a Young Contrarian* (Basic/Perseus 2001); his latest book, *God Is Not Great: How Religion Poisons Everything,* was released May 2007.

Tom Junod lives in Marietta, Georgia, with his wife, his daughter, and his pit bull. He's been a writer-at-large for *Esquire* for ten years. He's been a finalist for the National Magazine Award nine times, and has won twice.

Stuart Klawans, *The Nation's* film critic, is author of the books *Film Follies: The Cinema Out of Order* (a finalist for the 1999 National Book Critics Circle Awards) and *Left in the Dark: Film Reviews and Essays, 1988–2001.* His film criticism and reviews for the *Nation* won the 2007 National Magazine Award. When not on deadline for the *Nation,* he contributes articles to the *New York Times* and other publications.

Eric Konigsberg grew up in Omaha, Nebraska, and he lives in New York City with his wife and son. His writing has appeared in the *New Yorker,* the *New York Times Magazine, Rolling Stone,* and *Tin House.*

William Langewiesche is *Vanity Fair's* first international correspondent. Prior to this, he was a national correspondent at the *Atlantic Monthly.* During his tenure at the magazine, Langewiesche was nominated for eight National Magazine Awards in the past eight years (including this year), and won a Reporting award in 2002 for "The Crash of EgyptAir 990." His coverage has ranged from a profile on wine critic Robert Parker, to the space shuttle Columbia disaster. Langewiesche is the author of five books, among them *Cutting for Sign* (Pantheon Books, 1994); *American Ground: Unbuilding the World Trade Center* (Farrar, Straus and Giroux, 2002); and *The Outlaw Sea: A World of Freedom, Chaos, and Crime* (Farrar, Straus and Giroux, 2004). He is also a four-time nominee for the National Book Critics Circle Award.

SANDRA TSING LOH is a writer and performer whose radio commentaries appear regularly on American Public Media's Marketplace. She can also be heard on KPCC-FM, in Pasadena, California. Loh is a contributing editor to the *Atlantic Monthly* and the *Los Angeles Times* op-ed page.

BRUNO MADDOX has enjoyed a long and tangential relationship with the world of science. As the son of former *Nature* editor Sir John Maddox, young Bruno sat through dinners with such éminences grises as James Watson and Sir Fred Hoyle and once accepted the charges on a collect call from a hysterical Russian scientist who claimed to have invented a perpetual motion machine. Maddox retreated to the humanities during his school days in London and eventually fled to New York to edit *Spy* magazine and write a critically acclaimed novel, *My Little Blue Dress.* He currently writes *Discover* magazine's monthly humor column, "Blinded by Science."

RAJESH PARAMESWARAN is a writer from Missouri City, Texas.

IAN PARKER has been a staff writer at the *New Yorker* since May 2000. He contributed his first "Fact" piece to the magazine in

1994. Parker primarily writes profiles and has written about a range of cultural figures including the poet James Fenton, photographer Mario Testino, museum curator Thelma Golden, and Elton John. Parker came to the *New Yorker* from *Talk*, where he was a contributing writer. Before joining *Talk*, he was the television critic for the *London Observer*. He has also been a staff writer and a features editor for the *Independent*, and has contributed articles to *Granta*, the *New York Times Magazine*, the *Modern Review* and the *Sunday Telegraph*.

JANET REITMAN is a contributing editor at *Rolling Stone*. Her previous work includes coverage of the wars in Sudan and Sierra Leone, the crisis in Zimbabwe, and the Iraq war, which she reported on extensively for *Rolling Stone* in 2004. She has written for *GQ*, the *Los Angeles Times Magazine*, *Men's Journal*, *ESPN the Magazine*, and *Marie Claire*, among other publications, and is currently working on a book.

ALEX ROSS has been contributing to the *New Yorker* since 1993. He was named a staff writer in 1996 and covers classical music—from Baroque opera to the downtown avant-garde—for the magazine. He has also written about Bob Dylan, Radiohead, and Björk. Ross came to the *New Yorker* from the *New York Times*, where he served as a music critic beginning in 1992. He has also written for the *New Republic*, the *London Review of Books*, *Slate*, *Transition*, and *Lingua Franca*. Ross has won two ASCAP–Deems Taylor Awards for music criticism, and, in 2002, he received a Holtzbrink Fellowship from the American Academy in Berlin. His work has been anthologized in the *Best American Essays* and *Da Capo Best Music Writing* series. Ross's first book, *The Rest is Noise: Listening to the Twentieth Century*, a cultural history of music since 1900, will be published by Farrar, Straus & Giroux.

PAUL THEROUX published his first novel, *Waldo*, in 1967. His many subsequent novels include *The Family Arsenal, Picture Palace, The Mosquito Coast, O-Zone, Millroy the Magician, My Secret History, My Other Life*, and *Kowloon Tong*. His highly acclaimed travel books include *Riding the Iron Rooster, The Great Railway Bazaar, The Old Patagonian Express*, and *Fresh Air Fiend. The Mosquito Coast* and *Dr. Slaughter* have both been made into successful films. Theroux was the guest editor of *The Best American Travel Writing* (Houghton Mifflin, October 2001). He is a frequent contributor to magazines. Theroux divides his time between Cape Cod and the Hawaiian Islands, where he is a professional beekeeper.